TOWARD A NEW AGE
IN CHRISTIAN THEOLOGY

The American Society of Missiology Series, in collaboration with Orbis Books, seeks to publish scholarly works of high merit and wide interest on numerous aspects of missiology—the study of mission. Able presentations on new and creative approaches to the practice of mission will receive close attention.

Previously published in
The American Society of Missiology Series

No. 1   *Protestant Pioneers in Korea,*
         by Everett Nichols Hunt, Jr.

No. 2   *Catholic Politics in China and Korea,*
         by Eric O. Hanson

No. 3   *From the Rising of the Sun—Christians and*
         Society in Contemporary Japan,
         by James M. Phillips

No. 4   *Meaning across Cultures,*
         by Eugene A. Nida and William D. Reyburn

No. 5   *The Island Churches of the South Pacific,*
         by Charles W. Forman

No. 6   *Henry Venn,*
         by Wilbert R. Shenk

No. 7   *No Other Name: A Critical Survey of Christian*
         Attitudes toward the World Religions,
         by Paul F. Knitter

American Society of Missiology Series, No. 8

Toward a New Age in Christian Theology

Richard Henry Drummond

ORBIS BOOKS

Maryknoll, New York 10545

Copyright © 1985 by Richard Henry Drummond

Published by Orbis Books, Maryknoll, NY 10545

Manufactured in the United States of America
All rights reserved

Manuscript editor: Lisa McGaw

Library of Congress Cataloging in Publication Data

Drummond, Richard H. (Richard Henry)
  Toward a new age in Christian theology.

  Bibliography: p.
  Includes index.
  1. Theology, Doctrinal—History—20th century.
I. Title.
BT28.D78   1985   230′.09′04   85-5155
ISBN 0-88344-514-X (pbk.)

To Pearl,
with whom I have walked
the way to this faith-understanding

Contents

Preface to the Series   viii
Preface   ix

1   What Is Happening in Christian Theology?   1
    The Universal Significance of Biblical Covenants   2
    The Early Covenants in Genesis   5

2   Biblical Bases for the Happening   8
    The Old Testament   8
        The Covenant with Israel   8
        The Particularity of the Covenant with Israel   13
        The Missionary Responsibility   14
    The New Testament   16
        The Gospels   16
        Acts of the Apostles and Pauline Writings   20
    In Summary   23

3   Historico-Theological Bases for the Happening   25
    The Early Church and Theological Traditions   25
    Reincarnation in the Judeo-Christian Tradition   33

4   Some Suggested "Whys" for Reductionism in the Historical Process   36

5   The Long Way Out and Up   46
    The Age of Exploration and the Humanist Tradition   49
    Pietism and Evangelicalism   55
    The Enlightenment   58
    Christianity and Other Religious Traditions   61
    After World War II   66
    Eastern Orthodox Churches   83

6   Views of Contemporary Theologians: Roman Catholic   86
    Raymond (Raimundo) Panikkar   87
    Karl Rahner   93
    Heinz Robert Schlette and Hans Küng   96

Paul Knitter   102
Heinrich Dumoulin, Joseph J. Spae, and William Johnston   104

7 *Views of Contemporary Theologians: Protestant*   *114*
Hendrik Kraemer   114
Paul Tillich   118
Contributions of Indian Christians   122
Christian Presence: The Anglican Tradition   134
Schubert Ogden   138
John Hick   140
Don Cupitt   143
John A. T. Robinson   145
John B. Cobb, Jr.   149
   Cobb's Ethical Vision   152
   Cobb's Christology   154
Choan-Seng Song   155
Seiichi Yagi   160
Mikizō Matsuo   165
African Theologians   171
   John S. Mbiti   173
   African Traditional Religions and Culture   176
   Consultation on Global Solidarity in Theological Education   182

8 *Theological Epilogue*   *183*
A New Age in Christian Theology   183
The Christian Doctrine of God   189
The Christian Doctrine of Jesus Christ   190
The Role of the Holy Spirit   193
The Christian World Mission   198

Notes   *203*

Bibliography   *236*

Index   *251*

Preface to the Series

The purpose of the ASM Series is to publish, without regard for disciplinary, national, or denominational boundaries, scholarly works of high quality and wide interest on missiological themes from the entire spectrum of scholarly pursuits, e.g., theology, history, anthropology, sociology, linguistics, health, education, art, political science, economics, and development, to articulate but a partial list. Always the focus will be on Christian mission.

By "mission" in this context is meant a cross-cultural passage over the boundary between faith in Jesus Christ and its absence. In this understanding of mission, the basic functions of Christian proclamation, dialogue, witness, service, fellowship, worship, and nurture are of special concern. How does the transition from one cultural context to another influence the shape and interaction of these dynamic functions?

Missiologists know that they need the other disciplines. And other disciplines, we dare to suggest, need missiology, perhaps more than they sometimes realize. Neither the insider's nor the outsider's view is complete in itself. The world Christian mission has through two millennia amassed a rich and well-documented body of experience to share with other disciplines.

Interaction will be the hallmark of this Series. It desires to be a channel for talking to one another instead of about one another. Secular scholars and church-related missiologists have too long engaged in a sterile venting of feelings about one another, often lacking in full evidence. Ignorance of and indifference to one another's work has been no less harmful to good scholarship.

The promotion of scholarly dialogue among missiologists may, at times, involve the publication of views and positions that other missiologists cannot accept, and with which members of the Editorial Committee do not agree. The manuscripts published reflect the opinions of their authors and are not meant to represent the position of the American Society of Missiology or the Editorial Committee of the ASM Series.

We express our warm thanks to various mission agencies whose financial contributions enabled leaders of vision in the ASM to launch this new venture. The future of the ASM series will, we feel sure, fully justify their confidence and support.

William J. Danker, Chairperson,
ASM Series Editorial Committee

Preface

This book represents an attempt to identify and describe both the nature and the background of the new age into which Christian theology now finds itself moving. It also constitutes an attempt to cope with this situation in a responsible and constructive way. On every side are heard voices of intelligent and responsible persons who identify the present time as the end of an age in Christian theology and missiology and the beginning of a new. James I. Mc-Cord, president of Princeton Theological Seminary, in a letter to this author expressed his thoughts on this matter in the following words: "There is no doubt about our being at the end of a theological period. To date, we have not taken sufficiently into account the other religions of the world, nor have we taken into account the scientific advances that have been made in the twentieth century. The result is that theology is not as central to the life of the Church as it should be." McCord is also suggesting by these words what we shall note later as a critical need for Christian theology to expand both the parameters of its concerns and the ranges of its potential source materials.

One of the most important recent international conferences held under the auspices of the Roman Catholic Church was the International Congress on Mission held in Manila, December 2–7, 1979. The papers and addresses of this congress were published, three books in two volumes, in 1981 and reveal how deeply the conclusions of Vatican Council II have permeated almost all levels of leadership of the Roman Catholic Church throughout the world. Manila 1979 in particular represents a climax to a process of development seen in a series of conferences over the 1970s, which followed in direct continuity with Vatican II. A major emphasis of Manila 1979, also in conformity with Vatican II, is that "we can speak of a new age in human history." The title of the published two volumes of the congress materials is *Toward a New Age in Mission.*[1]

The point is not only that the Roman Catholic Church is itself in process of far-reaching change, of deep-seated renewal. (This process, to be sure, is not one to be slighted. Indeed, the Roman Catholic Church is now leading all Christian churches in its work-process of renewal, and the time has surely come, not for a counterreformation, but for a coreformation in all the churches.) But we must note that something wider than the ranges of the Roman Catholic Church or of all the churches is in process of change, as is suggested by the words of Pope John Paul II in Ankara, Turkey, on December 2, 1979, when he said that it is "precisely today when Muslims and Christians have entered a new period of history."[2] That is, Muslims and others are also involved. John Paul II's predecessors, John XXIII, Paul VI, and John Paul I, also expressed essentially the same perception of change in both word and deed. Malachi Martin, former Jesuit professor at the Pontifical Biblical Institute in Rome and a close associate of Pope John XXIII, has written of John's perception in the following graphic words:

> The essence of the change John saw was this: All the social, political, ideological, ethnic, and intellectual boundaries that had divided human beings for centuries had lost their validity. No one could explain it, but it was certain that gone from the human scene was some root persuasion, some deep conviction. Because of that conviction, men had preserved those boundaries up to John XXIII's very moment in history. But now a new unheard-of and frightening human unity was emerging. And all the old boundaries, all the things men and women had understood and lived by, were disappearing.[3]

We shall see that very important continuities are in fact being preserved in the midst of change and that there was also a long background of development leading up to the event of John XXIII. But there is no little significance in the forceful, graphic nature of Martin's language as he tries to describe what has happened as seen from his own Roman Catholic perspective. He thinks that "John's main contribution was his simple intuition that a change had taken place *already,* and that only the surface of previous things remained, like shells of buildings ready to collapse." And in comparison with his predecessors, "the newness and peculiarity of John's vision lay in its superiority to anything we find before him in the Popes. In fact, in one sense, no Pope ever had John's vision."[4]

This incisive and colorful language is not to be taken with total literalness, but is cited here as giving vigorous expression to an emerging and ever growing consciousness around the world. Clearly we are not dealing with a new awareness merely within the Christian churches, nor even within the larger ranges of human religious perception. James McCord refers to the scientific advances of the twentieth century, to which the new physics and other sciences like astrobiology have notably contributed.[5] We are in fact facing new and wider views of the cosmos, new and wider views of humanity and of what it means to be a human being living in human society in the context of these new and wider views. My intent, therefore, in this book is to try to identify and to delineate long-range developments in Christian faith-understanding, drawing upon both biblical and historical theology, so as to make it possible to understand these new views and to deal with them responsibly and constructively.

This preface is not the place in which to describe in detail the nature or scope of the changes that have been emerging over the past halfcentury and more. These multifaceted changes have been occurring throughout the whole world, although with considerable differences in both kind and degree in different places. Further explanations of the changes are offered at appropriate places in the course of the book. I would add only a few words at this point from Aleksandr Solzhenitsyn in his 1978 commencement address at Harvard University as he sums up some of the effects of recent changes upon persons especially within the geographical ranges of Western civilization:

> How short a time ago, relatively, the small world of modern Europe was easily seizing colonies all over the globe, not only without anticipating any real resistance, but usually with contempt for any possible values in the conquered peoples' approach to life. It all seemed an overwhelming success, with no geographic limits. Western society expanded in a triumph of human independence and power. And all of a sudden the twentieth century brought the clear realization of this society's fragility. We now see that the conquests proved to be short-lived and precarious (and this, in turn, points to defects in the Western view of the world which led to these conquests).[6]

Solzhenitsyn views the effects of this new realization as an aspect of what he calls "spiritual exhaustion" in the West. He considers this effect, this "present debility" of the West, as primarily the result of the "prevailing Western view of the world," which he sees as having been born in the Renaissance and finding political expression since the Age of Enlightenment. This view of the world he identifies as "rationalistic humanism or humanist autonomy: the proclaimed and practiced autonomy of man from any higher force above him." He more succinctly denotes this mentality as "anthropocentricity with man as the center of it all."[7]

I am personally in agreement with Solzhenitsyn's depiction of this phenomenon if taken as descriptive of one important development in the intellectual-spiritual life of Western civilization over the past six or seven hundred years. His description without doubt applies to substantial elements of our societies, which have been influenced, often profoundly, sometimes overwhelmingly, by the long-increasing momentum of this naturalistic—he calls it humanistic—mind-set. Readers of this book, however, will find identification and depiction of other streams of life-activity in Western civilization over the same time period. They will also detect a sense of liberation, even of immense gratitude, for certain developments within Western civilization and in the wider world of humankind in more recent years. I specifically feel grateful for certain developments in Christian theology and missiology. "Spiritual exhaustion" is indeed a fact of our times, but it applies to the world of eastern European—and Chinese—socialism as much as to western European and American "Christian" capitalism. It is at least in large part, I believe, the natural cosmic consequence of long-nurtured cultural and ethnic arrogance, of overweening pride of self and clan, which the events of the twentieth century in particular have shown to be poisonous to the inner life of persons as well as to interhuman relationships and the well-being of whole societies. In this book I fully acknowledge this past and its present effects. But at the same time I cannot but express both gratitude and joy over what I believe to be the rediscovery of authentic Christianity in our time. I feel joy over the current reperception of the wider presence and work of the living God in the whole world of his creation. There is joy also over rediscovery of the cosmic Christ of ancient Christian faith, over reperception of the wider significance and work of Jesus the Christ in both past and present.

Finally, I would note that this book is intended to give a background of understanding in order to cope responsibly from within Christian faith and practice with what has been called the present radically pluralistic religious condition of the world. In another volume I plan more specifically to deal with what Marcello Zago has called the most difficult challenge in the history of religions, the challenge that Buddhism presents to Christianity.[8] This will be in particular an attempt to understand the person and the teaching of Gautama the Buddha and to relate this understanding to the expanded reperception of Jesus Christ of which I speak.

Here, however, my intent is to focus on the background of biblical data and historical theological developments that can make such an encounter intellectually and spiritually responsible. I would add that there are many in our day who consider religious pluralism to be "the single most important issue facing Christian theology." Harvey Cox, for one, has said that such perception is declared "on every hand."[9] Patrick D'Souza, Roman Catholic bishop of Varanasi, India, has written that "the most acute problem of the mission in Asia [is] the new relationship of our Christian message with the existing living faiths of the Third World." He speaks of this as "one of the most difficult questions of present day theology."[10] This work is intended to offer at least a partial contribution to the resolution of the missiological problem as well as to the answering of the theological question.

Perhaps a brief personal word is in order to indicate the background from which I come to these studies. My formal theological education as well as earlier religious training were almost equally within two great branches of Protestant Christianity, the Lutheran and the Presbyterian-Reformed. I have, however, been a Presbyterian minister since 1947. Differently from most persons in theological education, I completed my doctorate before entering seminary. This was a degree in Classics, in the Latin and Greek languages and literatures. The gradual development of my personal Christian faith during the latter part of this course of studies may be somewhat suggested by the fact that my doctoral dissertation was on the theme of the historical thinking of the early Latin Christian writers, from Minucius Felix and Tertullian through Augustine.

After two years of service as a pastor in the inner-city of San Francisco, my wife and I went to Japan in 1949 as missionaries under what was then the Board of Foreign Missions of the Presbyterian Church, U.S.A. We served there for various blocks of time, which in all have amounted to fifteen years, the last year being 1978. The nature of my own work during these years involved various kinds of field work, including itinerant evangelism, as well as teaching. The schools in Japan where I have taught are Meiji Gakuin University, Tokyo Union Theological Seminary, and International Christian University. Since by far the greater part of my teaching and preaching was in the Japanese language, Japanese studies and increasingly wider ranges of Asian studies have constituted a major part of my adult professional career.

Another matter of great importance in my professional life-experience is that from the summer of 1969 until the summer of 1981 our seminary was privileged to share the same campus with a Roman Catholic seminary, Aquinas Institute of Theology. This school was primarily staffed by priests and nuns of the Dominican Order, to a lesser extent by Franciscans and others. This situation gave me a rare opportunity to enrich and correct my earlier ecumenical studies through personal contacts that in a number of instances resulted in warm friendships. I count it one of the high privileges of my personal as well as academic life that I was able to participate in these dozen years of delightful ecumenical cooperation.

I mention these matters because they indicate something of how I have been led, in a measure compelled—as I believe, by the providence of God—to take the whole world into account before God with increasing seriousness as a result of my own experiences and studies. With due modesty for my very great personal limitations, I believe that my entire past life and professional career have worked together to enable me to write the pages that follow. Furthermore, as will probably be evident to most readers, much of what I have written is the result of more than academic concerns; I write out of deep personal conviction and feeling. Not every statement in the book, of course, represents my personal conviction, but I trust that I have not hidden what is of me in the midst of what is cited from others.

I wish to thank most warmly various friends and colleagues who have consented to read and critically evaluate this manuscript. They are also persons from whom I have learned much over long years. These are, in alphabetical order, Benedict M. Ashley, O.P., Professor of Theology, Aquinas Institute of Theology, St. Louis; Donald G. Bloesch, Professor of Theology, University of Dubuque Theological Seminary; Harmon H. Bro, Theologian and Psychotherapist, formerly Dean of Drake University Divinity School; Charles Thomas Cayce, President, Association for Research and Enlightenment, Virginia Beach, Virginia; Minoru Kiyota, Professor of Buddhist Studies, University of Wisconsin, Madison; Paul F. Knitter, Professor of Theology, Xavier University, Cincinnati; James I. McCord, formerly President, Princeton Theological Seminary; Donald K. McKim, Associate Professor of Theology, and C. Howard Wallace, Professor of Biblical Theology, both of the University of Dubuque Theological Seminary. I myself assume, of course, full responsibility for any remaining errors or inadequacies.

I should like to thank in a special way my wife, Pearl, for her help in proofreading, and, above all, for both aiding and sharing the developments in my personal understanding, which are reflected in this book. Our sons, Donald and Lowell, have also been most helpful in proofreading and especially in doing the entire work of preparing the bibliography. I also wish to thank warmly our faculty secretary, Mrs. Marguerite Saunders, for her careful typing of the manuscript and sensitive concern for the accuracy of its content. Finally, I wish to thank Dr. Walter F. Peterson, President of the University of Dubuque, for his leadership in the creation of the climate of intellectual and spiritual openness in our school that has made the writing of this book a pleasurable adventure.

1

What Is Happening in Christian Theology?

The unity of humankind is clearly one of the perception-concepts most appealing to modern persons in all parts of the world. There are those who speak of the resurgence of ethnicity and of a widespread quest for "roots," in particular genealogical, cultural, and religious strands. Yet most who enter upon such a quest prefer to do so in continuing awareness of belonging to a larger whole. They wish to affirm their individuality and group allegiance on the basis of a glad consciousness of the solidarity of all humankind.

This perception is by no means new. The Stoic philosophers of Greece and Rome regarded humankind as a single family, and the covenantal relationships that in fact constitute the framework of the entire Bible show the whole of humanity, indeed all living things, as comprised within the range of their concern (cf. Gen. 3:15; 9:8–19; 12:1–3; Isa. 55:3–5; 56:3–8; Jer. 31:27–34; 33:9; Lk. 22:20; 1 Cor. 11:25; Heb. 8:13; 12:24). It is therefore a strange fact, as W. A. Visser 't Hooft once observed, that the Christian church and its theologians have been slower than humanistic philosophers in the West to recognize and affirm the solidarity of all humankind. Wilfred Cantwell Smith has set the dilemma before us in even more striking terms in stating that "the Christian Church has yet to discover, in any serious and profoundly theological fashion, how human, as it were, everyone else is."[1]

The pressures, however, which at the present time lead in the direction of both theory and praxis of wider unities, appear to be inexorable. To be sure, statements concerning the emergence of "one world" in our time, the world as a "global village," and the like are sometimes overdrawn or too facile. But there can be no doubt that, even with appreciable differences in degree, all persons everywhere are being drawn into new and wider experiences of interrelationship. Nineteenth- and twentieth-century achievements in science and technology, more recent developments in the techniques and extension of mass media of communication, the post-World War II massive increase in human travel and the even more recent movements of peoples—all have contributed to these wider experiences of interhuman relationship and some awareness of their meaning.

There are, however, deeper aspects to these developments. We appear to be

1

living in a time when previously largely disparate streams of historical experience are being drawn into one world-history. There are persons who view this phenomenon as more than merely an increase of contacts across the world at the level of socioeconomic, political, or even cultural activities. Some see also a "convergence of the historical processes of different religions" with the result of a "sense of participation in each other's ongoing religious history."[2] A distinguished Roman Catholic theologian, Ewert Cousins, has not hesitated to express this perception in even bolder words by saying that "all spiritual traditions are dimensions of each other and that at this point of history individuals throughout the world are becoming heir to the spiritual heritage of mankind."[3]

These are admittedly heady thoughts in the context of more reductionist trends, both cultural and theological, which have plagued Western Christian thought in varying degrees of intensity from the time of the Roman emperor Constantine (A.D. 272–337) and even before. But there is good reason to perceive them as authentically Christian, or at least as viable Christian options, even though for long centuries they did not constitute the dominant thought of either Roman Catholic or Protestant orthodoxy in western Europe and the Americas.

To some persons in our day concerns of this kind may appear as a diversion or distraction from what they consider the more primary issues of economic and social justice, the overcoming of racism and sexist discrimination, and related issues of practical human living. Certainly the themes of this book reflect a relatively quiet kind of theological activity in the midst of more strident voices of our time. Yet it is the conviction of this writer that this activity in fact can contribute to a deepening of faith-perceptions and theological convictions without which there does not appear to be a way to overcome the present polarization of views that exists so strikingly even among persons of goodwill within the Christian church and the wider ranges of those significantly influenced by perspectives of Christian faith. Hence let us move without further apology into a consideration of recent developments within Christian perception and theology, which are of the very greatest significance for Christian praxis as well as thought in the present and coming generations. This work is intended as a contribution of understanding that may give a deeper and firmer undergirding to Christian action than much of the activism of our day has yet known. What will emerge, one hopes, is a biblical and theological basis for mutual human respect, a respect for the dignity of all human beings that will give a new quality as well as stronger impetus to attempts to achieve better and nobler results in the practice of interhuman relationships.

THE UNIVERSAL SIGNIFICANCE OF BIBLICAL COVENANTS

We noted above that perceptions of the solidarity of humankind, of a common humanity, have become in a more significant way than for many centuries a part of the thinking, feeling, and living of persons all across the world. A recent work has spoken of a "silent but effective" activity over the past few generations that has served to bring about "a widening of horizons, a crumbling of dividing frontiers, and a drawing together of peoples once far apart."[4] It is the intent of this book to identify the religious dimensions of this activity, which, as we shall see, also involve mutual influences of the major religious traditions of human history upon each other. It is the intent also to relate these dimensions to older developments in the history of Christian theology so as to be able to see the emergence of more recent developments in Christian theology as in fact having their rootage in the sources of our theology in both the Bible and the early church. This activity should enable us to think more freshly and creatively about the possible theological significance for Christians of other religious traditions. In chapter 8 of this work we shall explore how this all relates to the meaning and reality of Jesus the Christ for our present generation.

To an appreciable extent, even though with certain differences of nuance, all major branches of the Christian church have participated in the solid theological work that lies behind the "widening of horizons" mentioned above. Christian theologians may have been slower than humanistic philosophers in perceiving the drift of historical developments of the past four centuries and more, but at least in the twentieth century an enormous amount of work has been done so that Christians are increasingly able to participate with theological understanding in the emerging spiritual awareness of contemporary humanity.

Part of this awareness is to sense not only that all human beings live in one world, but that in some measure all draw from the same spiritual and moral Source and, although in different ways, aspire to a common fulfillment. This has meant for Christians that the previously divergent traditions of human experience of, and reflection upon, the ultimate Mystery that, we believe, surrounds, permeates, and yet transcends our mortal lot become potentially bearers of theological significance. They may even serve, *in potentia* and with proper clarification of norms, as theological source materials for those of Christian faith; that is, they may serve along with, and yet with distinct subordination to, the classic sources of the Bible, the tradition and theology of the church, and the guidance of the Holy Spirit.[5] The astonishing aspect of this perception, in terms of the older orthodoxies, is that it is recognized as the result of the rediscovery and reformulation of the most ancient perspectives of Judeo-Christian faith.

Mention was made above of the fact that covenantal relationships of universal scope and significance constitute the framework of the entire Bible. A covenant is a promise or agreement between two or more parties, not necessarily of equal status or authority, whereby both or all concerned bind themselves to fulfill the commitments made. A covenant may be initiated by one party, but it is invariably an act leading to a relationship with mutual responsibility. Following the earlier work of Walter Eichrodt beginning in the 1930s and the pioneer work on covenants in the ancient Middle East by George

Mendenhall in the 1950s, there has developed an almost universal consensus among biblical scholars that the reality-concept of covenant was one of the basic elements in the religious self-understanding of the people of Israel and of the later Christian church.[6] The concept has become a key means for understanding and interpreting the central message of the Bible. Not always, however, has it been adequately perceived or taught how universal or inclusive are the covenants that provide the framework for the activities within the histories of both Israel and the Christian church. The roles of these two are now seen to be representative rather than to constitute totalities that are fully significant in themselves alone. Certain activities or events within their histories may serve as norms for those within the tradition, but they are not events without relationship either on the historical plane or in theological significance to other events—or persons—quite outside the "revelatory events" that have been the traditional theological sources of the Judeo-Christian tradition.

A particularly perceptive analysis of this theme of covenant with reference to its significance for Christian, and also Jewish, theological understanding of the other religious traditions of human history has been made by Donald G. Dawe. He notes that the two covenants that figure most prominently in the history of Christian theology are the one made with Abraham, which established the Hebrew people in a special relationship with the God of their faith (cf. Gen. 12:1-3; 15:1-21; 17:1-14), and the covenant made in Jesus Christ by which the Christian church was constituted (cf. Mk. 14:24, and parallels; 1 Cor. 11:25). Dawe rightly insists that these are by no means the only covenants in the Bible and that a focus on these two to the neglect of the others in fact distorts their significance because it ignores their context. He states: "The covenant is a conception that extends for biblical religion from the divine creation of the world to its hoped for consummation by God. The covenants were not simply the means for securing the particularity of certain communities but also the means for expressing the universality of God's sovereignty."[7]

Not a few scholars from every major tradition in the Christian church have written on this theme in recent years, but let us draw further on Dawe's analysis as we move toward a fuller statement of comparable perceptions in recent Christian theology. Dawe would have us turn from what he calls the interpretive tradition of "Christian triumphalism" to what the Bible really teaches.

In later chapters of this book we shall discuss the need for new perceptions with regard to traditional conceptions of the terms "salvation" and "damnation." For the present let it be sufficient to say that certain exclusivist notions of who of humankind are to be finally saved in the full cosmic sense of the word and who are not—notions that arose in certain strands of late, pre-Christian Judaism and were often given an even more particularistic twist in later Christian theology—represent a radical distortion of the teaching of the Bible. As Dawe has well put it, "the context for the call of Abram (Abraham) is the prior covenanting action of God reaching back through Noah to Adam."[8]

THE EARLY COVENANTS IN GENESIS

It is customary to denote the accounts of creation and the primal history of humankind as mythical and events like the call of Abraham as legendary. Persons like Rudolf Steiner suggest that other terms may be more appropriate and that it is more likely that Moses and others early in the Hebrew tradition "perceived" the events of creation with sufficient clarity to be able to compose the Genesis accounts, even as they drew upon older Babylonian accounts of creation.[9] However that may be, the Bible itself gives its own setting, and that setting is the divine creation of the whole universe and of a primal couple who are the ancestors of the whole of humankind. The book of Genesis begins with God's creation of "man" and "woman" and not with the Israelites. It is "man" who is made in the image of God (Gen. 1:26–27). It is a biblical commonplace to see the promise that God made to Eve as in fact the first of the biblical covenants (Gen. 3:15). It appears that already from the time of her son Seth and his son Enosh, human beings "began to call upon the name of the Lord" (Gen. 4:26), and the emergence of the nations was apparently according to the will of God (Gen. 10; cf. Deut. 32:8). The Jewish scribe Ben Sirach, who was active in the period around 180 B.C., in writing of the tradition of creation that had already become sacred Scripture by his time, begins with the use of the singular form for "man" (*anthropos* = human being) and immediately changes to the plural. He forthrightly affirms that the Lord "established a perpetual covenant with them and revealed to them his decrees" (Sir. 17:12, NEB). Ben Sirach understands the Lord as having given "them" the capacity for ethical discernment and knowledge of the Lord's law of life. If Israel is the peculiar possession of the Lord, the statement is made in the context of affirmations of God's providential ordering of the lives of the nations and of God's mercy as well as judgments operative upon both Israel and the nations. "He leaves a way open for the penitent to return to him, and gives the waverer strength to endure" (Sir. 17:24, NEB).

The second major divine covenant recorded in Genesis is that with Noah and his family, who are cited as preceding the call of Abraham and of course preceding the establishment of the people of Israel. This covenant is twice stated as not only including all human beings but "every living creature of all flesh that is upon the earth." The sons of Noah are said to be the ancestors of all peoples, and the covenant is with all (Gen. 9:8–19). The later Jewish rabbinical tradition came, on the basis of this Noachian covenant, to acknowledge the existence of a universal divine rule over all nations with specific implications for the potential divine blessing and, indeed, "salvation" of the nations. Raymond (Raimundo) Panikkar, following Jean Daniélou, has used the term "cosmic covenant" to denote the universal scope of this covenant with Noah.[10]

These two universal covenants, then, or larger structure of divine-human relationships, constitute the specific background and context for God's call of Abraham and the charge to create a particular people to fulfill particular purposes. But even the particularity or narrower ethnic scope of this call and covenant with Abraham is specifically stated to be effected only for a universal restorative purpose, that "by you all the families of the earth will bless themselves" (Gen. 12:3; cf. Gen. 18:18; 22:18; 26:4; 28:14). This affirmation is one way of stating the fact that, as Donald Dawe has put it, "the various covenants do not abrogate or replace one another. The prior covenants are the context of the later ones."[11]

The first eleven chapters of Genesis are generally thought to constitute an introduction to the first canon of Scripture in the Judeo-Christian tradition, the Pentateuch. The intent of the writers responsible for this work in the reign of Solomon (961–922 B.C.) was evidently to interpret both the liberation experience of the exodus and the revelatory events of Mount Sinai in the context of the whole world and of the needs of the nations. As Millard Lind has put it, the major biblical themes of grace and rebellion, judgment and salvation are universalized in these chapters "to show Yahweh's concern for the world behind his choice of Israel."[12]

This perception of the ongoing religious and theological validity of the older or prior covenants is an integral element of the self-understanding of the Hebraic tradition.[13] It has been a cause of misunderstanding, however, almost from the beginning of the Christian movement that some of its members perceived the new covenant in Jesus of Nazareth as abrogating the old rather than reforming it. But clearly the teaching of Jesus as recorded in the Matthaean tradition, like Jeremiah's, forthrightly affirms selective reform and a new interiority and rejects wholesale abolition (Mt. 5:17–48). The ideal Christian, or "scribe who has been trained for the kingdom of heaven, is like a householder who brings out of his treasure what is new and what is old" (Mt. 13:52). Subsequently we shall see in more detail how this perception is in fact the dominant biblical view.

These early covenants—which, as we see, constitute the structured context of understanding for all subsequent events, teachings, and persons recorded in the Bible—regularly include certain specific aspects. For one thing, they are based on divine-human encounters that include revelation or disclosure of the self and mind or will of God. This was clearly Ben Sirach's reading of the Genesis tradition of creation and the communication of Yahweh with Adam and Eve. The Genesis accounts of the covenants made with Noah and Abraham are similarly revelatory. The inescapable conclusion, one that the apostle Paul also drew in his letter to the Roman Christians (Rom. 1:19; 2:14–16), is that God's self and will have been revealed from the beginning in some measure to all peoples. And surely Paul Tillich was right in his insistence that it would not be proper to separate, even though we may distinguish, the revealing and the saving work of God.[14]

An aspect of the biblical covenants that emerges with particular clarity in the case of the call of Abraham is that of election. The influence of the "new theology" of Augustine and its repristination in Luther, and even more explicitly in Calvin, has given the concept of election an exclusivist meaning that was never intended in the biblical context.[15] Indeed, it has become a consensus of contemporary biblical studies to understand that the election of Israel as a "special" people was for special service, not for privilege.[16] The biblical concept of covenant, while rooted in God's free, sovereign choice, always carries the dual, inextricably intertwined polarity of divine grace and human response, of God's mercy and human responsibility. As we shall see, the nature of both divine grace and human response is as ineluctably ethical as it is personal. Nowhere in the Old Testament do we find the notion that God's salvation, a term whose meaning developed considerably over that period from concepts of delivery out of concrete situations of human need to more cosmic scope, is denied the nations because they are not of Israel.[17]

2

Biblical Bases for the Happening

THE OLD TESTAMENT

The Covenant with Israel

The covenantal relationship of Israel to Yahweh its God was, as we have seen, central to the self-awareness of the people of Israel. This covenant, constituting a contractual relationship with reciprocal responsibilities, was not one between equals.[1] It depended on the gracious initiative of Yahweh, particularly as this was manifested in the deliverance of the people of Israel from their bondage in Egypt and in the revelation basic to the creation of the covenant at Mount Sinai. Moreover, the liberation from Egypt is seen in our chief historical sources as the fulfillment of God's earlier promises to the patriarchs. Both the exodus from Egypt and the conquest of the "promised land" were viewed as a witness to Yahweh's faithful fulfillment of promises.[2] Hence what we may call the theology of Israel was rooted in this faith-understanding of the gracious initiative and dependable faithfulness of Yahweh.

In spite of this basic perception of Israel's election as resting not in any goodness or merit of its own,[3] and furthermore, in spite of the patriarchal tradition going back to a pattern of universal covenants, there are statements in the Old Testament implying that not a few in the history of Israel regarded Yahweh as the patron deity of their people in an exclusivist or partial sense. Especially in the early historical books that recount the process of the conquest of the land, we find the tensions implicit in such a crusading drive leading, as they have led in other later marches of "manifest destiny," to hostile and contemptuous perceptions of "the others." With reference to evaluations of the religious beliefs and practices of the nations other than Israel, we note the ferocity of Deuteronomy 7:2, 5, 16 and Elijah's command to kill 450 prophets of Baal (1 Kings 18:40). Long influential in western Europe was the Latin of Psalm 96:5 (Vulg. 95:5), "omnes dii gentium daemonia."

To be sure, there were ethical as well as theological issues of the profoundest import in the confrontation of the worship of Yahweh and the worship of Baal in Palestine of the time of Elijah, as later. The history of Israel as seen in the biblical record is primarily the account of its response, its varying degrees of faithfulness to its covenantal relationship with Yahweh. And this response was properly, at least according to the records of the literary prophets, ineluctably ethical. The will of Yahweh was for the people to show mercy, especially to the widow, the orphan, the poor, and the stranger at the gate. Oppression of the poor by the rich and powerful or any other form of economic or social injustice was seen as specifically constituting breach of the covenant. Furthermore, the strong and consistent concern of the Hebrew prophets for social and economic justice did not divert them from an equal concern for the inner intent and motives of persons. Joel, who cried out, "Rend your hearts and not your garments" (Joel 2:13), was but one of the many who proclaimed that Yahweh desires worship from a sincere heart that manifests its sincerity in appropriate deeds (cf. Amos 5:21-24).

The relationship implicit in the Abrahamic-Mosaic covenant of Israel with Yahweh was personal (corporate as well as individual) because Yahweh is personal. For this reason the term "adultery" was frequently used to denote breach of the covenant. The breaking of the most intimate of interhuman personal relationships seemed to provide the most apt metaphor to describe Israel's unfaithfulness to its Lord (cf. Hos. 7:4; Jer. 3:8; Ezek. 16:32). With reference, then, to the reaction of Elijah—we would now decidedly say "overreaction"—to the challenge of Baal worship, and the unfaithfulness of many in Israel to their covenant with Yahweh, the issue was profoundly ethical. The indignation of Elijah and the later prophets against Baal worship was not directed primarily toward the foreignness of the name. They were profoundly disturbed because Baal worship seemed to be integrally involved with practices of temple prostitution and the burning of children alive as a part of worship. The prophets thundered that such was not the will of Yahweh (cf. Jer. 32:35; Ezek. 16:20-22).

Furthermore, the modes of Baal worship seemed to involve a perception of cosmic totality wherein no significant distinction was made between the divine and the natural. In this world-view, unqualified religious sanction could be ascribed to royal authority and to the structures of society as they are. The practical consequence was that no transcendent criterion existed by which it was possible, on a religious basis, to criticize political or social injustice if perpetrated by the ruling powers of state or society. Perhaps the contrast is too sharply set here, for in comparable situations in other societies, as in the case of the religious ultimacy historically given to the caste system of India, there are frequently countervailing factors even where and when they do not appear to be theoretically or theologically possible.[4] In any case, it is significant that in the great confrontation on Mount Carmel, Elijah did not reprove the Canaanites; he addressed himself to the people of Israel. They had the responsibility to be faithful to what they knew (1 Kings 18:20-21).

The word of God in both the Old Testament and the New is addressed primarily *to* a people, not *about* them. And, as we shall see, when the judgment of God is proclaimed against particular foreign nations, it is not because of the nature of their religious faith but for their evil deeds, which represent faithlessness to an obligation (covenant) or knowledge already possessed (cf. Amos 1:1-2:8; Obad. 15; Nah. 1:2; Zech. 9:1).[5]

Our primary concern here, however, is for Israel's perception of the nature of Yahweh and of Yahweh's wider work in the world. At least from the beginning of the period of the literary prophets, the spiritual leadership of Israel had clearly come to regard Yahweh as Creator and Lord of the universe and therefore Lord of the nations as well as of Israel. We find also a basic assumption not only in the biblical descriptions of the creation of the universal covenants, but also, and consistently, in the prophetic literature, in the psalms and the wisdom literature. This is the assumption, frequently stated as well as implied, that the nations have some knowledge of Yahweh and of Yahweh's ethical character and demands. Not only Israel, but the nations, too, are enfolded within Yahweh's concern and care even as they are under Yahweh's lordship.

As early as the mid-eighth century B.C. the prophet Amos had come to a remarkably universal understanding of the providential lordship of Yahweh. This understanding appears implicit throughout the oracles of Amos, but we find it expressed in particularly graphic mode when he asserts that Yahweh regards the movements of the Philistines from Caphtor (Crete?) and the Syrians from Kir (their place of origin to the northeast?) as the result of Yahweh's providential guidance and of comparable significance with the deliverance of Israel from Egypt. The very Israelites who regard themselves as the first of the nations (Amos 6:1) are the same to Yahweh as the Ethiopians, a people who, to Israel's ken, reside in the remotest part of the world (Amos 9:7; cf. Isa. 14:16-27). Amos himself evidently believed that Israel participated in a unique relationship with Yahweh (Amos 3:2) and had gained its land with divine help (2:9-10). But Amos gave it as the word of the Lord that "Israel should not draw from this the conclusion that its God had guided only its history."[6]

The consistent understanding of the literary prophets was that on the day of the Lord—and before!—the nations are to be judged, like Israel, in accordance with their ethical conduct and in proportion to their knowledge (Amos 1; 2; Jer. 7:3-4; Ezek. 16:44-58; Zech. 1:15; 7:8-9; Zeph. 1:3, 9, 18; Mal. 3:18). If Israel has a unique measure of the knowledge of Yahweh and the divine will, this knowledge carries proportionate ethical responsibilities. Amos asserts flatly that because of a special relationship, *therefore* will the Lord punish Israel for all its iniquities (Amos 3:2). Ezekiel reports the word of the Lord that Israel has "wickedly rebelled against my ordinances more than the nations . . . *therefore* . . . *therefore* thus says the Lord God: Behold, I, even I, am against you; and I will execute judgments in the midst of you in the sight of the nations" (Ezek. 5:5-8, italics added; cf. Hos. 7:11-12;

13:4–16; Isa. 40:2; 51:7; Jer. 7:30–34; Mic. 3:1–4; Mal. 2:8–9). Indeed, the further affirmation is made that Yahweh uses the nations in both saving and punitive activity toward Israel (Isa. 44:28; 45:1–5).[7] Jeremiah, we may recall, had described Nebuchadrezzar, the king of Babylon, as the servant of Yahweh to execute the judgments of Yahweh upon the people of Israel (Jer. 25:9).

There are numerous references in the Old Testament to "just Gentiles": Abel, Enoch, Noah, Daniel (as in Ezek. 14:14), Melchizedek, Lot, Job, the Queen of Sheba, and so forth. Among these are specifically prophetic figures (as that term was used in Israel) such as Balaam and Job, as well as the priest-king Melchizedek (Num. 22:1–25; Gen. 14:18–20; Ps. 110:4). Other men and women from among the nations are approvingly depicted in the Old Testament. Judah, the son of Jacob, is recorded as having a Canaanite of Adullam for a friend and marrying the daughter of Shua, another Canaanite. Tamor, the wife whom Jacob chose for his first son, Er, was a Canaanite and is singularly praised by Judah for her righteousness. We note favorable mention of Pharaoh's daughter; of Moses' non-Israelite father-in-law Jethro, from whom he received counsel; of Rahab, the prostitute of Jericho; and of course of Ruth (Gen. 38:1–30; Exod. 2:5–10; 18:1–27; Josh. 2:1–21; Ruth). We find, furthermore, statements in certain cases that men and women of the nations truly worship the Lord (Exod. 18:10–12; Jon. 1:16).[8] In the wisdom books of the Bible we note a general recognition of the value of the wisdom of the nations. It is now widely acknowledged that the Hebrews were familiar, at least to some degree, with the wisdom literatures of Babylonia, Syria, Edom, and Arabia as well as of Egypt and that they borrowed extensively from them. In 1 Kings 4:30–31 the excellence of Solomon's wisdom is said to lie in surpassing that of "all the people of the east and all the wisdom of Egypt." The names of three Edomite sages are specifically cited in the passage, and we find references to the wisdom of Edom in both Jeremiah and Obadiah. We may recall that both Job and his friends were of non-Israelite origin, most of the latter evidently coming from Edom.[9]

A highly significant image of the prophetic understanding of divine providence at work among the nations is that given by Ezekiel in his "anointed guardian cherub," which he saw as assigned by Yahweh to the king and people of Tyre (Ezek. 28:14–16; cf. the Greek of Deut. 32:8; Dan. 10:13). This may be the origin, or at least an early expression, of the theological commonplace in later Judaism according to which an angel was assigned by God to each nation to signify, in personified form, the divine presence, protection, and vocation given to each. It is significant that the same belief is expressed in the late first-century Christian letter from the church in Rome to the church in Corinth known as 1 Clement (29:2) as in the later Jewish Christian (Pseudo-Clementine) *Recognitions* (II, 42).

We have noted with reference to evaluation of the religious beliefs and practices of the nations what we called the ferocity of Deut. 7:2, 5. Actually, this posture of wholesale condemnation lies in the context of what was perceived as a divine command to genocide and is by no means representative of the mainstream of biblical faith, even as the vengeful, pitiless spirit of Ps. 137:8–9 is by no means typical of the mentality of Psalms as a whole. G. Ernest Wright, for example, has argued, as a means of better understanding the message of the Old Testament with reference to this problem, that the so-called "woes" pronounced upon the nations (e.g., Isa. 33:1; Jer. 48:46; Nah. 3:1) represent not imprecations but laments, or, more often, statements declarative of Yahweh's ethical judgments in the context of universal covenants. The "ah, my brother" of Jer. 22:18 (RSV) and the "alas" of 1 Kings 13:30 are renderings of the same Hebrew word *hoy*, which is elsewhere translated as "woe." Furthermore, the Hebrew term *neqamah*, which is rendered in the Revised Standard Version as "vengeance" in Jer. 46:10 and 51:11 is more properly translated, Wright contends, by "vindication," as of the prerogatives of Yahweh in the world. The context is that of a concept of the universal suzerainty of Yahweh over the world wherein "the peoples and nations of the world are bound together in various ways by law." The prophetic "declarations" therefore relate to what the prophets believed to be specific transgressions of that law.[10]

Actually, in the Old Testament we generally find more discriminating appraisals of the nations and their religious faith and practices than that given in Deuteronomy 7. It is true that idols, in the literal sense of the word as graven images, are regarded, especially by the later prophets, as having no religious significance, as empty wind, a delusion (cf. Isa. 46:1–13). The gods of the nations (*ēl*), however, were generally perceived at this period as contingent realities, as representing the powers of nature. Thus in Deut. 10:17 Yahweh is called God of gods. But the same Deutero-Isaiah who is so critical of idols calls the Persian king Cyrus (who permitted the Jewish exiles in Babylon to return to their homeland) the shepherd of the Lord, Yahweh's anointed (Isa. 44:28; 45:1; 48: 14–15; 2 Chron. 36:22–23; cf. Ezra 1:1–4; 6:10; 7:12, 21, 23; Dan. 4:34–35; 5:23). For the prophet, Yahweh is the universal Lord; beside him there is no God (Isa. 45:5). This theological perspective leaves the prophet with no alternative but to identify the liberating work of Cyrus as a high expression of the providential work of Yahweh.

The widening historical experience of Israel brought widened views. The captivity in Babylon may not have been at first a religiously broadening experience (cf. Isa. 45:1–2), but Habakkuk saw the punitive role of the Chaldeans as directly expressive of the plan and work of God (Hab. 1:5, 6, 12). The experience in Babylon constituted the primary setting for the entire prophetic career of Ezekiel. But even if detailed evidence is lacking in the Hebrew Scriptures themselves, the whole development of later pre-Christian Judaism was clearly influenced by the Jewish experience with Cyrus and his successors in the empire of the Medes and the Persians. Acquaintance with the Persian empire brought Israel for the first time into contact with ethical monotheism of a high level outside itself, that of Zoroastrianism. Here the people of Israel met with religious faith of a different ethical and spiritual quality from what their ancestors had known in the worship of Baalim and Ashtarōt. Here was to be found as clear an example of "emissary prophecy" as in the history of Israel, and the role of Iranian (Persian) influence upon the development of Judaism, from the fifth century B.C., is undeniable.[11] Certainly we may speak of Malachi (ca. 450 B.C.) as a product of the tolerant atmosphere of the Persian empire, for it was he who averred that Yahweh is in fact worshiped throughout the world under the guise of every person's worship (Mal. 1:5, 11, 14; cf. Isa. 28:11).[12] We need also to take with full seriousness the inclusive affirmations of Psalms 65 and 87, as of 47:7-10, 46:10, and 48:10.

In Malachi are also to be found strong words expressive of Yahweh's disapproval of Edom. This was not because Edom was a heathen nation, but because the people were cruel and treacherous (Mal. 1:4; cf. Amos 1:3-2:8; Obad. 3-14; Nah. 3:1-4). In the day of the Lord the duty of God's people will be once more to "distinguish between the righteous and the wicked, between one who serves God and one who does not serve him" (Mal. 3:18). This is to make a distinction based primarily upon ethical conduct (cf. Jer. 7:3-4; Zech. 7:8-9).[13] Persons and nations are to be judged by their ethical performance, in accordance with their knowledge (cf. Zeph. 1, 3, 9, 18; Zech. 1:15). And in the Wisdom of Solomon we read the prayer, "But thou art merciful to all, for thou canst do all things, and thou dost overlook men's sins that they may repent. For thou lovest all things that exist, and hast loathing for none of the things that thou hast made, for thou wouldst not have made anything if thou hadst hated it. . . . Thou sparest all things, for they are thine, O Lord who lovest the living" (11:23-26). In this work, written in Alexandria in probably the second century B.C., we find notable expression of the compassionately inclusive spirit emergent within postexilic Judaism.

The Particularity of the Covenant with Israel

The question then arises, what, if any, particularity lies in the election of Israel and God's covenant with that people? There is a highly significant particularity, and it is similar to the particularity of any individual servant or group of messengers of God in relationship to the persons or groups whom they may serve. In the case of the servant as an individual, this person as an individual has unique aspects of self, of knowledge and power. He or she, by reason of these aspects or endowments and the call of God, may have a distinct mission to serve others. This is the person's role under God. And because of this role and its function to communicate specific knowledge of God and God's healing power, this servant-individual may at a point or period of time have specific knowledge of God and the divine will and a unique mode of relationship with God that certain others at that time do not have. But this "temporary" advantage or superiority is not intended to remain as such; it is certainly not a part of the will of God that it be a permanent privilege arbitrarily granted to one and denied to another. The principle applies with equal validity to servant-groups, whether ethnically characterized or not.

Furthermore, whatever the extent to which Yahweh may use Israel to fulfill Yahweh's saving purposes toward humankind, the prophetic eschatological position, as we have seen, views Israel as subject to judgment together with the nations. Th. C. Vriezen has written in this connection that the election of Israel is not to be identified with modern notions of certainty of ultimate salvation. Rather, "the Old Testament is not concerned in the first instance to lay the foundations of a certainty of salvation, but to place the fact of [Israel's] existence as the people of God in the right light: this privilege has not been extended to Israel that she might become infatuated with it, but that she might recognize it as a commission."[14]

In the relational mystery of God's cosmos, the destiny of all beings appears to be that of coming into relationship with all other beings in the spirit of love and the activity of service—all coordinated by the "one thing needful," love and service of God. In this relational mystery, where salvation in either its penultimate or ultimate sense is radically constitutive of quality of relationship, and sin is essentially severance or distortion of relationship, the role of the one or ones who "have" is to share with those who "have not." It is of course basic to the biblical view of human beings that no one or ones "have" totally, and no one or ones are totally without. We always operate in the context of relative degrees of knowledge, goodness, or quality of relationship. But a central conclusion to be drawn from this line of thought is that there is no single individual or group or people who "have" it alone. And insofar as any one does have a "temporary" advantage, it is to be shared. Such advantage exists to be shared and, in the economy of God, if it is not shared it "spoils."

The foregoing constitutes in a sense a rationale for mission. It evidently took centuries for the people of Israel to come to understand their election and covenant with Yahweh in this sense as necessarily involving mission to others. But the understanding comes to clear focus in Deutero-Isaiah when he perceives that for Yahweh the restoration of Israel is not an end in itself: "It is too light a thing that you should be my servant to raise up the tribes of Jacob and to restore the preserved of Israel; I will give you as a light to the nations, that my salvation may reach to the end of the earth" (Isa. 49:6; cf. Zeph. 3:9; Isa. 25:6–8). As Donald Dawe has well put it, this is "the particularism of a people that has been given a vision of God by which the world may be illumined."[15] As a very special aspect of Israel's election, it was to have a special role as the channel of preparation for the coming of the universal Messiah, universal in the range of his meaning and in the effect of his work.

The Missionary Responsibility

It is possible, then, to find in the universal perspectives of the Old Testament a valid basis for missionary witness (cf. Isa. 42:1–7; 55:5). It was not, however, until the intertestamental period, in the Jewish Diaspora, that the missionary implications were drawn to the extent of substantial practical implementation. In a sense anticipatory of this development, there is, however, one book in the Hebrew Old Testament that dramatically contrasts narrow nationalistic self-concern with the missionary responsibility that properly belonged to Israel's faith. This book is Jonah. Here we see a prophet called to preach repentance to a foreign people in spite of their cruel treatment of Israel, because Yahweh cares for them, because Yahweh has personal concern for the welfare of the people of Nineveh, even for their cattle (Jon. 4:11). The prophet addresses himself to the ethical issues and urges everyone in Nineveh to "turn from his evil way and from the violence which is in his hands" (Jon. 3:8). But the unique message of the book is that the Lord who delivers, who is gracious and merciful, slow to anger, and abounding in steadfast love, is also so disposed toward the nations, and the prophet (Israel) has been called to minister to that purpose. This is primarily the reason for the prophet's anguish of spirit, and presumably, in the author's mind, the reason for the anguish of the people of Israel.

Neither in the Old Testament nor in the New is there any acknowledgment that there are others who "have" precisely in the same sense or to the same degree as Israel or its extension in the form of the Christian church. Yet, as we have seen in the Old Testament and shall note in the New, there are clear statements that there are others than Israel who "have," even if the degree of their possession is not specified. And in fact it is an inescapable conclusion from the nature of the universal covenants which the biblical writers acknowledged as the very structure of their corporate life that all human beings be regarded as already "having" in an important sense. The apostle Paul acknowledges this fact clearly in his letter to the Roman Christians, the most systematic statement of his theology in the New Testament. He insists that God has revealed basic elements of the divine nature and will to all human beings (Rom. 1:19-20). The Gentiles do not have the law in the form given to Israel, but they have its essential content because "what the law requires is written on their hearts, while their conscience also bears witness" (Rom. 2:15).

The main thrust of Paul's message in the first three chapters of Romans is to affirm the paradoxical fact that in a basically important sense all human beings share in similar gifts from God and yet that there is "advantage" that the Jews have: "To begin with, the Jews are entrusted with the oracles of God" (Rom. 3:2). But Paul's conclusion is finally that all human beings are really "in the same boat" (Rom 1:18-32; 3:9-20). In this context he proclaims the universal saving intent of God and the great fact of God's work to that end in Jesus Christ (Rom. 3:21-31).

It would seem that a necessary conclusion of this understanding of God and God's ways with humankind is that all who have some awareness of divine call or election and accordingly feel that in a significant sense they "have" that which they may share with others—whether they who "have" be

Jews, Christians, or others—will approach all human beings with respect. Those who would share with others—and share they must if they are faithful to their call—may have some temporary advantage. It seems to be central to the mysteries of divine methodology that God use human as well as other instruments in the divine work unto the salvation and restoration of human beings and the entire cosmos; but we who belong to the Judeo-Christian tradition are not the only ones who "have." Such seems to be the right reading of the biblical message. And those from one tradition who believe that they "have" will carefully and patiently explore the extent to which others already "have" even as they endeavor to share with these others their own "possession."

As we have noted, the Bible gives us little help with reference to the specifics that others "have." But the solidarity of humankind, which the Judeo-Christian Scriptures affirm from their beginning, calls us to respect not only the fact of human solidarity and the shared personhood implied therein but also what these others already "have." This means that the mission to give is also a mission to receive, the mission to teach is also a mission to learn. This means that mission in the Judeo-Christian tradition is properly to be grounded in the profoundest of human mutualities: mutual human respect, mutual human sharing, mutual human learning and help. A purpose of this book is to explore some of the specifics by which these mutualities may be discerned and enhanced.

THE NEW TESTAMENT

The Gospels

One of the most important emphases of New Testament scholarship from the mid-twentieth century has been to stress the varieties of religious understanding and theological interpretation to be found in the New Testament. This position has not in general led to a denial of a basic unity as characteristic of the New Testament, but its effect has been such as to render quite untenable any notion of a total sameness. This means that the proof-text method, the selection of passages or verses without regard for context or relationship to other documents within the New Testament or materials from without, is not considered in most academic circles an acceptable method of study. Nevertheless, because there is also a basic unity discernible in the New Testament, the identification of common understanding on a particular theme in various parts of the Gospels and other "apostolic" writings is highly significant for knowledge of at least major segments of the broad mind of the apostolic generation and the early church.

The Gospel of John was probably the last written of the four Gospels of the New Testament, but as the product of decades of loving reflection on the deeper significance of the life of Jesus of Nazareth—the author presumably also made use of earlier records—it occupies a unique place among the Gospel accounts. From the first chapter we note universal perspectives quite in keeping with the best of pre-Christian Judaism and, as we shall see, probably expressive of the mind of Jesus himself.

John uses the Greek term *Logos* (Word) to give specific identity to the person and role of Jesus of Nazareth. This term was already used by Heraclitus of Ephesus (fl. 513 B.C.) in the sense of universal Reason, the cohesive principle constitutive of order in an otherwise ever changing physical universe (*panta rhei*). The concept was developed by Zeno (fl. 310 B.C.) and later Stoics as their basic religio-philosophical position moved from an early pantheism toward theism. John retains the universal significance of Hellenistic usage but affirms that the Logos became flesh and dwelt among human beings as a particular man (Jn. 1:14). The Logos, however, in this way was sent to the whole created universe, which already belonged to him *in toto* or was his by affinity (*ta idia*, Jn. 1:11).[16] God's love for the world is cited as the basic motivation of God's action (Jn. 3:16), as a reality prior to any distinction of nations or religions.

It would take us too far afield to attempt to consider in detail the teaching of Jesus with regard to the nations, but it is possible to paint a fairly coherent picture with a few strokes even amid the somewhat differing nuances of the various Gospel accounts. All the writers agree to the extent of depicting Jesus as utterly free of nationalistic or ethnically based prejudice himself and as rejecting all notions of arbitrary divine vengeance, eschatological or present, upon the nations (Mt. 19:30; 20:16 [Mk. 10:31; Lk. 13:30]; Mt. 11:21-24; 12:41-42; Lk. 9:51-56). Indeed, quite in accord with the ancient prophetic tradition, Jesus, even as he evidently considered the Jews to have been given certain spiritual endowments appropriate to their divine mission, forthrightly affirmed that they would for that reason be held to account all the more severely (Lk. 13:28-29 [Mt. 8:10-13]; Mt. 5:20; 10:15; 11:21, 23; cf. Jas. 3:1).

Among the synoptic Gospels we find in Matthew alone specific criticism on Jesus' part of Gentile religious practices (Mt. 6:7, 30 [Jn. 4:22]; but cf. Mt. 11:21-24; 10:15). But then again in no other Gospel is there found sharper reproof of common contemporary Jewish practices or more forthright affirmation of the sublime impartiality, or fairness, of God. Indeed, special notice should be taken of Jesus' appreciation of the religious faith and ethical conduct of certain Gentiles as recorded in Matthew (Mt. 8:5-13 [Lk. 7:1-12; Jn. 4:46-54]; cf. Lk. 10:30-37; 17:11-19). In the context of consideration of contemporary rival religious parties and groups, Jesus emphasized the importance of quality of attitude or intent as compared with formal allegiance, and we read that "he that is not against us is for us" (Mk. 9:40).[17] Again in Matthew we find Jesus resolutely refusing to ascribe any ultimate religious significance to merely formal acts or allegiances. That is, not those who proclaim the "name" or even perform miracles, but those who do the will of God shall enter the kingdom (Mt. 7:21-23; 25:14-46; cf. 1 Cor. 13; Lk. 10:25-37;

13:22–30). Also recorded in Matthew is the devastating statement of Jesus made immediately after his warm commendation of the faith of the Roman centurion whose servant he was about to heal: "I tell you, many will come from east and west and sit at the table with Abraham, Isaac and Jacob in the kingdom of heaven, while the sons of the kingdom will be thrown into the outer darkness" (Mt. 8:10–12). Equally devastating is Jesus' criticism of certain Jewish missionary practices whereby converts were won to the faith of Israel only to manifest ethical fruits of an even lower quality than their mentors (Mt. 23:15). In Matthew's account of the eschatological parable of the sheep and the goats, final separation is made not on the basis of ethnic or cultural affiliation or even of religious faith, but as a consequence of the presence or lack of ethical, in particular of compassionate, conduct (Mt. 25:31–46).

In the Gospel of Luke we find the clearest exposition of Jesus' teaching on the theme that is essentially one with the ancient prophetic tradition of Israel. This is the conviction that the judgments of God are primarily concerned with the ethical quality of the deeds and lives of persons and that greater knowledge brings greater responsibility (Lk. 12:47–48). The saying of Jesus in this passage, that the servant who knew but did not act in accordance with his master's will shall be more severely treated than he who so acted but did not know, expresses what H. J. Cadbury called the principle of proportionate duty, which is also the principle of utter divine fairness, or impartiality.[18] We note in Luke that when Jesus was refused entrance into a Samaritan village because his ultimate destination was Jerusalem and his disciples asked if they should bid fire to come down from heaven to punish the villagers, Jesus rebuked the disciples (Lk. 9:51–56). The particularities of election cited in the Bible and the diversity of the personal endowments of human beings are both properly to be understood by means of this principle, which seems basic to the whole of Jesus' teaching.

We are not given in Jesus' recorded teaching a systematic rationale for differences in the givenness of human endowments. We even have the paradoxical statement that "to him who has will more be given, and he will have abundance; but from him who has not, even what he has will be taken away" (Mt. 13:12). Perhaps the meaning of the saying is that all persons must attend to their several responsibilities, and smallness of endowment (at any one time) is no excuse for lethargy or despair. But Jesus appears to have devoted attention not only to the exploited or underprivileged of Israel; indeed as H. J. Cadbury has pointed out, many of Jesus' sayings were addressed to favored persons.[19] The rich are shamed by the relative generosity of the poor widow's offering (Mk. 12:41–44; Lk. 21:1–4). Simon the Pharisee is shamed by the costly offering and tender care of a sinful woman (Mk. 14:3–9, par.); a priest and a Levite are outdone by a foreign Samaritan in deeds of compassion (Lk. 10:29–37). And, as we have noted, Jews in spite of their privileges may be rejected, while others from east and west, from north and south, will come and sit at table in the kingdom of God (Mt. 8:11–12; Lk. 13:28–29).

Not just a neatly or arithmetically proportioned more, but *even* more, is expected of the favored. Jesus expects his disciples to exceed the righteousness of the scribes and Pharisees, that is, the righteousness of the carefully calculating (Mt. 5:20). He proclaims the special privileges of the persons of his generation and asserts that their less-favored predecessors, even the wicked of Sodom, Tyre, and Sidon, will find it more tolerable in the day of judgment than those who reject what greater thing God has offered them now (Mt. 10:15; 11:21-24, par.). The Beatitudes and Woes pronounced by Jesus are properly to be interpreted in this context of understanding. The rich have not acted in proportion to their advantages, whereas "the poor have often deserved better than might have been expected of them." In the same way the Jew is contrasted with Samaritan or Gentile. Thus we may say that the principle running through Jesus' teaching is more than a proportionate responsibility. It is a call to the giving of a surplus, in excess, a call to an uncalculating generosity of spirit and conduct.[20] For God is like that.

As a further example of Jesus' inclusive mentality, we note that the context of his assertion to his disciples of God's parental concern, that the very hairs of their head are all numbered (Mt. 10:30), implies that the affirmation applies to all human beings. For even in the case of sparrows, "not one of them is forgotten before God" (Lk. 12:6), nor will one fall to the ground apart from God's will (Mt. 10:29). God "makes his sun rise on the evil and on the good, and sends rain on the just and on the unjust" (Mt. 5:45). This last saying, of course, communicates the truth not only of the impartiality of God the Parent but also of God's generosity toward all. The high anthropology of Jesus is revealed not only in his teaching of a hierarchy of values in the cosmos, whereby a human being is "of more value than many sparrows" (Mt. 10:31; cf. "Of how much more value is a man than a sheep!" Mt. 12:12). Of even more significance is the confrontational colloquy recorded in the Gospel of John wherein Jesus replies to hearers critical of his own expressed self-understanding and quotes to them Ps. 82:6: "Is it not written in your law, 'I said, you are gods'?"; Jesus goes on in the passage to affirm that the psalmist "called them gods to whom the word of God came" (Jn. 10:34-35). The Gospel of John is as noteworthy for its high anthropology as for its high Christology.

A graphic summation of Jesus' inclusive posture can be found in the famous passage in the fourth chapter of Luke, which is a report of Jesus' first sermon in Nazareth, "where he had been brought up." The passage as a whole is a remarkable example of Jesus' selective use of Scripture to focus on the highest and the best of the past of Israel.[21] The first part of the sermon stresses God's—and Jesus'—social inclusivism, indicating God's concern for every class of society. The second part emphasizes God's—and Jesus'—international inclusivism, indicating God's concern (not only currently but also in the past) for those outside historic Israel. The reaction of violent anger from Jesus' hearers was probably as much because of the first kind of inclusivism as from the second (Lk. 4:16-30). A final point of the highest significance is the fact that the primary content of Jesus' teaching, especially as recorded in the synoptic Gospels, focuses on the kingdom of God, not on the people of Israel or any other narrower category.

Acts of the Apostles and Pauline Writings

When we turn to the book of Acts we come upon a statement that has been made much of by writers of exclusivist persuasion. This is the statement made by Peter to the Jewish assembly hastily formed the morning following the overnight detention of the apostles Peter and John. They had been held in custody because, in spite of firm strictures to desist, they had publicly and forthrightly given witness of their experience of the resurrection of Jesus. The assembly included the full Jewish establishment, "rulers and elders and scribes" and "all of the high-priestly family." The situation was confrontational to the extreme. The Jewish authorities were becoming increasingly nervous over the public statements of Jesus' disciples as witnesses to his resurrection from the dead. Their nervousness was compounded by the fact that on the previous day Peter and John had been the human instruments for the healing of a man born lame. Just after this event they made their further public witness to Jesus' resurrection, his messiahship, and the present power of his name. On that previous day the author of Acts records Peter as addressing his hearers in language as confrontational as it is rhetorical: "you denied the Holy and Righteous One, and asked for a murderer to be granted to you, and you killed the Author of life, whom God raised from the dead. To this we are witnesses" (Acts 3:1–26).

On the day following this healing and their detention, Peter and John were set in the midst of the aforementioned hastily gathered assembly. Once again Peter acted as the spokesman and once again insisted forthrightly that the power responsible for the healing of the lame man was not their own but "by the name of Jesus Christ of Nazareth, whom you crucified, whom God raised from the dead." This all was the larger context for Peter's further statement "and there is salvation in no one else, for there is no other name under heaven given among men by which we must be saved" (Acts 4:1–12).

This single verse has been the occasion for many exclusivist conclusions with reference to the possibilities of ultimate salvation available to human beings in the plan and providence of God. That is, it has been widely understood, in conservative Protestant circles at least from the beginnings of continental Pietism and English-speaking evangelicalism, as meaning that apart from explicit Christian faith and specific verbal expression of faith-commitment to Jesus Christ, there is no salvation possible for human beings.

We shall discuss the meaning of the term "salvation" in more detail in a later chapter, but in our present context let us take note that there is a variety of meanings for the term, either as noun or verb, in the New Testament, as indeed in the Old. Only about one-fifth of the 150 instances in the New Testament refer to a salvation to be consummated at the last day, that is, ultimate or eschatological salvation. Nearly a third refer to deliverance from specific ills, as in Acts 4:9 just preceding the verse we are considering. As is frequently the case with the healings of Jesus recorded in the synoptic Gospels, the fact of the man's healing is described in the Greek here with the verbal form of "save."²² The RSV renders the last phrase of Acts 4:9 as "by what means this man has been healed." The Greek original has "by what means this man has been saved." The immediate context of Acts 4:12 in the Greek is therefore not an exclusivist statement about limited possibilities of human salvation in any ultimate sense but a ringing affirmation of the incomparable healing power available to all human beings in the name of Jesus Christ. We may recall that in the controversy wherein Jesus was accused by the scribes of healing by means of Beelzebul, he assumes that God's power to cast out demons is available to others ("by whom do your sons cast them out?" Mt. 12:27).

If we follow through with the larger context of the Acts of the Apostles, we learn that in order to understand the full significance of Acts 4:12, we need to see it in the light of Acts 10:34–35 (cf. Lk. 2:14; 1 Clement 21:8). The latter passage in Acts cites the statement of Peter made in the home of Cornelius, a Roman centurion, and in the presence of a number of other Gentiles: "Truly I perceive that God shows no partiality, but in every nation any one who fears him and does what is right is acceptable to him." As we have seen, a statement like this is in accord with both a major stream of thought in the history of Israel and the teaching of Jesus himself. But Peter admits to having been caught up in the narrower views and practices of his time (Acts 10:14–15, 28–29; cf. Gal. 2:11–21) and confesses that the vision which led him to Cornelius' home—as Cornelius' vision had impelled him to invite Peter—was in fact divine revelation leading him to broader understanding and sympathies.

It is more likely than not that the author of Acts intended the entire incident of Peter's encounter with Cornelius, his family, and friends to be perceived as a corrective of possible misunderstanding of Peter's earlier statement in 4:12. Peter's affirmation of God's inclusiveness in Acts 10:34–35 appears later in the narration of events, as an event later in time. It is also specifically cited as correcting, or enlarging, his former narrower understanding (Acts 10:1–48). That such was the author's intent appears from his account four chapters later where Paul is recorded as asserting in Lystra of Lycaonia in Asia Minor a view of the wider work of God in the world, which is essentially similar to that of Peter's enlarged understanding. Paul specifically states that God "did not leave" himself without witness throughout the entire range of human history before the coming of the Christ (Acts 14:15–17).

A like reference to the bountiful providence of God is found in the account of Paul's address to the Athenians recorded in Acts 17:16–34. Here we find Paul critical of idol worship and assuming that he must instruct his sophisticated hearers (among whom were Epicurean and other philosophers) more particularly as to who and what God really is and what God had already done and would do through "a man whom he has appointed." But Paul boldly asserts the solidarity of all humankind, their oneness in origin by divine creation, their oneness in existence by participation in divine being. He furthermore states that the whole of the Greek past as well as the Hebrew had been under the providential care and within the structure of the purposes of God. He asserts that not only had the Greeks been zealous in their religious devotion, albeit in part mistaken, but even in their ignorance they had worshiped the one, true God. "He is not far from each of us."[23]

We have already taken brief note of Paul's views of the place of the nations in the economy of God in the discussion of election and particularity. To summarize briefly, however, his understanding as found in the New Testament letters generally acknowledged as authentically Pauline, we may begin with what is the *locus classicus* for his treatment of this theme, the first three chapters of Romans. Paul's contention in Rom. 1:19–32 is that the fact of God, God's nature as eternal power and deity, is knowable to all human beings through God's creation. But Paul does not say that this knowledge is attained by the use of human reason alone, for "God has shown it to them" (Rom. 1:19). This is in effect an affirmation of the universality of divine revelation in some measure and mode. Paul further contends that God's law, or basic moral requirements, is written in the consciences of the Gentiles, as human beings (Rom. 2:15). It appears from Rom. 1:21ff. that Paul follows in the tradition of historic Israel (cf. Isa. 44:9–20; Jer. 10:3–9; etc.) in regarding this universal knowledge as gravely corrupted in all humankind but yet of such a nature that it leaves human beings without excuse for their distorted modes of worship and life.

As suggested above in an earlier context, Paul's basic purpose is to put all human beings "in the same boat" so as to prepare their understanding to receive the same liberation-salvation that God has made available to all through and in Jesus Christ. But the basic structure of his thought, and the central theme of Romans 2, is what again we may call the principle of proportionate duty as a cosmic expression of God's utter fairness—and generosity. Israel's election and related "advantages" are real (Rom. 2:17–18). But if Israel is unfaithful to God and disobedient to the divine law, the whole structure of "advantage" is demolished, for God shows no partiality (Rom. 2:25, 11). "He will render to every man according to his works" (Rom. 2:6—an aspect of Paul's teaching often neglected in Pauline studies; cf. Gal. 6:7–10; 2 Cor. 5:10; Col. 3:25). If Jews are first, they are the first to receive judgment, as they are the first to receive praise (Rom. 2:9–10; cf. 1 Pet. 4:17). God is the God of the Gentiles as well as of the Jews (Rom. 3:29).

Paul shares the view of other New Testament writers that the Mosaic law itself was communicated through the intermediation of angels (Gal. 3:19; cf. Acts 7:53; Heb. 2:2). In light of the presence in later pre-Christian Judaism of the concept of the divinely assigned role of angels among the nations, this view, as we have seen, may well have constituted the predominant apostolic understanding of the mode of divine working among the nations as well as within Israel. Paul follows Deutero-Isaiah with his words: ''we know that 'an idol has no real existence,' and that 'there is no God but one' '' (1 Cor. 8:4). But he at once goes on to acknowledge, in the same prophetic tradition, that there are in fact many gods and lords in the heavens or on earth, even though all are subsumed under the dominance of one God, the Father, and one Lord, Jesus Christ (1 Cor. 8:5-6; cf. Eph 4:6).[24] Later in the same letter to the Corinthian church, Paul suggests that the food offered to pagan idols could be an offering to demons (1 Cor. 10:20-22). But whatever was Paul's criticism of the empirical condition of popular religion among the pagans, and we find no example of specific approval of pagan religious worship in any Pauline letter, nothing could alter his conviction of the universal lordship, gracious providence, and loving care for all beings on the part of God the Father and his Christ. God shows no partiality (Rom. 2:11).

We see Paul probably at his most mature and mellow stage of growth in the letter that he wrote from prison at the end of his life to the church in Philippi. Herein he urges the Christians of Philippi, whom he seems to have loved with especial appreciation and fondness, to be open to all truth and goodness wherever found (Phil. 4:8). We note comparably universal perspectives in Col. 1:12-20; 2:9-10 (as also in Eph. 1:22-23; 4:9-10).[25]

IN SUMMARY

We need not pursue this biblical inquiry in further detail. To summarize our conclusions at this point, we may confidently affirm an essential unity within both Old and New Testaments with regard to the following themes. Israel and the nations are equally the creation of God, equally the object of God's love and concern. All are subsumed within the scope of the pre-Abrahamic covenants, and these form a central and integral element of Israel's tradition and constitute the basic structure of Israel's understanding of itself and of the whole world of living beings. Within this structure specific particularities may obtain, and these particularities may constitute differences in the mode and degree of divine revelation to different persons and (ethnic) groups. Specifically, the biblical witness seems to reveal an essential agreement in self-understanding that the people of Israel and then also the ''people of God'' in the new aeon, the Christian church (as an expression of a reformed Israel), participate in a covenantal relationship with the living God, who is also the God of all living beings, that in some measure is unique.

This covenantal relationship, however, with reference to all its aspects, whether unique or shared, is for service, not for privilege. It exists in order that the ''people of God'' may serve as special instruments for the fulfillment of God's purposes toward all humankind, indeed toward all living beings. This service is properly performed in awareness of the ancient divine convenants with all living beings, which means an awareness of human solidarity, an ungrudging respect for all persons and beings, and an eager openness to explore the extent to which the Lord God has been revealed and worked in both their corporate cultures and personal histories. The biblical witness is in agreement that all persons have some light, revealed to them by God, and the judgments of the Eternal are proportioned—"lest any man should boast"—to the degree of the true light human beings have received and to the ethical quality of their response. The message of the prologue of the Gospel of John is of a universal divine acting and speaking, for the Logos is "the true light that enlightens every man" (Jn. 1:9; cf. Jn. 1:4, 16; 10:16; 1 Jn. 2:2; 4:7, 16).[26]

3

Historico-Theological Bases
for the Happening

THE EARLY CHURCH AND
THEOLOGICAL TRADITIONS

The conclusions of the preceding biblical inquiry may appear to some readers to be so obvious, given the nature of the supporting data brought together, that they may wonder how the Christian church, and Western civilization in general, was able to develop exclusivist views about the work of God in the world at all. And yet in the past, for long centuries, exclusivist views prevailed in the Christian tradition, indeed in all major branches of the church, though with some variations. Even today, as is well known, sections of the Christian church hold exclusivist views as extreme as any found in Europe of, say, the ninth or the seventeenth century.

Let us attempt, then, to trace the major lines of development of the tension between degrees of inclusive and exclusive understanding and practice, which in fact has existed apparently from the beginning of the history of the church. A religious narrowness or intransigence seems to have existed in the early church—along with wider views—whose tone and force were evidently largely derived from late pre-Christian Judaism, especially in its popular forms. The wider covenantal scope and comprehensive perspectives of biblical prophecy as perceived by recent Old Testament scholarship evidently did not characterize common Jewish attitudes after the Babylonian captivity. The impulses to develop and maintain national and religio-ethnic identity, which led to the Maccabean struggle and the development of Pharisaism and the institution of the synagogue, were not conducive to thoughtful, impartial evaluations of other nations and persons. The dilemma of Peter in his confrontation with the Roman centurion Cornelius, which we considered above (Acts 10), may be taken as representative of the views of many if not most pious Jews of his time, especially in Palestine.[1]

Furthermore, in spite of certain noble exceptions, the relatively low moral, especially sexual, practices of contemporary life in the Roman empire were certainly factors in the development of attitudes of religious superiority, as well as stimuli to missionary activity, among Jews in the Diaspora.[2] Not only the resolute and robust monotheism of Judaism, but also its noble ethical teachings and, in spite of not a few failures, the continuing aspirations of most Jews toward high levels of personal, familial, and communal ethical living acted as powerful factors in the building of the distinctive self-consciousness of the Jews of the first century A.D. both in Palestine and abroad.

Actually, there were two relatively distinct tendencies in pre-Christian Judaism: one issuing in the exclusiveness of Ezra and the later Pharisaism, the other stressing the inwardness of a denationalized religion and its independence of outer forms and expressing itself in love of God and all human beings.[3] The Jews of the Dispersion, whose faith and religious practices constituted the primary model for the life and practices of the emerging Christian church outside Palestine, tended to stress the ethical and spiritual content of historic Judaism. Even though they remained distinctly separate as a religio-ethnic group, for the sake of their own self-understanding and for missionary purposes they moved in the direction of mutual understanding and communications with their non-Jewish environment. The literary remains of Alexandrian Judaism, such as the Wisdom of Solomon, Sirach, 2 Enoch, and the works of Philo (20 B.C.?–A.D. 42?) show how Jews in the Diaspora could adapt and assimilate traditionally non-Jewish thought without sacrificing the essentials of their faith. Already two centuries before the time of Philo, Judaism had been presented as a kind of mystery religion in conformity with the esotericism then prevalent in Alexandria. Increasing Jewish openness to the deep-rooted esthetic tradition in non-Jewish religions is reflected in the mural art seen in the synagogue excavated at Dura-Europos (fl. A.D. 245–256).[4] To Philo, Plato (like Moses) was "holiest of the holy."[5]

Yet it would be unfair to the Hellenistic Jews to say that they were any less truly zealous for the faith of their ancestors than the Palestinian Jew of the more rigorous type. They were certainly more concerned for the conversion of the Gentiles. But their personal, existential contacts with Hellenism enabled them to appreciate its good, even its religious good, not only as a tool for more effective missionary activity, but as a good in itself that they could appropriate and learn from for their own sakes.

Much has been made in the twentieth century, particularly in Protestant neo-orthodox circles, of what we may call the party of religious and cultural rejection in the early Christian church. This party, which indeed came to form a tradition, was in the second and early third centuries most notably represented by Tatian of Syria and Tertullian of North Africa. But as in the case of earlier Judaism, this tradition was only one in a much larger spectrum and, in the first three centuries of the history of the church, was evidently the less typical theological position. The famous question of Tertullian, "What is there in common between Athens and Jerusalem, between the Academy and the Church?'' by no means represented the primary Christian tradition of his time.[6] Partly indicative of this fact is that both Tertullian and Tatian ended their careers as members of ascetic groups separated from the mainstream of catholic Christianity.

In a more acute way in the postapostolic period in the early church, the question came to be asked: Does acceptance of Jesus Christ as Lord and Savior, as the supreme and normative revelation of the living God, require the complete rejection of the wisdom of this world? Does committal to what the apostle Paul called the folly of the cross (1 Cor. 1:18–2:16) mean that the cultural and religious heritage of Hellenism has no truth or value and must be summarily rejected?[7] Or is Paul's statement in 1 Corinthians to be understood in its larger context, along with his insistence that he was concerned to impart wisdom to the mature? Is it consonant with Christian wisdom that pagan culture and learning, including the religious insights of philosophers, are in some way, at least in part, in accord with the "secret and hidden wisdom of God, which God decreed before the ages for our glorification" (1 Cor. 2:7)? May they be appropriated and openly acknowledged by those who have committed themselves to the one God through Jesus Christ? Both sets of views existed in the church from the earliest period, albeit in differing degrees, and both sides believed that they had apostolic precedent for their positions.[8]

It is a fact that the early church held a consistently critical posture toward the religious worship and practice of Hellenistic paganism, particularly in its popular manifestations.[9] Origen (ca. 185–253/4), the most learned biblical scholar and probably the most influential theologian in the early church, in writing against the pagan philosopher Celsus tells how Christian instruction of catechumens was designed to develop the will to reject all religious worship of idols and images.[10] Lactantius in the year 313 writes that the first step in the process of Christian instruction is to enable the hearers to "perceive the religions which are false, and to cast aside the impious worship of gods made by human hands."[11]

Intelligent and knowledgeable Christians, however, whose number in the church continued to increase over the first three centuries, were quite aware that idol worship and sexual immorality did not accurately describe the whole of paganism, in either its past or its contemporary modes of expression. For this reason one of the most significant of the theological developments in the early church was that which took the Johannine doctrine of the Logos and attempted to expound it in such a way as to appreciate and affirm certain elements of Hellenistic culture and, indeed, to understand thereby the wider work of God in the history of humankind. This theological activity was an expression of the general patristic concern to affirm both the fact of divine providence and grace from the beginning of human history and their "pedagogical" role in the divine economy of salvation prior to the coming of the Christ. Notable among the representatives of this theological tradition were

Justin Martyr, Theophilus of Antioch, Athenagoras, Irenaeus, Clement of Alexandria, and Origen.

The classic formulation of the patristic doctrine of the Logos is to be found in Justin Martyr (ca. 100–165). The intent of Justin, as of other writers in this major stream of Christian thought, was that (to use the words of A. C. Bouquet) of "relating the work and person of Jesus Christ to the larger world of Mediterranean thought and of defining His position in relation to other religious teachers."[12]

Justin taught that the divine Logos appeared in fullness only in Jesus Christ but that a "seed" of the Logos had been scattered among the whole of humankind long before its manifestation in Jesus of Nazareth. Every human being, therefore, possesses in his or her mind a seed (*sperma*) of the Logos. Not only the patriarchs and prophets of the Old Testament, but also pagan philosophers, many if not most of whom are to be classed as religious philosophers, bore a seminal element of the Logos (*Logos spermatikos*) in their souls. Justin was certainly critical of much of the pagan tradition; he saw it as full of debased practices and its religion degraded. But he held that those who have lived according to the Logos are to be regarded as Christians, even though in some cases they may have been considered atheists by their contemporaries. He gave as examples of these nobler pagans who are worthy of the name "Christian" Socrates, Heraclitus, and others of like spirit among pre-Christian Greek philosophers.[13] Justin's use of the figure of a seed implanted in the human mind admittedly suggests in some passages an impersonal process; in others, however, the context implies a more personalist and dynamic activity.

One of the most seminal of Justin's statements on this theme of the wider work of the Logos of God in the world and throughout human history is that whatever has been well (i.e., beautifully and truly) said among all human beings belongs to the Christian heritage.[14] This is a magnificent statement, which reveals the cosmopolitan breadth of this early second-century Christian apologist at the same time that it opens the door for questing Christians of every generation to the whole of human culture as well as of religion. Justin expected this openness to all truth and goodness wherever found to be accompanied with discriminating evaluation. On the one hand, he believed that all human beings who have written had at least a dim glimpse of the truth through the seed of the Logos implanted in them. But even in the case of philosophers and lawgivers who presumably functioned at a higher level, it is only what they expressed rightly that one may see as a result of their discovery and contemplation of some aspect of the Logos. Their knowledge of the Logos was not complete, and hence they often fell into contradictions. Although Justin regarded Socrates as the finest example of these philosophers, even Socrates's knowledge of the Logos was imperfect. Yet the Logos is in every human being.[15]

Irenaeus (fl. 185), writing a generation or more later, carried on this tradition of understanding with his conviction that God is one and the same to all human beings and has aided the human race from its beginning by various economies (*variis dispositionibus*). His word order is precisely the opposite of the popular claims of the medieval church and state, for he says that "where the Spirit of God is, there is the church and all grace." Irenaeus writes of the Logos as being always present with the human race, that from the beginning the Son has revealed God to all to whom, and when and how, God wills.[16]

The teacher-predecessor of Origen in Alexandria, Clement (ca. 150–215), the first Christian who may properly be called a scholar in the technical sense of the term, gave further specificity to the Logos theological tradition. He taught that "all authentic understanding or wisdom is sent by God and that the true teacher of the Egyptians, the Indians, the Babylonians and the Persians, indeed of all created beings, is the first-begotten Son, the Fellow-counselor of God. . . . Philosophy was given to the Greeks as a covenant peculiar to them; many are the different covenants of God with men. . . . The Lord is upon many waters (Ps. 29:3); his beneficence is not limited to particular places or persons." Clement's thesis that God has had many different covenants with human beings is a particularly illuminating concept in the light of our consideration of the universal covenants of the Bible. His perception is of God as good, "a Savior from age to age through the instrumentality of his Son, and in all ways absolutely guiltless of evil."[17]

Theophilus of Antioch (fl. 180), while a lesser-known writer, gives us an equally typical view of the mind of the mainstream of the early Christian church. In his apologetical work *Ad Autolycum* he strives to demonstrate the greater antiquity as well as moral and spiritual "superiority" of Christian faith with its ancient biblical roots over the Greek religious tradition. In the very midst of this line of argument, however, he shows a lively awareness of the whole of humankind as existing under God. Furthermore, he stresses the fact that things said by Greek poets, philosophers, and even the Sibylline oracle agree with elements of Christian faith. He asserts that they said things concerning the unity of God, God's righteousness, divine judgment, punishment, and providence that are essentially one with the understanding of Christian faith. The theological framework of Theophilus' understanding was that of the Logos, whom the Father of all, whenever he wishes, sends to a place, where the Logos the Father becomes present and is heard and seen. (Thus is the Logos distinguished from God, who is not confined to a particular place.)[18]

Minucius Felix (3rd cent.) as a contemporary of Tertullian was one of the earliest Latin Christian writers. His theological position, however, was in essentially the same tradition as Justin Martyr's. In his charming dialogue *Octavius,* written in elegant Ciceronian Latin in probably the first decade of the third century, Minucius affirms that the pre-Socratic Greek philosopher Thales, who taught that God is the mind that formed all things from water, was given this insight by God. Furthermore, Minucius writes, this insight is completely (*penitus*) consonant with the faith-thought of Christians. Minucius finds himself in similar agreement with concepts of Deity held by Anaximenes and Diogenes of Apollonia. Citing also the views of a number of other thinkers, he asserts that these views, particularly those of Plato, are almost the same as the understanding of Christians.[19]

An equally significant view comes to us from the document of Jewish Christianity known as the (Pseudo-Clementine) *Recognitions*. This work is extant only in the Latin translation of Rufinus (d. 410), but it is now generally believed that it goes back, like the so-called *Homilies* of the same genre, to a second-century common source and constitutes a primary witness to early Jewish Christianity. Here we find a high appreciation of the best of Indian religious faith and practice, which comports well with the author's concept, expressed in other passages, of what constitutes authentic worship and service of God. "There are likewise amongst the Bactrians, in the Indian countries, immense multitudes of Brahmans, who also themselves, from the tradition of their ancestors, and peaceful customs and law, neither commit murder nor adultery, nor worship idols, nor have the practice of eating animal food, are never drunk, never do anything maliciously, but always fear God." The author, however, proceeds to distinguish this lifestyle from that of other Indians: "And these things indeed they do, though the rest of the Indians act differently."[20] The author's view of the wider work of God in the world is that, among other things, "Christ, who was from the beginning, and always, was ever present with the pious, though secretly, through all their generations, especially with those who waited for him, to whom he frequently appeared."[21]

The theologian of the early church who deserves special attention in the context of our study is, of course, Origen, who, as we have seen, was the most learned biblical scholar and probably the most influential theologian of the first six centuries of the history of the church, especially in the Greek-speaking East, where the great majority of Christians lived. With his vast learning and breadth of sympathy, Origen followed the mainstream of Christian understanding by insisting upon discriminating evaluations of non-Christian religion and culture, for pagan philosophy "is neither at variance to the law of God at all points, nor in harmony with it in all." But Origen's understanding of the wider work of God in the world was that every wise person, to the extent that the person is wise, participates in Christ, for Christ is wisdom. He held, like Augustine later, that the church existed from the foundation of the world or even before, that it was in all the saints from the beginning of time.[22]

Given the long process of reductionism of Christian faith and understanding, which began in distinctive fashion with the politicization of the Christian Way under Constantine and his successors and proceeded rapidly with the breakdown of the Roman empire in the West, it is difficult for modern Christians to appreciate with existential feeling either the vast scope of early Christian thought or the comprehensive range of early Christian sympathies. Clement, Origen's predecessor in the theological school in Alexandria, had a faith-understanding of cosmic scope that comports well with the perspectives of his great pupil. There was no room in either for notions of "cheap grace" or shortcuts that downplay the New Testament insistence upon moral as well as spiritual transformation as the accompaniment of faith.[23]

Clement depicted the Christian life with the imagery of a ladder of ascent. The soul progresses from faith, as one step on the way, to knowledge as another. Not only by control of its wayward passions, but even more by positive attitudes and deeds of love, the soul ascends step by step to the beatific vision and union with God.[24] Following Jesus' teaching of the kingdom of God through parables of growth (Mt. 13:1-52), Clement saw the Christian life as properly involving both moral and spiritual progress. He put as strong an emphasis upon sanctification as early Protestant evangelicals did. And like other Christians of his time, he saw this process as also involving heavenly dimensions (we may recall the apostle Paul's reference to "the third heaven" in 2 Cor. 12:2). Clement wrote: "Leaving behind all hindrances and scorning all the distractions of matter, he [the mature or knowledgeable Christian] cleaves the heavens by his wisdom, and having passed through the spiritual entities and every rule and authority, he lays hold of the throne on high, speeding to that alone, which alone he knows."[25]

This kind of language may sound strange to modern ears, and those of polemical bent may wish to castigate it as indicative of some sort of Prometheanism, the titanic, self-assertive world-view of a soul that would thrust aside both God and fellow beings in its self-willed striving toward its goal. Such is, of course, a parody of the truth of the matter. Origen, Clement's follower, had similar perspectives and was the gentlest of persons. He was a churchman in intent and fact all his life. Like Clement he was utterly Christocentric, seeing Jesus the Christ, the Logos of God, as the central instrumental element in the saving plan and work of God. But also like Clement, he saw the plan and work of God as having cosmic scope, as working toward the progressive salvation and restoration of all beings. The central concept of Origen's theological system, as Jean Daniélou has pointed out, was his doctrine of *pronoia* and *paideusis* ("la Providence éducatrice"). This concept enabled Origen to place the work of God in Christ in the context of a vast view of "educational providence." The two presuppositions of Origen's thought were a gracious and beneficent divine providence and free creatures, with the latter free to choose either evil or good, but able to follow through with the choice of good only by the grace of God. Origen saw human beings as placed on earth for ultimately spiritual and moral purposes; that is, they are given "educational" opportunities here that they may return to perfect fellowship with their Maker.[26]

Brief mention should be made of an element of the faith and theology of Origen that he evidently shared with many Christians of his time and that enabled him to view the wider work of God in the world with perspectives and sympathies that most modern Christians have quite lost sight of. This was his belief in some form of metempsychosis, or reincarnation of souls, a term for the concept of the possibility of a series of human lives on earth experienced by the same soul or continuing "personal" focus of consciousness. It has long been recognized that Origen believed in the preexistence of souls, but more recently a number of patristic scholars, like the Englishman Henry Chadwick, have come to assert that Origen taught reincarnation as a "very plausible opinion."[27] Origen, for example, in his treatment of the differences between Jacob and Esau, which the apostle Paul, following Malachi, put into the sharp contrast of "Jacob I loved, but Esau I hated" (Rom. 9:13; cf. Mal. 1:2-3; Gen. 25:21-34), insists that there is no injustice on God's part. He suggests that by reason of his merits in some previous life Jacob had come to be preferred to his brother. But God's gracious compassion provides for all and works toward the healing and final salvation of all beings. With regard to Clement, we do not find in his extant works specific support for his own belief in reincarnation, although much later the ninth-century patriarch of Constantinople, Photius, charged him with teaching such. Clement, however, clearly affirmed the saving as well as purifying work of God in Christ operative after the physical death of human beings.[28]

The key point in this theological understanding is actually not whether human beings have lived on this earth before and may do so again but whether they may be given further opportunities for both repentance and spiritual growth beyond this present life on earth. In the late twentieth century a considerable number of theologians in the Roman Catholic and Orthodox churches seem to allow for this possibility, as do even a few Protestant evangelicals. Donald G. Bloesch, as an example of the latter, follows P. T. Forsyth in believing that such opportunities will be given "even if this be not in this life."[29]

This key point is of vital significance in our understanding of the term "salvation." In the case of Origen, as with most Christians in the early centuries of the church, salvation was viewed as comprising more than a single event. The dramatic conversion of Paul on the road to Damascus as depicted in the book of Acts (9:1-19; 22:1-21; 26:1-23) was evidently not typical of the modes of entering upon the life of faith in the early church. Soon catechetical instruction came to be required for church membership, and two years of such training before admission to communion were common. But from the earliest, apostolic period, as the New Testament makes abundantly clear, the term "salvation" had a wide range of meanings. As we have seen, in the original Greek the verb "to save" was frequently used in the synoptic Gospels to denote the healings of Jesus (Mt. 9:21-22; Mk. 5:34; 10:52; Lk. 8:48; 17:19; 18:42); it often meant to save from death or from some affliction or situation of grave danger. With reference to time, the word is used in the New Testament, now with reference to the past, now to the present, and again to the future. Paul included himself along with the Corinthian Christians as those "who are being saved" (1 Cor. 1:18—the continuative present tense of the verb; cf. 1 Clement 58, 2). In writing to the beloved church in Philippi at the end of his life, he speaks of the good work that God had begun in them but had not yet brought to completion (Phil. 1:6), urges them to continue to work out their own salvation, for God is at work in them (Phil. 2:12–13), and insists that he himself had not already obtained all, nor was he already perfect. "I press on to make it my own, because Christ Jesus has made me his own" (Phil. 3:12–15). Paul believed that he himself had been accepted, but he was acutely aware that he had not yet accepted, appropriated, and applied the grace of God as he was meant to. The position of the New Testament is consistently that which creates the paradoxical tension of much already received, much to be grateful for, and yet much still to receive, do, and become.

REINCARNATION IN THE JUDEO-CHRISTIAN TRADITION

Inasmuch as one of the major purposes of this book is to help those of Christian faith intelligently to understand and discriminatingly to evaluate other religious traditions, it is in order to say a bit more about the concept and role of reincarnation in the Judeo-Christian tradition. It was an integral part of the world-view of Hinduism and Buddhism from very early periods, as of almost all the religious traditions originating in India. Similar beliefs have been extensive in African religions, among Native Americans, and in pre-Christian Greece and Rome. They also have been found among the ancient European peoples: Finns, Lapps, Danes, Norse and Icelandic peoples, among Old Prussians and early Teutonics, Lithuanians, Letts, and the Lombards of Italy.[30]

Actually, the concept of reincarnation in one form or another has been held as an element of faith by many Christians from the earliest periods of the church. This fact does not, of course, constitute proof of its truth. That is a problem possibly to be resolved only by a very complex process of thought, study, and experience, although currently some responsible Christian thinkers are trying to follow through with this process.[31] It is clear from various passages in the New Testament that some form of a concept of reincarnation was widely held by Jews, including Palestinian Jews of more than one sect, at the time of Jesus (Mt. 17:9–13 [cf. Mal. 4:5–6]; Lk. 9:8; Jn. 9:1–12; Jas. 3:6 [note the original Greek]; Rev. 3:12 [again note the Greek]). In fact, if one is willing to confront the literal meaning of Mt. 17:9–13, it appears that Jesus himself believed that John the Baptist was the reincarnation of the prophet Elijah (cf. Mt. 11:11–15; Jn. 1:21).

It is clear from 2 Maccabees (12:38–45) that Judas Maccabeus, and presumably other pious Jews of the time (166–165 B.C.), believed in and practiced prayers for the dead and a related mode of ritual offering as an "atonement for the dead." More specifically with reference to reincarnation, the most natural interpretation of several passages in the works of the Alexandrian Jew Flavius Josephus, roughly a contemporary of Jesus, indicates that the Pharisees believed good souls return to earth in new bodies.[32] Then we may quote again from the so-called Pseudo-Clementine writings, which are generally classed as later forms of a primary witness to Jewish Christianity.[33] These materials indicate the presence of belief among Jewish Christians in the second century in a series of incarnations of Jesus himself prior to his birth and manifestation as the Christ in Palestine at the beginning of the Christian era. Here we find reference to the Christ as the one "who has changed his forms and his names from the beginning of the world, and so reappeared again and again in the world, until coming upon his own times, and being anointed with mercy for the works of God, he shall enjoy rest forever. His honour it is to bear lordship over all things, in air, earth and waters."[34]

Finally, a word should be added with reference to the persistence within the tradition of Jewish spirituality of belief in reincarnation, which can be traced with relative clarity to the earliest periods of this era. We have already noted its presence in New Testament times. We find the belief appearing in the Jewish Karaite movement of the seventh century, frequently in the writings of the Cabala and then among the Hasidim, the great movement of modern Jewish spirituality that has continued into the present time. The present-day Israeli rabbi Adin Steinsaltz, of whom it has been said that there is "probably none today [who] can compare in genius and influence" with him, is a significant example of this tradition. His "extraordinary gifts as scholar, teacher, scientist, writer, mystic and social critic have attracted disciples from every faction in Israeli society." Steinsaltz believes in reincarnation and presents the Jewish mystical tradition, the Cabala, as the authentic theology of the Jewish people, rather than the more rationalistic interpretations of Hebrew Scripture of the better-known rabbinical tradition.[35]

The American rabbi Herbert Weiner reports the presence in contemporary Israel of reincarnation as a "commonly held folk belief," especially among the religiously more conservative Sephardic Jews, who came to Israel from such areas as Iraq, India, Yemen, and North Africa. Weiner writes that belief in reincarnation (*gilgul nephashot*) became the basis of a popular form of spiritual therapy that is reminiscent of aspects of Jungian psychology. By various means, rabbis would identify a disciple's previous incarnation and thereby present him a "kind of archetype which could make sense out of his travails or problems." Upon this basis, then, specific advice and other help could be given. This kind of spiritual therapy has very ancient roots and reached a special height of popularity in the seventeenth century with the school of Rabbi Isaac Luria.[36]

The purpose of this discursus into the question of belief in reincarnation in the Judeo-Christian tradition is to make more intelligible its presence and role in the teaching of the Buddha and in the Asian tradition in general. Its significant presence in the Judeo-Christian tradition, however, can also give contemporary Jews and Christians fresh perspectives on how their ancestors thought about the nature of salvation, in its more immediate as well as ultimately cosmic aspects, and about the extent of the opportunities for salvation given human beings by God in the divine economy of work for the restoration of the entire cosmos. Belief in reincarnation, incidentally, as we learn from one of the letters of Jerome (ca. 340–420), the famous translator of the Bible into the Latin Vulgate, was widely held by Christians in his time, especially in the churches of the Greek-speaking areas bordering on the eastern Mediterranean.[37] Once again, the presence of such belief by no means proves its truth, but it should make it an intelligible option for contemporary Christians who are willing to explore the cosmic significance of the Christ event in all of its past, present, and future aspects. The concept of reincarnation also opens new avenues for consideration of the wider work of God in the world and for theological evaluation of religious traditions other than the Judeo-Christian.

The real issue here is the fact of God, of God's nature and the extent of God's presence and work in the whole of creation. The main thrust of the biblical witness in both the Old and the New Testaments is forthrightly open-ended and inclusive with reference to the universality of this divine presence and work, both revelatory and salvific.

The Bible itself, to be sure, is relatively reserved with reference to affirmation of authentic manifestation of the divine presence and work in other religious traditions of humankind. There are, as we have seen, not a few hints or intimations of such affirmation. We can say, moreover, that there are no statements whatsoever that totally deny the divine presence and work in the religious life of others, that is, of those outside the formal boundaries of Israel and of the Christian church. The unreserved praise that Jesus gave to the faith of the Roman centurion, who was clearly no proselyte and whose faith was praised more for its existentially religious than formally theological quality (active trust in the reality-power of God and in the possibility of their manifestation through an authentic human agent) is paradigmatic for the entire New Testament (Mt. 8:5–13; Lk. 7:1–10; cf. Jn. 9:46–54). The affirmation is clearly that the divine presence and work are not confined to the religious boundaries of Israel—or of the Christian church—and neither is authentic human response so confined, in either faith or obedience of life (cf. Lk. 4:16–30).

It remained largely for missionary or Diaspora Judaism and for missionary, mobile Christianity to identify—as Jesus identified the centurion—specific instances of the divine presence and work in other religious traditions. One reason was that they came to know these traditions more existentially, in all the kaleidoscopic variety of their forms and ranges of quality, both spiritual and ethical. They were able to perceive the good as well as the bad. Just as Philo, the Alexandrian Jew, was able to recognize and acknowledge Plato in the past of the Greek tradition as one of the holiest works of God, so the Christian apologist Justin was able to see in Socrates one of the noblest manifestations of the revealing work of the Logos of God. We have seen how this theological understanding and spiritual perception were developed and even expanded in the major theologians of the early church. The question must be asked: How and why did we stray from this understanding?

4

Some Suggested "Whys"
for Reductionism
in the Historical Process

We have been reviewing evidence for the massive presence in the first three centuries and more of the history of the Christian church of a cosmopolitan comprehensiveness of thought and sympathy that may appear astonishing to some contemporary Christians, for the reason that such cosmopolitan comprehensiveness has hardly characterized the mainstream of Western thought and feeling over the past millennium and a half. To the contrary, Westerners have been dominantly characterized by notions of religio-cultural and personal superiority, notions that at least in part have had deep theological rootage. These concept-attitudes have admittedly been shaken as a result of the world wars of the twentieth century. The extent and frightfulness of the wars themselves, the perhaps thirteen million lives lost through purges, imprisonment, and forced movements of peoples in the Soviet Union during the 1920s and 1930s, the deeds perpetrated in the name of German National Socialism—all have contributed to a crisis of self-understanding among the nations of the West. A related result was serious diminution of respect for Western peoples and culture in other parts of the world. The combination of all these events brought about the end of old forms of Western colonialism as nation after nation, first in Asia and then in Africa, shook off the shackles of Western colonial rule. One distinct effect of these events has been the loss, or at least the weakening, of centuries-long attitudes of Western cultural and racial as well as religious superiority toward other peoples of the earth.[1]

The question then naturally occurs: Was this mind-set essentially Christian? Our study up to this point would suggest that it was not, especially in many of its external expressions in the activities of the Conquistadores and other representatives of Western expansion. If, as we have seen, apart from some exceptions, the central thrust of the biblical witness and of the theology of the early church was more sensitively discriminating and characterized by more comprehensive and cosmopolitan religio-cultural appreciations, we may properly ask how Westerners, primarily Western Christians, developed the intolerant attitudes of superiority characteristic of much of their history.

The problem is highly complex, and we have space to consider only certain main lines of development. For one thing, Westerners are by no means the only peoples to have developed notions of cultural and personal superiority. Perhaps every nation or empire that has gained a distinct measure of military power or cultural achievement vis-à-vis its neighbors in the course of human history has shown something of this mind-set. It seems to have characterized the inhabitants of the four major examples of human civilization. The militarily powerful Aryan invaders of northwestern India in the middle of the second millennium B.C., as evidenced by the early Vedic materials, were characterized by contemptuous attitudes of superiority toward the darker-skinned, flatter-nosed but culturally superior remnants of the Indus Valley civilization whom they had conquered.[2] The Chinese and Japanese in their several ways for long centuries held views of their own racial and cultural superiority. Greeks and Romans, whether possessing imperial power or not, had their own distinct notions of superiority. But perhaps no other similar mentality has had such widespread repercussions upon the rest of the world as the Western. Whence this distinctive quality and force?

Arnold Toynbee has pointed out that the sharpening of Western attitudes of superiority characteristic of the nineteenth and twentieth centuries had distinctive origins in the industrial revolution and the access to new forms of economic and military power that this development gave to the West. Before that time the British in India, for example, were far more inclined to mingle socially on an equal basis with the Indians.[3] Lord Macaulay wrote in the mid-nineteenth century of the awe with which the first British in India viewed the achievements of Indian civilization before their eyes, as, indeed, we may add, did some elements among the Spanish Conquistadores in the Americas.[4] Yet in spite of these and other qualifications, the dominant Western mind-set over long centuries was clearly characterized by an overweening self-confidence. There is even something mysterious about the spirit of those responsible for the early distant voyages of Western exploration and subsequent colonial acquisitions: the heroic daring, the sheer nerve characteristic of many of the enterprises, from Columbus and Magellan to Drake and Cartier and the British in India. G. B. Sansom has shown that in terms of military or economic power the earliest confrontations of East and West often revealed the latter as actually the weaker party of the two. Some of their "victories" appear to have been no more than "flukes,"[5] but they were more than accidentally successful strokes of luck. The piratic depredations of the entire coast of eastern Asia by the Japanese Wakō from earlier centuries were unquestionably "heroic" but by no means had comparable effects upon the course of human history.

The early Portuguese and Spanish voyages of discovery seem to have been primarily motivated by the desire to drive the Muslims out of Europe and to lessen their power in the Mediterranean by circumnavigating their areas of dominance. But what qualified and literally inspired much of the derring-do of Europeans was their sublime self-confidence—which often degenerated into attitudes of superiority and even contempt toward other peoples, but which, there is strong reason to believe, was primarily derived from and nourished by religious faith.[6]

We have already explored some of the sources of this religiously based set of attitudes in the history of Israel and in the early church. We have also seen, however, that in both Judaism and the early church there were powerful streams of inclusive and sympathetic understanding that hardly account for the later narrowness, even ferocity of Western attitudes. Actually, we find that narrow theological views and related notions of Western Christian religio-cultural superiority seem to take on singular sharpness and focus from about the time of Augustine (354–430).

Two factors seem to have been primarily at work in creating this relatively new phenomenon in Christian history. As we have seen, the theology of Augustine was at significant points a "new theology." Augustine was not alone in representing this development. Ambrose of Milan (337/340–397), by whom Augustine was influenced in various ways, had already exhibited a mentality and policy of exclusivism that was to have wide theological and ecclesial consequences. By the time of Augustine, however, a primary causal factor came to be the experience of a crumbling empire in the western Mediterranean and to the north. This horrendous experience, given special poignancy for the entire Western world by the capture of the city of Rome by the Visigoth chieftain Alaric in 410 and for Augustine by the movement of the Vandals into North Africa and finally their successful siege of his own city of Hippo in 430, brought about not only political and social chaos, but increasingly a narrowing of cultural opportunities and activities.

From before the time of Augustine the other major factor had already long been at work. This was the fateful alliance between church and state, which began with the victory of Constantine over his rival for the empire in the West, Maxentius, on October 28, 312, and the subsequent Edict of Milan granting to the Christian church full legal rights as a religion in the Roman empire. This edict was promulgated by Constantine and Licinius, the emperor in the East, probably in early 313. The alliance between church and state, which at first was one of personal sympathy and legally constituted no more than full equality with other religions in the Roman empire, came into a quite new dimension with the imperial edict of 380. Theodosius, together with Gratian, issued an edict that all persons should "hold the faith which the holy Apostle Peter gave to the Romans." This phrase was more particularly defined as meaning that which was taught by the then regnant bishops of Rome and Alexandria. The practical significance was that henceforth there was to be only one religion legally allowed in the Roman empire, and that the Christian. The Christian movement had swung fully about from the status of an often persecuted, at best tolerated, religious minority in the empire to that of the only religious faith and worship legally permitted therein. This meant not only increasing political and financial support from the government, together with social prestige and power for its leaders, all of which constituted more than enough temptation for the generally quite ordinary persons who made up the bulk of the clergy. It also involved increasing responsibilities to serve the interests of the state and the formal structures of society.

The first name that the Christian movement gave itself as a distinctive activity within the larger spectrum of Judaism was "the Way" (Acts 9:2; 19:23; 22:4; 24:14, 22). For the adherents of the movement the name said much of who or what they were and what the activity was in which they participated. Because they spoke of "the Way," they saw themselves as travelers on a path, as practicers of a dynamic way of life, rather than adherents or members of a static organization. "The Way" was the way to life and salvation in the fullest sense of the terms, involving ultimately the total transformation of human lifestyle and character and the restoration of the entire cosmos (cf. Acts 3:19; 1 Cor. 15:28; Col. 3:11). "The Way" was not lonely or individualistic, for "all who believed were together and had all things in common" (Acts 2:44). A primary characteristic of their togetherness was worship in the temple, prayer, and "breaking bread in their homes . . . with glad and generous hearts" (Acts 1:14; 2:46).

This is all to say that we have to do with a comprehensively viewed religious activity looking toward the work of God within the disciples and through them, and then, in God's own time, decisively and massively in the larger world about them. The early church in Palestine was by no means unaware of the relationship between religious faith and leadership, whether priestly or prophetic, and political power and leadership. Israel had been one form or another of a theocracy throughout no small part of its history, and the ideal was still that of a Davidic king who would combine priestly and royal functions. Maccabean rule was inconceivable apart from priestly cooperation, and now under the Romans the high priests and related figures were very much involved in the government of the people, at least on the local levels.

There is no evidence, however, that the early Christian community aspired to a role like that of the priests in Israel. The evidence points, rather, to the acceptance of sectarian status within Judaism—even as the Christians aimed and moved beyond Judaism—and of the roles of both the Jewish synagogue and Greek mystery religions as providing models for structural formation within the Diaspora. In this context of activity we find a remarkable fluidity and variety within the life and thought of the Christian church throughout the first three centuries of its history. In particular, the focus of its witness seemed to be upon recital of the great events involving the Jesus of Nazareth whom they believed to be the Christ, the Messiah of God. Their statement of faith at first was of the simplest kind: "Jesus is Lord" (cf. Phil. 2:11).

To be sure, there were strong pressures from the beginning toward unity, but this unity was seen as best expressed in mutual love (Jn. 15:12–17; 1 Cor.

13:13; 1 Jn. 3:11). We find in the letters of Ignatius at the beginning of the second century a strong concern for the unity of the church, which expressed itself in a persistent emphasis upon the need for obedience to church authorities, as, indeed, had already been expressed a decade or more earlier in the first letter of Clement of Rome to the church in Corinth (1 Clement 1–2).[7] In Ignatius' letters we find clear evidence of the emergence of the system of monoepiscopacy, that is, the local congregation governed by "a single bishop who is supported by a council of elders and assisted by deacons."[8] This pattern came increasingly to the fore, even though as time passed the bishop became the leader of several congregations in a city or town and the surrounding countryside and presbyters became leaders of individual congregations. The leader, whether bishop or presbyter, was responsible for the right administration of the liturgy and, indeed, for the preservation of the unity of the faith.

This unity, which had to be preserved in the midst of various fissiparous trends, including extreme forms of Gnostic Christianity, Montanism, Donatism, and the like, continued to be focused upon unity of spirit and life. What is fundamental to Ignatius' faith-understanding is a "mystical nexus" between the church on earth and the realm above, and obedience to the bishop is seen as accord and harmonious love, which is a hymn to Jesus Christ.[9] It is true that the at first loosely organized Christian community, which signally marked itself out from other religious bodies in the Roman empire of the first century by its mutual concern and strenuous efforts for intercommunication among its scattered local fellowships as well as by its zeal for an enriched and subtle form of monotheism and sexual purity, increasingly came to be a closely knit corporate body. The official leaders of this body, the bishops, were acknowledged as having the authority to define the faith and then to exclude from its communion those who did not accept their definition of the faith and their authority. Brief statements of faith going beyond the confession that Jesus is Lord are found already in the New Testament (1 Cor. 15:3–8; Rom. 1:3–5; Phil. 2:5–11; 2 Tim. 2:8; 1 Pet. 3:18–20). And it is true that valiant efforts were made during the first as well as second apostolic generation to clarify and preserve the central perceptions of Christian faith (cf. Acts 15:1–35; 1 Cor. 3:1–23; Gal. 1–6; Col. 2:8–3:17; 1 Jn. 2:18–29; 2 Jn. 7–11). By the year 180 acceptance of *a* rule of faith and *a* form of the New Testament canon seems to have become a fairly general requirement for church membership. At first these rules of faith were in the form of interrogatory creeds, with the response of "I believe" (*credo*) to the questions, and this format only gradually changed to a declaratory one. The Apostles' Creed now used in all major branches of the Christian church has its origin in the old interrogatory form used in the church of Rome. The fluidity of the situation, however, is revealed in the fact that the Apostles' Creed did not develop into a close approximation of its modern form until the year 400 and came into its final form as late as the eighth century.

This is not the place for a detailed consideration of the development of the organization and creeds of the early church. The point of concern here is to show that the development, while constituting a movement from relative simplicity of faith and structure in the first apostolic generation to relative firmness of structure and expression of faith by the beginning of the fourth century, was still focused on the inner life of the churches. The process moved somewhat from confession of faith as personal commitment to creedal belief in propositional statements, but only somewhat, for the ethos of the churches remained dominantly concerned with faith as linked with obedience expressed in ethical living.

The new situation created by the church's alliance with the state, however, and then by the church becoming the imperial state church, meant that the church became also an instrument of government policy and an agency, perhaps the primary civilian agency, for the support and maintenance of imperial political control. The unity of the church became necessary, therefore, not only for its own inner peace and concord but also for the order of society. Christians had believed from the beginning that their prayers were an aid to the peace and prosperity of state and society. But from the time of Constantine they were increasingly under compulsion to serve that goal as an agency of the state, and Constantine joined with the leading bishops further to establish and maintain the unity of the church.

Out of this situation emerged a new ethos of compulsion to institutional loyalty, a required conformity to increasingly detailed creeds, and a shift from the primary concern of the early church for authentic interiority to acquiesence with conformity in externals. A highly significant consequence of this fateful shift was that a different mentality began to develop, especially in the leadership of the church, a hard mentality, exclusive rather than inclusive, narrow rather than cosmopolitan. Theological views emerged, even in the case of as great a figure as Augustine, which were frankly barbaric.

We may speak of elements in the later Christian thought of Augustine as ambivalent, an ambivalence not entirely to be ascribed to his background in Neoplatonism and Manichaeism. On the one hand, Augustine recognized God as Creator and Controller of the universe, of all things animate and inanimate. He wrote that there is no doubt that the nations, too, have their own prophets and indeed these prophets also have truth. Paul says precisely this, Augustine insisted, as does also Jesus.[10] Augustine affirmed, however, that the Christian religion constitutes "the simple way for the liberation of souls, for souls can be saved by no way but this." And outside the church no one receives or retains final salvation (*salutem beatitudinis*). Yet he wrote that this way, the reality that is now denoted by the name of the Christian religion, had never been lacking to the human race at any period of its history. Augustine, who was certainly possessor of one of the subtlest minds of his century, may have had a way of reconciling these statements that we do not have in his extant writings. The church rightly assigned him the title of *doctor gratiae* because of his luminous depiction of both the necessity and the utter generosity of divine grace.

The move into the barbaric, however, emerges with greater clarity in Augustine's teaching that unbaptized babies are condemned to hell. He also wrote that if Greek philosophers, especially Platonists, had said things that by some chance are true and conformable to our faith (*si qua forte vera et fidei nostrae accommodata*), we should not fear them but claim them for our use as if from unjust possessors.[11] A grudging and ungenerous attitude, to be sure, in comparison with the appreciative cosmopolitanism of Justin, Irenaeus, the Alexandrian theologians, and other like figures in the early church.

We confront a barbarism in full force, however, in Fulgentius of Ruspe (467–533), who drank deeply of Augustine and went on to draw the further conclusion that not only all unbaptized children but even those who die in their mother's womb without baptism are eternally damned. He held that all pagans, Jews, heretics, and schismatics who die outside the visible (*praesentem*) Catholic church will go into the everlasting fire prepared for the devil and his angels.[12] We need to recall in this context that Augustine had taught the sinful corruption of all humankind (*massa perditionis*) and the concept of double predestination to heaven and hell, from before all creation. His language was that God predestines whom he will, "to punishment and to salvation," with the number of each class already fixed.[13] This unusual language is one reason, as T. Paul Verghese has stated, why the Eastern churches have never recognized Augustine as a doctor or teacher of the church.[14] At least we can say that Augustine's extreme views were never accepted in the Eastern churches and that only a modified kind of Augustinianism came to be influential in the West during the Middle Ages.

Most modern theologians have rightly tried to identify the operation of certain historical and sociological factors as having significantly influenced the development of this exclusivist mentality. Perhaps "psychology" is a better term than "mentality," because the concepts involved seem to be more the expression of feeling and mood than of rational thought. As we have seen, the mentality was in some ways the expression of psychological and sociological panic at the experience of Augustine and his contemporaries in the West of an empire, indeed for them all human civilization, crumbling before their very eyes. Not only had the city of Rome fallen into barbarian hands, Augustine's own city of Hippo was being besieged by the Vandals at the time of his death in 430. The Vandals, a Germanic tribe originally from south of the Baltic Sea, had come to North Africa through Gaul and Spain and had victoriously made their way eastward to that point. Vandals were later (455) to sack Rome. Edward Gibbon in his *Decline and Fall of the Roman Empire* has skillfully depicted the long-range effects of these events upon the subsequent mentality of persons in western Europe.

Certainly one effect of the crumbling empire was the gradual breakdown of the old Pax Romana, with all that this peace had meant in support of diverse, sophisticated, and extended economic and cultural activity as well as political order. In the late fifth and the sixth centuries communal and personal life in western Europe fell increasingly into more primitive forms of activity, and there was a consequent limitation of geographical movement. A narrowing of cultural horizons was an almost inevitable result.

As is well known, many of the Teutonic and Frankish tribes had already accepted Christian faith, especially in its Arian form, before their migrations into the crumbling Roman empire. The Visigoths, who had been living north of the Danube in the fourth century, rapidly accepted Arian Christianity, as did their kinsmen in southern Russia, the Ostrogoths. The Vandals also became Christian, at least in part, and even more remote Teutonic tribes, such as the Burgundians and Lombards, became Arian Christians before they invaded the empire. The so-called barbarian invasions, therefore, in most cases did not mean the destruction of the Christian church. Quite to the contrary, its political and social roles were greatly enhanced, and the contest with Arianism came finally to be resolved. The church became perhaps the chief custodian of the older culture in the fullest sense of the term, even though a diminution of the range and power of that culture was inevitably the result of the larger situation. The church also became the chief nonmilitary agent of the new governing classes for the preservation of peace and order in their communities as well as custodian of the old culture. In increasing numbers of cases, the whole community was or became Christian in the formal sense of the term. This meant that the church came to have formal social and political as well as religious responsibility for the whole community—a phenomenon utterly without precedent in the Roman empire before Constantine and, indeed, anywhere before the late fourth century, except for the kingdom of Armenia in the east.[15] This phenomenon not only impelled the church into a new role of compelling social as well as religious conformity—with the aid of the military and police power of the state. It also subtly but distinctly influenced its theology, with reference to its understanding of the final salvation of those outside the formal bounds of the church as well as of the wider work of God in the world. In fact, the wider work of God in the world came to have little meaning for the bulk of persons in western Europe, for they had largely lost any existential knowledge or feeling for the existence of that world, especially from the sixth century on.

It must be remembered that the western European church as an entirety over the period of the Middle Ages did not adopt Augustinian theology "whole cloth." In fact, we may speak of a general medieval tendency to qualify rigid Augustinian views of predestination. An early example is the position of Prosperus of Aquitaine (fl. 450), who reflected the earlier patristic breadth of sympathy with his explicit concept of a general divine call and grace given to all human beings.[16]

The emergence of Islam in the East in the early seventh century can hardly be considered an aid to Christian thinking in its relationships with the wider world of humankind. Islam soon became, first for Eastern Christendom and later for the West, partly because of its geographical contiguity, the chief religious, cultural, and military competitor of the European, African, and

Middle Eastern Christian world. We may recall that the western end and later the larger part of the Mediterranean Sea became for long centuries a veritable "Muslim lake," on which Christian ships for most of that period could hardly venture apart from Muslim sufferance.[17] The Belgian scholar Henri Pirenne has argued that the end of Late Antiquity, whose cultural ecumenism largely transcended national and racial differences within the Roman empire, was not primarily caused by a process of decadence but by the abrupt appearance of the politico-military religion of Islam.[18] It is a fact that by the victory of the Byzantine emperor Heraclius over Persia in 627 after a protracted struggle, the power and prestige of the Roman empire in the East seemed assured. And yet within fifteen years after Muhammad's death in 632, the Roman empire lost Syria, Palestine, and Mesopotamia to Arab military rule. Then Egypt and the whole of North Africa came under this dominance. Subsequently these victorious armies were to move northward to Spain and southern France, eastward to the borders of India and beyond.

There is much truth to Pirenne's thesis, but perhaps its chief weakness is that it does not take sufficient account of internal developments in the West. The loss of all of North Africa and Spain to the Eastern empire and its subsequent inability, also because of increasing Muslim control of the Mediterranean, to exercise effective political control of the southern European continent, was a highly significant factor in the growing isolation of western Europe from the East. But, as we have seen, this isolation had rootage and major elements of its development well before the advent of Islam.

One final point may be made with reference to Christian-Muslim interrelationships at this period. The church father John of Damascus (d. ca. 752) was the first in the line of Christian Scholastics who considered Islam to be a Christian heresy, as earlier theologians had viewed Manichaeism. John was born about fifty years after the *hijrah*, the migration in 622 of the small Muslim community of Mecca to Medina, the event that marks the beginning of the Muslim calendar. Before entering upon monastic life John, following his father, had held high office under the caliph of Damascus. He had considerable knowledge of the faith of Islam, and the tone of his writings was generally calm and fair. But as a part of his methodology of theological controversy, he resorted to ridicule and began the long—and unfair— tradition of accusing Muhammad of pretending to receive revelations from God in order to justify his sexual license.[19]

Even though certain of the extreme views of Augustine and Fulgentius were qualified in some ways in the course of the European Middle Ages, a generally exclusivist view of God's saving work in the world came to be the almost completely unchallenged pattern of thought in the church in western Europe throughout the early and late Middle Ages. This pattern was, in effect, to see the God and Father of Jesus Christ as essentially the patron deity of Western peoples and his saving work as practically confined to persons explicitly Christian. The Fourth Lateran Council in 1215 restated in the most literal sense the formula of Cyprian (ca. 200–258) that outside the church there is no salvation. The extent of shift in the mind of the leadership of the church over subsequent centuries is clearly revealed in the fact that at the time of Cyprian himself the church of Rome had opposed Cyprian and his party in their interpretation of the formula. Cyprian had insisted that baptism administered by heretics is invalid and that the martyrdom of those not in communion with the Catholic church has no spiritual significance.[20] The mainstream of the church throughout the first three centuries of its history, however, consistently rejected any such identification of salvation with institutional adherence.

Following the Fourth Lateran Council, Pope Boniface VIII in his bull *Unam Sanctam*, issued in 1302, reaffirmed the Cyprianic formula, again in the literal sense and without qualification.[21] The Council of Ferrara and Florence (1438-45) made this position even more explicit by a declaration similar to that of Fulgentius: "It [the Council] firmly believes, professes, and proclaims that those not living within the Catholic Church, not only pagans, but also Jews and heretics and schismatics cannot become participants in eternal life, but will depart 'into everlasting fire which was prepared for the devil and his angels,' unless before the end of life the same have been added to the flock. . . . No one, whatever almsgiving he has practiced, even if he has shed blood for the name of Christ, can be saved, unless he has remained in the bosom and unity of the Catholic Church."[22] We may recall that Luther's opponent in the early Reformation theological debate at Leipzig (July 1519), Johann Maier of Eck, doubted whether Eastern Orthodox Christians could be saved.

5

The Long Way Out and Up

The process of liberation from the distortions of Christian faith described in the previous chapter has been long. Perhaps what we may call a massive momentum in the process is discernible only after the end of World War II. But distinct activities in this direction are to be perceived from the early Middle Ages. Admittedly, it is not until Abelard (1079–1142) that we find a forthright questioning of Augustine's teaching that unbaptized children suffer in hell. Abelard's primary concern, however, was to turn the punishment of such children into a privative separation from God rather than a positive suffering of the pains of fire. His view was not intended to speak to the condition of non-Christians, who hardly constituted existential realities for western Europeans in the geographical and cultural isolation characteristic of their time and place. Yet when Peter Lombard (1100?–1160) took up Abelard's concept—which later became known through the term "limbo," coined by Albertus Magnus—it spread throughout the universities of Europe that used the Latin language as the medium of instruction.[1] This perception, however inadequate, marked the reemergence of a certain religio-cultural independence and a more humane spirit in this part of Christendom.

Thomas Aquinas (1225–74) may properly be considered as at once the greatest systematic mind and most representative theological figure of the high Middle Ages. He accepted and developed the concept of "limbo" but generally affirmed the prevailing belief that outside the formal structure of the Roman church and its sacraments there is no salvation. He recognized, however, the possibility of the salvation of Gentiles in classical antiquity through implicit faith in divine providence. Furthermore, this distinction between explicit and implicit faith actually constituted a substantive open-endedness in Aquinas' system and became a significant basis for later developments in Roman Catholic theology. Aquinas clearly affirmed the possibility of wider ranges of divine revelation and the freedom of God to "deliver mankind in whatever way was pleasing to Him."[2] Bonaventura (John Fidanza, 1221–74), in some ways theologically more conservative than

46

Aquinas, was able through his use of the concept of "appropriations" to allow certain authentic knowledge of God among the Greek philosophers.[3] We see in the great Italian poet Dante Alighieri (1265–1321) essentially the same theological position but with a broader and deeper sympathy for classical culture and thereby for classical men and women that became one of the characteristic marks of the early Renaissance.

The emergence of a more humane spirit in noteworthy figures can be perceived in the fact that Francis of Assisi, Roger Bacon, and Ramon Llull objected to the religious basis as well as the inhuman methodology of the Crusades. Ramon Llull, almost two centuries earlier than Nicholas of Cusa, whom we shall consider in more detail later, came to hold essentially the same vision of a single humanity, with one faith and one religion, a goal to be reached by persistent, mutually respectful dialogue.[4] The issue is not merely one of cultural influences but of the quality as well as kind of Christian spirituality. Meister Eckhart, led in part by his perception of the nature of the essence of the human soul, occasionally reflected the cosmopolitan humaneness of many of the early church fathers.[5]

Actually, there were at least two strands of development in the process of liberation into more humane, and thereby more anciently Christian, understanding. One was, as we have noted, the influence of the more hopeful, expansive personages of the Renaissance, such as Dante, Petrarch, Nicholas of Cusa, Pico della Mirandola, and Giordano Bruno among the outstanding literary figures. Some of these, Pico and Bruno, for example, as a part of the larger Renaissance affirmation of the almost limitless possibilities for the development of human selfhood and its cultural expressions, assumed that more than one life might be necessary to complete the process of fulfillment of the possibilities for human life on earth. That is, they espoused the concept of reincarnation.[6] But the larger hopes for humankind held by leading Renaissance figures were not merely the product of the fresh study of classical, especially Greek, antiquity. They were in considerable measure derived from the biblical and early Christian aspirations toward growth in faith-understanding and in ethical obedience. These aspirations had been revived especially in the Franciscan movement of the thirteenth century and developed further in the fourteenth century, which was one of the greatest periods of Western Christian spirituality, even as it constituted an important element of the early Renaissance. The humanist movement at its best was specifically tied to renewed concerns for the inner life of persons and related spiritual experience which characterized the period.[7]

The continuity of high tension within the church and Western society, however, with regard to the issues of exclusivism and inclusivism is revealed in the creation of the policy and then the introduction of systematic inquisition. As a result of this development veritable crusades of terror and violence were unleashed, beginning in the late twelfth century, against substantial groups of varying "heretical" persuasion, of whom the Cathari (Albigenses) and Waldenses are the best known.[8] Giordano Bruno, as a later Renaissance figure, was burned at the stake in Rome in the year 1600 after seven years of largely solitary confinement and some torture.

And yet, the second strand was a theological development within the so-called mainstream of faith-understanding in the church that was to make this kind of ferocious policy and practice increasingly distasteful and then intolerable to the bulk of Christians. All the great theological masters of the Middle Ages taught the doctrine of the unity of the being of God, and the concept of the Trinity was somehow reconciled with the unity of God without destroying it.[9] Deeper perceptions of the nature of human beings were in time to make it possible to develop a higher anthropology in Christian theology that would in turn create new respect for human beings qua human beings.

William of Conches in Normandy (1080-1154), a member of the school of Chartres and a Platonic Scholastic philosopher, appears to have been a key figure in the development of a concept that in time led to the perception of the dimension of the unconscious in the human psyche in a formal sense by Sigmund Freud. This was the concept of a *sensus naturae*, an "unconscious, instinctive, supernatural knowledge," which animals as well as human beings were believed to possess. This anthropological perception, as formulated earlier by Avicenna (the Muslim philosopher Ibn Sina, 980-1037), was used to explain the gift of prophecy and telepathic capacities in human beings. The *sensus naturae* significantly came to be associated with the work of the Holy Spirit and thereby helped to recreate within Christian theology wider perceptions of the work of the Holy Spirit—first by William of Conches himself and then by some of the greatest philosopher-theologians of the Middle Ages. Among these may be cited Abelard, Guillaume de Paris, Albertus Magnus and, later, most Western alchemists.[10]

The doctrine of natural law, particularly as it came to be formulated by Thomas Aquinas, was also a factor in this process of theological development. The origins of this understanding are said to lie as much in later Stoicism as in the New Testament, but it does have clear rootage in the latter, as in Romans 1-3. The concept of natural law presupposes the existence of broad principles of human behavior, which are based ultimately on the eternal law existing in the mind or will of God but may be discerned by the reason of reasonable persons everywhere.[11] John Calvin also followed in this tradition.[12] The concept at times has been understood as almost exclusively an exercise of human reason, with the added assumption that human reason is somehow exempt from either finiteness or sin, or both.[13] But this is to push the context of discussion into the more limited perceptions of reason as mere rational process, which are more characteristic of post-Enlightenment European thought. In the Middle Ages reason (*intellectus, intellegere*) was as much a spiritual as a rational faculty or activity, often used in a sense akin to our modern term "consciousness." In any case the concept of natural law was another factor—and expression—in the historical process of the Christian humanization of western Europeans.

THE AGE OF EXPLORATION
AND THE HUMANIST TRADITION

Some sense of the wider world of human beings existed in western Europe in the Middle Ages, in particular as a result of the development of Venetian trade with the Byzantine East, the experiences of the Crusades, and contacts with Muslim culture and religion in Spain and Sicily. This awareness, however, developed into more explicit and existential knowledge as a result of the voyages of exploration. This remarkable movement in the history of humankind, so pregnant with consequences for both the West and the rest of the world, may be said to have begun with Henry the Navigator of Portugal in the first half of the fifteenth century. Christopher Columbus, Vasco da Gama, Ferdinand Magellan, Francis Drake, and Jacques Cartier are among the names that distinguish the early years of this activity.

At least in part as a consequence of these events, new perspectives began to emerge, especially in what became the Roman Catholic regions of Europe after the divisions of the Reformation. These were the territories closest to the Mediterranean Sea and, for a variety of reasons both cultural and political, were the place from which the earliest explorers went out. It is a fact, however, that certain of the early Protestant Reformers also participated in the emerging new perspectives. For example, the Swiss Reformer Huldreich Zwingli acknowledged the work of the Spirit of God beyond the formal "boundaries" of the Christian church. Certain early Anabaptist and "Spiritual" writers appear to have had similar views. Balthasar Hubmaier wrote that "God gives power and capacity to all men in so far as they themselves desire it." Sebastian Franck wrote in a letter to John Campanus, "God is no respecter of persons but instead is to the Greeks as to the barbarian and the Turk, to the lord as to the servant, as long as they retain the light which has shined upon them and gives their heart an eternal glow."[14]

These perceptions, reminiscent of the best minds of the early church, seem to derive in part from the religious insights of the persons themselves and in part as a heritage from the largely lay and often anticlerical, anti-institutional spirituality of the fourteenth-century Rhine valley. One thinks of the activity of the Friends of God, the Brethren of the Common Life, the Beghards and the Beguines, the last two of which are thought by some scholars possibly to be German-speaking reconstitutions of the Albigenses of France and Italy. These broader sympathies, however, do not represent the views of the major Reformers. The Apology of the Augsburg Confession expresses the general belief of these Reformers that the Christian gospel had been disseminated over the entire world by the apostles and therefore the nations are without excuse in their unbelief.[15] This severe view, however, in large measure did not lead to a following out of the missionary imperatives that seem implicit in it. Nearly two centuries were to elapse before European Protestants began, as a part of the great religious movement called Pietism on the Continent and evangelicalism or revivalism in English-speaking countries, seriously to consider these imperatives.

In the Roman Catholic Church, on the other hand, we note the emergence of broader views, with a more massive momentum developing in the period of the Counter-Reformation. In theologians of the sixteenth century such as Bellarmine and Suarez, concepts unknown to medieval Scholasticism were developed and then affirmed by the Council of Trent (1545-63). In particular, the affirmation was made that baptism, and thereby salvation, could be received not only, as by Christians, with water (*in re*) but by desire (*in voto*).[16] This development was a distinctive sign in a long process that began in the late Middle Ages and early Renaissance and was to enable Roman Catholics to make important qualifications to the Cyprianic formula that outside the church there is no salvation. The result, as we shall see, was to bring the Roman Catholic Church around full circle to the end of reaffirming the more inclusive position of the church of Rome of the time of Cyprian. This has meant that modern Catholics are able once again to share the spiritual sympathies and cultural cosmopolitanism of the early church at its highest levels.

To be sure, this development did not move forward evenly on all fronts. There were substantial holdovers from the medieval past, both attitudinally and in practice. Ignatius Loyola, shortly after his conversion in 1521, is said to have met a Moor (Muslim) in Spain and considered whether it was not his duty to kill the dog. Francis Xavier, the great Roman Catholic apostle to the Indies and disciple of Loyola, tended at first to identify the glory of God and the glory of Portugal. In his first area of missionary activity in South India, he encouraged the small boys whom he had won to a measure of allegiance to seize the small clay idols of the Hindu shrines, "smash them, grind them to dust, spit on them and trample them underfoot."[17] His notion of the spiritual condition of non-Christians was that God, who is always faithful, does not dwell with infidels and is displeased with their prayers, for all the gods of the nations are demons (*omnes dei gentium demonia*).[18] Xavier literally believed that all those who worship idols go to hell and, like Augustine, he held that unbaptized babies are committed to eternal fire. With regard to the Chinese captain whose pirate junk carried Xavier and his companions to Japan and who later died, a man "good to us," Francis sorrowfully declared that his soul was in hell.[19]

But the field experiences of a man as spiritually sensitive as Francis Xavier led him to certain modifications of what we must call this savage theology. Earnest Japanese inquirers, for example, were troubled because they could not reconcile the infinite goodness and mercy of God as taught by the Jesuit missionaries with the fact that God had not been revealed to them and their ancestors before the Jesuits arrived. But if, as the latter also taught, all who did not worship the true God and participate in the sacraments of the Roman Catholic Church went to hell, then their ancestors must have gone there. Xavier reported in a letter to Europe that the Lord helped the missionaries to deliver the Japanese from this terrible misgiving. This existential situation in fact forced the missionaries to reach back into the depths of their tradition in the New Testament and the theology of the early church, and they explained to the inquirers that the moral law and knowledge of God were imprinted from the beginning in the hearts of all human beings. They also affirmed that the Creator of all peoples had taught them apart from human (i.e., Christian) mediation. Xavier also came to appreciate that in the Japanese past "were men of old, who were (so far as I understand) persons who lived like philosophers."[20]

Just as Francis Xavier's personal experience of the wider world led him—and later the seventeenth-century Jesuit missionaries in China: Matteo Ricci, Johann Adam von Schall, Sabatino de Ursis, and others—to more appreciative views of the work of God in that world, so had the wider experiences, as well as studies, of a major ecclesiastical figure in the Renaissance. This was Nicholas of Cusa (1401–64), who became a cardinal in the Roman Catholic Church and, although of German origin (Cues on the Mosel River), was an outstanding figure in the cultural as well as religious activities of the Italian Renaissance. As an expression of both his personal experiences and humanist studies, he returned from a diplomatic mission to Constantinople in 1437 with the vision of reconciling Christianity with Islam. We may recall that this was almost on the eve of the Council of Ferrara and Florence (1438–39), which explicitly declared that "all pagans, Jews, heretics and schismatics have forfeited eternal life and are destined to everlasting fire." In his book *De pace fidei* Nicholas anticipated the position of the European Enlightenment of the eighteenth century by stating that there is in fact only one religion, the cult of those who live according to the principles of wisdom. The worship, he affirmed, even of the gods of pagan polytheism witnesses to the one God, and the divine Logos affirms the essential concord and harmony of the great religions.[21]

Views of Islam like those of Nicholas of Cusa were admittedly rare. The prevailing practice was to furnish *Schauermärchen* and *Greuelpropaganda* regarding Muhammad and the religio-political tradition that he initiated.[22] But as we have seen, Nicholas of Cusa, while somewhat unusual in the specificity of his proposals, was only one of many humanists of the fifteenth and sixteenth centuries who began to concern themselves with the problem of Christian evaluation of other religious traditions on the basis of perspectives different from those of the medieval church. Through their studies of the great writers of classical antiquity they came to appreciate in a new way particularly their ethical concerns. Early Renaissance humanism had a strong moral purpose and found much in Homer and Plato, Cicero, Virgil, Seneca, and Plutarch that accorded with their own sense of Christian morality.

This intellectual and cultural activity-process needs to be correlated with the specific effects of the veritable knowledge explosion effected by the aforementioned voyages of exploration. Alfred North Whitehead once observed that in the year 1500 European scholars knew less, scientifically, than did

Archimedes, who died in 212 B.C.[23] But an enormous expansion of knowledge, due largely to the impetus of the voyages of exploration, occurred in the course of the sixteenth century. This new knowledge was at first more the possession and instrument of Roman Catholics than of Protestants. The new knowledge had its focus in European discoveries in both geography and astronomy. A key institution was the Jesuit Collegium Romanum, where the man who was responsible for the execution of the new Gregorian calendar, Christopher Clavius, taught mathematics in the second half of the sixteenth century. Clavius and other Jesuits were personal friends of Galileo Galilei, a fact also indicative of the ambivalence of the church as a whole to the new knowledge. But this was the age of Tycho Brahe, Johannes Kepler, Giovanni Antonio Mazzini, and other great pioneers in natural science. New perspectives of humankind, as of the physical universe, were in the making.

This background of events enables us to understand the emergence of the views of the religious situation of the non-Christian world of the Spanish Jesuit Juan Cardinal de Lugo (1583–1660), who, like Nicholas of Cusa, was a high prelate of the Roman Catholic Church. De Lugo held that

> God gives light, sufficient for its salvation, to every soul that attains to the use of reason in this life. . . . the human soul, in all times and places, has a certain natural affinity for, and need of, truth. . . . the various philosophical schools and religious bodies throughout mankind all contain and hand down, amid various degrees of human error and distortion, *some* truth, some gleams and elements of divine truth. . . . the soul that in good faith seeks God, His truth and love, concentrates its attention, under the influence of grace, upon those elements of truth, be they many or few, which are offered to it in the sacred books and religious schools and assemblies of the Church, Sect, or Philosophy in which it has been brought up. It feeds upon these elements, the others are simply passed by; and divine grace, under cover of these elements, feeds and saves this soul.[24]

This understanding of de Lugo was assuredly not typical of the bulk of Roman Catholics, clerical or lay, of his time. But he was representative of what we may call, from the perspectives of the present, the best thought of his time and, even more importantly, pointed the way to the future development of the mind of the church. Perhaps this area of understanding was not what John Henry Newman had in mind when he worked out his famous concept of the development of doctrine, but historically it was the result of a process of development, even as it constituted a repristination of the best of the old.

It should be noticed that de Lugo presupposed the work of divine grace in all human beings. He did not ascribe their knowledge of truth, and consequent action in accordance therewith, solely to the exercise of their reason functioning on the basis of a rational perception of the "natural law." De Lugo understood the total divine-human activity-process in a more relational and existential way. Nevertheless, whether perceived primarily in a relational or in a rationalistic manner, the doctrine of natural law in Thomistic-Aristotelian theology was characterized by an optimistic view of nature. This outlook, nourished by many of the ideas of the Christian humanists of the Renaissance and later by the more tolerant perspectives of the Enlightenment, the traumas of the French Revolution, and the Napoleonic period and finally by the love-hate relationship with the developments of natural science and freedom in the modern world (developments summed up by the word "modernism"), all helped to keep the humane tradition of world understanding alive in the Roman Catholic Church. This tradition in turn came increasingly to constitute a movement with growing momentum, a movement that burst forth with astonishing power and beauty in Vatican Council II (1962–64).

We do not have space to trace in detail the more particular developments of this theme in the twentieth century leading to Vatican Council II, but there were of course specific persons and activities involved. We have space only to cite the names of Roman Catholic Islamic scholars like Louis Massignon and Louis Gardet, both men of profound spirituality whose studies in the Muslim mystical tradition led them and other Catholic scholars to a new empathy and consequently different theological understanding of Islam.

Another Roman Catholic who contributed significantly to the momentum of thought-understanding that made Vatican II possible was Raymond (Raimundo) Panikkar. We shall discuss Panikkar more in detail in the next chapter, but note should be taken particularly of his work contributory to the results of the council. His highly significant and influential book *The Unknown Christ of Hinduism* was first published in 1957, and his previous writings with their specificity of data drawn from the Hindu tradition served, like Louis Gardet's notable work on mystical experiences outside the Judeo-Christian context and the Swiss diplomat-scholar Jacques-Albert Cuttat's reflections on the significance of developments in Mahayana Buddhism for the history of salvation as a universal sacred history, to inform the Catholic theologians who made the results of the council what they were.[25] Among these latter theologians may be cited particularly the names of Maurice Blondel, Yves Congar, Jean Daniélou, the then young Hans Küng, Henri de Lubac, and Karl Rahner.

The Declaration on the Relationship of the Church to Non-Christian Religions (*Nostra Aetate*) was clearly one of the most significant documents of Vatican Council II, one which in particular constituted a theological watershed for the Roman Catholic Church.[26] It was subsequently noted by Catholic thinkers that the Roman Catholic Church, by explicitly recognizing in the Declaration theological meaning and value in other religious traditions, "has abandoned officially an exclusive claim to religious values for the first time in history."[27] In the Dogmatic Constitution on the Church (no. 16), the council asserted forthrightly that, even without explicit knowledge of God in Christian terms or of the gospel of Christ, human beings may yet so receive and respond to divine grace as to attain to everlasting salvation. The understanding revealed in these documents is essentially the result of the long process that we have outlined. It constitutes a revival and a refinement of the ancient Logos theology to the end of affirmation of the openness of the Roman Catholic Church to the concept of religious pluralism. Gregory Baum has come to the point of stating that religious pluralism is part of the divine dispensation.[28] In the years following Vatican Council II, even greater attention has been paid to the issue so that it is now one of the major theological themes in the Catholic church. This is one reason why Raymond Panikkar has claimed that the meeting of religions is the *kairos* of our time.[29]

Certain statements in the Declaration on the Relationship of the Church to Non-Christian Religions (no. 2) of Vatican II may be profitably quoted at this point in support of the conclusions given above.

> From ancient times down to the present, there has existed among diverse peoples a certain perception of that hidden power which hovers over the course of things and over the events of human life; at times, indeed, recognition can be found of a Supreme Divinity and of a Supreme Father too. Such a perception and such a recognition instill the lives of these peoples with a profound religious sense. Religions bound up with cultural advancement have struggled to reply to these same questions with more refined concepts and in more highly developed language.
>
> Thus in Hinduism men contemplate the divine mystery and express it through an unspent fruitfulness of myths and through searching philosophical inquiry. They seek release from the anguish of our condition through ascetical practices or deep meditation or a loving, trusting flight toward God.
>
> Buddhism in its multiple forms acknowledges the radical insufficiency of this shifting world. It teaches a path by which men, in a devout and confident spirit, can either reach a state of absolute freedom or attain supreme enlightenment by their own efforts or by higher assistance.
>
> Likewise, other religions to be found everywhere strive variously to answer the restless searchings of the human heart by proposing "ways," which consist of teachings, rules of life, and sacred ceremonies.
>
> The Catholic Church rejects nothing which is true and holy in these religions. She looks with sincere respect upon those ways of conduct and life, those rules and teachings which, though differing in many particulars from what she holds and sets forth, nevertheless often reflect a ray of that Truth which enlightens all men. Indeed, she proclaims and must ever proclaim Christ, the way, the truth, and the life (John 14:6), in whom men find the fullness of religious life, and in whom God has reconciled all things to Himself (cf. 2 Cor. 5:18–19).

The Church therefore has this exhortation for her sons: prudently and lovingly, through dialogue and collaboration with the followers of other religions, and in witness of Christian faith and life, acknowledge, preserve, and promote the spiritual and moral goods found among these men, as well as the values in their society and culture.

There follows a similar statement about Islam, beginning with: "Upon the Moslems, too, the Church looks with esteem."[30]

Of very great significance is the fact that the first encyclical of Pope John Paul II, *Redemptor Hominis*, crystallizes with fine clarity and succinctness the conclusions both of the declaration on non-Christian religions and of the many Roman Catholic theologians who have written on this theme since the council. He refers to "the firm belief of the followers of the non-Christian religions" as "a belief that is also an effect of the Spirit of truth operating outside the visible confines of the Mystical Body." He states that "the Fathers of the church rightly saw in the various religions as it were so many reflections of the one truth, 'seeds of the Word.' " He writes also of "the magnificent heritage of the human spirit that has been manifested in all religions." "Jesus Christ becomes, in a way, newly present" in our world. This is "in spite of all the limitations of the presence and of the institutional activity of the church." The high anthropology characteristic of the entire encyclical is further supportive of these affirmations, "for, by his Incarnation, he, the son of God, *in a certain way united himself with each man*." Pope John Paul II writes also of "the later covenants [following the first covenant with Adam and Eve, Gen. 1:26] that God 'again and again offered to man.' "[31]

PIETISM AND EVANGELICALISM

As we have noted in the context of our brief discussion of Protestants in the early period of the Reformation, there were Protestants who, like Nicholas of Cusa, Juan de Lugo, and other humanist Catholics, broke with the exclusivism of the dominant orthodoxy. The names of Huldreich Zwingli, Balthasar Hubmaier, and Sebastian Franck were mentioned. The latter two were representative in a more distinctive way of the deep spirituality found in German-speaking Europe from the fourteenth century and before. This is the German mystical tradition that we meet again in the Lutherans Jakob Böhme, Johann Arndt, and others, and which was a prelude to the later great movement of spiritual renewal in Protestantism known as Pietism in Germany, Holland, and Scandinavia, and as evangelicalism or revivalism in English-speaking lands. The impact of the thought of Böhme on later German philosophy, on men such as Hegel, Schopenhauer, Nietzsche, Heidegger, and the French Bergson, was marked; his influence upon the speculative theology of the nineteenth century was also noteworthy. Johann Arndt's *True Christianity* had a strong influence upon Philipp Jacob Spener (1635–1705), who was the central figure in the early development of Pietism in Germany.

An important consequence of this great movement was that faith, in Christian context, was taken seriously in a highly personal and explicit way. On the one hand, faith in God through Jesus Christ was understood, on the basis of the experience of the Reformation, to be the sole means of salvation. The further consequence was drawn that personal unbelief must necessarily entail personal damnation, and in this consequence Pietism was in accord with the views dominant in the bulk of Protestantism. But this perception was given a new and existential explicitness of meaning as knowledge of the wider world increasingly penetrated the countries of central and northern Europe as a result of the voyages of exploration. In particular, among the men and women participating in the developing spirituality of Pietism, the new awareness of the peoples of Asia, Africa, the Americas, and the islands of the seas led them, differently from the mainstream of early Protestant orthodoxy, to a lively concern for the horrifying fate of "those without Christ," as this category was then understood.[32] Through their Christian faith these men and women understood God to be boundlessly compassionate and the cross and resurrection of Jesus Christ to be the primary expression in human history and in the cosmos of that compassion. They believed that God had a boundless desire for the salvation of all human beings and that their own missionary concern and activity were properly specific consequences of that prior divine concern. The Moravians, who were also in the direct line of the tradition of German-speaking spirituality, had the conviction, surprisingly akin to that of the early church, that Jesus Christ, through the Holy Spirit, had long been present and at work in the whole world to create disciples for his church. This was to give a wider understanding to the doctrine of prevenient grace.

Like the later pioneer English missionary to India, William Carey, the Moravians preferred to focus upon simple obedience to divine call as the primary motivation to Christian witness. An example of even broader perspectives was George Fox (1624–91), the prophetic founder of the Society of Friends, who followed directly in the tradition of the "spiritual writers" of the early Reformation period. Fox came to believe that every human being receives from the Lord an inner light, which if faithfully followed will lead to a direct and saving knowledge of God. Of similar spirit in the last years of the seventeenth century were the Cambridge Platonists in England "with their inner illumination" and the Dutch Arminian Remonstrants "deep in love with God's wisdom." In the midst of the prevailing temper of theological writing of the time, which, as has been said, had "little of either calm or toleration" and ran "from intolerable rudeness to intolerable barbarity," we find among the Cambridge Platonists, such as Henry More and Ralph Cudworth, rather a "general courtesy and politeness . . . reasonableness and breadth of view." Like the Dutch Remonstrants, with whom there was a history of long and close association, they combined, in the tradition of the noblest spirits of the Renaissance, profound spirituality, relatively conservative biblical scholarship, and religious understanding open to the data of natural science.[33]

The point to be made, however, with reference to the role of Pietism and evangelicalism in the historical process that we are considering, is essentially a positive one. That is, while important elements of this great tradition of faith were uncritically in accord with the exclusivism of the medieval theological tradition, the spiritual sensitivity and concern of many of the men and women themselves contributed in time to more adequate theological understanding of the wider presence and work of God in the world of his creation. If missionaries of this tradition believed themselves to be expressive of the divine concern in their own lives and work, their personal experiences "on the field" led the more perceptive into an awareness of wider manifestations of that concern than they had been taught in their homelands to expect. Specifically, some came to see signs of the divine presence and work in traditionally non-Christian lands in both past and present quite outside "the visible confines of the Mystical Body," to use the phrase of Pope John Paul II. They saw that apart from some such awareness they were in danger of depicting the God and Father of Jesus Christ as a tribal deity of Western peoples. They began to perceive increasingly the need for Christian inquirers and converts to understand the spiritual and ethical traditions of their own peoples in a positive as well as a critical light. It was vitally important (as we noted from the experience of Francis Xavier) for the Christian self-understanding of men, women, and children in these lands to know that God and Christ and church belonged in some way to their own past as well as to their present and future.

Significant examples of this development in Protestant context can also be seen in Japan. Among the early leaders of Japanese Protestantism, Hiromichi Kozaki (Congregational) was among those who tried to combine sensitive appreciation with careful criticism as they reflected on the religious past of their nation. Kozaki saw Christianity as the fulfillment of the basic spirit of the teaching of Confucius, which he recognized as a positive good in the history of east Asia and meaningful in the history of salvation as Christians understood the term. Yet he sharply criticized the role of Neo-Confucianism as a bulwark of the rigidly class-structured, feudalistic patterns of traditional Japanese society. Danjō Ebina, also of Congregational affiliation, had a similarly high view of the best of the Confucian tradition. Masahisa Uemura, the pioneer leader of Presbyterian-Reformed Christianity in Japan, saw *Bushidō* (the Way of the Warrior) as a singular gift of God to Japan and a veritable Old Testament for Japanese Christians. He believed that the Christian doctrine of the redemptive sacrifice of Jesus Christ for the world was particularly possible of comprehension by persons reared in that tradition. He objected to the overweening pride and class consciousness that it frequently begot and felt that it had lost the perception of authentic humanity that he found in the Christian gospel. But he believed that this tradition, fed by many sources including the simple piety of native Shinto, had true meaning and theological validity as preparation under God.[34] Inazō Nitobe similarly saw the seeds of the kingdom of God as having blossomed in *Bushidō*.[35]

THE ENLIGHTENMENT

To return again to the European situation, there are other factors of importance to be noted in the developments that we are considering. Perhaps more than any other single factor of the time, the wars of religion in the seventeenth century, as they combined with the northward movement of the Renaissance and the effects of the voyages of exploration, led numbers of sensitive Europeans to more critical appraisals of the teaching and claims of institutional Christianity of every branch. The further developments of early modern science had certain effects also upon the humanities. For example, in 1705 the Dutch scholar Hadrianus Relandus (1676–1718), who was professor of Oriental Languages at the University of Utrecht, published a two-volume work *De religione Mohammadanica libri duo*, the first scientifically objective representation of Islam to appear in European history. Another factor that served to broaden the cultural sympathies of Europeans was the relatively wide diffusion of the *Lettres curieuses et édifiantes* sent back to Europe by Roman Catholic missionaries in China during the late seventeenth and early eighteenth centuries.

The Jesuit missionary theologians in Peking made use of the Logos theology of the early church fathers to interpret for themselves and then for the recipients of their letters the theological significance of the greatness of the Chinese civilization in the midst of which they were serving. Following the developments in Roman Catholic theology in early Renaissance Europe, they moved beyond the tentative efforts of Francis Xavier in Japan and developed the doctrine of natural revelation and knowledge of the divine law among all human beings as potentially salvific, as instruments of divine grace, outside the institutional means of salvation provided by the Roman Catholic Church. In his journals written in China from 1583 to 1610, Matteo Ricci (1552–1610) wrote:

> One can confidently hope that in the mercy of God, many of the ancient Chinese found salvation in the natural law, assisted as they must have been by that special help which, as the theologians teach, is denied to no one who does what he can toward salvation, according to the light of his conscience. That they endeavored to do this is readily determined from their history of more than four thousand years, which really is a record of good deeds done on behalf of their country and for the common good. The same conclusion might also be drawn from the books of rare wisdom of their ancient philosophers. These books are still extant and are filled with the most salutary advice on training men to be virtuous. In this particular respect, they seem to be quite the equals of our own most distinguished philosophers.[36]

From this notation of Ricci it is clear that the perspectives of the Council of Trent on our theme and, indeed, the conclusions of men like Juan de Lugo, had already become theological commonplaces among the intellectual and spiritual leaders of the Roman Catholic Church. With reference to European knowledge of China, however, Ricci's journals took Europe by surprise. Written originally in Italian, they were translated into Latin by Nicola Trigault and published in 1615. Four Latin editions followed the first, and within a very few years editions appeared in French, German, Spanish, and Italian, with excerpts in English. Three French editions followed, in 1616, 1617, and 1618. The book in fact opened a new era of Chinese-European relations, and together with the letters aforementioned, helped to create such enthusiasm for Chinese culture among educated Europeans as to effect distinctly new styles in architecture, painting, furniture, earthenware ("chinaware"), and so forth, which have remained a part of the Western cultural heritage to the present day. Voltaire expressed himself as favoring Chinese civilization in contrast with "Christian Europe."

All these influences were factors in creating the great movement called the Enlightenment, which has had such enormous effects upon the formation of the modern Western world in both its inner and its outer aspects. In one sense the Enlightenment (*Aufklärung*) represents the delayed northward movement of the free spirit of the Italian and larger Latin Renaissance, as, indeed, did the Reformation, although in a more restricted religious and theological sense. Nevertheless, the time difference was important. The wars of religions had profoundly shaken the confidence of ethically sensitive Europeans everywhere in the claims of the institutional churches. The mentally expansive effects of the voyages of exploration had been compounded with the passage of time. Actually, Pietism itself broke the hold of earlier Protestant confessional orthodoxy and, as a more profoundly religious activity in its depths of feeling than the preceding orthodoxy, exercised a distinct role in the movement toward religious and cultural freedom.

The Enlightenment proper is commonly viewed as a movement originating in the German Protestant states in the early eighteenth century, with Christian Wolff (1679–1754) as the most noteworthy of its early leaders. The Deistic, Unitarian, and other so-called rationalistic movements in England had emerged somewhat earlier and had a distinct influence upon developments in Germany. Wolff had been influenced also by the earlier Christian Thomasius (1655–1728), who was a "rationalist" akin to the English John Locke and a defender of religious toleration. Wolff's religious position was actually a kind of Protestantized version of Roman Catholic concepts of the natural law with an additional thrust in the direction of creating a world-view that tried to include both the religious dimension and the fast-developing natural science of the time. Wolff had also been influenced by the thought of the great German mathematician, historian, statesman, and philosopher Gottfried Wilhelm Leibnitz (1646–1716), who taught that human beings may gain knowledge by the elucidation of ideas innate to them.

It is customary to view the Enlightenment as a primarily "rationalistic" movement with cognitive reason consistently taking priority over the distinctly religious dimension in the characteristic leaders of the movement. It is true that men like John Locke, David Hume, and Immanuel Kant evaluated all religions, including Christianity, by the criterion of "reasonableness." But this posture does not constitute the whole of the movement. We do not have space for a detailed discussion of the various nuances of the Enlightenment, but a few points are in order to correct, or at least restore balance to, traditional views. The movement was, at least in part, a protest against seventeenth-century Protestant orthodoxy, but it was profoundly religious in its own way. In fact, the issue was basically one of perception of the nature of salvation and of the Christian life on earth. Protestant Scholastic orthodoxy of the seventeenth century, perhaps primarily in the Lutheran churches but also in the Reformed, tended to view salvation in juridical terms, in the sense that one is "declared" righteous and thereby acceptable to God through faith in the atoning sacrifice of Jesus Christ for the sins of all. This is of course one valid way of expressing the great gospel truth of the divine forgiveness of sin wrought through the person and work of Jesus Christ. The problem was that orthodoxy, including both theologians and leading pastors, too often yielded to the temptation to consider this aspect of the gospel the totality of salvation available in this earthly life and to leave the needs for transformation of human character to the state and to life after death. There was great resistance to the Roman Catholic concept of *gratia infusa* (as against *imputata*), whereby emphasis tended to shift toward recognition of the importance of the Christian daily life. This latter more existential understanding of faith tended to generate expectations for change and growth in human character in this life as a proper, indeed necessary, response of Christians to the divine grace freely given them in Jesus Christ. Both Pietism and the Enlightenment, with important analogies, as we shall see, as well as differences, constituted a protest against the tendency of Protestant Scholastic orthodoxy to rest content with the "declaration" without appropriate human response. The orthodox position, we may say, represented an egregious misunderstanding of the Pauline message. For Paul the essence of the gospel from the human side, that is, from the side of human response, appropriation, and application, was "faith working through love." Love, in turn, was the consummation of all ethics, and without the totality of faith working through love, for Paul there was no salvation (cf. Gal. 5:6, 13–15, 21; 6:7–9).[37]

To return to the Enlightenment and more particularly to Christian Wolff, we may note as characteristic of his religious position clear affirmations of the fact of God, the possibility of revelation and miracle, as well as a high role for human reason. He also stressed, following Leibnitz—and the major stream of Roman Catholic understanding—the presence of moral awareness in all human beings. He differed from the older Protestant orthodoxy but followed the perceptions of the early Renaissance in his more hopeful, expansive anthropology. In his concepts of salvation as progress under God toward individual and racial perfection, Wolff differed, therefore, from the low expectations for personal or group development in this world characteristic of contemporary orthodoxy and followed the higher expectations of both the Renaissance humanists and the fathers of the early church.[38]

The Enlightenment, then, was a protest against certain presumptions of prevailing Protestant orthodoxy in favor of more inclusive religious understanding as well as, in not a few cases, in favor of aspirations for deeper and broader expressions of personal religion. Perceptive readers will be able to recognize in the libretto of Wolfgang Amadeus Mozart's *The Magic Flute* an example of this latter posture, an example that is also indicative of the fact that important aspects of the Enlightenment were shared by many of the educated classes in Roman Catholic as well as Protestant lands. With reference to the dimension of personal religion, Mircea Eliade has pointed to what he calls "an unknown or perhaps carefully neglected dimension of the Enlightenment—the religious concern of a great section of European intelligentsia," which had long been considered "antireligious or religiously indifferent." Eliade stresses the importance of the work of a number of French scholars in this area, beginning with Auguste Viatte, the publication in 1928 of whose two-volume work, *Les sources occultes du romantisme: Illuminisme-Theosophie*, was a highly significant event in clarifying the issue. Admittedly, the genuine religious sentiment involved was at times expressed in perhaps unusual forms, and the corporate formation was often in what may be called "esoteric groups and secret societies." But Eliade stresses that these groups were "animated by a profound hope in an imminent *renovatio*," both personal and corporate. He rightly notes the analogies of these secret societies with the larger religious milieu of the eighteenth century, especially with German Pietism. The activity as a whole is to be classed as in the tradition of creative Christian spirituality, which in one form or another had stirred the soul of Europe from the early Middle Ages, especially from the time of Gioachino da Fiore (1145?–1202). Eliade insists that aspirations for spiritual rebirth, both personal and collective, which he sees as the "Christian objective par excellence," were consistently characteristic of this tradition, the raison d'être for which, as distinctive activities, lay largely in the fact that these aspirations were for many reasons "less and less present in the institutionalized religious life" of the churches.[39]

CHRISTIANITY AND OTHER RELIGIOUS TRADITIONS

Friedrich Schleiermacher (1768–1834), the first major Christian thinker in modern Europe to grapple theologically *in extenso* with the themes of the present study, was himself a product of the Enlightenment. Somewhat earlier, the distinguished German dramatist, literary and artistic critic, Gotthold Ephraim Lessing (1729–81) had written his *Education of the Human Race*, which, with its theme of the development of humanity as akin to the maturation process of an individual, expressed an important element of the spirit of the Enlightenment. He also expressed that spirit in his *Nathan the Wise*, which represents the three religions of Christianity, Islam, and Judaism in a parable of three brothers. In the story Lessing does not say which of the three religions is the true one that makes human beings acceptable before God and others (*vor Gott und Menschen angenehm*), but the implication is that they are of at least relative equality in salvific value. Both Lessing and his later contemporary Johann Gottfried von Herder (1744–1803) in fact maintained that all human history is a single process through which God is working and within which all religions are only partially true, and none perfectly. Schleiermacher, however, differed somewhat from the apparent relativism of Lessing by assigning to the religions of the world varying degrees of development as differences of kind and quality. He affirmed Christianity to be the best but clearly attributed significant theological meaning and value to the others.

Schleiermacher became the leader of an important school of thought in German-speaking Europe and a major formative influence in the development of nineteenth-century German theological liberalism. He was distinctively Christocentric, albeit in ways that differed at points from Lutheran orthodoxy. He held Jesus Christ to be the central element of the Christian religion but perceived his mediating role in the reconciliation of the finite with the universal to be primarily significant for Christians. By implication other ways have been divinely appointed for others. Thus while he held to "the exclusive superiority of Christianity," he insisted that the proper Christian posture toward "at least most other forms of piety" should not be the attitude of comparing the true with the false.[40]

This kind of evaluative thinking had great influence throughout the nineteenth century. For a long time men and women continued to think in terms of the historic religions as self-contained and largely consistent units, and it remained for Ernst Troeltsch early in the twentieth century to break the hold of the notion of the superiority of "Christianity." Increasing knowledge not only of the other religions of the world but also of "Christianity" as a total reality in the historical process made it impossible any longer to compare these vast conglomerates of human activity in such a way as to assert the superiority of one over another. It became increasingly clear as the twentieth century proceeded, especially as the frightfulness of the fact and consequences of World War I was better known, that notions of the superiority of any historic religion—or culture or civilization—however imposing the external edifices it had created, are almost meaningless in the light of any in-depth consideration of their concrete expressions. All have their varying shades of light and darkness, their heroes and villains; all have their several periods of relative glory and decline. Increasingly it became clear that any "comparison of religions" worthy of the adjectives "objective" and "informed" had to refrain from facile evaluations that historically had so often been the product of ignorance and doctrinaire presuppositions.

An important element in this process was the greatly increased knowledge of other religious traditions that became available to educated Europeans, beginning, as we have seen, with the early eighteenth century. Subsequent to the expanded and more reliable knowledge of Islam and Chinese civilization came, first in the latter part of the same century, the discovery and translation of Sanskrit, Pāli, and then Chinese, Tibetan, and other Asian religious texts. The work of pioneers like A. H. Anquetil-Duperron, F. Max Müller, and C. A. F. Rhys Davids and his wife contributed enormously to an expansion of mental horizons and a general enrichment of the intellectual life of the West as well as to a renewal of appreciation among Asians for their own religious and larger cultural heritages. Americans will recall the great influence of these materials upon the early nineteenth-century movement in New England known as Transcendentalism. Though the movement as such was of relatively brief duration, through the lectures and writings of its best-known leaders, such as Ralph Waldo Emerson, Henry David Thoreau, Bronson Alcott, and others, it significantly influenced the New Thought or Metaphysical movement in American religious history. It exercised weighty influence upon the Pragmatism of William James and John Dewey, upon the architecture of Louis Sullivan and Frank Lloyd Wright, and upon various later developments in American art and environmental planning. In a quiet but decisive way the Transcendentalists were an important factor in forming the tone and ethos of American liberal theology of the late nineteenth century and increasingly that of the mainline churches in the twentieth.

Among the pioneers themselves and also among their readers were men and women of earnest Christian faith who made some attempts, especially from the latter part of the nineteenth century, to understand the larger meaning of these materials, as of the contemporary manifestations of the religious traditions, from the perspectives of Christian faith and theology. Much of the early work was necessarily philological, and all the pioneers named above were in the first instance linguistic specialists. We may also cite Cornelis P. Tiele and Pierre D. Chantepie de la Saussaye as pioneers oriented more toward historical studies. Even as they interpreted materials that dealt directly with dimensions of the sacred and/or transcendent, these scholars were concerned to use the tools of critical scholarship without being bound by the procedures, categories, and attitudes of orthodox theology.[41]

This approach aimed at a certain *epoché* or suspension of judgment, liberation from preconceived ideas and principles, and at least provisional contentment with descriptive, as contrasted with normative, statements. Since orthodox Christian theology of the nineteenth century generally seemed averse to this mode of inquiry and procedure, the early decades of the gradually emerging discipline of history of religions manifested a certain antitheological bias.[42]

The nature of religious data, however, is such that, as Mircea Eliade has written, properly "the historian of religions does not act as a philologist, but as a hermeneutist."[43] From the early years of the twentieth century a number of scholars accordingly began to move beyond the early emphasis upon philology, ethnology, and other forms of technical expertise in order to seek integration of the materials and an understanding congruent with their kind. They began to consider the nature of religious experience itself and to explore questions that were of an epistemological and even metaphysical nature. An important reason for this broadening of interest was the participation in the work of history of religions by distinguished Christian theologians such as Friedrich Heiler, Rudolf Otto, Nathan Söderblom, Ernst Troeltsch, and William Temple. Among missionaries of distinction who contributed notably may be cited J. N. Farquhar and Karl Ludwig Reichelt. The name of the American philosopher William Ernest Hocking should be added to this list, not least for his contributions to the document *Re-Thinking Missions*, which was published in 1932 as the report of the Laymen's Foreign Mission Enquiry. On the European continent the *Religionsgeschichtliche Schule* developed with the intent to apply to the area of biblical studies the abundance of data being uncovered in the larger Middle East regarding the religions and cultures surrounding Israel. We may add that the views of men like Frederic William Farrar, John Frederick Denison Maurice, George Rawlinson, and others of the Broad-Church movement in the Church of England in the late nineteenth century also contributed notably to the emergence of this climate of thought.

A significant expression of these developments within the mainstream of the Protestant churches was the Jerusalem Meeting in 1928 of the International Missionary Council (IMC). Already in 1910 the Anglican missionary Temple Gairdner, of Cairo, was writing of the need for Christians to recognize the light of Christ, however "broken," to be found among other religious traditions. The American Presbyterian missionary William Ambrose Shedd urged that Christians ought to be "ready to learn from Orientals truths which we have not apprehended." The report of the Jerusalem Meeting, however, revealed among the churches a new degree of understanding and appreciation of the other religions. The apologetic note is still strong, and there is a tendency to identify alleged faults of character or inadequacies of understanding in others that comports more with the period between the wars than after. But there is discernible a distinct effort to separate "Christianity" from Western culture or modern civilization and a serious concern to appreciate the great personages and high truths of other faiths in the light of adequate theological understanding. The following is a brief part of the International Missionary Council's official statement:

> We rejoice to think that just because in Jesus Christ the light that lighteth every man shone forth in full splendor, we find rays of that same light where he is unknown or even is rejected. We welcome every noble quality in non-Christian persons or systems as further proof that the Father, who sent His Son into the world, has nowhere left himself without witness.
>
> Thus, merely to give illustration, and making no attempt to estimate the spiritual value of other religions to their adherents, we recognize as part of the one Truth that sense of the Majesty of God and the consequent reverence in worship which are conspicuous in Islam; the deep

sympathy for the world's sorrow and unselfish search for the way of escape, which are at the heart of Buddhism; the desire for contact with Ultimate Reality conceived as spiritual, which is prominent in Hinduism; the belief in a moral order of the universe and consequent insistence on moral conduct, which are inculcated by Confucianism; the disinterested pursuit of truth and of human welfare which are often found in those who stand for secular civilization but do not accept Christ as their Lord and Savior.

The great Orientalist Max Müller had contended that "other religions are languages in which God has spoken to man." This understanding was given powerful expression at Jerusalem by Rufus Jones, Kenneth J. Saunders, and others. The other religions were cited as "allies in our quest for perfection," and Saunders affirmed that Buddhism could contribute "wonderful treasures" to the Christian church.[44]

A word may be added at this point about the document *Re-Thinking Missions*, of which mention was made above. It created a great amount of opposition upon its publication, and in the Barthian-weighted theological climate of the time, it seemed for a while as if its influence had been effectively negated. It appears, in the 1980s, to have been a surprising harbinger of the future of Christian theology in the second half of the twentieth century. *Re-Thinking Missions* strongly affirmed the obligation of the Christian church to continue and even to extend its mission to the whole world. But in place of aiming at the destruction and displacement of other faiths, it urged Christians to regard earnest men and women within the other religions as fellow workers and fellow disciples of Christ "in the wider Christian fellowship." Christianity also may "find itself bound to aid these faiths, and frequently does aid them, to a truer interpretation of their own meaning than they had otherwise achieved." The Christian will "regard himself a co-worker with the forces which are making for righteousness within every religious system."[45] We shall see below how these perceptions reemerge with even greater force in contemporary theologians of every branch of the Christian church.

Another result of the developments that led to the Jerusalem Meeting of the IMC was the veritable vogue of so-called comparative-religion studies in theological seminaries in North America from around the turn of the century until the 1930s. This phenomenon was also aided in part by the influence of Protestant liberal theology, especially in English-speaking lands. Actually, however, the developments outlined above had had relatively little influence upon the mainstream of Protestant orthodoxy and its missiological or theological thinking. The late 1920s and early 1930s were to see a unique kind of confrontation in the United States between "Fundamentalism" and "Modernism" with reference to both biblical and theological interpretation. Europe did not experience quite the same kind of confrontation, but the development after World War I of crisis, or dialectical, theology under the leadership of Karl Barth, Emil Brunner, and others constituted a distinct

German-speaking response-reaction to earlier German biblical and theological liberalism. Even as this movement led to a kind of general theological renaissance, it also carried with it a relatively negative appraisal of other religious traditions than those produced by the "biblical message." Within this movement, also known as Neo-orthodoxy, there were those willing to acknowledge value and truth in the ethical teachings of other religions; but few, if any, in the movement seemed to be able to allow these religions any significance in the "history of salvation." The person who most clearly and resolutely represented this position besides Karl Barth was the Dutch missiologist and theologian, Hendrik Kraemer, and the heyday of his influence was the 1938 meeting of the IMC at Tambaram, Madras, India.[46]

It is necessary to note, however, that in one sense Neo-orthodoxy has made a distinct contribution to all subsequent developments in the theology of understanding the religions of humankind. This was its insistence that Christian faith, or the gospel, transcends Christianity as a historical movement. The leaders of Neo-orthodoxy stressed the universality of human sin as rebellion against God and tended to see human religions as Promethean creations of human beings in a vain attempt to find justification for their self-centered willfulness. As M. M. Thomas has noted, this made all religions suspect, including Christianity. A major problem in Neo-orthodoxy, however, was that in its actual ethos the other religions were considered much more suspect than Christianity. Nevertheless, its relativization of Christianity as well as culture in the light of the biblical message about Jesus Christ has made it easier for later theologians to look for the wider work of God in the world. Concepts of an exclusive tie between the risen Christ and either the Christian church or the movement known as Christianity have thus largely disappeared from the mind-set of contemporary Christian theologians.

AFTER WORLD WAR II

If World War I brought about a crisis in the personal and cultural self-awareness of Western peoples, the results of World War II were even more traumatic. As we have seen, a distinct effect of these events has been the loss, or at least the weakening, among thoughtful Westerners of centuries-long attitudes of Western cultural, racial, and religious superiority toward the other peoples of the earth. These events were evidently primary factors in giving a new force and momentum to trends that were long in the making. Beginning approximately in the late 1950s, a movement became noticeable in Protestant as well as Roman Catholic and Eastern Orthodox theology wherein Christian theology began in a massively new way to take seriously for its task the data and perspectives of the discipline of history of religions. We have already seen the results of this development in the Roman Catholic Church. In the Protestant churches comparable results are to be seen, and before we examine in the next chapters the thought of specific individuals, it would be well to identify certain larger or corporate consequences.

For one thing, it is probably true that theologians of the late twentieth century are better informed with regard to the data of the phenomenology and history of religions than any other generation since the period of the early church. The World Council of Churches (WCC) in recent years has given increasing attention to study, as a significant theological problem, of the relationship of Christian faith to the other living faiths of humankind. Many persons and groups in its worldwide constituency are currently engaged in serious dialogue with traditional or new religions in their various cultural contexts. A specific focus in the background of this development can be found in the work of the various Christian Study Centers related to the Division of World Mission and Evangelism of the WCC. In and through these centers Christians came to be engaged not only in academic study but in some of the first attempts at dialogue with persons of other faiths and ideologies at the ecumenical level.[47]

A particular theological principle that came into new focus and prominence in the early postwar years significantly helped to inform this activity. This was the understanding—which came to be an almost universal assumption—that God is present and at work in the secular realm of human activity as well as in the traditionally sacred or religious. This perception, one of the primary perceptions of Dietrich Bonhoeffer, captured the imagination especially of younger theologians in the West as perhaps no other single concept did. In the context of missiological thinking, this understanding led to a shift from emphasis on the church as the primary if not sole agent of God's mission, to the world as the locus for God's mission. The role of the church came to be seen more modestly as that of a participant in the *missio Dei* by its witness in word and deed.[48]

Perhaps the first action at a high level taken by the World Council of Churches was the decision of the Central Committee at its meeting in Galyatetö, Hungary, in 1956 to follow up in a more specific way the preparatory consultation that had been held the previous year in Davos, Switzerland. That is, the Central Committee made the decision to approve the creation of a study project entitled "The Word of God and the Living Faiths of Men." A further step can be identified in the meeting at Mexico City in 1963 of the newly formed Commission of World Mission and Evangelism, as the expression within the WCC of the former International Missionary Council. Although the attention of this meeting was directed mainly to the problem of Christian attitudes to their neighbors in the secular milieu, it did take into consideration also the relationship of dialogue with various religious traditions to practical issues of Christian witness. Basic to this approach was the affirmation of the conference that Christians must "discover a shape of Christian obedience being written for them by what God is already actively doing in the structures of the city's life outside the church."[49]

In the meantime, however, the Third Assembly of the World Council of Churches was held in New Delhi, India (Nov. 18–Dec. 6, 1961). In the statements and addresses of this assembly we find many of the developments in ecumenical thought and action over the preceding decade coming into expression. For instance, the belief is expressed that before we speak to our fellow human beings of Christ, Christ has already sought them. The Holy Spirit, the report of the assembly states, leads Christian witnesses to where Christ already is and is ceaselessly working among human beings in all times and places. Christian witness therefore is, properly, to the whole activity of God in the world. The report speaks particularly of the wisdom, love, and power that God has given to persons of other faiths and of no faith. This means that wise and sensitive expressions of Christian witness will not aim at the total displacement of other religious traditions but at changes that will alter all partners in the dialogic process, even though Christians may rightly continue to work and hope for the formal conversion of others to God in Jesus Christ.

A final point to be mentioned from New Delhi is the gentle way in which the report suggests a modification of the tendency of the older Protestant orthodoxies to prejudge the eternal destinies of human beings according to humanly contrived criteria of faith and religious allegiance. The report states that "Because God in Christ has reconciled the world to himself, we may no longer judge our brother man by ordinarily accepted standards. God has not condemned us; we may not condemn any man."[50]

Also of decisive importance in the ongoing process of development was the WCC-sponsored Assembly of the East Asia Christian Conference (EACC; now the Christian Conference of Asia) held in Bangkok, Thailand, from February 25 to March 4, 1964. Here certain basic principles were enunciated which have since become an integral part of the accumulating theological heritage of the WCC. With reference to the witness of Christian mission, the affirmation is forthrightly made that "It is Jesus whom men must encounter. The concern of the Christian is not to confront men with Christianity but with the event and person of Christ." The mode of enunciation was a statement entitled "Christian Encounter with Men of Other Beliefs," which was adopted by a commission of the EACC Assembly and commended to member churches and councils for action.

The statement goes on to affirm that all human beings are created by God through Jesus Christ, and when they are illumined, "it is he who illumines them." All persons live by the providence of God. "His love broods over all, and is present in the life of each man, both in judgement and in mercy." Similarly, affirmation is made of God's searching judgment of all religions, including Christianity. Therefore dialogue with men and women of other faiths impels Christians to combine witness to the truth as they know it in Jesus Christ with "the necessity of subjecting themselves to that process of mutual correction and learning which belongs to a conversation when it is truly open." Furthermore, "when Christians are aware of the wonder of the treasure which they have in Christ, they will be able, not with fear, but with joy and expectation, to enter into the lives of those of other beliefs so as to discern in them their treasures. . . . The point is that Christians must learn to discern the working of God wherever it may be, whether through the religious or the secular life." This work of God is not only a creating activity but the work of the Holy Spirit whereby the light of Christ is made to shine for every human being. No one in all human history is left without evidence of this light of Christ. And yet the Christian church is not merely communal; it is also missionary and it will witness to the light of Christ by the word of Christ.[51]

The next step in the development can be said to be the consultation at Kandy, Sri Lanka, in February and March of 1967 on "Christians in Dialogue with Men of Other Faiths." At Kandy, Roman Catholic scholars participated in the ecumenical debate on this theme for the first time; the Eastern Orthodox had been involved from an earlier period. The statement issued from Kandy, following in the spirit of New Delhi, also affirms that Christ can speak to the Christian through his neighbor, of whatever background, as well as to his neighbor through him. This is because "through the Spirit Christ is at work in every man's heart." The Christian church is "that community within humanity which, in spite of manifest weakness and failures, consciously responds to Christ in trust and obedience." But the church "is not conterminous with the historical community that openly bears His name."

Again in the spirit of New Delhi, the statement insists that "Christ brings grace and judgement to all men." After referring to Acts 10:34–35 and Rom. 2:6–16, the document quotes approvingly from Vatican II's Dogmatic Constitution on the Church: "Those also can attain the everlasting salvation who through no fault of their own do not know the gospel of Christ or His Church, yet sincerely seek God and, moved by grace, strive by their deeds to do His will as it is known to them through the dictates of conscience." The Kandy statement also affirms the need of Christians to be "more joyfully and responsibly aware" than they often are of their solidarity with all their fellow human beings, "no matter what their colour, culture, faith or unbelief." This document, too, states that "all mankind is furthermore being caught up into one universal history, and made increasingly aware of common tasks and common hopes." Therefore the proclamation which Christians must make and which is the sharing of the good news about God's action in history through Jesus Christ "should always be made in the spirit of dialogue."[52]

In the same year as the Kandy consultation, the United Presbyterian Church, U.S.A., issued a new confession of faith, to be affirmed along with older historic confessions, entitled "The Confession of 1967." In this statement we find the following:

> The Christian finds parallels between other religions and his own and must approach all religions with openness and respect. Repeatedly God has used the insights of non-Christians to challenge the church to renewal. But the reconciling word of the gospel is God's judgment upon all forms of religion, including the Christian. The gift of God is for all men. The church, therefore, is commissioned to carry the gospel to all men whatever their religion may be and even when they profess none.[53]

This statement, however reflective of the still powerful influence of Barthian theology, is yet a clear call to carry out the mission of the church, including proclamation of the gospel, with humility, openness, and genuine respect for the great historic religions. It asserts that the living God has used and may continue to use them to correct the Christian church as well as to instruct it. The mission of Christian witness is therefore properly to function in the context of a process of mutual respect and mutual learning. Similarly, a statement was issued in July 1970 by the East Asia Christian Conference calling for a new sensitivity to the Holy Spirit in order to discern "Christ's work since history began in all our societies and spiritual 'worlds.' "[54]

Prior to 1970, of course, was the Fourth Assembly of the World Council of Churches, held at Uppsala, Sweden, in 1968. In large part as a result of the mood of the time and in smaller part in consequence of the 1966 Geneva Church and Society Conference, new emphases came to the fore. Practical issues arising from deep concern for the worldwide human experiences of racism, sexism, and economic, social, and political injustice led to a focus on themes such as conscientization and the liberation of peoples. But like New Delhi and Kandy, Uppsala affirms dialogue with persons of other religious faiths as indispensable to authentic Christian living in this age. It insists that "a genuinely Christian approach to others must be human, personal, relevant and humble." And the humanness of this approach has its basis as well as its appropriateness in "our common humanity, its dignity and its fallenness." Dialogue "opens the possibility of sharing in new forms of community and common service"; even when we remain distinct in our separate religious traditions, Christians believe that "Christ speaks in this dialogue, revealing himself to those who do not know him and correcting the limited and distorted knowledge of those who do."[55]

Since 1970 the World Council of Churches has continued its activities in this area with great seriousness. We shall here identify only the most salient events. The election of M. M. Thomas, director of the Christian Institute for the Study of Religion and Society in Bangalore, India, to chair the Central Committee of the WCC had much significance in this context. This was because of his creative theological work in interpreting the Hindu religious tradition from the perspectives of Christian faith. Also of great importance was the appointment in August 1968 of Stanley J. Samartha, formerly principal of Serampore College in India, as associate secretary in the Department on Studies in Mission and Evangelism. His primary task was to coordinate studies on the relationship of "the Word of God and the Living Faiths of Men" and to support and coordinate the work of the study centers in different parts of the world that were related to the WCC Division of World Mission and Evangelism.

In January 1971 a new organizational pattern of the WCC was approved by the Central Committee. This was to create a set of subunits under the Programme Unit on Faith and Witness. Parallel to the three other subunits on Faith and Order, Church and Society, and World Mission and Evangelism, a new subunit was created entitled Dialogue with Men of Living Faiths and Ideologies. Stanley Samartha was appointed director of this subunit, and its primary task was to implement the most recent recommendations of the Central Committee, as of the previous assemblies of the WCC.

Already, however, in 1970 important events had occurred. The first was the Ajaltoun (Beirut) Consultation in March, which had been authorized by the Central Committee at its Canterbury meeting in August 1969. Forty people from seventeen countries participated at Ajaltoun to constitute a landmark in the history of the WCC. For the first time in that history the WCC brought together under its own auspices adherents of four major faiths—Hindu, Buddhist, Christian, and Muslim—to consider the theme of "Dialogue between Men of Living Faiths—Present Discussions and Future Possibilities." The nature of the meeting was admittedly experimental and exploratory, but as Stanley Samartha has written, "the keynote of the Consultation was the understanding that a full and loyal commitment to one's own faith did not stand in the way of dialogue, but on the contrary, was the very basis of such meetings."[56]

Several of the significant contributions of Ajaltoun have been identified by Samartha in another article of his. One of the most important of these contributions was experience of the "acceptance of common human interests, the convergence of the historical processes of different religions, a sense of participation in each other's on-going religious history, an openness to the strangely other, even the occasion of sharp disagreements and unresolved conflicts." Concretely, this came to mean the development of understanding that dialogue can be a "new theologizing experience" if the participants are ready to look beyond themselves. Such understanding seems to call for a new ecclesiology appropriate to it and a more humble practice of mission. In many parts of the world Christians seem increasingly to sense that Christian mission means to participate not only in a mission identifiably Christian but also, as a pilgrim people, in the larger life activity of multireligious communities. Because "God has not left himself without witness in the history of all mankind" and men and women of other faiths are also within the love and grace of God, Christians need to understand with greater theological sophistication what it means to be a part of "the converging historical processes of men of all faiths," which all persons in this generation are experiencing consciously or unconsciously.[57]

A further discussion with only Christian participants was held at Zurich, Switzerland, in May 1970 on the theme of "Christian Dialogue with Men of Other Faiths." Twenty-three theologians from fifteen countries, among whom were four Eastern Orthodox and three Roman Catholic representatives, took part in this Zurich Consultation. Its purpose was to evaluate the Ajaltoun Consultation and then to work out the theological implications of dialogues of this kind, and on that basis to offer suggestions for future action to the World Council of Churches. It may be helpful to identify a few of the conclusions from the aide-mémoire issued by the Zurich Consultation.

The aide-mémoire (available from the World Council of Churches, 1970) phrases some of its conclusions in particularly seminal language. For example: "Christ releases us to be free to enter into loving, respectful relation with all human beings. . . . God is at work among all men and he speaks to a Cyrus or a Cornelius and bids them do his will." "We now have an opportunity for a renewed understanding of the universality of God's work," for "an extended understanding of the universality and fulness of Christ." This understanding is based upon perception of God's activity for the salvation of the whole world, an activity of God's love, which Christians see particularly embodied in Jesus Christ. It is, however, in Christ that all things are held together now, even as all things will be summed up in him in the End. Therefore the mission of the people who are Christian is concerned, as part of its task, to discover Christ where he is already holding things together. In this time, "when different streams of history are being drawn into one world history," the Christian church, insofar as it is the body of Christ, is "essentially related to the centre of that sacred history in which we are to see God moving all things through Christ to their salvation." This is to see a central but not controlling role for the church in the divine history of salvation.[58]

The next important meeting on these themes sponsored by the World Council of Churches was the Broumana (Lebanon) Consultation held July 12–18, 1972. This was a Christian-Muslim Dialogue, which consisted of forty-six persons from twenty countries, with the participants almost equal in number from each community. They came not as representatives but in their personal capacity, by invitation. Because of their diverse cultural backgrounds and widely different places of geographical origin, they were nevertheless significantly "representative." The Broumana Consultation was one of the first major consequences of the decisions made by the 1971 Addis Ababa meeting of the Central Committee of the WCC.

The memorandum (available from the World Council of Churches, 1972) issued by the consultation, which of course took place in the aftermath of the 1967 war and in the context of continuing Middle East tensions, contains a number of statements which are yet pregnant with meaning and hope even as that context continues today. Among the guiding principles for the dialogue, mutual respect was held to be paramount. The participants felt that this involves "a sensitive regard for the partner's scruples and convictions, a sympathy for his difficulties and an admiration for his achievements." Both sides "wished to retrieve more positive evaluations of each other" and "shed all caricatures of each other's social and theological position." For this reason they "also dared to hope for some convergence, not in impatient syncretism, but in openness to God's further guidance." This posture was understood as properly including a willingness to reconsider "many of our theological and legal constructions," even while this reconsideration, the statement affirms, should be carried on in continuity with the past.

One of the significant aspects of the consultation was the attempt to have "devotions" together in mixed groups of Christians and Muslims. Each morning these groups met in the specific context of worship to listen to readings from the Bible and the Qur'ān, to pray and to meditate. These experiences of common worship, which were very well attended, helped the participants to realize, as Kenneth Cragg later wrote, that "God is one and the same in both faiths, [even though] God is understood and invoked by differing dogmatic languages. God is affirmatively the same, but predicatively the other: an inclusive focus of worship, with exclusifying patterns of vocabulary." What happened was an "interpenetration of mutual recognition and responsiveness to God."

One of the final statements of the Broumana Memorandum was that "we reaffirm the urgency of avoiding all polemic, and of providing text-books, teacher-training and seminary programmes which should be worked out in consultation with each other." The spirit of the consultation was well expressed by Stanley Samartha in an interpretive paper written after the event. This was that each community of faith would neither question nor neglect its own historic continuities. And yet a kind of "inter-spirituality" can emerge that will lead to a certain "dogmatic openness" as well as effective cooperation in service to society. What is needed now is "an inter-penetration of sympathy, of awareness, of recognition, and of responsiveness, and the will to a positive 'discerning' of each other, as the necessary context" of both dialogue and common action.[59]

The need to take the whole world seriously both as the locus of God's mission and as the place of Christian participation in that mission—with all that this acceptance implies in mutual human respect and openness to learn as well as readiness to teach—seems to have become an integral element of contemporary ecumenical theology. Since Uppsala 1968, however, with "its heavy emphasis on social and political affairs as points of opportunity for mission," a distinct shift in the direction of this emphasis became discernible in the deliberations and documents of the World Council of Churches. At the same time Uppsala saw the participation and active contribution of Protestant evangelicals in the ecumenical debate on mission on a new level of intensity, and the liveliness of that debate is a noteworthy feature of the contemporary scene. The WCC Commission on World Mission and Evangelism Conference held at Bangkok in 1973 on the theme of "Salvation Today" tried in its own way to synthesize the different emphases in the larger Christian movement by its comprehensive depiction of the salvation proclaimed in the Christian gospel. This was to see the essence of salvation as God's gift of new life in Jesus Christ, which is intended to mean fullness of human life on earth as well as life eternal. There was still the same call "to engage in spoken witness and to enter into dialogue with all those, of one faith or another, of one conviction or another, who are also loved by God." These persons must be regarded "through Jesus Christ as a brother or sister through whom God wants to enrich us." For "we see God at work today both within the Church and beyond the Church" for the achievement of his purposes.[60]

Mention must also be made of the Multi-Lateral Dialogue that took place under the auspices of the World Council of Churches in Colombo, Sri Lanka, from April 17 to 26, 1974. This was a meeting of fifty persons drawn from five religious traditions: Buddhist, Christian, Hindu, Jewish, and Muslim. Jews had not been present at Ajaltoun and they added significantly to the range of perspective and discourse at Colombo, as did the presence of Muslims from outside the Middle East. Christians, though forming the largest single group, were here in the minority, an element of the situation that also differed from Ajaltoun. Many of the participants at Colombo had had previous experience in similar dialogues, either international or regional, and this fact, together with the participation of persons of other faiths than Christian in the planning sessions, led to a new level of sophistication in method as well as to an atmosphere of mutual trust and understanding.

One evidence of the increased sophistication was the questioning of the polarities in views of world history commonly attributed to the East and the West. That is, the neat ascription to the Asian tradition of a "cyclical" view of history and to the Western of a "linear" view, or describing the entire cultural tradition of one or the other as "life-negating" or "life-affirming" was seen as "far too simple" and "too often an artificial construction of the colonial mind."

Increasingly in meetings of this kind, express recognition has been made of "the fundamental unity of human beings as one family." Indeed, it is highly significant that such language has become the common property of many religious traditions; in this case all five were able comfortably to share it. At Colombo this assumed reality-fact was noted as consisting of "real common links, based on a sense of universal interdependence and responsibility of each and every person with and for all other persons." This sense, however, was not merely the perception that one world already exists on the level of exchange of physical resources. The participants in their quest for "provisional" world community did not wish to exclude from "common endeavour on the level of social action" those persons who derive their inspiration toward world community from other than distinctly religious sources. But they strongly stated that all their religious traditions at their best have taught and emphasized responsible concern, indeed love, for others. The language of the Colombo Memorandum made clear the conviction of the participants that a specifically religious perspective gives a depth and strength of support to human interrelationships and common practical endeavor quite beyond the mutual economic benefits and concepts of "economic man" that are central to the usual discourse of modern industrial society.

The intent of the meeting was thus to reaffirm for religious people the universal scope of their interrelationships and responsibilities and at the same time to suggest something of the unique contributions that they can make qua religious persons, especially in community. The Colombo meeting said that it might be "the special task of religious groups to stress the importance of the model of concrete local community as the first reality of world community, but also as the reality which mediates world community." The way to this community, whether local or world, was not seen to require "syncretism." Rather, a larger framework was in part sought, in part seen as already existing, within which "differentiated interrelatedness" may permit, even encourage, harmonious living together and effective cooperation without glossing over differing particularities. Colombo "found helpful the recognition of particularity as a universal empirical fact, and the affirmation of universality as our common goal."

Significantly, the primary responsibility of religious persons in contributing toward the task of living together as a world community was seen to be the endeavor toward "a higher and more just quality of life" as well as "a new sense of community." In spite of real differences, even tensions, in understanding among the participants, all felt that they could share in "the common goal of world community, based on a readiness for responsible change and an openness to the future." This was possible because all shared the "faith that our present human condition does not exhaust reality," a faith in turn based upon the conviction that "human reality has a transcendental aspect" whether this aspect be described as a relationship with God or with Ultimate Truth. It is this conviction, the participants insisted, that makes it "our right and duty not to submit to the human situation as it is but constantly to strive towards its betterment in human history." In this context religious dialogue can be considered as a "major resource towards world community."[61]

The Fifth Assembly of the World Council of Churches, held in Nairobi in 1975, continued this effort to put and to keep the entire Christian movement in touch with and in service of the whole world. It also continued the WCC tradition of concern for dialogue in the report of Section III on "Seeking Community: The Common Search of People of Various Faiths, Cultures, and Ideologies." For the first time in any assembly of the WCC, guests had been officially invited from other faiths, and they shared in the work of this section. As we have seen, few issues in the history of the ecumenical movement have been more controversial than that of the relationship of Christian faith to the other great world religions, and the first draft of the report met with sharp criticism, chiefly from Scandinavian churches. As a result the draft was referred back for rephrasing. Significantly, it was Olle Engstrom of the Mission Covenant Church of Sweden who introduced the revised text, which was accepted, with the insistence that for many member churches of the WCC the search for a wider community, including relationships with persons of other faiths, is not an academic but an existential issue. He urged, doubtless with reference to the geographical and cultural situations of the Scandinavian churches, that those persons who are somewhat removed from direct encounters should listen carefully to members of churches for whom they are matters of primary concern.

Among the Nairobi Report's recommendations to the churches are highly significant proposals. The call is for study of the Bible as well as of the traditions of the churches in order "to relate the uniqueness of Christ to God's larger work among all peoples and in the whole creation." Christians are asked to examine and revise their catechetical, liturgical, and theological materials in order "to remove all caricatures and misrepresentations of other people's faiths, cultures, and ideologies, and in the teaching about other religions in theological seminaries." The churches are asked to prepare for wider dialogue by "continued reflection, on a regional and local basis, on the relation between dialogue and evangelism, taking into account experiments in actual dialogue with people of various faiths and ideologies." The preparation will properly include efforts to acquaint the members of churches with "the wide spectrum of the Christian spiritual heritage, ranging from the ancient Oriental Christian traditions of Asia to the contemporary spiritual practices, for example, of African independent churches."

The Nairobi Report calls Christians to continuing commitment to their own faith and convictions "while maintaining sympathetic openness to others." The report also renewed the call to "discernment of spirits" and the need for clarification of the proper criteria that make such discernment biblically, theologically, and spiritually responsible. It notes that Christians need specific preparation in order "to discern what could be seductively demonic or dangerously misleading in any religious or spiritual tradition."

A highly significant part of the process of debate was the strong espousal of the principle of dialogue by Asian Christian participants. For example, Russell Chandran of the Church of South India insisted that the process of deepening "theological insights and convictions about the presence and work of Christ and the Holy Spirit in other religions and cultures," which has been a part of the contemporary experience of all branches of the Christian church, is in fact "deeply rooted in our confession of Jesus Christ as Lord and Saviour and our commitment to the trinitarian faith." He held that "in a genuine sense, our knowledge and experience of Christ is enriched by the response of the people of other faiths. Witnessing to Christ is, therefore, a two-way movement of mutual learning and enrichment." This is in part because we do not possess the Christ: "he possesses us and all peoples."

Lynn A. de Silva of the Methodist Church of Sri Lanka also insisted that "dialogue does not in any way diminish full and loyal commitment to one's own faith, but rather enriches and strengthens it." Furthermore, "dialogue, far from being a temptation to syncretism, is a safeguard against it, because in dialogue we get to know one another's faith in depth. . . . The real test of faith is faiths-in-relation." De Silva held that "above all, dialogue is essential for us to discover the Asian face of Jesus Christ as the Suffering Servant, so that the Church itself may be set free from its institutional self-interest and play the role of a servant in building community."[62]

Brief mention has been made of the emergence of Protestant evangelicals as a distinct voice and power at the Uppsala Assembly (1968) of the World Council of Churches. A few more words on this matter seem in order at this point. The reference of course was to evangelicals who through their respective churches are members of the WCC and participate in its activities in various ways. At Uppsala the British Anglican John R. W. Stott and the

American David A. Hubbard, who is president of Fuller Theological Seminary, were noteworthy in representing this tradition in the discussions. By the admission into membership of the Pentecostal Church of Chile (in 1961 at New Delhi), the WCC had given formal notice of its intent to welcome into its fellowship churches of the charismatic tradition. The presumption was and is that churches and persons of the evangelical or biblically and theologically conservative stream of Protestant Christianity would be given a respectful hearing in the councils and debates of the WCC.

There are, however, especially in the United States, many churches that designate themselves as evangelical or conservative-evangelical and do not associate themselves with the World Council of Churches or the National Council of Churches of Christ in the U.S.A. Some of these churches, such as the Southern Baptist Convention or the Lutheran Church, Missouri Synod, are quite large bodies. Certain churches, and part of the membership of others, may be designated as fundamentalist. This latter term refers less to theological differences from other evangelicals than to differing views on the Bible and certain other matters. Fundamentalists tend to espouse "a meticulous definition of biblical inerrancy," as compared to other evangelicals "who feel that the focus on the details of science, geography and history distracts . . . from the saving message and the spiritual teaching of Scripture." This latter group represents a growing number of evangelicals who view themselves as "conservative without necessarily espousing some of the more negative traits of fundamentalism." Among these "more negative traits" may be cited a certain anti-intellectualism, lack of social concern, and a tendency toward separation in relations with other churches.[63]

Since 1966, however, Protestant evangelicals around the world have drawn closer to one another and have increasingly expressed their agreements—and disagreements—in fellowship through various organizations and conferences. The National Association of Evangelicals in the U.S.A. is a key organization for this tradition in the United States. The two largest missionary organizations of the tradition, the Evangelical Foreign Missions Association and the older Interdenominational Foreign Mission Association of North America, are responsible for sending the majority of evangelical overseas missionaries who go from North America. It should be mentioned in this context that if we add to this number the missionaries of churches and societies unaffiliated with either of these associations, such as the Southern Baptists and the Wycliffe Bible Translators—also to be classed as evangelicals—they constitute a very large proportion of all Protestant overseas missionaries. Thomas Stransky has reported that if one should add Roman Catholic missionaries to these Protestant evangelicals, the total number would reach 95 percent of the whole Christian overseas missionary force.[64] This means that evangelicals have become a weighty factor in the contemporary religious scene.

There is no need for our present purposes to describe in detail the development of the evangelical movement over the post-World War II period. We may merely note that the first major meeting of evangelicals in this period took place at Chicago in 1960 under the sponsorship of the International

Foreign Mission Association. Subsequently, two major congresses were held at Wheaton, Illinois, and Berlin, Germany, in 1966. The event, however, which elicited the greatest public attention was the International Congress on World Evangelization held at Lausanne, Switzerland, in 1974. This last meeting, to which 2,500 delegates came, was no doubt intended somewhat as a counterthrust to the Fifth Assembly of the World Council of Churches that was to take place in Nairobi in 1975. Many persons who attended Lausanne were also members of churches in the WCC. John Stott, whom we noted as a figure of importance at Uppsala, was perhaps the outstanding theological leader at Lausanne. Among various reasons for growing tension between the WCC and the evangelical movement, possibly the chief one was the mode of economic and social analysis as well as theological undergirding that evangelicals had come to feel was increasingly characteristic of the elected leadership and staff personnel of the WCC. The use of Marxist modes of social analysis and an apparent shift from serious concern for obedience to the Great Commission (Mt. 28:16–20) tended to lessen for evangelicals the credibility of the otherwise valid efforts of WCC leadership to relate the Christian gospel to the contemporary economic, social, and political conditions of humankind. It is significant that even as this tension was growing, the evangelicals, particularly at Lausanne, came to insist with new vigor that their own emphasis upon evangelism requires serious study of the various contexts in which such activity is to be carried on. They, too, came to lay strong emphasis, as had evangelicals in the eighteenth and nineteenth centuries, upon social service and related action as a necessary complement to, or expression of, evangelism.[65]

With reference to the present theme of discourse, it may be helpful at this point to identify certain of the most salient characteristics of thought of each of the major traditions that we have been considering. This will be how each views the possibility of the final salvation of human beings with reference to the theological principle—which all accept—that God is and always has been present and at work throughout the whole of creation. This issue relates to the subject matter of this book because views on the possibilities of human salvation have a direct bearing on how persons or churches can evaluate theologically other religious traditions than the Christian.

As we have seen, the Roman Catholic Church in the most explicit and official way, through Vatican Council II and through statements of the papal office, has affirmed the possibility of human salvation outside the formal boundaries of the church and apart from explicit Christian faith. This is to envisage salvation as available to those who respond in faith and obedience to the light and power granted them by the grace of God in their own place and time. We shall see that even if comparable official action has not been taken by Orthodox churches in concert, major theological leaders of the Orthodox tradition are in essential agreement with the Roman Catholic Church on this issue.

The World Council of Churches has not been able to gain a full consensus from its member churches on this issue and has therefore not expressed itself officially with the clarity of the Roman Catholic Church. We may say, however, that pronouncements of the WCC that we have already considered in this chapter point in the same direction as the position of the Roman Catholic Church. We shall see in the chapter on the views of Protestant theologians that many of these also express themselves as explicitly as Roman Catholics, including some elected officials and staff personnel of the WCC.

Protestant evangelicals, however, whether affiliated with the WCC or not, are generally understood as holding that while all persons have some knowledge of God and his will through the revelatory signs of divine creation as well as through their own consciences, this knowledge does not lead to salvation. The older evangelicalism, as seen in continental European Pietism or the evangelical-revivalism of English-speaking lands, tended to add that apart from explicit faith in Jesus Christ as Lord and Savior, that is, apart from "naming the name" of Jesus Christ in this lifetime, there is no salvation possible. Many contemporary evangelicals, however, are more sophisticated in handling this theme. For one thing, there is a far greater existential awareness of the many millions, indeed billions, of human beings in the course of our collective history who have apparently never had the opportunity to hear the Christian gospel or even the "name" of Jesus Christ.

Mention has been made earlier of the distinguished contemporary evangelical theologian Donald G. Bloesch. Bloesch follows in the tradition of "Jonathan Edwards, P. T. Forsyth and many others" in believing that "God in his mercy will see to it that no person is bereft of the opportunity to come to Jesus Christ." Probably the very great majority of contemporary Protestant evangelicals would share this conviction. Most, however, would not wish to specify how this extension of divine mercy is, or has been, made possible for the untold millions who have not had the "Christian opportunity" in their lifetime. They would simply trust the mercy and wise providence of God. Bloesch, on the other hand, is willing to be specific. He joins with Forsyth in believing that the opportunity will most assuredly be given "even if this be not in this life." Bloesch, indeed, considers it a heresy to hold that persons who have never had the opportunity of hearing the message of salvation in Christian context are nonetheless condemned to hell.[66]

A significant statement on this theme made by an evangelical group is the affirmation of the second National Evangelical Anglican Congress, which met at Nottingham, England, in April 1977. Under the heading of "Salvation" the following statement occurs: "Though the Bible excludes the hope of universal [guaranteed] salvation, it envisages the presence in glory of a countless multitude of the redeemed. We are not fully agreed, however, as to the ultimate extent of salvation. . . . Jesus Christ is the only name given by God by which Man must be saved. Therefore if there are people who are saved without hearing the name of Christ, they are saved on the basis of his work."[67]

This understanding is in principle no different from Bloesch's. It is, on the one hand, to identify the Christ-event—the life, death, resurrection, and ascension of Jesus Christ—as central and indispensable in the divine work for the salvation of humankind, as Bloesch does elsewhere. This conviction, on the other hand, clearly allows for the effects of the work of Jesus Christ, by the merciful and wise providence of God working through the Spirit, to reach the uncounted multitudes who over the course of human history have never had the opportunity to hear the name of Jesus because of the circumstances of their place and time. This theological understanding in fact makes it possible for Protestant evangelicals to share in the cosmic perspectives of the early church. It also allows room for consideration of the possible theological meaning and value of "secondary" factors in the larger process of the divine work of salvation, namely, the other religions of humankind. Some of the great personages in these traditions can properly be seen as having perceived divine truth, indeed as having received divine revelations. They may be regarded, if examination of the pertinent data so warrants, as authentic instruments of God within God's larger work, as persons who have contributed significantly within the category of *preparatio evangelica*.

There are those who would consider this kind of theological position as condescending and offensive to members of other religions. But the cosmic scope of the salvific process implied in the view properly removes such understanding from the category of "spiritual imperialism." In this view the saving, judging Christ of God is confined neither to the Christian church nor to Western culture. This is admittedly a conviction of faith, but it is a conviction that excludes no one from God's best and highest for external or arbitrary reasons.

Another point of some significance in this context is the wide popularity among evangelicals of the late C. S. Lewis. Lewis's fiction, essays, and letters are quite consistently evangelical with reference both to theology and to views of Scripture. And yet Lewis believed in a mode of purgatory and in prayers for the dead. Lewis was an Anglican, and perhaps his views at this point have been taken by some evangelicals as simply a reflection of his Anglican background. On the other hand, might it not be that Lewis's long and continuing popularity among Protestant evangelicals lies in his compatibility with the perceptions of not a few even at these points?

A final word may be added with reference to the WCC Conference on World Mission and Evangelism held at Melbourne, Australia, from May 12 to 24, 1980. This is not the place for an analysis or evaluation of the documents as a whole; but with their keen probing of the meaning of the kingdom of God for Christian faith, they form a truly noble statement as a whole. They represent a distinctly holistic approach to the Christian gospel and its application to life. The concerns expressed for implementation of the gospel in the whole of life, interiorly, individually, and corporately, within and without the churches are both beautiful and moving. One criticism might be that the documents seem to lack an adequate awareness of what Thomas Stransky has called "the discipline of limitations." A friendly critic could say that here, too, we should pray for "the courage to change what can be changed, the patience to accept what cannot be changed and the wisdom to know the difference." Perhaps what is especially needed is deeper exploration both theologically and practically of the realities of the providence of God at work in the world, as of the deeper spiritual significance of the "powers and Principalities."[68]

With regard to the theme of our present concern, Melbourne sets the goal high, quite in the tradition of the best theology of the early church: "God is working for the total liberation of the whole of life—indeed, for the redemption of the cosmos." The churches are urged to "be open to self-criticism and willing to enter into dialogue with people of other convictions, faiths and ideologies about their own involvement in their situations as others see it." The document sees the specific task of the churches to lie in disclosing "the final revelation of God himself in Jesus Christ," but as those entrusted with this revelation, Christians can best become aware of the specific modes and forms of their witness through "open and sincere dialogue." They should look toward joint efforts wherever possible "with other people of good will," especially "with groups outside the churches who show signs of the kingdom of God at work on behalf of those who are marginalized." "There is a common hope for humankind and for the whole of creation in the life and death, the resurrection and the ascension of the Son of God." But the Son of God is not confined, and "wherever a religion or its revival enhances human dignity, human rights and social justice for all people, and brings in liberation and peace for everybody, there God may be seen to be at work." This is of course to apply Jesus' criterion of discerning the quality of persons by the quality of their fruits in life (Mt. 7:15-27), as was evidently originally intended, to all the religious traditions and activities of human history.

In keeping with the "Guidelines on Dialogue" document, which was received by the Central Committee of the WCC in Jamaica in 1979, Christians are urged to combine a dialogic approach to neighbors of other faiths and convictions with authentic Christian mission. This means a mission "carried out in the spirit of our Lord, not in a crusading and aggressive spirit." It means "a mind of openness, respect and truthfulness" and also "courage to give an account of the hope we have in Jesus Christ as our Lord." Basic to Christian mission and witness is to "honour the inheritance of each person (culture, language and ideals)," for in this way Christians "witness to the personal care of God." There is frank avowal that as Christians "we have no proprietary rights on the kingdom, no claim for reserved seats at the great banquet. Therefore we seek the mercy and grace of God that we might be open to all those who are in the kingdom, whether or not they are part of the institutional churches." "The church is only an emergency residence (*paroikia*)," for the abiding citizenship of God's people is as citizens of God's kingdom.

Melbourne has been criticized for inadequate perception of the transcendent dimension. This may be true at some points. At other points there is discernible a profound spirituality, as in the statement that "we acknowledge our need to engage more faithfully in profound wrestling in prayer as essential to our commitment. It becomes therefore a missionary obligation for the churches to develop a dynamic spirituality." But it is precisely at this point that the affirmation is made that "God has many ways of working out his purposes of mercy and judgement far beyond the borders of the visibie church. His instruments often include the courageous witness of those who do not name his name, the actions of individuals and groups of other faiths and in secular bodies, with whom we can join in common action."

Perhaps it could be said that the framers of these documents are really not much interested in the concept of salvation with its emphases heavily weighted toward the dimensions of the hereafter and "other-worldly" as found in much traditional Protestant evangelicalism. No doubt the same could be said of those responsible for the documents of Bangkok 1973. But Melbourne 1980 is not only concerned with the large scale and the grand issues; the statement is made that "it is through the small events of our daily lives that the wider changes in society may come about in the direction of the kingdom of God." But in another passage, as the faithfulness of disciples in "small things" is said to be honored by the crucified and risen Christ, the statement is added, "this does not exempt us from responding to the wider vision." This all seems to mean that the writers, and the conference participants who amended and received the documents, are trying to retain a proper awareness of the importance of the individual, of one's person and activities, and of one's destiny both here and hereafter. But even as the writers make this effort, they clearly wish to emphasize that the proper Christian focus is upon the here and now and that it is of the essence of Christian faith to be and to function in community.

A beautiful spirit of compassion appears throughout the documents, compassion for the poor of the world, for the marginalized of our societies. The insistence is that such compassion is in accord with the mind of God and such is the priority of his Christ. The writers would mark the special significance of the crucifixion of Jesus outside the city wall. They see this as "a sign, consistent with much else in his life, that he who is the centre is constantly in movement from the centre towards the periphery, towards those who are marginalized, victims of the demonic powers, political, economic, social, cultural and even—or especially—religious." This is surely true, but perhaps in a broader sense than the writers intended. The older evangelicalism was also right in insisting that we have all been victims of the demonic powers whether in their spiritual or their temporal manifestations.[69]

The significance of all this has been for many in the Christian church an experience of liberation. It has not been liberation from authentic Christian faith or from responsibility to Christian witness in word and deed and life. It is, rather, to participate once again in the cosmopolitan, inclusive spirit of major segments of the early church, to sense once more the cosmic dimensions of the person and work of the Christ and to perceive "Christic values" more widely in the experience of humankind than most Christians have dared for fifteen centuries. This is a "renewed understanding of the universality of God's work," an "extended understanding of the universality and fullness of Christ" far beyond the previous—largely tacit but nonetheless real— theological confinement of Christ's manifestation to "places" of explicit Christian faith. This is aspiration to discover and realize more fully "all that is involved in Christ, the Son and Word of God."[70] Karl Rahner has reminded us that we have heretofore looked too ineptly and with too little love at the other religious traditions of humankind to perceive the "traces" (*Spuren*) of the divine handiwork in them.[71] Many Christian men and women now feel free, however, to look for traces of the divine presence in the whole of human history and once again to share in the total spiritual life of all humankind.[72] We shall see in subsequent chapters how these developments may be variously analyzed and classified, but at this point we stress the profound religious as well as theological significance of what has been happening.

EASTERN ORTHODOX CHURCHES

A brief word should be added here regarding the Eastern Orthodox churches. Consideration of their theological views and attitudes is largely left out of the purview of this book. A primary reason is that in a significant sense they did not experience the problem in the same way as the churches of western Europe. As we have seen, the Orthodox churches did not experience the fall of the Roman empire in the same way nor to the same degree as the Western churches. This was one reason why they refused to recognize Augustine as a doctor or teacher of the church. After the incursions of Islam, many of the Eastern churches became minority movements, in some cases tiny religio-ethnic enclaves, within the vast complex of Islamic society and culture. The Greek Byzantine empire remained the great center of Eastern Orthodox faith and culture, but after the Turkish invasions and final conquest of the whole of Anatolia, its power and external religious effectiveness were greatly reduced. Until the emergence of the great Slavic and Romanian Orthodox communions to the north, there was little sociological leeway in the Middle East proper for the Eastern churches to develop attitudes of superiority such as came to be found in the West.

On the other hand, the vision of the cosmic Christ in the theology of the early Greek fathers was never lost in the Eastern Orthodox churches.[73] We find certain of their theologians moving with consummate skill and ease among the newer currents of thought of Roman Catholics and Protestants. Among these may be mentioned Nicholas Cabazilas, Georges Khodr, Leonidas J. Philippidis, and T. Paul Verghese. It will be sufficient for our present purposes if we concentrate upon Georges Khodr. Khodr, longtime metropolitan of Mount Lebanon, a diocese of the Greek-Orthodox Patriarchate of Antioch, Beirut, Lebanon, at least in part because of his geographical location and personal responsibilities has reflected long and sensitively about the theme of our study. He writes, "if obedience to the Master means following

Him wherever we find traces of His presence, we have an obligation to investigate the authentic spiritual life of non-Christians. . . . The strikingly evangelical quality of many non-Christians obliges us, moreover, to develop an ecclesiology and a missiology in which the Holy Spirit necessarily occupies a supreme place."[74]

In keeping with the Orthodox theological tradition, Khodr emphasizes that basic to a right approach to our theme is awareness of an eternity transcending history and a "conception of the Church in which Christ is seen 'not merely chronologically but also and above all ontologically.' " He cites examples from his rich knowledge of the church fathers and notes the uniqueness of the Nestorian Church's missionary methodology. This was by way of spiritually adopting the whole of creation and thus seeing it as a legitimate part of Christian mission to "nurture the spiritual development of the religions it encountered by 'improving' them from within," as in the case of Buddhism in Tibet and China, while not "alienating" them.[75] Similarly, the Nestorian Church in Mesopotamia represents the boldest historical attempt of any church body to make a positive approach to Islam. This was to allow specific prophetic authenticity to Muhammad on the basis of careful analysis of the Islamic materials, especially the Qur'ān, even as they allowed "no blurring of the centrality and ontological uniqueness of Christ Jesus."

Khodr's central point is that contemporary Christian theology must go beyond limited concepts of salvation history in order to rediscover the true meaning and scope of the divine *oikonomia*. "The economy of Christ cannot be reduced to its historical manifestation but indicates the fact that we are made participants in the life of God Himself." From this cosmic perspective Khodr affirms that the church is "the instrument of the mystery of the salvation of the nations . . . the sign of God's love for all men," but "to say mystery is to point to the freedom of God who in His work of providence and redemption is not tied down to any event." Thus, vis-à-vis the historical religions, the task of the church is to reveal to "the world of the religions the God who is hidden within it, in anticipation of the final concrete unfolding and manifestation of the Mystery."

Khodr, too, emphasizes the universal nature of the pre-Abrahamic covenants and sees in Abraham the nations of the earth as already the object of divine election. The election of Israel is "particular but from it the economy of the divine mystery is deployed for the whole of humanity. . . . Israel is saved as the type and representative of the whole of mankind." Indeed, "the other nations have had their own types of the reality of Christ, whether in the form of persons or teachings."

> Christ is hidden everywhere in the mystery of his lowliness. Any read-
> ing of religions is a reading of Christ. It is Christ alone who is received
> as light when grace visits a Brahmin, a Buddhist, or a Muhammadan
> reading his own scriptures. Every martyr for the truth, every man per-
> secuted for what he believes to be right, dies in communion with Christ.

The mystics of Islamic countries with their witness to suffering love lived the authentic Johannine *agape*. For if the tree is known by its fruits, there is no shadow of doubt that the poor and humble folk who live for and yearn for God in all nations already receive the peace which the Lord gives to all whom He loves (Lk. 2:14).

Khodr follows the great tradition of the Eastern Orthodox churches with his affirmation of faith that the "work of salvation outside Israel 'according to the flesh,' and outside the historical Church, is the result of the resurrection which fills everything with the fulness of Christ." But "the economy of Christ is unintelligible without the economy of the Spirit. . . . The Spirit is everywhere and fills everything by virtue of an economy distinct from that of the Son. . . . Between the two economies there is a reciprocity and a mutual service." It is the Spirit who fashions Christ within us. Khodr quotes Irenaeus to the effect that "where the Spirit is, there is also the Church" and goes on to add his own perception that "all who are visited by the Spirit are the people of God."

Khodr draws a number of specific conclusions from this theological understanding with regard to the Christian mission and the approach of Christians, individually or as a community, to others. For one thing, "the Christian who knows that, within God's plan, the great religions constitute training schools of the Divine mercy will have an attitude of profound peace and gentle patience . . . and a secret form of communion with all men in the economy of the Mystery whereby we are being gradually led towards the final consummation, the recapitulation of all things in Christ." Khodr asserts that "there is a universal religious community which, if we are able to lay hold of what it offers, will enrich our Christian experience." Therefore, in Christian missionary witness we must treat the other "as someone who has something to teach us and something to manifest to us of God." "A Christian community purified by the fire of the Spirit, holy unto God, poor for the sake of God, can in the weakness of the Gospel, take the risk of both giving and receiving with equal simplicity."

The last quotation is clearly a perception-testimony born of the suffering and the love of the centuries-long experience of the minority Christian churches of the Middle East. In the midst of this situation, made even more desperate in some ways since he wrote these words, Khodr is yet able to discover and appreciate the profound intention of all religious persons and positively to relate their apprehension of the divine mystery to the object of Christian hope. Therefore he can say that "the supreme task is to identify all the Christic values in other religions" and from this perspective to show them the Christ who unites them and whose love is their fulfillment. "Our task is simply to follow the tracks of Christ perceptible in the shadows of other religions . . . to name him whom others have already recognized as the Beloved."[76]

6

Views of Contemporary Theologians: Roman Catholic

A basic theological issue necessarily emerges from the discussion in previous chapters. This is whether or not the kind of conclusion toward which the discussion was moving and which was intended to be summed up in a special way by the quotations from Georges Khodr removes all distinctiveness from Christian faith and in particular from the significance of the person and work of Jesus the Christ. This issue appears to be one of the most serious confronting Christian theology at the present time and is one that we shall consider in various ways from this point on.

Ever since the theological direction of Vatican Council II became clear, the mood of the great majority of Roman Catholic theologians has been one of immense gratitude for the privilege of freely working again with the concept-principle of the wider work of God in the world. The same could be said of very many in the Protestant and Eastern Orthodox churches. At the same time almost all of these persons have been concerned to assign a distinct role and authority to Christian faith and a universal meaning to the person and work of Jesus Christ. Thus they have not regarded all religious movements simplistically, nor all religious leaders as necessarily bearing cosmically or historically the same level of meaning, value, or truth. They have wished, rather, to live a "universal life in the concrete," by which posture they have hoped to universalize their faith without losing its specificity or basis for mission. Cosmically and historically viewed, this is to say that the kind and degree of the manifestations of the Logos have varied over the sweep of human history. It is of the essence of Christian faith, these theologians seem to believe, to affirm that the manifestation in Jesus of Nazareth was unique in its moral and spiritual quality and also in its cosmo-historical significance and effects. Yet there are differing nuances in the expression of these views. Let us consider first how a number of representative contemporary Roman Catholic theologians view the problem.

RAYMOND (RAIMUNDO) PANIKKAR

Raymond Panikkar has been and remains one of the most bold, creative, and wide-ranging figures in twentieth-century Roman Catholic theology. Born in Barcelona in 1918, son of a Hindu father and a Spanish Catholic mother, he was reared in an environment that included study of the Hindu Scriptures along with the Bible. Over the decades since his ordination as a Roman Catholic priest in 1942, Panikkar has spent almost equal periods of time in India, Europe, and North America. The book that brought him to the attention of the larger public, *The Unknown Christ of Hinduism*, was first published in 1957 and was thus a significant background factor in the formulation of the documents of Vatican Council II. Panikkar's periods of study in Germany and his writings in German—as well as in French, Spanish, and English—had made his thought increasingly well known and influential in almost all parts of the Roman Catholic Church. He has doctorates in philosophy and chemistry as well as in theology.

Panikkar was one of the first contemporary Catholics to attempt to show that there is substantial evidence in both the Bible and the church fathers for a more inclusive Christian view of the religions of the world, and almost all subsequent writers have depended upon him to some extent with reference to both methodology and data. We may note, however, that A. C. Bouquet, whose more massive *The Christian Faith and Non-Christian Religions* was first published in 1958, was doing his basic research and writing concurrently with Panikkar and came to very similar conclusions out of his own Anglican background and experience in India.

One of the basic insights of Panikkar in this earlier work was to understand the reality of Christ broadly in accordance with the perceptions of the church fathers, both Greek and Latin. This led him to the conclusion that "there is a living Presence of Christ in Hinduism. . . . Christ is not only the ontological goal of Hinduism but its true inspirer, and His grace is the leading though hidden force pushing it towards its full disclosure. He is the 'Principle' that spoke to men and was already at work before Abraham."[1] This understanding is perhaps appropriately called an application of Teilhard de Chardin's cosmic vision to the issue of the relationship of Christian faith to the other faiths of humankind and seems to be a significant factor in almost all contemporary Roman Catholic theological work.

At this time Panikkar still saw "Christianity [as] the fullness of religion and thus the real perfection of every religion." As we shall see, he later came to avoid the use of the term "Christianity" in this context of thought because of the usual limitation of its meaning to the historical movement with all of its lights and shades of moral and spiritual quality. But even then he insisted that "the relation of Christianity to other religions is neither one of simple contiguity nor one of total refusal or totalitarian dominance. It is a *sui generis* relationship.'' Panikkar's understanding was that "growing Christianity is also on pilgrimage. Such is the mystery of the cross.'' He felt that humility is required of Christians, as of others, "because no religion can boast to have deciphered fully the mystery of man and God . . . [and] a missionary zeal without knowledge and love would have disastrous consequences.'' Besides, there is the fact of "the presence of 'Christian' truths within other religions.''[2]

Panikkar's view of the Christ is "not *only* as the historical redeemer, but *also* as the unique Son of God, as the Second Person of the Trinity, as the only one ontological—temporal and eternal—link between God and the world.''[3] Thus Christ

> is the ontological meeting point of any religion as well as of any ultimate value. . . . It is Christ who leads every man to God; there is no other way but through him. It is Christ who inspires the prayers of man and "hears" them. It is he who whispers to us any divine inspiration and who speaks as God, whatever forms the "patient" of the divine may believe in or think of. He is the Light that illumines every human being coming into this world. . . . Hence, for Christianity, Christ is already there in Hinduism in so far as Hinduism is a true religion; Christ is already at work in any Hindu prayer as far as it is really prayer; Christ is behind any form of worship, in as much as it is adoration made to God. Christianity will not judge Hinduism; only God in Christ will judge. Christianity will not and has not the right to sift and sever the wheat from the chaff, so long as men are pilgrims on earth. It will take and meet Hinduism as it is and will find Christ there because he is already there, as he is also with the poor and the thirsty and the prisoner and the persecuted.[4]

Panikkar was as aware of the limitations and flaws of empirical Hinduism as a movement in human history as he was of empirical Christianity. He knew that in Hinduism "Christ has not unveiled his whole face, has not yet completed his mission there." Hence Hindus and Christians properly meet "in the depths of death," that is, "in the denial of ourselves," by which we may accept the divine life which was "deposited germinally" in the death and resurrection of Jesus Christ. But for Panikkar the presence of Christ in Hinduism made it not merely another religion but a "vestibule of Christianity."[5]

Panikkar was not thinking of an encounter of religions on the level of mere doctrine or cognitive intellectuality. He wanted from both sides, "but especially from the Christian side," a profound and sincere spirituality, an asceticism of self-denial and a detachment from preoccupation with doctrinal categories and dogmatic formulae. He looked not for a denial of orthodoxy but for "its integration into 'orthopraxy' (right action)." It was a basic principle of his faith-understanding that "only when a man is completely empty of himself will Christ fully dwell in him." Thus the Christian encounter with

Hinduism had to be the profoundest of ethical and spiritual challenges for Christians, as also for Hindus in their own way.[6]

From his own life experience as well as from his studies, Panikkar was already well aware of the trends toward a wider ecumenism in the years following World War II. "One of the most encouraging phenomena of our times is a worldwide and sincere desire for mutual understanding and a real thirst for universality." He quotes the French Catholic writer Jean Carbon to the effect that "an ecumenical vocation which limited itself solely to the re-union of the baptised would not be faithful to the call of Christ within history." He then adds, "Christian ecumenism is really universal, inserted in the very dynamism of history, or it is not true ecumenism. . . . The idea of Christ at work in history is not alien to Christianity." The specific theological consequences of this perspective for Panikkar are that "Christ is present in one form or another in every human being in his religious way to God." Any human being who is saved is saved therefore by Christ, the only redeemer, but "we know by reason and by faith God provides everybody with the necessary means of salvation."[7]

Panikkar, however, does not mean to imply by this kind of language a merely individualistic kind of salvific process by which Hindus may be saved, as it were, in spite of Hinduism. Rather, "there is a Christian economy in history in which Hinduism cannot be fully rejected, but in which it would find its providential place." True, "the good and *bona fide* Hindu is saved by Christ and not by Hinduism, but it is through the sacraments of Hinduism, through the message of morality and the good life, through the *Mysterion* that comes down to him through Hinduism, that *Christ* saves the Hindu normally. This amounts to saying that Hinduism has also a place in the universal saving providence of God."[8]

At this point in the development of his thinking Panikkar was still espousing a form of the fulfillment theory of the role of Christianity as a movement in human history. He saw Hinduism as a kind of Christianity in potency, already possessing authentically Christian seed because Christ had been in its midst. But it is "the starting point of a religion that culminates in Christianity." "Christianity as an historical religion has the fullness of divine revelation—ultimately because it possesses the eucharist."[9] Panikkar, however, was neither a naïve sacramentarian nor an uncritical apologist of a church "without spot or stain." "If it is true that 'outside the Church there is no salvation,' this 'Church' should not be confounded with its outer appearance, not even with an explicit adherence to Christianity." For those who have followed with care the historical developments outlined in previous chapters, it is highly significant to note that Panikkar insists that this understanding has been "so explicitly expounded" within Roman Catholic theology in recent years as to have become a veritable theological commonplace. What he is in fact expounding is a universal idea of Christianity, "an idea which makes possible the Catholic embrace of every people and religion." This is because there is a divine link between the religions of humankind and the religion of God's Son, based on the ontological link between God and the world constituted by "the unique Son of God, the Second Person of the Trinity."[10]

In his later writings Panikkar does not differ in any essential way from this understanding except to refine his views on the nature of the relationship of the church and Christianity to the other religions and to apply the results of his ongoing studies in the history of religions to a deepening of Christian theological self-understanding. He continues to demand that the dialogic process be conducted on the basis of a profound as well as sincere spirituality that will enable a penetration "within," into the interior life of the other religious traditions. He now asks, however, for a radical Christian "stripping" or loss of self-centeredness to the extent that Christian faith will "strip itself of the 'Christian religion' as it actually exists and free itself for a fecundation that will affect all religions both ancient and modern."[11]

Panikkar's thought at this point is subtle, and it is necessary to follow his language with care in order to preserve the precise nuances of his actually well-modulated views. He is himself a participant in the contemporary "awareness of and openness to the community of mankind, the world, nature and history." As a specifically Christian perception, however, arising out of this experience, he feels that "we can detect a thrust, as it were, of the Spirit pushing the Christian forward beyond what we call 'Christianity,' beyond, I am tempted to add, even the institutional and visible Church." The proper Christian response to this leading of the Spirit of God he denotes as "collaborating towards the *universalization* of Christianity, towards the actualization in fact of its catholicity," a process which he believes is contributing to the development of all religions in the direction of convergence unto unity. This will mean the conversion of all religion, or religions, including Christianity. Panikkar notes that the dominant form in which Christianity is at present expressed is "incontestably that which it has adopted little by little in the course of the history of the western world. We have no right at all, however, to identify this particular sociological form with Christian faith itself. To do so would involve on the one hand a particularism incompatible with catholicity and on the other an anachronistic theological colonialism that is absolutely unacceptable."

Panikkar clearly means to say with this line of thought that becoming "Christian" in a formal or institutional sense of the term is not necessary for the final salvation of human beings. He himself, however, prefers to continue to use the term "Christian" to denote this faith that is *in statu nascendi*, in a state of becoming. He also would not sever this faith from the historic claims of tradition, which he sees "as the historical link between past and future. To act thus would be not only barbaric but false. Continuity must not be ruptured; development must occur harmoniously, enrichment progressively and transformation in accordance with nature. This process must involve a *sui generis* assimilation of new values or else it may come about through the coming to light of hitherto neglected aspects—in a word, by a vital process of growth in which substitution happens less by rejection than by assumption."

This is the process that Panikkar calls "the very *kairos*, the moment of destiny, of our age." And Panikkar insists that rightly understood his views are both "orthodox" and "ecclesial."[12]

Panikkar tries in the most serious way to make use of this faith-understanding and of the data and perspectives that are opened to it by the process to reexamine, reperceive, and reformulate some of the great Christian affirmations of faith. Panikkar, in particular, has wrestled with the doctrine of the Trinity, the nature of God, and the nature of human beings. He has used the term "ecumenical theandric spirituality" to denote the somewhat revised, but deepened and enlarged Christian faith that exposure to the Hindu religio-philosophical tradition from the Upanishads and the Bhagavad Gita to the present has helped him to perceive and embrace. He describes this Christian faith as follows:

> What I wish to understand by the word *theandrism*, then, is a spirituality which combines in an authentic synthesis the three dimensions of our life on earth as well as in heaven (in time and through it): a *contemplation* which would be something more than thought, *action* which aims beyond the building up of the merely spatial city, a God who is not simply a Judge or a scrutinizing Eye, a love that surpasses all sentimentality, prayer not limited to petition or even praise—but also a *silence* that does not fall into indifference, an *apophatism* that does not become stuck in nihilism, a *supernaturalism* that is not anti-natural—in short a sense of the Spirit that is not discarnate and a sense of Incarnation that does not neglect the Spirit, an *affirmation* that is not exclusive and a *negation* that is not closed in upon itself.[13]

For Panikkar the divine unity is God, Christ, and Spirit—and a human being is more than "man." A human being is a theandric mystery.

We have space only to identify a few insights from Panikkar's later writings. He tries to formulate the dilemma facing contemporary Christians by asking the question: Can one lead a universal life in the concrete? But "I may only universalize my belief and reform my religion if at the same time I let my neighbor do the same with his." He holds that the Christian economy of salvation should be reinterpreted as constituting in fact "the framework of a universal economy of salvation and a certain mysterious presence of the Lord in a multitude of epiphanies." "The Christian fact cannot be confined to a given religion; it must be recognized as that leaven at work in every religion until it has brought them all to a higher fulness. . . . The Christian understanding of faith can inform more than one religion, not blotting it out but transmuting and resurrecting it (which is what conversion means)."[14] From his encounter with Hinduism, Panikkar has come to stress that

> the Church is a living organism and . . . as such can very well live without the present-day organization. . . . What the church could learn from Hinduism is that ecclesial consciousness does not need to be a

closed-group consciousness. . . . What is fundamental in the Church, or in other words the central ecclesiological character, is its *sacramental structure*, the Body of Christ in Pauline terms. The *sacramentum mundi* is certainly material, visible, historical, but this is only the external aspect of an inner core, a living soul which manifests itself in as many forms as the universal saving will of God may deem it convenient. . . . What the Church could learn from Hinduism is confidence in the Spirit . . . for God does not discriminate among persons; all those who are moved by His Spirit are sons of God.[15]

Panikkar makes a number of historical analyses that are helpful for the future of what he calls "the Intrareligious Dialogue." His goal of relationship is not a mere parallelism of religions, because in fact "the different religious and human traditions of the world have usually emerged from mutual interferences, influences and fertilizations." "Religions do not stand side by side, . . . they are actually intertwined and inside each other." Panikkar then draws the conclusion that, as we have noted, a number of the deepest thinkers of our day have also drawn, namely, that each religious tradition "is a dimension of the other." For Panikkar, therefore, the aim of the intrareligious dialogue is understanding unto a pluralism that stands "between unrelated plurality and a monolithic unity."

Panikkar feels impelled to state his case boldly, at least in part because of his perception of Christian need. He calls it an almost self-evident fact that "the Western Christian tradition seems to be exhausted, I might almost say effete, when it tries to express the Christian message in a meaningful way for our times." And his conclusion is that "only by stepping over present cultural and philosophical boundaries can Christian life again become creative and dynamic." "It is precisely because I take seriously Christ's affirmation that he is the way, the truth and the life (Jn. 14:6) that I cannot reduce his significance only to historical Christianity." "This is a conviction that the living and ultimately the real Christ is not the kerygma of the Lord but the Lord himself."[16]

A brief word should be added in this context regarding other distinguished Roman Catholic missionaries in India who have worked and written in the same spirit as Raymond Panikkar. Among the pioneers may be listed *Jules Monchanin* (1895–1957), whose ideal of a monastic life was one "totally Indian and totally Christian" and desired that "what is deepest in Christianity may be grafted onto what is deepest in India."[17] Another was *Henri Le Saux* (1910–73), the French Benedictine who came to live in the style of an Indian holy man and took the Sanskrit name Abhishiktananda (Bliss of the Anointed One). Le Saux worked in part with Monchanin and wrote of the "Hindu-Christian Meeting Point" at the deepest levels of open-ended spirituality.[18]

Among contemporaries we may cite *Dom Bede Griffiths* (b. 1906), who has long served the cause of Hindu-Christian dialogue by living, as he has

written, "as an Indian among Indians, following Indian ways of life, study-
ing Indian thought, and immersing myself in the living traditions of the Indian spirit."[19] *Klaus Klostermaier* (b. 1933), a German missionary-priest who
now teaches as a layman at the University of Manitoba in Canada, has written with delightful humor and graphic vividness of the existential differences
in doing theology at 120 degrees Fahrenheit as compared with 70 degrees. But
the central point of his account of two years in the north India town of Vrin-
daban as the only Christian in a place especially devoted to the worship of
Krishna (Kṛṣṇa) is that Christ was already there before him.[20]

KARL RAHNER

Karl Rahner (1904–1984) is clearly one of the most highly respected,
perhaps the single most influential, of contemporary theologians in the Roman Catholic Church. The documents and later results of Vatican Council
II are almost unthinkable apart from his contributions (along with those of
the Dutch Piet Schoonenberg and Edward Schillebeeckx, the French Yves
Congar, Jean Daniélou, and Henri de Lubac, the American John Courtney
Murray, and others). Rahner's thought on the relationship of Christian
faith and church to the religions of humankind is most fully expressed in an
essay that was first given as a lecture in Bavaria on April 28, 1961.[21] It will be
noticed at once that much Catholic thought has moved beyond Rahner's
views of this time, but they are foundational for almost all subsequent development.

Rahner begins his essay with a discussion of the "open Catholicism" that is
basic to his thought. He notes that the non-Christian religions, which he also
denotes as "extra-Christian," were formerly, for Western Christians, elements of other cultural units, parts of a history with which one communicated only at the edge of one's own history. Now they have become both
question and existential possibility for every person. Rahner's first thesis is
that Christianity is the absolute religion, which is determined (*bestimmt*) by
God for all human beings and which can acknowledge no other beside itself
as equally authorized.[22] Rahner at this time had not reflected as deeply, nor
with as much historical realism, as Raymond Panikkar on the problems inherent in overstatements about the term "Christianity" with its necessary
connotations of the social dimensions and therefore of the lights and shades
of empirical Christendom. Rahner, to be sure, repeatedly emphasizes the
social dimension as a necessarily constitutive element of religion, but he appears still at this time to have identified the historical presence of Christ in the
world with the church.[23]

Contemporary Christians of almost every theological position tend to bris-
tle at the use of the term "the absoluteness" of Christianity. As we have seen,
it has been a contribution of Protestant Neo-orthodoxy to relegate the term
to the place of a historical relic, a product of the theses methodology of
Hegelian philosophy and of the early Troeltsch and having no longer a place
in intelligent theological discourse.[24] Rahner, however, affirms the absolute-

ness of Christianity in no exclusive sense, and the main burden of his thought is in fact in another direction. He specifically states that Christianity as a historical phenomenon is not always and everywhere the way of salvation for human beings. Central to his thought is perception of the universal salvific will and work of God, which comprises the entire extent of the perhaps million years of human life on earth, compared to which the span of particular salvation history in Israel and the Christian church is short indeed.[25] Every human being is truly exposed to the influences of divine grace by which God is disclosed and offers communion with the divine. Human beings, according to Rahner, must always have the possibility of participating in a genuine relationship to God. Rahner insists that we have every reason to think optimistically about God and God's will to save.[26] Theologically we may affirm, he insists, that the supernatural grace given human beings beyond the limits of the visible church and formal or explicit faith in Christ are given on account of Christ, but given they are.

The second thesis of Rahner is that the non-Christian religions, as social as well as religious entities, contain not only elements of a natural knowledge of God but are vehicles of the supernatural grace given human beings by God on account of Christ. They may, on a different level from Christianity, be considered as authentic (*legitim*) religion.[27] Rahner contends that it is utterly perverse to deny that human beings in the concrete situation of their religions are also given divine grace and revelation in the salvific sense. There may be authentic religious acts that refer to the one true God even in polytheism.[28] Other religions have their own elements of religious validity and God-willed authenticity, even though they may be mixed with much that is false and depraved. True religion cannot exist without a social and institutional dimension, and the grace of God properly works through the concrete social and historical circumstances in which persons are placed.[29] Every person is pursued by the grace of God, and there are traces (*Spuren*) to be found in human history of this confrontation with divine grace. Rahner says that they may be difficult to discern even by the eye of the enlightened Christian, but they must be there (*vorhanden sein müssen*). Perhaps, he suggests, we have heretofore looked too ineptly and with too little love at the non-Christian religions to see these traces of grace.[30]

Rahner affirms that we cannot speak a certain word about the final destiny of individual human beings within or without formal Christianity, and of course there can be no talk of the "heathen" as abandoned by God and Christ.[31] But men and women in the religions are also confronted with the necessity of concrete decision for that which is of God insofar as it is available and known in their concrete historical and social situations. To affirm the legitimacy of the religions is not to say that they are legitimate in all their elements or that every religion is equally legitimate with every other. The individual person must decide which elements and structures of what is existentially before him or her constitute the better and for that person the solely permitted way to find God.[32] Human beings are given the right and certain limited possibilities for selective criticism in their concrete religious situations; the contemporary social morality that constitutes a person's environment is normally the concrete form in which the divine law is presented to the person, but it (perhaps always) needs prophetic correction. Rahner stresses the responsibility of human beings to give heed to the impulses to reform which by the providence of God again and again emerge in the non-Christian religions.[33] It is a significant contribution of Rahner to affirm that reform movements within the religions may be seen by Christian faith as authentically of God.

Rahner thinks of the religions as theologically pre-Christian and states that they have no right further to exist in the moment when they confront "Christianity" really and in historical force (*real und geschichts-mächtig*). Christianity is the only way of salvation for a human being when it truly confronts the person in the concrete situation of one's life.[34] But Rahner refuses to make judgments regarding the ultimate salvation of individuals, for God can conquer with secret grace where the church may not. He assumes that the religious pluralism of our contemporary experience will not disappear.[35] He denotes the person in the religions who has been touched by the grace and truth of God and has responded positively according to the opportunities divinely given in the concrete situation by the term "anonymous Christian." The missionary witness of the church confronts this person not simply as a non-Christian or anonymous theist but as an anonymous Christian to whom the grace and revelation of God in Christ have already been given. The proclamation of the gospel to such a one is an objective, explicit statement of what one has to an authentic extent in the depth of one's existence already consummated (*vollzogen*) or could consummate. Salvation has already in *potentia* become available to that person. But to come to conscious Christian faith represents a higher stage of spiritual development (*höhere Entwicklungsphase*), and the empirical proclamation of the gospel is a necessity in the divine plan.[36]

Rahner writes that the coming to self-consciousness of anonymous Christianity through empirical Christian faith is required (*gefordert*) because the incarnational and social structure of divine grace in Christianity offers a clearer and purer reflective comprehension and therefore a better chance of salvation (*grössere Heilschance*) for the individual. This last notion of a better chance appears to be contrary to the implications of Rahner's previous arguments and is explicitly rejected by later Catholic writers. Rahner was evidently too anxious to find theological basis for the missionary obligation of the church.[37] But he insists that God is greater than the church, that the church is not an exclusive community of candidates for salvation. It is the historically discernible vanguard (*Vortrupp*), the socially structured expression of what the Christian expects God also to give to men and women outside the institutional church. It is the community of those who can confess expressly what they *and* the others aspire to be.[38] Rahner apparently sees no theologically legitimate role for the extra-Christian religions in the moment of their "real" confrontation with Christianity, but this is not to say that they will actually cease to be vehicles to human beings of the salvific grace of God. Rahner has probably completely demolished for the mainstream of Roman Catholic theology any lingering notions of salvific grace as confined to the institutional church; he has established for the church and its mission a dogmatic basis for potentially profound appreciation of both the persons and the religious values of the non-Christian religions.[39]

In his later work Rahner has developed certain themes to give further specificity to these principles. Thus he now sees the history of salvation—and of revelation—as coextensive with the whole history of the human race, even if not identical therewith. He of course allows for the possibility of human rejection of God with its accompanying sin and guilt. He insists upon Jesus Christ as the criterion, for Christian faith, of what is authentic in the "transcendental experience of God," which is offered to every human being. But he asserts that "God communicates himself absolutely to the whole of mankind." Even as he affirms a categorical and special history of revelation, which is recorded in the Old and New Testaments, he goes on to state that "revelation in such essential purity" is not found only therein. There can be "such brief and partial histories" within the collective history of humankind and in the history of its religions in which a part of the "self-reflection and reflexive self-presence of universal revelation" that are recorded in the Judeo-Christian Scriptures "is found in its purity." But basic to the whole of his thought is the fundamental premise that God in freedom offers the divine self to absolutely all human beings in their freedom.[40]

HEINZ ROBERT SCHLETTE AND HANS KÜNG

Next we consider the views of two German-speaking theologians who represent the process of rapid digestion of the conclusions of Vatican Council II even as it was going on in the Roman Catholic Church. These are Heinz Robert Schlette and Hans Küng.

Heinz Robert Schlette begins his work with the thesis of Henri de Lubac and Karl Rahner that all human life is set in a supernatural orientation and perspective. This is part of the human "given" following the prior fact of the goodness and salvific will of God, who wills to take part in a sacred history with humankind as a whole. The term "sacred history" is expressive of human reflective self-awareness that a "history of revelation" has actually occurred in world history as a whole.[41] Schlette affirms it as the normative doctrine of the Roman Catholic Church that "there is always a genuine possibility of salvation for non-Christians, that they are never absolutely abandoned by grace, that is, by the living God, the author of salvation, despite in particular their remoteness from the special revelation of God that occurred in Jesus Christ."[42]

The historical religions of human history, moreover, are an imposing reality which must be theologically confronted. Schlette conceives of the history of salvation as universal; he notes an "intrinsic legitimacy in all religions and forms of religion" and therefore affirms their role positively in the history of salvation. The covenant of Noah constituted, he contends, a fundamental divine sanctioning of all non-Israelite religions. He sees, however, the revelation of God in Jesus Christ as "something new" and makes, therefore, what is for him an important distinction between general and special sacred history. The latter is the special course of divine revelation and action centering in Jesus Christ and his church, and by reason of this special sacred history one is enabled to understand that the whole of human history is also sacred.[43] The religions of humankind, which in Schlette's view fall into the category of general sacred history, are also by God's will ways of salvation in the true sense, independent of the special way of salvation of Israel and the church, although according to the faith of the church this salvation is "fundamentally" that from Christ as mediated by the church. The way of the "non-Christian" religions is the ordinary way of salvation for the bulk of humankind in history and that of the church the extraordinary way. God in his salvific work has not been confined to special sacred history; God's saving presence can be recognized also in the other religions. This means, then, that the primary significance of special sacred history does not lie in the "salvation of souls"; nor does its "superiority" and that of the church consist of a more advantageous chance of salvation.[44]

Because of the coming of the Christ the religions, objectively speaking, are already superseded in God's salvific plan, but they are not so on the concrete individual plane as long as there are human beings who still live them with a good conscience. They "possess a relative providential right to existence," although theirs is a theologically prior position in the history of salvation.[45] Schlette repeatedly expresses his view of the "superiority" of Christian faith over the religions; it is as the perfect to the less perfect. There is in the manifestation of God in Jesus Christ "an absolute quality, clarity and binding character which essentially transcends the level of general sacred history." The principle, however, is that of different degrees in the self-communication of God. The enduring meaning of the Christian mission Schlette finds in "God's invitation" to human beings through Jesus Christ, not in notions of God's total absence from the non-Christian world nor from fears for the eternal damnation of persons if unreached by empirical Christian witness. The primary meaning of special sacred history he affirms not to lie in the "salvation of souls" but in the revelation, the complete epiphany, of the divine *doxa* to human beings. This divine glory, however, is "representative" of the whole of sacred history.[46]

Schlette is concerned over the question of truth, but he has a high appreciation of the common though differently patterned life of human beings in the presence of the transcendent mystery that surrounds and permeates us all. Although in his rather scholastic schema the religions are already superseded objectively, that is, theologically, from the coming of Jesus Christ, they have an authentic *continuing* role as potential instruments of God for the salvation of all humanity and the cosmos.[47]

Hans Küng (b. 1928) has become best known for his confrontations with the Roman Catholic hierarchy (and with Karl Rahner) on the issue of "infallibility" and for a generally liberal stance in Catholic theology. His influence, as a younger theologian, was considerable during Vatican Council II; in the area of our present concern his contribution has been largely to follow through on the implications of the documents of the council. The views of Hans Küng on the religions are given most fully in a long essay in his book *Freedom Today*, written after the appearance of Schlette's work. Küng develops his argument in the context of a fresh consideration of the dogmatic formula "Outside the Church No Salvation." His first conclusion is that no one disputes any longer the fact that human beings can be saved outside the Roman Catholic Church. Salvation is given to us in Christ alone, he contends, but Christ does not confine his salvific grace to those who are within the visible communion of believers. Küng suggests that we consider the problem of the destiny of non-Christian humankind by looking, not primarily at the church, but at God; the church itself is properly "to be understood not as a closed society of those in possession, but an open community of those who serve and help."[48] Following Vatican Council II's *Dogmatic Constitution on the Church* (*Lumen Gentium*), Küng affirms the universal salvific will of God, God's nearness to all persons of goodwill, and the working of God's grace among them to their attainment of eternal salvation.[49]

Küng affirms that the world religions have truth concerning the true God but are also in error; though in error they proclaim the truth of the true God. The gospel of Jesus Christ summons human beings in the religions to conversion but does not require them to renounce whatever therein "is true, whatever is honorable, whatever is just, whatever is pure, whatever is lovely, whatever is gracious" (Phil. 4:8). Even though he insists upon the right to call all persons to explicit conversion to God in Jesus Christ, Küng, like Schlette, removes the question from the issue of their eternal salvation. He also calls the world religions the ordinary way of salvation for non-Christian humanity and the church the extraordinary way. The latter represents special salvation history, the former universal salvation history, but both are bound together in a common origin, meaning, and goal in God, subject to the same grace of God.

Küng posits it as an integral element of Christian faith, based upon the will of God that everyone be saved, that all persons are intended to find their salvation within their own historical situation, which includes the religion that is "socially imposed" on them. Every historical situation, outside the church as well as inside, is included in advance within the grace of God. God, therefore, although not sanctioning every element in the religions, sanctions them as social structures and potential vehicles for the operation of divine grace. They are in their own way "legitimate religions," although in different senses and degrees. Küng follows Schlette in affirming that they have a "relative validity" and a "relative providential right to existence." They are, however, theologically pre-Christian.[50]

While affirming "every ground of hope for the church and her mission,"

Küng seems to envisage a continuing salvific role for the religions in the providence of God. The service of the church to the world properly includes service to the world religions; the church has to exist for the people in the world, even when and as they remain in the religions. Rather than coexistence, there should be pro-existence, all being for each other. Küng affirms therefore that the role of the church is to offer brotherly help to the world religions, to share responsibility with them, past and future, in word and in deed. The church is the representative before God of all persons, including those in the religions; it is not alien to them, for all alienation has been brought to a close in Christ, as the future has been opened in him. The church, as the *pars pro toto*, the minority to serve the majority, is the sign of the invitation of God to all peoples, yet it is itself but an imperfect and obscure image, albeit clear enough to be recognizable, in the power of the Spirit, of the ultimate and universal kingdom of God, which has already been inaugurated but is still awaited in its completed form.[51]

This approach focuses on the eschatological aspect of the nature both of the church itself—as a German-speaking Catholic Küng prefers the feminine gender—and of its mission. No longer is the Christian church in the present aeon seen to be the sole repository and expositor of truth; no longer is the mission of the church seen to be the total displacement of other religions and cultures. The church shares in the imperfections and ambiguities of all human beings in this age, with reference to perception and expression of truth as well as to quality of moral and spiritual life. The church may be *the* sign of the invitation of God to all peoples, but as an imperfect and obscure image-sign its mien before the world and to itself is properly modest. Neither our present Christian ecclesial structures nor our present Christian activities and being can be identified with the kingdom of God. Rather than the pose of triumphalism, we owe others the offer of brotherly help and affection. A legitimate part of the mission of the church can therefore be to help—and be helped by—men and women in other religious traditions as we grope toward the goal that lies before us all and that we all may perceive, albeit with varying degrees of clarity. This is to recognize that authentic Christian missionary activity may be carried on even when its effects, humanly speaking, remain under the name of another religious tradition.

In a later book, *On Being a Christian*, Hans Küng shows that these themes have been much a part of his reflection in more recent years, and he writes as always with passion, rich learning, and insight, even though occasionally with some carelessness. His basic theological position remains essentially the same as in his earlier treatment, but certain different nuances emerge. He continues to "stress the universal perspectives of the Bible (in Genesis, Romans, Acts, John's prologue): that God is Creator and Conserver of all men, that God operates everywhere, that he has made a covenant with all men (the 'cosmic covenant' with Noah), that—according to the New Testament— he wills the salvation of all men without respect of persons and that non-Christians too as observers of the law can be justified." Even more forthrightly than before, Küng emphasizes that there is salvation outside the visible bounds of the Christian church and that the other religions may be ways of salvation under God and therefore have authentic theological legitimacy.[52]

Küng writes with fine perception and telling eloquence of the commonality of the human quest lying behind the origins and developments of the major religions of human history. He asks, "Were not Buddha, Confucius, Lao-tse, Zarathustra, Muhammad, impelled by the same great, final questions to which we have been alluding?" And he adds, "Least of all can we merely decree in dogmatic, 'dialectical theology,'—following in the footsteps of Luther, like the earlier Barth, Bonhoeffer, Gogarten, and (less radically) E. Brunner and H. Kraemer—without a closer knowledge and analysis of the real world of the religions, that religion is nothing other than 'natural theology,' self-important, sinful revolt against God and unbelief; that Christianity is not a religion since the Gospel is the end of all religions." Küng, rather, insists that the great world religions, formerly mainly an external, quantitative challenge to Christendom, have now become an internal, qualitative challenge for the Christian churches themselves, as indeed, on the other hand, the world religions themselves are being challenged by Christianity.[53]

Küng rightly emphasizes the important contextual and qualitative differences in faith and practice to be found within and among the major world religions, as well as from prevailing Christian modes. He occasionally makes the mistake in his analyses of giving generalizations that are not strictly correct. As we shall see later, it is not true that "the experience of absorption" is central to Hinduism and Buddhism. Historically, it has been only one option among a number, and, in the case of early Buddhism, or in the numerically massive Pure Land School of Mahayana Buddhism, distinctly not the central theme or goal. It is also not true of "the great religions of the East, especially Hinduism, Buddhism and also Jainism" that "they have a *cyclical world picture*, in the light of which everything—both the course of the world and the life of the individual—is predetermined." Such may be found abundantly in popular forms of these traditions, but at their best or highest levels they are as open-ended as Christianity, or even Islam, at *their* best.[54]

Küng is correct in his emphasis that we must not overlook the immense contributions that the Christian churches in their missionary activity in all parts of the world over the past centuries have made to the liberation and betterment of human life. In his seven-volume classic work, *A History of the Expansion of Christianity*, Kenneth Scott Latourette has provided a wealth of data in chapters or sections of every volume on the effects of Christianity upon its environment, as indeed on the effects of the environment upon Christianity.[55] (I myself can attest from my own experience and study in Japan to the very great significance of these contributions.[56]) Even though Küng can speak of "the striking failure of the Christian missions" in achieving the goals set by nineteenth- and early twentieth-century Christian missionary activity, he would have us remember "the enlightenment and liberation, demythologizing and de-demonizing, the spiritualization and humanization which the Christian faith can bring" and in fact has brought in some measure to almost all parts of the world. This fact constitutes for Küng a powerful rationale and motive for Christian mission.

Küng, however, is too knowledgeable of the facts and developments of universal human history not to be aware of "the manifold failure of Christianity *and* the world religions in regard to the humanizing of man, to involvement in the struggle for justice, peace and freedom, and their influence—more divisive than unitive—on mankind as a whole." Therefore he asks from Christians a more modest posture than before, for a missiology that no longer aims at

the arrogant *domination of a religion* claiming an exclusive mission and despising freedom. . . . We do not want a narrow-minded, conceited, exclusive particularism which condemns the other religions *in toto*, a proselytism which carries on unfair competition and takes too restricted a view not only of the religions but also of the Gospel. . . . What we must strive for is an independent, unselfish Christian *ministry to human beings in the religions*. We must do this in a spirit of open-mindedness which . . . destroys nothing of value in the religions, but also does not incorporate uncritically anything worthless. Christianity therefore should perform its service among the world religions in a dialectical unity of recognition and rejection, as *critical catalyst and crystallization point* of their religious, moral, meditative, ascetic, aesthetic values.

For Küng the real aim of this kind of Christian missionary activity would be "to enter into genuine dialogue with the religions as a whole, giving and taking, in which the most profound intentions of the latter could be fulfilled". Christians would thus abandon fruitless attempts to prove the superiority of Christianity and manifest an inclusive Christian universalism claiming for Christianity *not exclusiveness, but certainly uniqueness*.[57] The open-endedness inherent in this posture means for Küng that "even Christendom [sic] within its own field would *not simply* remain in *possession* of the known truth, but *would be in search* of the ever greater and so constantly new unknown truth." This forward-looking spirit would reckon that the philosophers and religious thinkers of other nations than the Western could be "pedagogues" leading persons to Christ as much as Plato, Aristotle, and Plotinus. "Have not certain forms of Hinduism, Buddhism, Islamic mysticism grasped at a far deeper level than the Greeks—and still more than the 'Critical Theory'—the New Testament Truths of God's love, of peace, of vicarious suffering, even of justification by faith (Amida Buddhism)?" The consequence could be a Christianity "without a false, antithetical exclusiveness, but with a creative rethinking, resulting in a new, inclusive and simultaneously critical synthesis," which is at the same time not "a crippling, dissolving, agnostic-relativistic indifferentism."[58]

PAUL KNITTER

A significant contribution to the current discussion is being made by a younger Roman Catholic theologian, Paul F. Knitter (b. 1939), professor of theology at Xavier University in Cincinnati, Ohio, where he has taught since 1975. He has published over a dozen articles in several American and German journals and has given a very perceptive account of continental European Protestant thought in this area of concern with his doctoral dissertation, published under the title of *Towards a Protestant Theology of Religions.*[59] Knitter has more recently written an article in *Horizons,* the official journal of the College Theology Society, sharply criticizing Hans Küng for some of the claims made in the latter's book *On Being a Christian.* As we have seen, Küng is distinctly in the tradition of Catholic theologians who are in accord with the spirit of Vatican II. He is a bit careless, however, in some of his statements, making claims, at times without adequate qualifications, that *both* Christianity and Jesus Christ are unique and universally normative for all human beings, including the adherents of other religions.

Knitter quickly disposes of such claims with reference to Christianity as an empirical movement in human history but then goes on to assert that they are not applicable even to Jesus Christ except with careful qualifications. He insists that these claims, in the mode of Küng's formulations, are not necessary for religious commitment to Jesus Christ or for fidelity to Christian tradition. He further asserts that they are not only detrimental to genuine dialogue with other religions, but actually not possible according to the norms of proper theological or historico-critical methodology. Knitter in fact lifts the whole discussion to a somewhat different level from that of Küng and Schlette and shows his closer affinity to Raymond Panikkar and a large group of contemporary theologians.

Knitter shares with others of this critical perspective, such as Catholics Gregory Baum and David Tracy, and Protestants John Cobb and John Macquarrie, the conviction that Jesus of Nazareth has "universal significance" and that "the difference he makes is vitally important" for all persons of whatever background or faith-commitment. But he then asks whether it is not possible to "give oneself over wholly to the meaning and message of Jesus and at the same time recognize the possibility that other 'saviors' have carried out the same function for other people?" Knitter suggests, for example, that Christians can and should be open also to recognizing "the vitally important difference" of Gautama the Buddha. He asks why we cannot speak of other incarnations whereby "at the most the difference between Jesus and these others would be one of degree, not essence." Therefore "Christianity can and should learn from the religions."[60] The connecting link among the variety of incarnations in Knitter's thought seems to be "the Logos, the reality of Christ," who may be truly present, for example, in "the Krishna-myth"; and the uniqueness of Jesus lies, at least in part, in the uniqueness of the degree to which the Logos is present in him.[61] This also means that the great personages of human religious history all drank from the same Source, albeit in different ways and degrees and with differences in the kind and therefore significance of their several roles.

Knitter read a paper at the annual convention of the College Theology Society (May 1980) on the theme "Jesus and Buddha: A New Conversation," in which he gave a critical survey of recent literature and developed his views with a new refinement and precision of thought. This is his best work yet, mature, perceptive, creative. Amid the abundance of recent literature Knitter quotes most copiously from three persons, Heinrich Dumoulin and William Johnston (Roman Catholics), and this writer, Drummond (Protestant). It is interesting and probably of some significance that all three have had long missionary experience in Japan.

Knitter summarizes the literature by saying that "the majority of the authors approach the conversation with Buddhists with a firm conviction that there is much for Christians to learn and, given the crisis of Western Christianity, an urgent need to learn it." The phrase "the covenant with the East" is currently being used to indicate the prior fact of a divine covenant with "the East," just as the church fathers had recognized a divine covenant with the Greeks. Knitter suggests that precisely as the early church had learned from the Greeks in the context of such a category of theological understanding, so today a similar kind of transformative encounter can take place with "the East."

For the dialogue to be fruitful, Knitter contends that "it must have as its starting point [from the Christian side] a deep commitment to Christ and to the truth discovered in him." At the same time "the depth of this commitment must be matched by the breadth of one's openness to the truth that may be contained in Buddha's message." It seems to be a consensus of the authors whom Knitter surveys that especially at the points where Buddhism historically has seemed to differ most from Christianity the latter has most to learn. He states that "Christian writers are discovering their 'other eye' in Buddhism."

Part of the problem of difference is, of course, the fact that the Buddhist and Christian traditions have historically developed largely (not entirely) in isolation from each other and have "no common language." But Knitter contends that "we can perhaps discover that our 'words,' with all their baffling differences, are more complementary than contradictory." He agrees with Thomas Merton that the theology appropriate to dialogue must have rootage in religious experience, in contemplative prayer. Hence while Christians must cling to God, they "need not and ought not to cling to views and ideas about God." Knitter wishes to affirm to Buddhist dialogic partners that words and doctrines are important, even necessary, and yet he makes the significant addition that "no words or doctrines can share in the absoluteness of God. No doctrinal or biblical statement can be infallible in the sense of being irreformable or the final and only way of talking about the Mystery of God."

Knitter has some seminal thoughts with regard to understanding more perceptively the main themes of the teaching of the Buddha as well as early Buddhism, which we shall take due note of in the next chapter. He sums up his own theological conclusions with an appeal to Christians to take a "new and more critical look at the *exclusivism* that has marked their understanding of the uniqueness of Jesus." He further explains his position:

In the dialogue with Buddhism, Christians can—and I feel must— recognize that both Jesus and Buddha are mutually unique. Both preserve their distinctive difference and importance. And in a sense, both can be said to remain absolute in that they present their followers with a salvific revelation or *Dharma* which calls for total commitment and which is claimed to be meaningful for all peoples of all times. But this will be an absoluteness which is not defined by its ability to exclude or include other revelations; rather, Jesus and Buddha will be *proven* absolute insofar as they are able to relate to each other, complement and correct each other, discover and fulfill each other's truths, include and be included by each other. Christians, then, can continue to be totally committed to Jesus the Christ and to claim that for them God has been decisively revealed in him; but they will also feel not only the possibility but the need "to clarify, complete and correct" their understanding of Jesus and of God through dialogue with Buddhism as well as with other religions. . . . In understanding better their Buddhist brothers and sisters, Christians have the opportunity to understand better that their God is beyond all words and truly immanent in the world, that they themselves are radically social beings able to transform society only if they mystically realize this, and that their Savior is a Christ who defines God but does not confine Him.

Knitter's brilliant *magnum opus* on this theme, his book *No Other Name?* (1985), was published after the above section was written. His central thesis in this work is toward a "theocentric nonnormative interpretation of the uniqueness of Jesus Christ" that allows a personal and full commitment to Jesus at incarnation, but not the sole incarnation, of God's saving purpose and presence. I personally do not see how it is possible to have *full* commitment to Jesus without accepting him as normative, in a way to be discussed later in the Theological Epilogue. Knitter, however, is powerfully and winsomely persuasive in his clarion call to Christians to develop the depth and breadth of sympathy, the participative imagination now required for a truly global theology. This "new" theology, he avers, in fact requires a new type of unconsciousness, a multi-dimensional, cross-cultural consciousness.[62]

HEINRICH DUMOULIN, JOSEPH J. SPAE, AND WILLIAM JOHNSTON

We turn now to Roman Catholic theologians who have served for long years as missionaries in Japan. This writer has personally met them all and counts one of them, Joseph Spae, as a close friend and colleague in various activities. All represent the Roman Catholic Church at its best. They are immensely learned: in the languages, cultures, and religions of Asia as in the traditional disciplines of the West. They are cosmopolitan and at the same time profoundly spiritual. They meet representatives of other religious traditions at the deepest levels of both academic knowledge and spiritual experience because they come from those levels in their own tradition.

Heinrich Dumoulin (b. 1905) is a German Jesuit who first went to Japan in 1935 and was for many years professor of philosophy and history of religions at Sophia University in Tokyo. Since his formal retirement in 1976 he has continued his activities in Japan and also lectures widely in German-speaking lands. He is a leading Western authority on Zen Buddhism and became well known in the academic world for his *A History of Zen Buddhism* published in 1963.

Dumoulin was asked to write an article on "Buddhism—A Religion of Liberation" for a volume in the Concilium series. The article is characterized not only by wide and deep knowledge of historic Buddhism but also by the author's ability perceptively to correct a number of the facile half-truths of common Western understanding of Buddhism. For example, Dumoulin states that "the ideas of *karma* and reincarnation [commonly in the West] are linked with a *cyclical concept of history* which can be understood in a nihilistic sense, as Nietzsche did in his myth of the 'eternal return of the same.' But, as understood in the Far East, this concept, though linked with the path toward religious salvation, is in no way nihilistic." He notes that many Buddhists are critically examining the doctrine of reincarnation, without necessarily abandoning it, as they have increasingly come to recognize the importance of the historical dimension in the larger human experience. At the same time, in the West "modern psychology shows great interest in the idea of reincarnation."

Dumoulin, while noting that recent Buddhist scholars are pressing for a demythologization of certain traditional Buddhist views of karma as imperative, holds that the principle (as cosmic compensation or retribution) is of the essence of both Buddhism and Christianity. He defines karma in the Buddhist view as "the general intertwining of all human behavior, the weaving of an unfathomable, impenetrable yet meaningful net with all its connecting lives running in every direction." He then insists that this perception-experience is "in no way alien to Christianity," and in fact he uses it to clarify and deepen traditional Christian understanding of "the solidarity of mankind, that interrelatedness which is first of all experienced in the general wretchedness of human existence but then opens up a hopeful looking forward towards salvation. Both Buddhism and Christianity, profoundly involved in the fact of suffering, are aware of a human solidarity in suffering and a universality [universal availability] of salvation." Dumoulin observes that "the Buddhist view does not limit this solidarity to mankind but draws the whole cosmos within the scope of the changing interrelationship." This perception helps him better to understand Paul's words about the whole creation groaning in travail (Rom. 8:22).

Dumoulin follows one Western interpretive tradition in stating that "according to early Buddhist sources, man proceeds on the way towards liberation alone, without any outside help, simply on the strength of his own effort." We shall see that this is probably a mistaken view, but it is interesting that almost immediately after making this statement Dumoulin confesses that whatever theory appears in these sources, "in actual practice an 'other force,' namely transcendence, asserts itself. . . . the final stage of the way towards liberation was already open to this transcendency in very early Buddhism, and, I feel I may say, in Buddha's own mind." The present writer agrees with this latter understanding, as would the distinguished German-British Buddhologist Edward Conze.[63]

Finally, Dumoulin works to contradict the common Western nihilistic interpretation of Nirvana as simply extinction or total annihilation "of awareness, of individuality and of existence." He notes that actually none of the earliest modern European specialists in Buddhist studies, men such as H. T. Colebrooke, B. H. Hodgson, A. Csoma Körös, and E. Burnouf, understood the final state of Nirvana as simply extinction or total annihilation; but it is surprising how widely this interpretation later came to be held. Dumoulin rightly sees one important part of the meaning of Nirvana in early Buddhist texts as indicative of a radical change in the present modes of human existence. Furthermore, the vast majority of believing Buddhists of all schools from the earliest times to the present have understood Nirvana as entailing a "happy ending." That is, like New Testament Christian faith, Buddhism at its best holds an authentic eschatological orientation in wholesome tension with expectation of a "Nirvana here and now" to be attained in the present life.[64] Dumoulin's reflections constitute a significant example of the power of an open-ended Christian theology to liberate persons from the bonds of distorted academic opinions however long and deeply entrenched.

"Buddhism—A Religion of Liberation" is in a sense a distillation of elements of Dumoulin's earlier book *Christianity Meets Buddhism* (1974). In the book we learn some of the basic theological principles that inform his understanding. For example, he interprets the language of Vatican II's Dogmatic Constitution on the Church, which speaks of God whose "saving designs extend to all men," as meaning that "the Christian can recognize God's saving action at work in all religions. He can, if he turns to others with an open heart and mind, grow to see that the Far Eastern religions, which disclose precious values of inner life, could not have emerged without some kind of divine assistance." Dumoulin goes on to assert that the very writing of his book "proceeds from the conviction that the non-Christian religions contribute to the salvation of mankind."[65]

Simple as this language may be, it carries the profoundest theological significance. Dumoulin himself recognizes that what he calls "the new Christian theology of the Second Vatican Council" in fact "rediscovered basic values and attitudes which had been lost for centuries in the West." This is also to say that the dialogue with the East is impelling Christianity to give heed once more to the depth and fullness of its own spiritual tradition. Dumoulin, like many others on the frontiers of contemporary Christian mission and theology, is seeking means for in-depth renewal of Christian life and finds help in the perceptions and perspectives of Teilhard de Chardin both for such renewal and for wise understanding of, and sensitive relationship with, the other religions of humanity. The goal is not unity of religions, he believes, but "to gain and deepen mutual understanding and cooperation, on the personal level." He feels this is necessary for the common welfare of all humankind. One of Dumoulin's greatest contributions to this activity, besides the breadth and warmth of his spirit, is his attention to the specifics of detailed knowledge as well as general considerations in the dialogue.[66]

Joseph J. Spae (b. 1913), a Belgian priest of the Immaculate Heart of Mary Mission Society (CICM), first went to the Orient in 1939 and began his studies in Chinese language and culture in Peking. A year later he was transferred to Kyoto, Japan, and began the studies that were to make him one of the most competent Japanologists of his generation. Those who know him personally and marvel also at his extraordinary command of English, including its colloquial forms, soon learn that part of the foundation for this facility lies in his wartime internment in Japan (from 1942 to 1945) with American construction workers captured on Guam! All of Spae's numerous books, most of which were written at the Oriens Institute for Religious Research in Tokyo, which he founded, show him to be at once a leader in the forefront of Roman Catholic missiological theology and possessor of a heart ever yearning to share the riches of the Christian gospel with the people of Japan.

Some of the most perceptive of Spae's thoughts on the theme we are considering are to be found in the book *East Challenges West: Towards a Convergence of Spiritualities,* which resulted from his lecture series given in Australia in 1979. He rejects the notion of any "challenge" (in a negative or competitive sense) offered the West by the East. He contends, rather, that there can be only "invitation towards mutual growth." Everything, he says, "points to the fact that the new unity of mankind, pressed upon us in the economic, cultural and political field through the ever-widening influences of a common technology, is drawing people's minds and hearts together to the point where mutual esteem is heightened to that 'intercommunication of goods which is the quintessence of charity.' "[67]

Spae states that an integral element of an incarnational Christian theology is that Christianity remain "wide open to that complementarity of charismata which are found throughout the nations and which it is called upon to integrate within itself so that they may be put into the service of all mankind." This incisive statement is a call not only to a broader theological activity within the church but also to a more inclusive spirituality as a background for a more effective mission in the world. Spae understands this kind of activity as a true *imitatio Christi* because—he quotes Augustine—the Lord Jesus "is that unique person [now] present throughout the whole world, *Christus, homo ille toto orbe terrarum diffusus.*"[68] The "challenge" of the East to the whole church in the true sense is that the church recognize the great fact that there are "spirit-laden aspects of other cultures and religions." He calls it an inspired word of Ambrose (337?–397) that "whatever is good and just and beautiful, by whomever and wherever it be said, comes from the Holy Spirit" (cf. Phil. 4:8).[69] We may recall similar words from Justin Martyr (ca. 100–165) quoted in chapter 3, above; but Spae is anxious not only to admire them but to apply them. He insists that the church "has much to glean in fields other than her usual own, that of the Greco-Roman tradition. The *Mater et Magistra* must humble herself and go to school."[70]

This open-minded, open-ended theological position enables Spae, like Dumoulin, not only to enter upon a learning process which leads to an enrichment of Christian faith and life and which is actually a rediscovery of "what Christianity really is, a movement toward comprehension of what is the breadth and length and height and depth" (Eph. 3:18). It also enables him to understand what other religions are trying to say even when they use language that polemicists have at times vilified with scorn. Thus Spae states that Buddhist concepts like "Emptiness" and "Nothingness," which are of course not unknown in the history of Christian spirituality, are emotionally pregnant terms that, among other things, point to the goal of selfless interiority, which plays a highly significant role also in the teaching of Jesus (Mk. 8:34–35, etc.). In both the past and the present of Japan, in Buddhism, Shinto, and the New Religions, as well as in the at times glorious history of Christianity in Japan, Spae sees the mystery of salvation unfolding before the eyes of Christians who have eyes to see as the most "challenging and tantalizing object of research and wonderment." His passion for the crossing of boundaries has enabled him to draw out comparable yearnings already at work in the hearts of others. For example, he quotes the distinguished Buddhist professor at Ryukoku University in Kyoto, Ryōgon Fukuhara, as saying: "I hope that, in the years to come, we Buddhists and you Christians shall learn to talk from heart to heart!" Spae notes that the Buddhist professor's words are remarkably similar to the motto of John Henry Newman, *Cor ad cor loquitur.*[71]

Like other perceptive Christian specialists in Buddhist studies, Spae perceives that although Buddhism and Christianity have significantly divergent ways of expressing their perceptions of truth, they "yet converge in their soteriological intentions." He realizes that, for both, a central element of the process-event of salvation is that a human being be saved from self "so that he might become his 'true self.' " The Japanese Buddhist philosophers Keiji Nishitani and Masao Abe are both cited as stressing this understanding. Nishitani, in looking toward "the religion of the future," which should be a religion relevant not only to the life of human beings on earth but to the cosmos as well, stresses that such a religion should be "the force that can eradicate the deepest roots of our self-centered ego."[72]

Spae, like almost all contemporary Roman Catholic theologians, tends to reject the "type of Christian dogmatism which peremptorily claims to capture all divine realities in exact, verbal formulations." He prefers to see "the deeper meaning of salvation as an intimate event in which a loving God is perceived and accepted by an intuitive thrust of the heart." Spae is helped in this development of faith-understanding by what he sees in the whole Japanese historico-cultural experience and, indeed, in a flexibility in the use of terminology in all the religious traditions stemming from India. He sees the East as "relaxed and expansive in its definitions . . . illustrative rather than logical in its doctrinal statements. . . . Varying symbols do not contradict; they reinforce one another."[73]

Spae is not one to be accused of either advocating or practicing loose thinking. His concern is, rather, to learn from the Eastern emphasis on the existential-visceral in order to expand the ranges of the intellectual-conceptual. He understands the Buddhist ideal perception of enlightenment—seen as one part or aspect of a larger, more encompassing salvation—not as an array of ideas but as "a state of being at the level of total awareness," a perception that Christians may properly use for the sake of enlarging common Christian understandings of salvation. Spae sees a new mode of spirituality emerging across the world, namely, that of an expansive type of person "whose religious life is not tied to a monolithic culture fencing in one's self-identity." It is the responsibility of Christians, he believes, to respond to this "deep-running religious change" with the very compassion of their Lord, therefore with openness and flexibility and the willingness to participate in growth that is also self-transformation as well as transformation of the cosmos.[74]

Spae, like most other contemporary Roman Catholic theologians, has been significantly influenced by both Teilhard de Chardin and Thomas Merton, and he frequently builds on their insights and spiritual visions. His own intimations of an "East-West spiritual convergence" have been significantly influenced also by their emphasis on the vital importance of the instrumentality of mysticism, a term, we should recall, which retains a noble connotation in the Catholic terminology of spirituality. Spae, in particular, sees Christian monasticism as being called to stand "in the vanguard of a valid and powerful modern mysticism which will gather what is best in the religious traditions of East and West." This will be a "mysticism of tomorrow, a living-in by East and West at the peaks of interiority; the meeting of Christianity's ascensional force toward a Transcendent, a loving God, and the Eastern propulsive force toward an Immanent, a *Tao*, Way or Spirit, whom we breathe and in whom we live." Like his mentors, Spae asks for a new balance between the contemplative life and the active, between mysticism before God and social mysticism oriented to love and service of the world.

It would be a mistake to infer from the foregoing that Spae would not work, given the opportunity, to win others, including Buddhists, to conscious faith in, and commitment to, God through Jesus Christ and to fellowship in the Christian church. He has a high view of "the mystery of the church, seen in her universality and in her existential presence within cultures and nations," and perceives the significance of the role of the church in the divine economy of salvation as great indeed. But he knows that it is of the best theological tradition of the church and a practical imperative for a wise mission strategy in this age to try "to detect God's saving action within and without the monotheistic religions." He asks for "an advanced study of the world religions undertaken with prayerful attention to whatever is good and true in them, and with the desire to learn from them a better understanding of God's will towards his church." In this context of understanding he asks for "joint projects of interreligious collaboration in the whole sphere of immediate needs and concerns, and among them, all that is related to international and national justice and peace."

If Spae speaks of "ever-converging tendencies" in the dialectical relationship between Buddhism and Christianity, he yet states that the church is not asked to compromise or to "acquiesce to irrationality, syncretism, emotionalism or intuition. She is merely asked to see them [in herself as well as others] as ambivalent cultural realities strewn upon man's path like stepping stones toward a final goal. . . . Christianity and Buddhism instinctively know that the contest between 'the mystery of salvation' and 'the mystery of iniquity' admits of no solution except in an eschatological dimension. But Christians know that they dare not wait for the end of the world to attempt an at-one-ment between the Church and the world."[75]

A few points of significance may be added from Spae's *Buddhist-Christian Empathy* (1980). With reference to the theme of the "intercommunication of goods" mentioned above, Spae more specifically defines the term as "a mutual illumination which radically banishes all thought of superiority" over other religions among Christians. This illumination that Christians may receive from others Spae further identifies as a kind of *Fremdtprophetie*, or prophetic knowledge received from persons outside the Christian faith and church, which is potentially an authentic *locus theologicus*. It may serve, moreover, as a factor for Christian self-identification, as significantly helpful feedback information "from outsiders." Spae believes that Christian faith and, indeed, Christianity as a historical movement, may yet use this "factor for self-identification" to claim "a specific, universally valid role, different from that of Buddhism" even as it eschews "all thought of superiority." This is because of the Christ, for "he is *the* revelation of God to man; . . . he, and no other, is the supreme manifestation of all perfection; . . . in him God has reconciled all things to himself" (cf. 2 Cor. 5:18–19). "But Buddhism could and should enrich the Christian heritage with new forms of thought, with new opportunities to penetrate more deeply into the mystery of Christ, with a renewed understanding of the comprehensiveness and the uniqueness of the Gospel."

Spae gives further insight into his own understanding by quoting with approval a passage from Carrin Dunne: "From a Christian perspective, I see Buddha as a precursor, preparing the way of the Lord. From a Buddhist perspective, I see Jesus as a true successor of the Buddha." On the basis of this theological understanding, Spae, then, asks "whether it is an impossible dream that Buddhists and Christians, in more advanced encounter, should reach out toward a symbiosis, a kind of synergistic merger, in which, with mutual respect for one another's identity, they coordinate their response to urgent human concerns. Already the encounter fleshes out this dream." In order to move further in this direction Spae believes that for Christians a "Christocentric rather than an ecclesiocentric approach" will be both more effective and more authentically Christian.[76]

William Johnston (b. 1925) is an American Jesuit priest who has served for many years on the faculty of Sophia University in Tokyo, Japan, especially in its International College. Like almost all Roman Catholics concerned with the practice and theory of Christian spirituality, he has been deeply influenced by Thomas Merton; he dedicated his book *The Still Point* (1970) to Merton "in memoriam." Even though we are not treating Merton in this chapter, because he does not belong to the category of "contemporary theologians," it should be stated that he is a masterful model in consideration of our particular theme as well as of the larger ranges of Christian spirituality. Merton's suggestions, for example, in his *Mystics and Zen Masters* for proper Christian understanding and appropriation of the insights and practices of Zen Buddhism represent the finest kind of open-ended and sensitive Christian theological work from his generation.[77]

Brief mention should also be made of another Roman Catholic predecessor of Johnston in Japan, Hugo Enomiya-Lassalle. While "Lassalle" is the name used in the Library of Congress catalogue of his books, he evidently prefers the hyphenated form. Enomiya-Lassalle is a German Jesuit priest, born in 1898, who first arrived in Japan in 1929 and served in a variety of activities, including work in the Tokyo slums and at Hiroshima. He was in Hiroshima at the time the atomic bomb was dropped and suffered personal injury from its effects. He became a naturalized Japanese citizen and thus adopted the Japanese surname of Enomiya. He became widely known for his attempts to introduce the methodologies of Zen meditation into Christian spiritual practices. Enomiya-Lassalle believed that the methodologies of Zen could be divorced, or at least distinguished, from Zen Buddhism because "there is no dogma at stake in Zazen, but only the development of the natural powers of the soul." There may be some who would wish to question this assertion, but Enomiya-Lassalle has made a significant contribution through Christian-Zen meditational groups, which he sponsored over the years. He also contributed greatly in a beautiful way in stressing mutual understanding, learning from each other, between East and West. "Soul speaks to soul, heart to heart, and in this dialogue all prejudices are dissolved and the more noble future of man is assured. And this future will surely be one in which a new spiritual culture is born and valued above all material things."[78]

Johnston himself is a boldly creative figure in this noble tradition. Like his predecessors, he has entered deeply and empathetically into the Japanese cultural and religious experience, particularly that of Zen Buddhism. Also like the others, he enters into dialogue with a rich background of study and experience in the tradition of Christian spirituality. This fact has enabled him to focus on the unitive element of religious experience, which, in spite of being "poles apart" in philosophical formulations, has made it possible on occasion for Buddhists and Christians to meet in an atmosphere of "delicate charity and understanding," "of great cordiality, forming deep friendships and laying the foundations for further union." Johnston believes it to be a fact that "not only Zen but all forms of Buddhism are going to make an enormous impact on the Christianity of the coming century. If there has been a Hellenized Christianity (which is now about to succumb with the passing of the so-called Christendom), there is every likelihood that the future will see the rise of an Oriental Christianity in which the role of Buddhism will be incalculably profound."[79]

Johnston wishes to make clear, speaking especially from the Roman Catholic standpoint, that, relatively and historically, orthodox Christianity has put less stress on mystical intuitive religious experiences in the formal conduct of its affairs. Specifically, it has not built its doctrines upon them, at least not since the apostolic generation, although this could not be said of the Protestant denominations, especially in their emergence, and perhaps not entirely of the Eastern Orthodox churches. He notes the difficulty, within the Christian context, historically as well as at present, of finding fully reliable norms for judging the authenticity and relative validity of such experiences. But he will not let go of their importance, and we too may ask whether or not Christianity could have developed as it did without them. In any case, Johnston stresses that the persons best fitted to participate in meetings between Buddhism and Christianity will be those who come from backgrounds of intuitive-perceptive religious experience transcending the cognitive-rational dimension.

Johnston believes that the common Christian practice of prayer can be significantly enriched by study of the Zen way. He suggests that the Zen techniques of meditation "can teach the Christian how to relax, how to be calm, how to think in a deeper way, how to dispose himself to receive God's love, how to conceive the truths of faith not only in his brain but in his whole body. . . . It is not impossible that Eastern techniques can teach more mysticism than nineteenth-century spiritual direction dreamed possible." Johnston rightly perceives that even Zen Buddhism, which is popularly supposed to be utterly divorced from all cognitive concepts and views, actually has its own "philosophy of life" and related presuppositions. He would have Christians continue to "sit" on their own philosophy of life; but he goes on to ask whether or not what he calls vertical meditation, which has been highly developed in Asia, can be introduced into Christian prayer. He asks, "Is it possible to *teach* to Christians a prayer that is imageless, silent and vertical, which will unite the personality in radical detachment from all things?"[80]

Johnston believes "that this silent concentration lends depths to the personality, that it strengthens convictions, that it puts things into the whole body in a psychosomatic way, and that man is convinced of ideas that he conceives, not just in his brain, but in his whole body." He contends that this vertical meditation "liberates the mind from inordinate desires and distractions, enabling it to seek the deepest truth lying at the heart of realty. . . . [It] promotes psychic growth and emotional maturity." This vertical meditation is what

Johnston believes "leads to that serene detachment and interior liberty which is the hallmark of Buddhist art and culture." Yet he is convinced that vertical meditation has relevance for, indeed a profound affinity with, specifically Christian prayer centered on Christ and God. He reminds us that because of our Western tradition of emphasis upon the cognitive aspects of human thought, we are frequently tempted to "smother the tiny flame" of love of God and fellow creatures with endless thinking when we should be "silent, empty and expectant before our God."

Johnston suggests that Christian modes of *satori* (enlightenment) are possible, as "a deep experience and a true change of consciousness." And this experience of change, which may be a gradual process, "reaches its climax when one's ego is lost to be replaced by that of Christ. 'I live, now not I, but Christ liveth in me'; when one's consciousness is lost to be replaced by that of Christ: 'Let that mind be in you which was in Christ Jesus'; it reaches its climax in a Trinitarian experience: 'Now this is eternal life that they may know Thee the One true God and Jesus Christ whom Thou hast sent.' "[81]

In his later writings Johnston continues to develop these themes. He continues to insist that the model for Christian mysticism is Jesus himself and that Christian mysticism in practice is a transformation into Christ. But no one religion in the empirical sense of its present historical manifestations "can answer the needs of modern man." This is, of course, because none adequately manifests the fullness of the cosmic Christ, who has been working in all human cultures and religions. And "in her dealings with the East, Western Christianity must humbly admit that she has much to learn. If she does this, she will find her encounter with the Orient no less enriching than her meeting with Greco-Roman thought in the early years of her existence."

The mission of the church goes on. Persons are invited into specifically Christian modes of faith. However, the faith that does not cling to words and concepts and images of God but aims at the reality of God recognizes "that such faith is not the prerogative of Christians alone." Buddhists also speak of the necessity of faith, and as their faith "flowers and develops into the naked faith" that Johnston calls mysticism, a union with Christians of the deepest kind becomes possible. "This is the union of people who are in love without restriction or reservation and whose love has entered the cloud of unknowing. They are one at the center of things; they are one in the great mystery which hovers over human life and toward which all religions point."[82]

7

Views of Contemporary Theologians: Protestant

With reference to the theme of Christian understanding of the other religious traditions of humankind, the two great Protestant protagonists of the generation ending about 1965 were Hendrik Kraemer and Paul Tillich. Even though our primary concern is with contemporary theologians, it may be helpful to set the stage with a brief description of the views of these two men. We may say at once that with the "demise" of Barthian theology as a more or less formalized movement by the end of the 1960s, the influence of Hendrik Kraemer (1888–1965) greatly lessened and can now be considered minimal among theologians of the mainline denominations in the English-speaking world. At the same time the position of Paul Tillich (1886–1965), while it has been considerably developed, corrected, and refined by others, has become in a sense basic material for perhaps all the Protestant theologians whom we shall consider in this chapter.

HENDRIK KRAEMER

As we noted earlier, Hendrik Kraemer, while by no means offering an unqualified espousal of dialectical theology, was its greatest missiological exponent. He was also the outstanding spokesman for the understanding of that school with reference to the religions of the world. Kraemer, of Dutch origin, served for sixteen years in Indonesia (then the Dutch East Indies) as a lay missionary of the Netherlands Bible Society. He also represented in a sense the dominant mentality of German-speaking conservative Protestantism from before World War I. It is significant that Tillich, who was German by birth and education, came to give theological expression to a new form of Anglo-Saxon liberalism rooted in the earlier Broad-Church movement of Anglicanism as well as to the older German liberalism of Schleiermacher and Troeltsch.

The dominant position of German Protestantism from the early twentieth century with regard to the world religions can perhaps be said to have been set by Julius Richter, professor of missions in the University of Berlin. In 1913 he wrote that Christianity is an exclusive religion and that the responsibility of the Christian mission is to oust the non-Christian religions and "to put Christianity in their place."[1] Richter constituted a watershed in the history of German Protestant missiology. He lacked the eschatological perspective that has strongly characterized almost the whole of German theology and missionary thinking from the end of World War I.[2] In spite of this new perspective, however, German Protestant theology largely continued to hold views of the religions essentially akin to Richter's until after World War II.[3] Notable exceptions were Rudolf Otto, Friedrich Heiler, and Ernst Benz. A significant leader in certain new developments in German Protestant theology has been Wolfhart Pannenberg. In the second volume of his *Basic Questions in Theology*, Pannenberg has a long chapter entitled "Toward a Theology of History of Religions." In this chapter he quotes with approval the passage of Ernst Benz in which the latter had written in 1960 of the "frightening isolation" into which much Christian thought had fallen as a result of the "unfounded claims of dialectical theology."[4] Paul Knitter in his careful study of the views of recent continental European Protestant and Catholic theologians notes a significant change from the position of Richter in that most German-speaking Protestant theologians are now willing to acknowledge the possibility of God's revelatory work outside the "places" and context of explicit Christian faith. He also shows their hesitancy, as contrasted with most contemporary Roman Catholic theologians of note, to admit a salvific dimension in this divine work.[5]

Hendrik Kraemer, therefore, was not a lone voice in his time but the man who gave the most trenchant and theologically thorough expression to ideas then held by considerable numbers of Christians in both East and West.[6] Kraemer's most influential work was the book that he wrote by request in preparation for the Tambaram, Madras Conference of the International Missionary Council in 1938. His purpose, at least in part, was to correct the primary stance and ethos of the Jerusalem Meeting of the International Missionary Council in 1928 and of the report of the Laymen's Committee on Foreign Missions published in 1932. Kraemer followed the emphasis of dialectical theology that there is an absolute qualitative difference between God and human beings, between the Creator and the creation. This was in accord with Karl Barth's rejection of the medieval Thomistic affirmation of *analogia entis*, or analogy of being between God and the created world. We shall see later that there are some reasons to consider with new seriousness the medieval view. Kraemer's theological foundation was "the prophetic and apostolic witness to a divine, transcendental order of life that transcends and judges by virtue of its inherent authority the whole range of historical human life in every period."[7] This order of life is communicated uniquely through the revelation of God in Jesus Christ, which "erects the absolute superiority of God's holy Will and judgment over *all* life, historical Christianity included."[8] Kraemer thus radically distinguished between the Christian revelation and empirical Christianity, which as a historical religious movement is thoroughly human. Christianity, however, he contended, even as an empirical reality can be differentiated from all other religions because of the radical self-criticism that is one of its chief characteristics deriving from the divine revelation in Christ to which it testifies.[9]

Kraemer saw the Christian revelation as placing itself over all the many efforts of human beings to apprehend the totality of existence. It gives knowledge of God of a special kind, which "upsets all other conceptions of God or of the Divine."[10] Kraemer conceived of the natural conditions of human beings in history to be dialectical, that is, characterized by a fundamental and demonic (or horrid) disharmony.[11] He saw God as working in humanity and shining through nature. The religious and moral life of human beings is their own achievement, but it is also indicative of God's wrestling with them. He wrote: "It manifests a receptivity to God, but at the same time an inexcusable disobedience and blindness to God."[12] Kraemer was concerned to avoid all attitudes of superiority and pride, but his conclusion with regard to the religions of the world was that all religious life, the lofty and the degraded, apart from the revelation of God in Jesus Christ, which he conceived solely in terms of Christ's manifestation as Jesus of Nazareth, is *misdirected*.[13] The religions as such bring neither true knowledge of God nor of humanity. The message of "Biblical Realism" must be brought to human beings, but the sole agent of real faith in Jesus Christ is the Holy Spirit. All the religions are but the various efforts of human beings to apprehend the totality of existence.[14] Neither fulfillment nor point of contact between them and the Christian revelation can be entertained as a possibility. The groping and persistent aspiration of human beings reflect the working of God, but the religions in themselves can be said only to be radically and *in toto* misdirected.[15]

Kraemer came to make certain qualifications to these extreme views in his *Religion and the Christian Faith* (1956). He here affirmed that, although Christ is the Crisis and the Caller-in-question of all religion, there are in fact evidences of God's revealing activity in the religions, indicative of God's uninterrupted concern and travailing with humanity. "All religions are huge systems of manifold, partly more or less positive, partly more or less negative, responses to God." He could now say from the perspective of revelation in Christ that both "continuity" and "discontinuity" can be affirmed with regard to the complex of spiritual reality constituted by the religions. He criticized Karl Barth for saying, as he does, that the Bible knows no other mode of revelation than Jesus Christ; at this point, Kraemer averred, the Bible is against Barth.[16]

Kraemer's last public expression of his views on the religions is the book that was published in English under the title *Why Christianity of All Religions?* In this book, in place of the earlier terms "Christian revelation," "Biblical Realism," and even "revelation of Christ," he prefers to speak of the "Person of Jesus Christ," who is *the* Revelation of God and alone has the power to judge every religion discriminately and with complete understanding. The work constitutes a magnificent affirmation of faith in Jesus Christ, not as the sole revelation of God but as Lord and the objective Criterion by whom human beings, in faith, evaluate all things, including the religions (and empirical Christianity).[17] Kraemer continues in this book to distinguish sharply between revelation, which is God acting and speaking, and religion, which signifies the various ways in which human beings believe and their consequent activities. But the God of revelation does not stand aside from the "struggling, questing, discovering and errant human spirit."[18]

Kraemer, apart from the craving for God awakened by the Holy Spirit which he finds widely in evidence in "non-Christian lands," nowhere (to this writer's knowledge) cites concrete instances of how God is involved in the religions.[19] In *Why Christianity of All Religions?* he affirms that by the light of the reality disclosed in God's self-communication in Jesus Christ and in full commitment to him, one is to search out evidences of revelatory activity on the part of the same God in all religions, an enterprise that properly includes empirical Christianity within its scope and must not fail to discern demonic as well as divine forces at work in them. In spite of these evidences or traces, which presumably may be found, the non-Christian religions, Kraemer contends, are all in error "in regard to their deepest, most essential purport." They are noble but misguided and abortive attempts to answer the fundamental religious questions in their own (human) terms. Humanity's greatness as well as depravity and failure are seen in their religious and moral activities; yet the demonstrable traces of God's active concern with human beings are not disclosed positively in the religions themselves but in the fact that they represent a negative reaction to God's activity, which is a fleeing from God. "The main thing about all religions—the heart and soul of them, as it were—is that they are a *fleeing* from God." Every religion, even a considerable part of the Christian religion, is shown to be primarily characterized as a religion of self-redemption, self-justification, and self-sanctification and therefore, in its ultimate and essential meaning, *erroneous*.[20] The key word in them all is "self-realization."[21] Jesus Christ presents us with an *entirely new* world of facts and norms, which involves a total uprooting, an *Umwertung aller Werte*.[22]

Kraemer affirms that at the very heart of "error" itself, we are to recognize that "God has passed this way" and that Jesus Christ does not quench the smoking flax (Isa. 42:3) but "discovers" whatever has an affinity with him. We are left, however, entirely in the dark as to what specifically in the religions has an affinity with Christ or where God has passed. For the "grace" proclaimed in Buddhism is always a "soft option"; in Hindu *bhakti*, grace refers solely to a private relationship between God and the individual soul. The concept of love (*mettā*) in Buddhism is wholly different from the love (*agape*) "for which Jesus Christ stands." The religions "never give any real weight to the one basic fact which the Bible calls 'sin.' " Kraemer therefore affirms that surrender to Jesus Christ means to make a break with one's own (religious) past, however impressive that past may be. The Christian church "is in duty bound to require this break, because one must *openly* confess Him."[23] Kraemer urges that we enter into dialogue with persons of other religions, that one of the most fruitful forms of communication would be to "steep ourselves in one another's problems and be ready to serve one another in word and deed." In our contemporary world where the inward and spiritual life of humanity needs to find new forms of expression as a consequence of the disintegration or inadequacy of the old, the paramount problems are the same for all the major religions. Also, even though the religions are erroneous, they "contain a great deal which really does have something to say to us and give to us. We can learn a lot from them; and we must be ready and eager to do so. . . . we shall be able to think afresh, in the light they shed for us, about the Christian faith." But "the differences between the various religions are unbridgeable and irreconcilable."[24] Kraemer never specifies what it is that we can learn from the religions, and one wonders to what extent he had a real openness at this point.

The changes or developments in Kraemer's thought that appear in his later books are, therefore, more theoretical than real. Of more serious moment, however, is that his critical statements regarding sin and grace in the other religions appear to be factually not true (on the basis of this writer's studies, at least). The concept of love in Buddhism is not wholly different from that in the gospel of Jesus Christ. Grace in Buddhism is not always a soft option. Nor is it true that other religions never give real weight to the basic fact of sin. We cannot, accordingly, take with full seriousness theological conclusions that are based on fundamental errors of fact, however much we may appreciate Kraemer's concern to establish the priority of Jesus Christ as the unique revelation of God and therefore the criterion of all things for persons who accept him in faith as their Lord. Kraemer's "Biblical Realism," therefore, at least with reference to his views of the religions, appears to be more representative of a doctrinaire theological position than of either the Bible or historical reality.

PAUL TILLICH

The thought of Paul Tillich on the world religions is given in its most systematic form in his Bampton Lectures in 1961, which were published under the title *Christianity and the Encounter of the World Religions*. Certain of his basic principles of thought on this theme, however, appeared in earlier works. In the James W. Richard Lectures given in 1951 Tillich stressed the primary need for human beings in their nations to make ultimate decisions that decide their destiny. These become an ethical decision for or against the Christ. "But this decision for or against the Christ is made by people who do not even know his name. What is decisive is only whether they act for or against the law of love, for which the Christ stands."[25] This was in effect to affirm the concept of the Logos as the universal principle of divine self-manifestation and the universality of the revelatory and salvific work of God. Tillich perceived an inner aim (*telos*) in the movement of history generally and in particular in the history of religions.[26]

Equally central to Tillich's thought, however, is a particularity that at some points is akin to Hendrik Kraemer's. Tillich affirms that revelatory events underlie all religions and quasi-religions, but the revelatory event on which Christianity is based has "critical and transforming power for all religions." This event is "the appearance and reception of Jesus of Nazareth as the Christ, a symbol which stands for the decisive self-manifestation in human history of the source and aim of all being." If one is grasped by the spiritual power of this event, he is enabled to evaluate both Christianity and the other religions.[27] Like Kraemer, Tillich accepts the Christ-event as his sole and ultimate criterion,[28] but he is more concerned than Kraemer to specify the universal presence and working of the Logos. Indeed, the problem of reconciling the polarities in tension of the universality and particularity of divine manifestation is a major concern of his thought.

Tillich contends for the presence of a "long line of Christian universalism" which affirms "revelatory experiences" in the world religions, a line that he sees as starting in the prophets and Jesus, carried on by the church fathers, interrupted for centuries and taken up again in the Renaissance and the Enlightenment.[29] This principle of universalism, however, has been under continual attack by its opposite, the principle of particularity with the claim to exclusive validity, with the result of the unsettled and contradictory attitude of contemporary Christianity toward the world religions.[30] Tillich accepts the particularity of the Christ-event as ultimately significant but normative, that is, as constitutive of the ultimate criterion but not exclusive. He sees the event as a personal life that shows no break in Jesus' relation to God and "no claim for himself in his particularity. What is particular in him is that he crucified the particular in himself for the sake of the universal." Tillich considers this fact as constituting liberation of "his image" from bondage to a particular religion and to what people call the religious sphere. The principle of love in the Christ embraces the cosmos, including both the religious and the secular spheres. The Christ thus constitutes an image that is particular yet free from bondage to particularity, religious yet free from bondage to religion; with this image are given the criteria by which Christianity must judge itself and other religions. Christianity is a bearer of the religious answer as long as it breaks through its own particularity.[31] Justice as a universal principle transcends every particular religion and makes the exclusiveness of any particular religion conditional. This principle of conditional exclusiveness is Tillich's guide in the inquiry.[32]

Tillich thus applies to the problem of the understanding of the religions the theme of prophetic criticism, or the "Protestant Principle," which appears in his earlier writings. He is deeply serious about the importance of mutual judging as opening the way for proper encounter of the religions and fair evaluation. He sees the foundation of Christianity in the Christ-event as giving freedom to accept critical judgment and presumably correction from the religions.[33] Tillich does not discuss the problem that emerges if men and women of the religions refuse to accept his criterion of judgment, and apparently their judgment could be accepted by Christians only if it accorded with the Christians' criterion. He affirms, however, that openness to such judgment was the glory of Christianity for centuries. The church learned anew from polytheism to discern concrete manifestations of the divine in the world. It learned from Persian dualism through Gnostic groups something of the seriousness of the problem of evil, the importance of mystical and transpersonal aspects of religion from ancient and modern mysticism. For almost two hundred years Christianity, by way of liberal humanism, has indirectly received Jewish judgment and transformed the critique into self-judgment. At present it could learn from Islam with regard to the solution of the racial problem and wisdom in dealing with primitive peoples.[34]

Tillich sees Judaism, Christianity, and Islam as all having the prophetic quest for justice as their essence. Neither Hinduism nor Buddhism gives "decisive motives for social transformation."[35] Tillich contrasts the respective *telos* of Christianity and Buddhism in the kingdom of God and Nirvana. The former is a "social, political and personalistic symbol," the latter ontological. Their principles are respectively "participation" and "identity," the first leading to the ethical perspective of love, the second to that of compassion.[36] Both faiths are based on a negative value of phenomenal existence, but in Christianity this is directed against the world in its existence, not in its essence. In Buddhism the very existence of the world is the result of an ontological Fall into finitude, a statement, we shall see, inadequately descriptive of the ethical ethos of early Buddhism.[37] Tillich also contrasts the symbolization of the Ultimate in Christianity in personal categories with the symbolization in Buddhism in transpersonal terms; he notes the differing explanations of the cause of the problem-situation of empirical human beings. He contends that the basic intent of Buddhism is not transformation of reality but salvation from reality, that there is no belief in the new in history, and no impulse for transforming society can be derived from the principle of Nirvana.[38] Tillich's views here, too, require considerable correction.

Tillich, however, suggests that the nature of the Holy, which both religions authentically experience, has forced each of those religions subsequently to include elements that initially predominated in the other. He understands the emergence of personalistic faith in the Mahayana on the basis of this principle, as also the transpersonal concept of God as *esse ipsum* in classical Christian theological formulation. Human experience of the Holy alternates between emphasis upon the Holy now as "is" (being) and now as "ought to be," and none of the elements of the Holy is ever completely lacking in any genuine religious experience.[39] Tillich wishes to tell us that the potential for the whole lies in every great religion and that the Logos of God has in fact worked to lead certain individuals and religious movements to positions of understanding significantly different from the original emphases of a particular faith. Men and women in the religions may also play a consciously contributory role in this process by the exercise of critical judgment working through dialogue. Tillich, therefore, asks for dialogue rather than conversion as the proper aim of communication among the religions.[40] Dialogue properly takes place in the context of the conviction that God has already accepted all persons.[41]

Tillich's last public lecture, given only ten days before his death, was entitled "The Significance of the History of Religions for the Systematic Theologian." It reveals how important this problem appeared to him in the latter part of his life, and he indicates therein the need for a "longer, more intensive period of interpenetration of systematic theological study and religious historical studies."[42] In this lecture Tillich affirms that revelatory experiences are universally human, given to persons wherever they live. But revelation is a particular kind of experience that always implies saving powers, and one can never separate revelation and salvation. Tillich's "first presupposition of thought" (affirmation of faith) is thus that God has left witnesses, that there are revealing and saving powers divinely provided in all religions.[43]

With reference to the specific problem of a theology of the history of religions, Tillich distinguishes between history of religions and history of salvation—they are not to be regarded as identical—and affirms that the history of salvation is something within the former, expressed in great symbolic movements, or *kairoi*.[44] He denotes his approach to the problem of identifying these *kairoi* as dynamic-typological. The universal religious basis he affirms to be the experience of the Holy within the finite. Over against this element there is need of two critical elements. One is the mystical, which with its thrust from the manifested manifold to the ultimate One constitutes a critical movement against the demonization or "utilization" of the sacramental. The other critical element is the ethical, or prophetic, which criticizes the demonic consequences of the sacramental insofar as the latter denies justice in the name of holiness. The unity of these three elements constitutes for Tillich the inner *telos*, or aim of the history of religions, and presumably constitutes both true religion and the criterion by which we may identify the *kairoi*. The term that he uses for this unity of elements is the "Religion of the Concrete Spirit," although he expresses hesitancy as to its aptness as a term.[45]

Tillich regards the thrust toward the manifestation of this "Religion of the Concrete Spirit" as a fight of God against religion within religion. He sees the whole history of religions as the scene of this fight of God, which "could become" the key to understanding the otherwise extremely chaotic, or at least seemingly chaotic, history of religions. Tillich does not hold to the concept of progressive development at work as a process inherent within history, but to the continuation of critical moments in history, of moments of *kairoi* wherein the "Religion of the Concrete Spirit" may be fragmentarily actualized here and there.[46]

Tillich speaks of another *telos*, or inner aim of the history of religions, which he calls *theonomy*, from *theos* (God) and *nomos* (law). He sees this end to be the pointing of the autonomous forces of knowledge, of esthetics, of law, and of morals beyond themselves to the ultimate meaning of life, to the Ultimate. Another dynamic struggle takes place in this context of the relation of the sacred to the secular between a heteronomous consecration of life, that is, life consecrated to the Ultimate as "Other," and an autonomous self-actualization of all the cultural functions. This theonomy appears as an element in the structure of the "Religion of the Concrete Spirit" but, apart from its full manifestation in Jesus the Christ, it appears historically only in fragments, never fully. Its fulfillment is only eschatological, beyond time in eternity.[47]

CONTRIBUTIONS OF INDIAN CHRISTIANS

The fact that the mind of Christians associated with the World Council of Churches had already shifted decidedly in the direction of the understanding of Paul Tillich is evidenced by the documents of New Delhi. These results of the Third Assembly of the World Council of Churches (WCC), which met in New Delhi, India, in 1961, affirm (as we noted in chapter 5) that before we speak to our fellow human beings ("our brother man") of Christ, Christ has already sought them.[48] The conviction is that the Holy Spirit leads persons to where Christ already is. The Holy Spirit is also seen as ceaselessly working among the whole of humanity, and Christian witness should refer to the whole activity of the triune God in the world. The report also speaks of the wisdom, love, and power that God has given to persons of other faiths and even of no faith. The assembly saw theological significance in the fact that other faiths are not being merely displaced but changed by their encounter with Christianity. "The story of God's dealing with Israel is the clue for our understanding of God's will for all nations and his present work among them." This is to say that God's work within Israel does not constitute the totality of divine work in the whole of human history but is a sign indicative to faith of the manner of God's dealing with all peoples and individuals and, presumably, this "manner of his dealing" could have used other instruments as well as Israel and its successors.[49]

It is especially appropriate to recall these statements from New Delhi as we begin to consider contributions from Indian Christian theologians. Indian Christians in general had long been particularly concerned with the problem of rightly interpreting the significance of the religions as a consequence partly of their position as a small minority group in India and partly of the trenchant criticisms of Christian missionary activity by Mohandas K. Gandhi, Sarvapalli Radhakrishnan, and other Hindus. David G. Moses was one of the first Indian Christians to write on this theme after World War II, and he gladly acknowledged the religious validity of reform movements and change within Hinduism as affirmed by Radhakrishnan. But he contended that this is also to imply that not all religions are equally true, as educated Hindus often affirm, and that some historical expressions of the Divine may contain more truth about God than others. Moses criticized in part the position of William E. Hocking, but he felt that "it does not fit the facts of the case" to describe, with Kraemer, the relation between the religions as one of utter discontinuity.[50]

An important study was published in 1956 by the Gurukul Theological Research Group of the Tamilnad Christian Council entitled *A Christian Theological Approach to Hinduism*. This work consists of a number of studies in the theology of three noted Indian Christians, Aiyadurai Jesudasen Appasamy, Vengal Chakkarai, and Pandipeddi Chenchiah.

Appasamy (1891–?), best known in the West for his works on Sadhu Sundar Singh, has as the basis of his theology the conviction that the eternal Spirit is constantly kindling the hearts of all human beings, that our life of oneness with God is possible because God is already in us. He feels that the Christian church has much to learn from the Hindu devotional tradition of *bhakti* with reference to its own practice of meditation and prayer, and the chief aim of his theology is to relate Christianity to Indian mysticism, or even to achieve a synthesis of the two. The writers of the critique frequently point out the dangers that they see inherent in Appasamy's position, but he is a clear example of an Indian Christian who recognizes religious authenticity in an important element of the Hindu tradition.[51]

Chakkarai (1880–1958) was a layman, an attorney, not a professional theologian; but as a Christian convert from Hinduism, of great learning, and one of the founders of the movement called Christa Samaj, he made important contributions to the theological thought of India. He is deeply convinced that God has spoken not only to ancient Israel but also to other peoples. He discerns in the religious past of India a "long stream of prophetic consciousness from the days of the Rig Veda down to Kabir, Nanak, Chaitanya and Keshub Chunder Sen. These were sent by God as witnesses of the Light." He concludes that "the religious genius of India must form the background of Indian Christianity just as the religious past and heritage of Israel from Abraham to John the Baptizer formed the precondition of Christ and His *avatar*."[52] Chakkarai, however, does not hold to the theory that Christianity is the fulfillment of Hinduism and has pointed out what he believes to be the limitations of the theory. He believes that the reason for the proclamation of the Christian gospel to the Hindu does not lie in "the alleged supremacy of Christianity over Hinduism, but in Christ Himself who reveals Himself to the preacher." When God calls a person, "what moves him is not that his old country is bad but that he has to obey the heavenly invitation."[53]

For Chakkarai, however, Jesus is *the Avatar*, absolutely unique, and in spite of his use of a large number of terms borrowed from Indian philosophy and Hindu religious literature, he believes the Bible to be "the final authority and the store house for our thinking." His theology is thoroughly Christocentric, but he sees the salvific work of God in Christ broadly, as present in the Hindu tradition as well as the Christian. Thus he writes: "The salvation of each, as understood by each, is by the grace of the Lord; the former by the grace of God without the historical Christ and the other by the grace of God in Christ."[54]

Chenchiah (1886–1959) was also a convert from Hinduism and an attorney; for a time he was chief judge of Pudukkottai. He contrasts the converts of an earlier day who hated Hindusm and gave themselves to what they supposed to be Christianity with the (proper) converts of his day. The latter regard Hinduism as their spiritual mother who has nurtured them in a sense of spiritual values in the past. "He [the convert of Chenchiah's time] discovers the supreme value of Christ, not in spite of Hinduism but because Hinduism has taught him to discern spiritual greatness. For him, loyalty to Christ does not involve the surrender of a reverential attitude towards the Hindu heritage." Chenchiah believes that by committing himself to Jesus and his demands only, the Christian is emancipated from bondage to both the traditions of Hinduism and the traditions of Christianity. Like Chakkarai, Chenchiah stresses the central importance of the experience of "contact with Jesus" for faith and theology, and in this context he does not hesitate to look to Indian philosophy for guidance as well as to the Christian Scriptures. Chenchiah is more critical than either Chakkarai or Appasamy of the institutional church and believes Hinduism also to be a guide to a better understanding of Christ. He looks therefore for the interfusion in spirit of the religions, the coalescence of the "revelations of God, now bottled up in different religions."[55]

Chenchiah sees Jesus of Nazareth not as "the absolute-unapproachable, incomprehensible" but as God's coming "down to us to abide with us forever as a new cosmic energy." The message of Christianity is that the word has become flesh and God has become human; in this event the longing of Hinduism is fulfilled. He sees Jesus as "the manifestation of a new creative effort of God, in which the cosmic energy of *śakti* is the Holy Spirit, the new creation is Christ and the new life order, the Kingdom of God." Therefore India will not be afraid of claiming Jesus as belonging also to itself, because he is the head of humanity, the "Son of man." Because the Christian gospel is for Chenchiah witness to the fact that God in Jesus has made a new creation, has initiated a new creative order in him, the real uniqueness of Christianity consists in the fact of new creation and new birth. "Jesus is the first fruits of a new creation, Hinduism the final fruits of the old creation." For Chenchiah this concept is not to be understood as precisely equivalent to the fulfillment theory, that Christianity is the "Crown of Hinduism." He evidently understands, however, the reality of new life in Christ as constituting something radically new that is also integrally related to the old. The truth in the fulfillment theory is that in all religions there is a residue of unfulfilled desire and Jesus stands in relation to the residuary problems of humankind as a new creation stands toward the old. Both are expressive of the work of the one Creator.[56]

The opinions of these three men—Appasamy, Chakkarai, and Chenchiah—are taken by the writers of the critiques as constituting individual, though important, expressions of Indian Christian faith, and they do not hesitate to make pertinent criticisms from a somewhat more traditional Protestant theological point of view. They are concerned to emphasize that religious experience must be subjected to the test of the gospel and that this gospel is known through the apostolic witness in Scripture.[57] They affirm that the form, not the content, of the gospel should be "Indianized;" "it is the Spirit of the Church universal that should be expressed in Indian forms." Yet the conviction of the three theologians that the religious past of India is at significant points indicative of the work and spirit of the God whom they know in Jesus Christ is also representative of many other Indian Christians. The constitution of the Church of South India expresses a similar understanding in its affirmation that it desires to conserve "all that is of spiritual value in its Indian heritage" as it endeavors "to express under Indian conditions and in Indian forms the spirit, the thought and the life of the Church universal."[58]

Paul Devanandan (1901–62) was an ardent exponent of Christian dialogue with Hinduism until his death in 1962. He emphasized that Christian theology in the past had too often passed value judgment on the religions without knowing them, and he greatly regretted that Christians in India, especially in recent years, had neglected to cultivate scholarly acquaintance with the creed, cultus, and culture of Hinduism at its many levels. He was particularly concerned to encourage cooperation in service with men and women of other faiths.[59] Devanandan's address ("Called to Witness") at New Delhi in 1961 was one of the first open pleas for dialogue with persons of other faiths in such a world meeting. He called for a new respect for the truth claims of partners in dialogue and stated his conviction that in encounters of this kind authentic communication could occur. Devanandan believed such communication would in fact reveal Jesus as "the radical renewer" of all values that human beings cherish anywhere.[60]

In his writings that were published after New Delhi, Devanandan gave further specificity to his convictions. He saw the solidarity of all humanity as manifest in "a common universe of discourse based on spontaneous reactions to the totality of life," which is shared by all. Like M. M. Thomas, whom we shall consider later, Devanandan believed the cross and resurrection of Jesus Christ to have effected a "New Humanity," which is realized in the risen Christ and is the source of the potential reconciliation of Christianity and other religions. Thus the word of the cross and the resurrection is the word of reconciliation because God in Christ has destroyed the basis of enmity between them even as he abolished the wall of partition between Jew and Gentile.[61] We should note that both Devanandan and Thomas were in no small part motivated in the development of these theological positions by their concerns for nation-building in post-liberation India. They were able to give specific theological expression to the significance of the experiences of many Christians in India that they could in fact participate with Hindus, Muslims, Parsees, Jains, and others in building a new Indian society-nation. Such participation, they felt, was a natural and compelling consequence of their shared humanity from creation and of the power of the New Humanity that is being "shed abroad" through the Spirit of the Christ.

Another Indian Christian theologian of distinction who has written on this theme is *Vinjamuri E. Devadutt* (b. 1908). Devadutt was born in India of orthodox Brahman parents and grew up in that environment until he left home to attend high school in Burma. While in Burma he was converted to Christian faith. Because of his background in the highest caste of Hinduism and his desire to share his Christian faith with both Hindus and Muslims among his compatriots, he began in-depth studies in both Hinduism and Islam, with special emphasis upon Indian philosophy. He later went to the United States, where he held a number of distinguished academic posts, culminating at Colgate-Rochester Divinity School and the University of Rochester.

A key element of Devadutt's thought is to see not only the redemptive aspect of the work of Jesus Christ but also his role in representing both the divine creative energy and the meaning of the created order. This enables him, like the fathers of the early church, to perceive theologically the common humanity of all peoples, their common rootage in God and their common nearness to him (Acts 17:24–29). He affirms "the priceless worth of all men before God." Therefore it is only proper to say that "God's activity . . . has not been and is not confined to only one stream in history. If God is the God of history, he is the God of all history. . . . The Christian affirmation then is not that God has not acted outside the Hebrew-Christian stream of history but that wherever he has acted, he has acted as in Christ." Similarly, "wherever God revealed himself, he did so and still does so as in Christ."

Devadutt wants to affirm of Christian faith at once "a broad universalism and an uncompromising particularism." This is to take the Christ event as the particular expression of God's activity, both revelatory and salvific, which is "definitive, decisive and normative." But this "revelation of God and his purposes in Christ . . . is not delimiting." "God's revealing activity as learned in Christ" is accepted by Christian faith as of supreme significance and therefore normative, setting the criterion or standard by which all else in life may be evaluated. Yet even as Christians cleave to the Christ-event, they perceive that God's activity "is not confined to one period of history or to one section of the human race." Rather, it is possible to see "in all aspects of the history of peoples everywhere unmistakable signs of witness to Christ himself and the way the God of Christ acts freely."

This openness of mind and heart has enabled Devadutt to appreciate with gratitude and gladness the presence within both Hinduism and Buddhism of significant commonalities with Christianity in faith and practice. He notes the similarities in teaching of the grace of God as prior to all human effort or righteousness between Christianity and certain schools of both Hinduism and Buddhism. He reminds us of the insistence upon the limitations of the cognitive intellect made by the writers of the Hindu Upanishads, as by the Buddha. He points to the Hindu Vaishnavite focus upon *prapatti*, or unconditional surrender to God in faith, as having elements in common with Paul's teaching of justification by faith. And finally he stresses the need for Christians to be alert to the actually many evidences of the work of God in Christ among persons who are not Christian by name. He notes that "The common word on the lips of Hindus at the time of Mahatma Gandhi's death was not Karma but the Cross."[62]

A considerably better-known Indian theologian is Madathilparampil M. Thomas, usually cited as *M. M. Thomas* (b. 1916). Thomas, director emeritus of the Christian Institute for the Study of Religion and Society in Bangalore, India, has served the World Student Christian Federation, the East Asia Christian Conference (now the Christian Conference of Asia), and the World Council of Churches in various capacities. In particular, he was moderator of the Central Committee of the WCC from 1968 to 1975 and continued for some years as a member of the Central Committee. M. M. Thomas is a lay member of the Mar Thoma Church (reformed Syrian Orthodox) of South India, and some may object to his inclusion in this chapter on "Protestant" theologians. Actually, some Anglicans also object to this designation for themselves, but we hope that they, as well as Thomas, will not object to being included in a classification that in this case is more convenient than precisely designative.

Thomas has long been concerned for the relationship of Christian faith with the whole of life, in particular with the political and social dimensions of human existence. In one of his first books, *The Christian Response to the Asian Revolution* (1966), he summarizes much of the thought and feeling of Asian Christians as they participated in the post-World War II revolt of almost all Asians against various forms of imperialism and traditionalism. He argues forcefully for an open democracy suited to the needs of Asia and insists that "the Christian mission is of tremendous relevance to the Asian revolution." Like other Asian Christians, Thomas strongly affirms human solidarity in the common humanity "given through Christ in creation" to all human beings. The redemption given through Christ effects therefore a renewal of that common humanity which we all in a basic sense already share. Like Paul Devanandan, Thomas has a perception of the cosmic Christ who is Lord of the created universe and therefore present to reveal and to save as well as to control throughout the whole of human history and in every culture.[63]

Thomas's major work is *The Acknowledged Christ of the Indian Renaissance* (1969), which as the name suggests was written to give another facet to the theme of Panikkar's *The Hidden Christ of Hinduism*. The book is a massive study of the largely sympathetic understandings of Jesus Christ (less so of historic Christianity) by the leaders of various reform movements in modern Hinduism, including Rammohan Roy, Keshub Chunder Sen, Vivekananda, Radhakrishnan, and Mahatma Gandhi. He adds accounts of responses to the various positions taken from both Indian Christians and Western missionaries. In conclusion he gives his own theological position to undergird what he feels to be a proper response and at the same time shares his perceptions of the theme of our present study.

Thomas notes that Hindus of the reform movements as well as Indian Christians came to see the British presence in India and the contributions of British civilization, especially the British educational system introduced into India, as examples of divine providence. He then notes the later shift in thinking away from that of the early educational missionaries, such as the Scotsman Alexander Duff, who aimed at "the total displacement of Hindu culture and religion and their substitution by Western culture and religion." By the early decades of the twentieth century, educational missionaries like C. F. Andrews, the noted friend and biographer of Gandhi, and Arthur Mayhew had begun to advocate a policy of Christian assimilation. In particular, this meant that, especially, educated Indians should be helped not to discard or compartmentalize their indigenous traditions, but "to reinterpret them in the light of the scientific approach and values of Western culture." This last phrase represents of course an identification of Western culture with Christian faith, as indeed the quotations from both Duff and Andrews clearly reveal, which then became utterly impossible for thoughtful Western as well as Asian Christians after the two world wars of the twentieth century.[64]

Actually, in this book Thomas tends largely to leave his own theological position in the form of assumptions that are implicit in the views of the Hindus and Christians studied. Even in the final chapter where he says that he intends to make some of these assumptions more explicit, he usually does so by means of a quotation from another writer. For instance, one important element of his thought is well revealed in his quotation from the late Ceylonese Christian D. T. Niles, that "The work of the Spirit is often evident in people's lives before they confess 'Jesus as Lord.' " Thomas further agrees with Niles that this very fact makes the mission of the church to proclaim Jesus as Lord a pressing one. It appears to be the conviction of Thomas as well as of Niles that "only in Jesus is the fruit of the Spirit secure." This is to say that the whole range of ethical fruit that may be brought forth through the guidance and power of the Spirit of God—a relationship-process available to both Christians and others—finds a "security" (perhaps an ongoing, long-range consistency of performance?) through explicit faith in Jesus that it does not find elsewhere.[65]

Another quotation significant for Thomas's own position is one from B. H. Streeter that reveals much of the way Thomas views the larger work of God in the world. "The barrier which separates the Buddha from [the] Christ is due, in the last resort, more to the intellectual theories which he inherited than to disagreement in the finds of his own very original moral insight. When the Buddha was most himself, there he was most like Christ." Thomas suggests that this is in effect to say that "the same moral insights may find themselves expressed in diverse doctrines depending upon the different world-views they are clothed with." He seems to hold that this understanding points to the fact that the "ultimate truth of salvation in Christ" will take to itself, even while transforming them, a great variety of "inherited intellectual theories" and world-views.[66]

Thomas is one of the more cautious among contemporary Indian theologians, and he makes fewer comments with reference to the content of the Asian religious traditions. A primary concern of his, however, has been to check the not infrequent tendency of Christian orthodoxy to absolutize the traditions of "the creeds and the historical confessions and the teaching authority of the Church," although he recognizes the importance of their role as "safeguards against heresy in the reformulation of Christian faith." He would stress that "theology is always explication of the truth of the contemporary encounter between the Gospel and the situation." And for Thomas "the situation" includes the full reality of the religions of the world. He, too, would protest against concepts of the restriction of salvation to conscious assent to a doctrine about Jesus Christ and against any identification of salvation history with church history. He also would try to discern the revealing and saving work of the Christ outside the formal boundaries of the institutional church. This is possible for him because he believes that "God's saving act in Jesus Christ has objectively made a difference in the existential potentiality of all mankind." Therefore the Christian mission must be carried on, if it is to be carried on wisely and sensitively, in the context of ongoing spiritual discernment of this work of the Christ and of the ferment of the kingdom of God in all human histories.[67] We may properly summarize Thomas's thought on the theme of the present study by identifying the conclusions of his later book *Man and the Universe of Faiths*. His choice of this title, purposefully related to and yet contrasted with John Hicks's *God and the Universe of Faiths*, was dictated by his conviction that our "common humanity and the self-transcendence within it, more especially the common response to the problems of humanisation of existence in the modern world, rather than any common religiosity, or common sense of the Divine, is the most fruitful point of entry for a meeting of faiths at spiritual depth in our time." Thomas's own stance of faith is also revealed in his criticism of Raymond Panikkar as "too preoccupied with religiosity to recognize the Christian significance of the 'new anthropology' in the meeting of religions."

Thomas is hardly a Barthian in the strict sense of the term, but he prefers to begin his approach with what he sees as a specific contribution of dialectical theology to contemporary Christian thought. This is the theological relativization of all religions, including the Christian, "in the name of the Grace of God in Jesus Christ." A key element of Thomas's theological understanding is his use of the concept of "the New Humanity of Christ." He sees the risen Christ as working throughout all the world in new modes since the time of the Christ-event, working with the power of his divine humanity, to create a New Humanity. He believes that it is possible for all human beings to be "caught up in the New Humanity of Christ through implicit or explicit faith" and thereby, as one consequence, to be "released from the absolute claims of religions or quasi-religions."

Drawing upon both the Indian Protestant Paul Devanandan and the Dutch Roman Catholic Edward Schillebeeckx, Thomas suggests that "the New Humanity in Christ," as a divine process at work within history, may serve as the source of the reconciliation of Christianity and other religions and of "the formation of Christ in other religions." This, then, is Thomas's key point. "If Jesus Christ transcends the Christian religion, as its judge and redeemer, it opens up the possibility of Christ reforming all religions and in-forming Himself in them." Thomas in fact sees all the religious traditions of the world to be "in various stages of renaissance and reformation." In one sense this is a process to which the risen Christ contributes apart from the efforts of the Christian community. In another sense it is a process to which Christians may distinctly contribute and thereby renew "the indigenous traditions themselves to become the vehicle of Christ and His divine humanity." This is the larger framework within which Thomas sees Christ as being formed in all human beings and the church as taking shape in the form of a larger fellowship in Christ. This vision calls for the transformation of all religions and ideologies, including atheism, but it sees the conversion of men and women to "Jesus as the Christ of God" as they remain "in integral relation" with their traditional religions and ideologies, "as it were, en route."[68]

A name that in the 1970s came to receive wide public recognition as representative of Indian Christian theology is that of *Stanley J. Samartha* (b. 1920) of the Church of South India. After a distinguished career in India, he became in August 1968 director of the World Council of Churches Programme on Dialogue with People of Living Faiths and Ideologies. One of his major services has been to arrange a number of important consultations or dialogues between representatives of the WCC and those of other traditions and to edit the publication of the major addresses and statements of the conferences. Samartha, however, has also written articles of his own for these volumes and in the process has made significant contributions to an emerging ecumenical theology of the religions of humankind. Samartha is distinctly representative of the Indian Christian tradition and at the same time an articulate exponent of this wider ecumenical mode of understanding the relationship of Christian faith to the other faiths and ideologies of humankind. The works that he has edited are as a whole also of great significance as expressions of the thought of others, many of whom we discuss in more detail in this book.[69]

At the outset one must say that in certain articles it is not always easy to identify with precision Samartha's personal thought as distinguished from the thought and language of those whose contributions it is his responsibility to edit and/or evaluate. By focusing upon those articles of his that aim more at interpretation than summarization we can, however, give a fairly adequate account of his own theological position. Like many other Christians of this generation, in both East and West, Samartha perceives "converging historical processes of men of all faiths" and believes that it is a vital aspect of the role of the Christian church to be a fully conscious participant therein, "in the name of Christ." This participation will involve a glad acceptance of our total human "inter-dependence and inter-involvement," because "God has not left himself without witness in the history of all mankind" and "no human formulations of revelation can claim absolute validity over against others." Such understanding leads Samartha to ask, fully conscious that he is departing from the narrower interpretations of the *Heilsgeschichte* theology popular on the European continent a generation ago: "Are Christians alone to be described as 'the people of God' in India? Are men of other living faiths outside the love and grace of God except through the Christian corridor?" Samartha's own negative answer to these questions impels him to call for a new conception of the Christian church and a fresh understanding of Christian mission.[70]

For Samartha dialogue with men and women of other faiths is a contemporary imperative of Christian faith. "It is Christology not 'comparative religion' that is the basis of our concern. Our primary interest is not in 'interreligious conferences'; it is to be with Christ in his continuing work among men of all faiths and ideologies. Christ draws us out of our isolation into closer relationship with all men. In his name people have gone to the ends of the earth as humble participants in his continuing redeeming activity in history." Samartha also speaks of "the continuing work of the Holy Spirit in judgment, in mercy and in new creation." But this divine activity, which for Christians can never be separated from faith in Jesus Christ, is not intended to limit the Christian goal to the building of Christian communities. Obedience to their Lord in this day requires that Christians join with others to cut across old religious boundaries and reach out with persons of other faiths "to form new communities of greater freedom and love." Indeed, "Christians must at all times be actively involved in building up a truly universal community of freedom and love."[71] Like other Indian Christians in the early post-World War II years, Samartha wrote out of a background of concern for nation-building in India. But as his thought came to maturation in the 1970s, it is clear that his concern for Christian participation in the building of wider communities had come to have a much wider frame of reference.

In introducing the papers on "Living Faiths and Ultimate Goals," which were in part a consequence of the Bangkok Conference (1973) of the WCC Commission on World Mission and Evangelism, Samartha identifies certain guiding principles of his own faith and theology. The theme of Bangkok was "Salvation Today," and Samartha gives us his own perception of the context of discussion with his statement that "all classical conceptions of religious salvation are today being seriously challenged by revolutionary change." But for Samartha this fact does not mean that Christians should abandon "commitment to the Truth as it has become known to us. It is, rather, gratefully to acknowledge that the fulness of Truth is always wider and deeper than our present apprehensions of it and that the Spirit is at work, in ways such that we do not know where He comes from nor where He is going, to guide us into all the Truth."[72]

Samartha gave further expression to his developing understanding at the Theological Consultation on Dialogue in Community held at Chiang Mai, Thailand, in April 1977 under the auspices of the Central Committee of the WCC. Samartha's thought, we may note, tends to reflect developments in the WCC itself, but these developments can also be said to be at least in part the result of his own leadership. In the opening address he identified the primary issue for the participants by asking the question that was both his own and theirs, namely: How can Christians living and working together with their neighbors, with concern both to serve and to witness, be "a committed fellowship in Jesus Christ and an open community at the same time"? This is to ask for "a fresh theological framework that can hold together the universality of God's love for all humanity and the particularity of his revelation in Jesus Christ."

Samartha believes that there is an urgency compelling Christians to move forth into larger communities of relationship, indeed, to seek community with the larger family of humanity, without waiting "until all doubts are removed and every question answered." "Common human concerns for justice, peace and the survival of humanity" are central elements of the ethos of the late twentieth century and as cultural values of previously separate traditions are increasingly being shared across the world, persons of different backgrounds are more and more willing, Samartha stresses, to transcend narrower religious and ideological loyalties in their quest for new modes of cooperation and for new forms of community to effect such cooperation. Ultimately, he avers, "our loyalty is not to the forms of our particular communities nor to our particular formulations of truth, but to God himself." Samartha is not unaware of the dangers of "syncretism" within developments of this kind, specifically the danger of a loss of specificity and identity, without which all human beings are unable to cope with the complexities of human experience. As we have seen, Samartha strongly insists upon the need for continuance of historic particularities and identities as the sine qua non of both dialogue and wider community. But he is convinced that the interiority of true Christian faith compels us to brave the dangers. Otherwise, "the syncretistic wolf could be kept at bay outside the gate (of a ghetto living in stifled isolation) but the Christian sheep within could be sadly under-nourished."[73]

Samartha later wrote an interpretation of the Chiang Mai Consultation, which in substantial measure also gives us a summation of his own thought. He identifies certain key points in the statement adopted by the conference, which in his treatment give us insight into both Chiang Mai and himself. The first point of emphasis is that dialogue as an indispensable element of human community must first begin—when perceived from the standpoint of Christian responsibility—*within* the community of Christian faith. Here there is yet much to be done, not only in the quest for unity in the classic sense, but even more in building the "relationships expressing mutual care and mutual understanding," which are vital essentials of any fellowship that would meet the existential needs of the present time. Only out of such heightening of the quality of human relationships, both interiorly and in external expression, can authentic Christian community emerge, and apart from such a base it is only "shallow sentimentalism" to work for a "wider community of peace and justice."[74]

Samartha, however, would have the Christian community or communities move toward a wider range of relationships even as they work for improvement of quality of life and action within their own. He agrees with the statement of the conference that dialogue is specifically one of the ways in which Jesus Christ can be confessed today.

A second point of emphasis of Chiang Mai, and of Samartha, is that of a vision of a worldwide community of communities in which the Christian community within the human community has both a common heritage with all and yet a distinct message to share. There is no way to resolve the tension inherent in this situation, and also no need—at the present "time" of human history. Within this tension "we discover the character of the Christian Church as a sign . . . of God's promise of a restored human community in Christ" and at the same time perceive the possibilities of Christian contribution to the realization of this vision without "any trace of condescension towards our fellow human beings."

A third point is the contribution of the statement toward a "more co-ordinated theological reflection on the inter-relationship between the search for intra-Christian unity, the Christianly perceived call to mission and evangelism and the invitation to dialogue which the Lord himself appears to be issuing." The specificity of being disciples of Jesus Christ is not now or in the future to be lost, the statement avers, and yet the participants specifically refuse to limit the Christ "to the dimensions of our human understanding." Samartha notes that it was particularly helpful for sharpening the focus in perception of this essentially wholesome tension to have as participants at Chiang Mai persons who were "deeply committed to faith and order and world mission and evangelism." In a sense their presence reflected the concerns in important segments of the constituency of the World Council of Churches, which came to be expressed with new vigor from the time of the Nairobi Assembly of 1975, that this emphasis continue to be a significant part of the life and theology of the member churches. Yet the wider perspectives that had been developing for decades were by no means to be put aside. They had become a part of the heritage of almost all, and the problem was how to effect some measure of balance in the tension, in both understanding and activity.

Samartha sees Chiang Mai itself as providing a theological framework for ongoing wise utilization of these challenges. He emphasizes the need for discussion of questions not merely in theory but in the context of perception of the larger picture, "in terms of what God may be doing in the lives of hun-

dreds of millions of men and women who live in and seek community together with Christians, but along different ways." Like other Indian Christians, Samartha will not let us forget the fact that authentic Christian
theology cannot be done apart from this larger perception of the presence and
work of God in the world. The Chiang Mai Consultation gives focus to this
truth by its call to renewed attention to the doctrine of creation and the comprehensive, inclusive implications of this doctrine. Considerations of the nature and activity of God as of the work of the Holy Spirit "must take place
with this comprehensive reference."

Christians will see the doctrine of creation as particularly illuminated by
their faith-understanding of "God as one Holy Trinity and by the resurrection and glorification of Christ." They will not, however, let the precious
particularities of their own faith keep them from dialogue with persons of
other faiths who also have their own particularities of esteemed value and yet
share with Christians participation in the creation of the God of all and in
comparable measure also in his divine providence. Samartha reminds us that
authentic dialogue does not lead to a "reduction of living faiths and ideologies to a lowest common denominator." To the contrary, the continued presence of differing particularities may lead all to a "quest for that of spirit and
life which is only found at those deepest levels of human experience [which
are] variously symbolized and conceptualized in different faiths." This is not
to say that all particularities of faith are of only superficial or transient significance but that commonalities and modes of relationship may emerge which
are beyond our present perceptions. It seems incumbent upon all Christians
who believe in "God the Father Almighty, Maker of heaven and earth" ear-
nestly to seek for all possible commonalities with the whole of God's creation.[75]

CHRISTIAN PRESENCE: THE ANGLICAN TRADITION

We have already noted the role of the Broad-Church movement in
nineteenth-century Anglicanism. We have seen the same spirit expressed in
men like Temple Gairdner (1873–1928) of Cairo in the early part of the twentieth century. The Anglican contribution to the Jerusalem Conference of the
International Missionary Council in 1928 in the person of William Temple
(1881–1944) was in the same tradition. After World War II this tradition
came to a singularly significant focus in the men who became in succession
the general secretary of the Church Missionary Society (CMS), namely, M.
A. C. Warren (1904–77), John V. Taylor (b. 1914), and Simon Barrington-
Ward (b. 1930). The CMS is generally regarded as an agency of the Broad-
Church (now more often called Low-Church), or evangelical (a term not to be
understood in the contemporary American sense of conservative evangelical), wing of the Church of England.

Warren was educated at Cambridge and served both as a missionary in
northern Nigeria and in parish work in England. As general secretary of the

Church Missionary Society from 1942 to 1963 he became one of the most influential missionary statesmen and seminal theological thinkers of his time. As editor of the four- to eight-page monthly *CMS News-Letter*, he reached an astonishing number of Christian workers in all parts of the world and contributed as much if not more than any other single Protestant theologian-missiologist to the emergence of the postwar change in Christian views of the other religions of the world. His successors have followed in essentially the same tradition of thought and spirit.

Both Warren and Taylor wrote books as well as their theologically sophisticated and well-informed news-letter, and we shall briefly take note of these later. Of particular significance, however, for the larger activity of which these men were leaders was the series of "Christian Presence amid. . . ." volumes. Following the word "amid" in each case was the name of another religion, for example, "Buddhism" or "Islam." Thus George Appleton wrote "Christian Presence amid Buddhism" with the specific title *On the Eightfold Path*, and Kenneth Cragg wrote "Christian Presence amid Islam" with the title *Sandals at the Mosque*. Max Warren was the editor of the series, and John Taylor wrote *The Primal Vision* as the "Christian Presence amid African Religion" volume in the series. The writers of these volumes were, almost without exception, first-rate specialists in their various fields, as well as one in sharing the general perspectives of the series.

The term "Christian presence" as indicative of an approach or mode of relationship to the adherents of other religious traditions seems to have come from the methodology of the innovative Roman Catholic worker-priests in France after World War II. In attempting to find new ways of relating to the French workers and their families who had become alienated from the church and often from Christian faith, these priests came to feel that a quiet presence among the workers, sharing as much as possible their labor and their life-style, had to precede, if not to displace, traditional methods of preaching and teaching.

Implicit in this approach to persons of other religious backgrounds is a certain restraint or reserve as contrasted with a quick or obtrusive witness to Christian faith. It may not carry a particular theological interpretation of other religions but, as we shall see, most of the leaders in this activity have come to espouse definite, and usually similar, theological interpretations. Persons acquainted with the Anglican tradition will recognize in the activity something of the reasonableness, the feel for the middle way, and the generally low-keyed approach characteristic of the tradition—and of the English upper classes.

Basic to the approach is the sense that the way to start in interhuman relationships is simply to be there, quietly appreciative of the commonalities of human being and human experience. Basic also is intent to take with full seriousness the ancient Christian emphasis upon the theological order of creation whereby one may recognize and acknowledge the full theological authenticity of the personal beings of others and the fact of the presence of the God of all in their personal histories and in their corporate traditions. This understanding makes possible an openness to others, a readiness to respect and even revere other religious faiths as well as persons, and therefore a willingness to learn as well as to teach. Christians are, of course, not expected to remain forever silent but to be ready to witness to their faith in this context. But the context is properly to be that of openness to the extent of expecting even to learn new things of God from these others.[76]

Central to the faith stance of this Christian-presence activity is the theological inclusiveness expressed by John V. Taylor in an issue of the *CMS News-Letter*. Taylor had studied at both Oxford and Cambridge and after some years of parish work in England served as a CMS missionary in Uganda. He succeeded Warren as general secretary in 1963 and remained in that position until he became bishop of Durham in 1975. Taylor emphasizes that however we may go on to formulate the details of Christology in Christian faith, the understanding that is basic to both the New Testament and the theology of the early church is that Jesus Christ must be considered as representative of the Creator Spirit who has been present and at work in all ages "at the heart of all being and in every human soul."[77] On another occasion Taylor wrote that "God is the Lord of every nation's history and he has shown his saving arm in the exodus of more than one people." This was in the context of his quoting Amos 9:7 and insisting that the covenant with Israel is not the only one in the Old Testament. "The Covenant with Noah, embracing all the sons of men, and, indeed, all creation, reverberates through the later words of prophets and psalmists." He reminded his readers that the early exponent of Logos theology, Justin Martyr, had written, "We have been taught that Christ is the firstborn of God, and we have declared above that he is the Word of whom every race of men were partakers; and those who lived according to the Logos are Christians, even though they have been thought atheists."

Taylor and others in this movement are not naïve; they by no means affirm uncritically all that is or has been in human religious experience and practice. If they can acknowledge that the Creator Spirit has been "at work anonymously, in every redeeming event and action through which the basic humanness of men is being saved and brought to its full stature," this is not to say that the whole history of human experience that we call religious has been equally "redeeming." Taylor sees Jesus of Nazareth as the fulfillment of Judaism in a way that was also a protest. This was, for example, a protest in the name of freedom under God "to act freely with each fresh situation," a protest against the burden of divinely prescribed legislation having become the foundation-stone of the tradition. Only in this way of combined protest and affirmation will Christ fulfill also "Hinduism and Islam and Buddhism and all the secular hopes of man."

Taylor allows that "the slow formation of a man's personal being may be through a history of Hinduism and in the terms of Hinduism." It may also be in the context of Christian culture or "according to the best values of scientific humanism." But the divine redeeming element, or that which we may

call salvation (which also has degrees or stages of development in its operation, he avers), in fact "comes by revolution, not evolution." This is as a
divine "irruption, a revolution, a new nature," which is as much a protest
against, as well as affirmation of, the old and the current.[78]

Writing on another occasion, Taylor expressed his conviction that if Christians are right in believing Jesus of Nazareth to be the incarnation of the word
that has been universally at work from the beginning, "the marks by which
we are to discern the Eternal Word in other faiths are wound-prints." He
meant by this pregnant phrase that the signs of the word's presence are "to be
discerned not so much in the orthodoxies of other faiths and ideologies, as in
the yeast of nonconformity and challenge which is always inherent in them.
He is the Source of that stream of revival which flows through all religions by
the grace of God. He is also to be found in the movements of history which
compel men of faith to break old moulds and think new thoughts. . . . The
creative Word is essentially the great disturber, speaking of life through
death." Taylor reminded his readers that the founders of religions were not
innovators so much as reformers, as, indeed, William Foxwell Albright had
insisted was true of the Hebrew prophets from the time of David on.[79]

Taylor insists that "the Church has never allowed the bold claim 'No salvation outside' to stand literally and unmodified." He himself is not one to
"believe that the mercy of God is ultimately limited to those who are within
the visible Church. We can leave the destiny of men in the hands of him who
was slain before the foundation of the world." He would see the imperative
to Christian mission not in panic over the eternal destiny of others but in the
conviction that through conscious allegiance to Jesus of Nazareth human
beings "may rise to their full stature as the adult sons of God, through attach-
ment to Him who was and is and ever shall be the complete Man because he is
the perfect Son."

Almost all of those who have written as representatives of the stance of
Christian presence are or have been missionaries and affirm the right and the
need for explicit verbal Christian witness at the proper time and place. But
they see this witness as requiring a specific context of heart and hand on the
part of the witnesser. This context should include "friendship, unassuming
and undemanding, offered to the other man." It would also include "humble
reverence that never desires to manipulate or possess or use the other." The
way of presence finally means compassion, a word that "sums up the listen-
ing, responsive, agonizing receptivity of the prophet and the poet." This is all
possible because "the God whom, all along, Africa has guessed at and
dreamed of, is One who is always and wholly present for every part of his
creation."[80]

We have space only for a few concluding observations under the present
rubric. The first is that the spirit of those who have tried to practice the way of
presence has enabled them to achieve new levels of sympathy and understanding in their treatment of specific religious traditions other than the
Judeo-Christian. Some of the volumes of the "Christian Presence amid . . ."

series are masterpieces of this kind. In addition to John F. Taylor's *The Primal Vision*, one may cite especially George Appleton's *On the Eightfold Path*, not only for its freshly appreciative approach to Buddhism but also for its openness to making the encounter a. means of deepening as well as broadening traditional perceptions of Christian faith. Kenneth Cragg's *Sandals at the Mosque* initiated a new level and a new era of Christian-Muslim dialogue with its extraordinarily knowledgeable as well as sympathetic perceptions of Islam.[81]

Perhaps the spirit of the entire movement could be summed up in a few words from the introduciton that M. A. C. Warren wrote for John V. Taylor's *The Primal Vision:*

> We remember that God has not left himself without witness in any nation at any time. When we approach the man of another faith than our own it will be in a spirit of expectancy to find how God has been speaking to him and what new understandings of the grace and love of God we may ourselves discover in this encounter.
>
> Our first task in approaching another people, another culture, another religion, is to take off our shoes, for the place we are approaching is holy. Else we may find ourselves treading on men's dreams. More serious still, we may forget that God was here before our arrival. We have, then, to ask what is the authentic religious content in the experience of the Muslim, the Hindu, the Buddhist, or whoever he may be. We may, if we have asked humbly and respectfully, still reach the conclusion that our brothers have started from a false premise and reached a faulty conclusion. But we must not arrive at our judgement from outside their religious situation. We have to try to sit where they sit, to enter sympathetically into the pains and griefs and joys of their history and see how those pains and griefs and joys have determined the premises of their argument. We have, in a word, to be "present" with them.[82]

SCHUBERT OGDEN

We turn to a number of writers—American, British, and East Asian—who have written specifically on the theme of the present study. Some of these are representative of what we may term a more liberal stance in the overall spectrum of Protestant theology. The first person in this category whom we shall consider is Schubert Ogden (b. 1928), a professor of theology at Perkins School of Theology, Southern Methodist University. He received his doctorate from the Divinity School of the University of Chicago and also taught there before going to Perkins.

Already in the early 1960s Schubert Ogden argued that "it is not only possible on Scriptural grounds, but in fact necessary to affirm that authentic human existence, or faith in Christ, can be realized apart from faith in Jesus or in the specific proclamation of the church."[83] He made this affirmation even as he insisted that in his understanding of Christian faith the event of Jesus of Nazareth is the "decisive manifestation of God's love" and "fulfills and corrects all other manifestations."[84] As a somewhat critical disciple of Rudolf Bultmann and perhaps less critical follower of the philosophical tradition of Alfred North Whitehead and Charles Hartshorne, Ogden took up the thesis advanced a century earlier by the Anglican theologian Frederick Denison Maurice, one of the leaders of Broad-Church Anglicanism of the time. This is that the event of Christ is to be understood more widely than the event of Jesus. The former is really "not one historical event alongside others, but rather the *eschatological* event, or *eternal* word of God's unconditioned love, which is the ground and end of all historical events whatever." Put in another way, "the word addressed to men *everywhere*, in all the events of their lives, is none other than the word spoken in Jesus and in the preaching and sacraments of the church."[85]

Ogden did not identify precisely the modes by which this word is addressed to all persons, although he affirmed that it "is everywhere spoken in the actual events of nature and history." At the same time he asserted that "from the standpoint of the word spoken in Jesus"—an assertion of the properly normative role of the event of Jesus, who is also the Christ—the "several attempts at self-understanding," which constitute the history of humankind's religions, may in fact reflect authentic answers to the question and yet be "fragmentary and inadequate—and even false." Ogden, however, held that there is an "original possibility of existence *coram deo*," which belongs to humankind as such. The God-human relationship that was actualized in Jesus is an *"eschatological* event" because it is "the essential reality of every human life." And Jesus re-presents *to us* the possibility of such a relationship.[86]

Ogden in his later writings has not significantly deviated from this qualifiedly Bultmannian existentialist position, but he has increasingly tried to ground his affirmations more in the biblical witness. Working from the Pauline thesis in the first three chapters of Romans, Ogden stresses an original revelation of God to humankind, God's original and universal self-disclosure. Every human being has an inextinguishable knowledge of God, "in the sense of the ultimate reality which is the final source and end of all things." It is basic to Christian faith, Ogden asserts, to affirm "that the whole of nature and history is . . . the beneficiary of God's love." Thus all persons constantly receive the original revelation, which is also the ever repeated free and unconditioned offer of God's love to persons, who are both free and responsible, to accept.[87] God in fact is at work to redeem *every history* among the multitude of histories in the total human experience.[88]

Employing what we may call a high anthropology, Ogden affirms that because a human being is *"logos* himself, he is able to grasp the *logos* of reality as such and to represent it through symbolic speech and action."[89] At other points, however, Ogden uses even stronger language to affirm the unique significance of the particular human life of Jesus of Nazareth as the "decisive re-presentation to all mankind" of the same promise and demand given in the Old Testament revelation and "attested by the whole of creation and man's conscience as well." The word spoken in Jesus Christ is not a "different word from that which always confronts men in their actual existence before God" but came and comes with unique clarity (Ogden's term is "transparently") and "with all the force of final revelation."[90] Jesus represents as a continuing event God's primal word to all humankind but with a decisiveness and precision ("not thus expressed elsewhere" seems to be the implicit if unstated meaning of Ogden's thought) that enable us to accept his word as normative.[91]

Ogden tends to consider as "plainly mythological" certain historic affirmations of Christian faith such as Jesus' resurrection from the dead, ascension into heaven, and virgin birth. He holds what he calls subjective immortality to be an open question, which (in 1966) he could not find sufficient reason to answer affirmatively. In speaking of the New Testament, especially the Pauline view of the cosmos as encompassing levels of reality and being that are different in spiritual and ethical quality, he writes, "We today no longer share such a mythological picture of ourselves and of the world, and there is something at once tragic and comic about theologians that try to pretend otherwise." This understanding is, one may say, a posture still to be found in sections of the academic community and is really an amalgam of post-Enlightenment philosophical reductionism and late nineteenth-century scientism.[92]

Ogden, nevertheless, has made a significant attempt from an existentially philosophical as well as, in part, a biblically based theological position to understand the uniqueness of the person and role of Jesus of Nazareth even as he completely rejects any exclusivist interpretations thereof. This he does without ascribing any "cosmic" significance to the work of Jesus the Christ, in the sense that the person and work of Jesus of Nazareth have made a "difference," a qualitative and structural change in the potentialities of the divine-human relationship, and thus in the cosmic situation of humankind. For Ogden, Jesus of Nazareth is worthy to be taken as normative, although presumably for those who know him not or do not accept him as normative there are other reliable or adequate norms by which the Christ, who is available to all, may be authentically discerned in his potentially manifold manifestations. As Ogden does not attempt to specify the nature of the relationship of Jesus of Nazareth to the universal Christ, except to say that Jesus *is* the Christ without further explanation, so he does not identify with specificity other manifestations of the Christ that could be religiously meaningful for persons for whom Jesus does not function as normative.

JOHN HICK

John Hick (b. 1922), longtime professor of theology in the University of Birmingham in England and subsequently teaching at Claremont Graduate

School of Religion in California, is one of the most lucid of contemporary expositors of the emerging understanding of the religions of humankind in Christian perspective. With both forthrightness and wealth of argument, he applies his understanding to the development of what he believes to be an appropriate Christology.

Like many others whom we have considered—Eastern Orthodox, Roman Catholic, and Protestant—Hick prefers not to conduct the discussion on the basis of a comparative evaluation of the major religions as historical movements. Specifically this means, for Hick, a rejection of any notion of Christianity, in the sense of a movement in human history, as absolute or superior to others. Hick emphasizes this point by the very title of the book that gives the fullest exposition of his thought on this theme, *God and the Universe of Faiths*. Calling for what he terms a Copernican revolution in theology, he states that the needed radical transformation in our conceptions "involves a shift from the dogma that Christianity is at the centre to the realisation that it is *God* who is at the centre, and that all the religions of mankind, including our own, serve and revolve around him."[93]

Hick is, of course, aware of the patristic support for this position and sees himself as advocating "an Irenaean type of theology" as contrasted with an Augustinian one. He stands with what he calls "the more open systems of Origen and of the Christian Platonists."[94] Sharing the strong patristic emphasis upon the theological order of divine creation, Hick draws the conclusion that "if God is the God of the whole world, we must presume that the whole religious life of mankind is part of a continuous and universal human relationship to him." Concretely this means that instead of thinking in terms of mutually exclusive systems, "we should see the religious life of mankind as a dynamic continuum within which certain major disturbances have from time to time set up new fields of force." Hick identifies these "disturbances" as "the great creative moments in human history from which the distinguishable religious traditions have stemmed. Theologically, such moments are intersections of divine grace, divine initiative, divine truth, with human faith, human response, human enlightenment. . . . Christianity, Islam, Judaism, Buddhism, Hinduism are among the resulting historical-cultural phenomena."[95]

This means, for Hick, that the several religious movements identified should not be viewed as essentially rivals. The basic reason is that their founders were the bearers of authentic divine revelation, of what can be perceived as communications from the same Source. Hick affirms that the great figures of religious creativity who began to emerge across the world around 800 B.C., in a veritable golden age (Karl Jaspers's "Axial Period") extending for about five hundred years, and became the initiators of various movements are the subjects of "a remarkable series of revelatory experiences." Somewhat strangely in terms of his own thought ("the ultimate divine reality—in our Christian terms, God—has always been pressing in upon the human spirit"), Hick holds that "the natural condition of man's religious life" before the appearance of these creative personages was "religion without revelation." Perhaps he means that before this Axial Period the nature of human evolution was such that the "divine pressure" could not properly be designated by the term "revelation" with its associations of cognitively intelligible communication. Nevertheless, Hick emphasizes in the strongest way the revelatory authenticity of these great figures, citing as examples first the early Hebrew prophets Amos, Hosea, and First Isaiah; then, in Persia, Zoroaster; in China, Lao-tsu and Confucius; in India the writers of the Upanishads, Gautama the Buddha, Mahāvīra the founder of Jainism, and later the author of the Bhagavad Gita. In Greece, Hick cites Pythagoras and, toward the end of the five-hundred-year period, Socrates and Plato. Like A. C. Bouquet, Hick sees this schema as properly meaningful only if the figure of Jesus of Nazareth is included as coming after a gap of over three hundred years, and then Muhammad after a longer gap.[96]

Like Paul Tillich, with whom he appears to find much in common, Hick concludes that the Christian theologian is now compelled "to include all forms of religious experience within his data, and all forms of religious ideas among the hypotheses to be considered." He further concludes, without wanting, as he says, to "water down" the essential Christian understanding of Jesus Christ, that " the divine presence in the life of Christ does not preclude an equally valid awareness of God in other religions." The theologically key phrase here is, of course, "equally valid." In the immediate context of this statement, Hick adds that "it may be that Christ is also present in these other religions, and their several awarenesses of God likewise present in Christianity."[97]

Hick seems to affirm by the last sentence his conviction that "equally valid" perceptions of God are possible in all human situations because God is *in potentia* equally present. As to the presence of Christ, however, it does not otherwise appear to be a part of his thought to regard the influence of Jesus of Nazareth, whom he frequently calls "the Christ," as directly operative from the spiritual realm in an ongoing way in human history. Hick does note the term "cosmic Christ" as one of the Christian names for "God acting savingly towards mankind," but he prefers to use the term "Logos" to denote what "we call God-acting-towards-mankind." And "the life of Jesus was one point at which the Logos—that is, God-in-relationship-to-man—has acted." Hick further insists that "under their various images and symbols men in different cultures and faiths may encounter the Logos and find salvation." And "we gladly acknowledge" that in fact Ultimate Reality has thus "affected human consciousness for its liberation or 'salvation' in various ways" within the life of humankind. Salvation he defines as the "creating of human animals into children of God," clearly laying emphasis upon the transformation of human character and quality of life. Hick's Christological understanding is given further specificity by the affirmation that "what we cannot say is that all who are saved are saved by Jesus of Nazareth." This is in effect to state that while the Logos savingly acted in Jesus of Nazareth, "we are not called upon nor are we entitled to make the negative assertion that the Logos has not acted and is not acting anywhere else in human life."[98]

Hick is not unaware of the need for discrimination in using this inclusive mode of thinking and qualifies his previously noted statement on validity by saying that "not . . . any and every conception of God or of the transcendent is valid."[99] He seems to see "the tremendous revelatory moments which lie at the basis of the great world faiths" as constituting valid criteria severally for the persons who accept and live by their respective faith-traditions; for these revelatory moments challenge "men in their state of 'natural religion,' with all its crudities and cruelities."[100]

The criterion-role played by the great revelatory moments is without doubt a fact of human history, and its theological validity for adherents of the various traditions can be acknowledged by Christians as natural and proper in the context of a patristically based Logos theology. The chief point of difference from the historic Logos theology in Hick's thought would be that he appears to see no abiding cosmic significance or, in particular, any direct, ongoing influence from a higher plane as a result of the union of Jesus of Nazareth and the Logos in a distinctive way.

Jesus as mediating the presence and claim of the transcendent God, as God's agent in the world, was, for Hick, apparently a matter of functioning in a role no different from that of the prophets of historic Israel. Hick does speak of the primitive Christian community as that "which had experienced Jesus raised beyond death into a life continuous with God's saving activity toward mankind."[101] Beyond this faith-event, however, there appears to be no distinctly discernible manifestation of Jesus in historical experience. And yet, Hick avers, in that life of Jesus of Nazareth Christian faith finds the divine agape to be uniquely manifest and at work.[102] Hick affirms that any moment of divine revelation has an "absolute" character, since it is God, the Ultimate Reality, who is being encountered. But "this experienced absoluteness need not entail exclusiveness." Jesus Christ is the Christian's image of God and, presumably, not an image necessary for human beings in other historical-cultural contexts as a condition that they may participate in authentic divine salvation. One of Hick's main theses is to reinterpret the traditional Christian doctrine of the unique incarnation of God in Jesus of Nazareth so as to allow full religious authenticity, that is, divine revelatory and salvific effect, in other "revelatory moments" and yet retain a unique and normative role for Jesus Christ in Christian faith. Whether Hick is able in this way to transcend religious relativism is not entirely clear.[103]

DON CUPITT

Don Cupitt (b. 1934), dean of Emmanuel College, Cambridge University, and university lecturer in divinity, enters the discussion with what he calls a "constructive proposal, which seeks to steer a midcourse between the pure religious relativism which says that every major religion is an equally valid way to God, and the absolutist language in which traditional Christian faith has so often been expressed." His argument is that Jesus' finality lies not in his person, ontologically considered, but in the content of what he proclaims and the way in which he bears witness to it. Cupitt rejects the use of the term "absolute" as inappropriate to the historical dimension, but asserts that "Jesus' life is a final paradigm of man's relation to God," that his "ethical teaching is final" and constitutes the ultimate moral value that "cannot be superseded." "And Jesus' spirituality is final," is a statement that Cupitt makes to indicate Jesus' relationship of both affirmation and transcendence of the total historical situation in which he was set. This was the situation of a particular time and place within the history of Israel in the context of a theological understanding of that locus as germane to the tradition.[104]

In order to describe Jesus' relationship to history as being at once in it and yet above it, Cupitt speaks of "the ever-present note of mocking irony in every recorded utterance of Jesus." He sees this irony, or "ironical spirituality," as the clue to a proper understanding of Jesus and as his way of evoking in others a sense of the presence of God. Cupitt holds that Jesus "forces upon us a critical and questing spirit of restless dissatisfaction with all mundane values, institutions and achievements, and a longing for that absolute good which we shall have to die to attain."[105]

A basic problem inherent in Cupitt's thought and procedure emerges in this second part of the last quotation. In a way similar to Kierkegaard and the early Barth, Cupitt seems to assume a radical ontological dichotomy between God and humankind, between history and transhistory. Thus he asserts that "the eternal God, and a historical man, are two beings of quite different ontological status. It is simply unintelligible to declare them identical."[106]

In an earlier essay on this theme, entitled "One Jesus, Many Christs," Cupitt had stressed the great variety of interpretations of Jesus as the Christ that have emerged both in the New Testament and in the subsequent history of the church. His own view, not essentially different from John Hick's, was that "Jesus was a signpost, not a destination. He pointed men to God and told them about the claims of God and the nearness of God . . . . It was always a mistake to make Jesus himself the direct object of worship." Cupitt wrote that he could refer to Jesus as the Christ "insofar as I respond to this summons [made by Jesus] and find in the gospels the pattern or shape of what it is to obey it." But with reference to other models of human worship and obedience, Cupitt seemed to acknowledge their potential validity quite on a par with that which emerges from the pattern of Jesus of Nazareth. Thus he wrote: "In the Christian tradition Jesus is the paradigm of faith, but that paradigm may be re-enacted in a great variety of ways, and we need not labour to reduce their number."[107]

As we have seen, Cupitt came to sharpen his concepts with an affirmation of the finality of Jesus that still differed from most traditional notions of incarnation. Thus he regards a certain reserve toward the entire situation of humankind-in-history as appropriate to the church because of the "seed of saving self-doubt'' that Jesus has planted within it. And therefore "Christianity must never be allowed to become a mere religion, a positive symbolic system built around the idea of the incarnation. For it is infinitely more than that. It is a religion and a critique of religion, a religion which speaks of God by negating itself, which affirms a man who teasingly denied himself."[108]

Cupitt is essentially one with the mainstream of contemporary biblical scholarship in affirming that the primary intent of Jesus was not to draw attention to himself but to point to the living God. We shall consider later certain exceptions to this thesis. Cupitt vitiates, at least in part, his claim to base his rejection of the possibility of divine incarnation upon scriptural grounds insofar as he makes use of his ontological presuppositions. It is an open question whether or not his view of a radical ontological discontinuity between God and human beings comports with the high anthropology found in at least parts of Scripture (Gen. 1:26–27; Ps. 8:5–8; 82:6; Jn. 10:34–35; Acts 17:28–29). What Cupitt is really about is to affirm a distinct finality in Jesus of Nazareth—"Jesus' life is a final paradigm of man's relation with God"—that avoids traditional Christian notions of either incarnation or exclusiveness. "The finality I attribute to Jesus is not in any sense exclusive."[109]

Once again, as in the case of John Hick, we are dealing with an understanding of Jesus of Nazareth as constituting in his historical life—whose main outlines, together with the teachings, are presumed to be knowable from the Gospels—a "final" model of human relationship with God. Cupitt seems to say that the finality of Jesus is indeed an objective fact of human history but is acknowledged as such normally only within the tradition of Christian faith. The objective facticity, however, of Jesus' finality disallows neither the historical possibility nor the religious authenticity under God of persons' accepting other religious personages or symbols as final. Again like John Hick, Cupitt appears to restrict the influence of Jesus of Nazareth to that which functions on the historical plane as a result of the documents that witness to his life. There is no word as to the abiding presence of Jesus as the Christ.[110]

JOHN A. T. ROBINSON

Another British witness is John A. T. Robinson (1919–83), who developed from a populizer of Bultmann and Bonhoeffer to become a creative theologian and biblical scholar in his own right. Robinson bases his Christology on the humanity of Jesus, preferring to focus on Jesus' unique manner of representation of God. This is to put aside questions of ontology, even that of whether or not Jesus bore "peerless human perfection." He writes also: "Yet Jesus is not exclusively the Christ, as if he personally and individually constituted the entire 'Christ-event.' "[111]

For Robinson the essence of Christian faith is the conviction that the representation of God that we see in Jesus of Nazareth continues. The entire Christ-event, including the crucifixion and resurrection of Jesus, is properly repeatable and repeated in the lives of those who now represent "the human face of God." Robinson uses the term "the provisionality of Christ" (in preference to "the finality of Christ") to indicate the open-endedness of the representation of God in Jesus. He sees this latter historical event as marking a new mode, a higher degree, in a process that reaches back to the "beginning" and will continue to the "end." "Jesus thereby represents a new mutation in the development of spirit, as evolution begins, not merely—as Julian Huxley has expressed it—to become conscious of itself, but through personal responsibility to incarnate God."[112]

Robinson has made his own a world-view of cosmic evolution that evidently owes much to both Teilhard de Chardin and process theology. In this context of thought he affirms that the fullness of the Christ is yet to be revealed in human history, and certainly we cannot say that Jesus as the Christ is exclusively the expression of God. This understanding enables Robinson to acknowledge authentic truth and meaning in the Buddha, Muhammad, and other great figures of human religious history. In language, however, that is not entirely clear as to what is his own view, Robinson appears to say that Jesus the Christ is the definitive revelation of God for the Christian, the manifestation of God in human terms as pure, unbounded love. Furthermore, it is of the nature of Christian faith to believe that "ultimately everything is summed up and included in him." Robinson states that one cannot say this last of any of the other great religious figures of human history. And yet as Christians we may "freely and gratefully learn" from them and, indeed, at points be corrected, clarified, completed in our faith and practice by their lives and teaching.[113]

Robinson states that Jesus the Christ is final for the Christian in a way that he will normally not be for the non-Christian. "For the latter the path home will be by another way." This is because the mystery of the Christ is not limited to Jesus; God has other true paths to salvation that God has made available to humankind. This of course leads to the conclusion that "Christianity as a religion is not the only true path to salvation." "The Christian sees in Jesus the clue to (though not the exclusive embodiment of) the Christ, who in turn is the clue to the nature of God as personal and the meaning of man's destiny *as love. The Christ is God with a human face.* Yet there are other faces of God and other aspects of reality."

The main thesis of Robinson, then, is to emphasize the manifestation of the Christ in Jesus of Nazareth as a model for a potentially ever wider manifestation in the whole of humankind. All of the aspects of the Christ-event in Jesus, including atonement, resurrection, ascension, and parousia, are properly to be considered "as present realities or possibilities in human experience," even though they were "new" realities cosmically and historically in Jesus. Robinson, however, quotes Teilhard approvingly that "the Incarnation is an act co-extensive with the duration of the world."[114]

Robinson therefore emphasizes the need "for discernment, for obedient sensitivity, more for prophecy than philosophy" in order to perceive the Christ in others in our own time. "Jesus is but the clue, the parable, the sign by whom it is possible to recognize the Christ in others," who may or may not bear the name of Christian, or even of religious person. Robinson, we may note, affirms with a clarity beyond any of the Protestant theologians whom we have yet considered the reality of the spiritual realm. He sees the fact of Christ "as a new corporate reality, at the level of spirit, around us and within—the Christosphere, the Christ-continuum, the divine field or milieu." But this Teilhardian language does not mean for Robinson any notion that the *kosmos* is already the *Corpus Christi*, for "in the world there is much un-Christlikeness." Hence the need for discernment of spirits. Robinson, however, would have us also see the embodiment of "the beyond," even if not perfect, in persons and lifestyles that we have traditionally tended not to recognize as conveyers of "the meaning of Christ," such as the "clown or harlequin, whose pathos and weakness and irony, as well as whose gaity and freedom, 'all begin to make a strange kind of sense again.' "[115]

It is also appropriate to note that Robinson seems to take the resurrection of Jesus as an event both historical and transhistorical more seriously than some others. In keeping with the generally greater openness of the British to the data of parapsychology, Robinson prefers to lay emphasis upon what he calls "the appearances" of Jesus to his disciples after his death. He regards them as belonging to "the realm of paranormal psychology, or extra-sensory perception" and as constituting materializations. He notes that the New Testament evidence requires that we sharply differentiate the resurrection from any form of resuscitation, as in the case of Jairus' daughter or Lazarus, where the person dies again. We, rather, have to do with the conviction in the disciples of "a vivifying presence," "a life-giving power, signalling a new world-order and the beginning of the End." Yet even here Robinson insists that this conviction that Jesus *lives* is possible for us now only as present experience joins with evidence from the past to substantiate it.[116]

Robinson gives us further clarification of the developments of his thought in his *Truth Is Two-Eyed*, written as a result of an extended lecture tour and study experience in India. The main thesis of this work is suggested by the provocative title, namely, that every culture, and also every religious tradition, has historically been limited in perspective and is therefore "one-eyed." But truth, Robinson contends, needs two eyes, that is, inclusive perspectives, to be perceived aright. He made good use of his stay in India to learn from Indian Christian thought as well as from Hindu and Buddhist insights to the end of deepening and enlarging his own Christian faith and, in particular, his understanding of Jesus Christ.

We do not have space for detailed consideration of this richly documented work but must confine ourselves to data related more directly to our own theme. Robinson believes that "reality is multi-polar, and its unicity comes not from a single fixed point but from its co-inherence at every level." This perspective enables him to clarify what has become a central element of his world-view: reality is supremely personal, in a more sophisticated way than to posit "God as a supernatural person, a separate personified Being." Robinson, while recognizing that Hindu philosophy, especially in its Vedantist expressions, has specific limitations on its own side, finds its perspectives helpful in working his way through to a world-view that he calls "panentheism." This is to affirm unicity "in the sense that everything and every centre of consciousness and energy is interdependent. Yet by the same token it is relational through and through, preserving rather than absorbing differentiation and freedom, multiplicity and movement. God, or *Brahman*, is neither a person outside the process as in theism nor is he identical with it as in pantheism."

Robinson recognizes that the language of paradox is necessary at points in order properly to express his thesis, but his concern is to affirm the "thouness" of everything, to see God as not precisely identical with all and yet as bearing ultimate responsibility for everything that happens. This is not to say that God is morally evil but precisely the opposite: God is love, "love which all along is taking up, changing, Christifying everything." This reality is the basic reality of God, which Robinson sees expressed in Jesus of Nazareth, supremely in his death and resurrection. This latter is a victory "of resurrection, of incorporation in which all others may also participate."[117]

Robinson gives us the depths and breadths of his thought in his Christology. First, he insists that the titular term "the Christ" is wider than Christianity. It is of course Jewish, but for Robinson the Christ figure represents "the broader notion of the 'visibility of the invisible' " and therefore stands for the ultimate reality or mystery of God made manifest or embodied in any or every history. This understanding allows for a multiplicity of such events, and yet Robinson insists that it is of the essence of Christian faith to see in the life, death, and resurrection of Jesus the Christ the clue to the whole process. At the same time he does not wish to see the Christ-event as an isolated, anomalous exception but prefers to view it as the "supreme exemplification" (Alfred North Whitehead's term), "the normative expression, of the relation between the Word [the Christ] and the world." For Robinson this is not merely intellective ideology. He is rightly critical of the overspiritualization or historical escapism found in certain characteristic elements of figures of the Hindu tradition, even in the Bhagavad Gita or in Sri Aurobindo. But he has learned sufficiently from the Indian tradition to be able to say that the prophetic focus, which is the glory of the Judeo-Christian tradition, needs equally the mystical, interior approach to reality "if it is not to become arrogant, narrow and unlovely."[118]

A further conclusion of this line of thought is that if we understand Jesus of Nazareth as "the normative expression of the relation between the Word and the world" we should employ key Christological terms of the New Testament, including the sonship of Jesus, the son of God, and so forth, as true but not exclusive statements. Such metaphorical language drawn from our experiences of human interrelationships is intended to indicate in Jesus "the supreme exemplification or focal point of what should be true of every son of God." This emphasis upon the vital importance of the appropriation and application aspect of Christian faith is an inescapable corollary of Robinson's *distinctive* understanding of the Christ as distinguished from an *exclusivist* understanding. His view can be called a contemporary exposition of the fulfillment theory, seeing Jesus the Christ, somewhat like J. N. Farquhar in earlier days, as the crown of all truth and goodness but not their sole expression. Thus Robinson writes, "The recognition that the light that enlightens every man found its focus and fulfillment in Jesus (John 1:1-18) in no way cancels but on the contrary crowns the revelation in and through the multiplicity of lights. The unique does not absorb or exclude the many."[119]

Robinson's major Christological chapter goes on to develop this theme with a rich combination of personal insights and scholarly data. He insists that Jesus claimed no exclusive powers for himself, and in place of the term "uniqueness" he prefers to follow Norman Pittenger in using the word "specialty" as more accurately denotive of Jesus as the Christ. The Gospels, he says, point to a special relationship of Jesus with God, which is intended also to serve as a paradigm of what all human beings are divinely intended to attain. Robinson is clearly more concerned with the obedience of faith than ontology. He sees it of "the very core of the New Testament message" to perceive Jesus as truly and fully human, that is, a human being as the Creator had designed him, "in unbroken fellowship with God." "The essential thing is that in this man, the indivisible divine reality becomes visible, surfaces, breaks through." "In utterly powerless humility he allows God to be everything." Robinson follows the Indian Christian Vengal Chakkarai in affirming that this "most ego-less person known in history" has become "therefore the most universal of all," a *kenosis* or self-emptying that "was achieved by the slow process of learning obedience" (cf. Heb. 5:8). This is admittedly not precisely the Christology of the Athanasian or Chalcedonian creeds, but Robinson is not trying to indulge in a theological put-down. It is supremely important to him to believe that God is decisively represented in Jesus of Nazareth, that in Jesus humanity is uniquely transparent to divinity, indeed to know that God is Christlike. For Robinson all roots in the fact that God is love, that God first loved us and continually manifests that love. Therefore Robinson can conclude, quoting William Sloane Coffin, "to believe that God is best defined by Christ is not to believe that God is confined to Christ." The truth of God is thus not confined even to the definition given "in the person, cross and resurrection of Jesus." But Robinson would "dare the conviction, always to be clarified, completed and corrected in dialogue, that it is this [definition] which offers the profoundest clue to all the rest." This is for him to affirm the vital importance of both the particular and the universal, the temporal and the universal in God's universe.[120]

JOHN B. COBB, JR.

John B. Cobb, Jr. (b. 1925), is one of the most creative and influential of contemporary American theologians, and his book *Christ in a Pluralistic Age* could be called the most significant Christological work to appear in the United States in the 1970s. It therefore deserves careful study and evaluation. Cobb is best known as a process theologian and belongs to the inner core of "the students of the students" of Alfred North Whitehead. This is a group of theologians, sometimes called the Chicago School, who have been striving to create a theological tradition significantly informed by the religious philosophy of Whitehead. The treatment here, however, will be largely confined to consideration of those aspects of Cobb's thought that relate primarily to issues of Christology and the relationship of Christianity to other religious traditions.

As the title of the book suggests, Cobb intends to take with the utmost seriousness the awareness of living in a religiously pluralistic world that has become an existential part of the consciousness of almost every person in the West and increasingly in every part of the world. He insists that Christians today can no longer view the other great Ways of humankind in a negative or condescending fashion. "It is impossible to dismiss the Zen master as a benighted pagan, and 'Buddha' must be recognized as rightly naming the reality which is for vast numbers of people supremely important." Pluralism in effect has now been recognized as reaching a level or degree that carries meaning for Christology itself.[121]

We shall consider subsequently the special meaning that Cobb assigns to the term "Christ," but in the context of consideration of the great contemporary fact of religious pluralism, he has some sharp things to say about a narrow-minded approach. He warns also against "an unqualified relativism," the notion that "all beliefs and attitudes are equally true or desirable." "But when Christ becomes a principle of closedness, exclusiveness, and limitation, he ceases to be what is most important for the Christian and the appropriate expression of the efficacy of Jesus. In short, what would then be called Christ is in fact the antichrist."[122]

This is in effect to say that the development of Christian theology and biblical studies in recent years has moved to the point that, in spite of the momentum of centuries of Western cultural arrogance and religious exclusiveness, such closed exclusiveness can be called radically unchristian. It also means a new understanding of certain aspects of church history, for, as Cobb says, "much that we have meant by Christ in the past, when we did not acknowledge pluralism, becomes destructive in our new situation."[123]

Cobb, however, differently from David L. Miller, would not have us understand pluralism as necessarily leading to new expressions of polytheism.[124] He wishes to retain the universal significance of Christ and does so by identifying Christ as the image of creative transformation, which latter term he uses to denote a process. Christ thus "can provide a unity within which the many centers of meaning and existence [in the religious history of humankind] can be appreciated and encouraged and through which openness to the other great Ways of mankind can lead to a deepening of Christian existence." "Christ is the Way that excludes no Ways."

The phrase "a deepening of Christian existence" identifies at least one of Cobb's personal as well as theological goals. He is aiming precisely at "creative transformation" of the quality of Christian faith and life, a constructive reformation of the church. In place of the older closed-minded exclusiveness, an openness to dialogue and learning from other religious traditions, above all from Buddhism, will lead, he believes, to our creative transformation as Christians both individually and corporately. Cobb states that "to become open to real otherness while remaining in one's own tradition provides an opportunity for the creative transformation of that tradition."[125] He notes that this is not a new experience for the Christian church. After an initial resistance, Christian theology in the first centuries of its activity opened itself to Greek philosophy and, "without ceasing to be Christian," was inwardly transformed by its interiorization of that contribution. Similarly, "today, after an initial struggle, Christian theology has opened itself to the traditions of Asia, and without ceasing to be Christian, it will be transformed." This transformation is made possible by a process of self-criticism that properly emerges as a result of the encounter of the Christian tradition with other religious traditions.[126]

Cobb cites certain concrete possibilities as to how such transformation may be effected. He thinks, for example, of the possibility of interiorization of images from other traditions, such as merging the image of the Logos with that of the cosmic force called Yin in Chinese Taoism and the image of the kingdom of God with that of the Yang.[127] He is intrigued by the traditional Buddhist rejection of substantialist concepts of the human self and finds therein suggestions for better Christian understanding of what actually constitutes the self of human beings, especially of what is a proper goal of selfhood in Christian faith.

Cobb has not fully understood, we should note, early Buddhist teaching on this theme, for he states that "Buddhism has negated the self and thus inhibited the development of strong, isolated selfhood."[128] It is true that Buddhism does not aim at any form of isolated selfhood, and certain historic expressions of Buddhism, within both the Theravada and Mahayana, seem to disallow any reality to the self, especially in a particularized mode. But the earliest recorded Buddhist teaching on the self does not negate the self. It refuses to identify the self with anything "substantial," that is, with any of the elements of the transitory stream of phenomenal existence. Its goal is, rather, the integrated self, the self-at-one, the self transformed from selfish self-centeredness by a self-transcending relationship with Dharma, which is seen as the transcendent "lovely." This mode of selfhood can no longer be described by the categories of phenomenal existence. Its abode is in the Deathless. One can say that the Buddha understood the self in this mode not in terms of static being but of activity charged with value. The human self becomes therefore more of an axiological than an ontological reality. Awareness does not depend upon substance, but by the nature of its relationship and thereby the transformation of its own quality it participates as in a deathless reality. This condition would imply continuity of consciousness, to use modern Western terminology, but without totally separate individualization.[129]

Nevertheless, Cobb has correctly perceived the basic ethos of the Buddhist teaching on the self. He rightly recognizes that there is much to be learned therefrom to correct certain tendencies in the Western tradition, some of which we could call Promethean or titanic. Thus he affirms that "the Christian goal is to go beyond fully developed personal individualization. It is an expansion of the self to include others."[130]

Cobb proposes as a significant challenge to the entire Christian community that "through inward encounter with Buddhism, Christian existence may transcend its individualism toward a community of perfect love." He makes this proposal in the context of discussion of the thought of Paolo Soleri and Teilhard de Chardin with regard to the future of humankind. Both of these men contribute, for Cobb, particularly significant concepts for the concrete application of his own theological insights. But for the appropriation of these concepts by the Christian community, Cobb sees that the latter must transcend its centuries-long western European cultural heritage of both closed-minded exclusiveness and a limited sense of the self. Cobb seems to feel that apart from this "creative transformation," the kind of community active in love, which he envisages as truly Christian, can hardly be expected to emerge. For this transformation Christians need Buddhist help, Cobb believes, and Buddhists need Christian help. Cobb anticipates, we note, an internal development in Buddhism as well as in Christianity. He looks for a new "Buddhist-Christian existence" in which we may expect a "transcendence of separating individuality in a fuller community with other people and with all things."[131]

Cobb's Ethical Vision

Cobb insists that universality is integral to Christian faith but that this universality is not to be dissociated from the historical particularity of Christian origins. The ongoing community of Christian faith can "accept the historical relativization of beliefs, images and practices" as part of its experience precisely because of its rootage. Cobb sees the transformation of Christian faith through openness to other faiths as its proper development. Since he uses the term "Christ" to denote creative transformation, "the creative transformation of theology that leads toward universality can responsibly be identified as Christ." This creative transformation, which Cobb specifically sees as a process in operation, is the consequence of the universal presence of the transcendent Logos. This means for Cobb that "Christ" is the term used to denote the incarnation, or activity in history, of the Logos. But Jesus of Nazareth is seen as "the full incarnation of the Logos" in a distinctive way. And the encounter of others with the words of Jesus together with "incorporation into the field of his influence" effects creative transformation in them. "Christians can only name Christ in responsible relation to Jesus."[132]

Cobb gives considerable specificity to his concept of creative transformation. He means among other things cultural creativity, with particular focus upon the arts; for example, in the first part of *Christ in a Pluralistic Age*, Cobb gives an extensive treatment of the religious significance of the artistic work of André Malraux. Cobb also sees the ethical dimension as inextricably involved in the process of creative transformation. Even though Cobb sees the "self-other relation of Christian existence" as requiring some ontological modification, as we have noted, he insists that the "strong self" that has emerged in the Christian tradition is not only capable of self-objectification, but also properly includes a forthright acceptance of moral responsibility for past actions and future commitments.

But Cobb would have Christians move somewhat from the particular ethos of this tradition of ethical understanding and practice, and he believes that Buddhist perceptions of the self can be of help to us in the move. He holds that "the thrust of the New Testament is to subordinate ethics to love rather than to view love as one ethical requirement among others." He is impressed by recent stress upon the concept of a "social self," that is, a self that emerges out of the social matrix. Indeed, Cobb at points seems to be so strongly influenced by this concept that he occasionally uses language that implies a rejection of any real identity or continuity of the human self. If one views his book as a whole, however, such rejection does not seem to be his conclusion.[133]

Cobb's ethical vision could be called holistic. He sees ethics as involving the whole person. He believes that both the New Testament and Alfred North Whitehead's philosophy—the latter has been a powerful but by no means the sole structural influence in the formation of Cobb's process theology[134]—lead to "an emphasis upon the inner condition of a person." Cobb is perhaps second to none in his perception of the importance of the social dimension in Christian ethics. He states that Christian understanding at its best "has always regarded persons as existing in community and community as constituted through mutual love." As we have seen, he even presses for an expansion of the Christian understanding of the self so as to include others not only within the range of self's concern but somehow within the range of self's being.[135] But Cobb insists that "the new age expected in the New Testament requires an inner purity and wholeness as much as an outer and social virtue." The reason why we act is as important as the act itself, and our states of "feeling, anticipation, and decision" are really the primary issue. External manifestations or consequences are in fact secondary. And yet, "history must be transformed by the Kingdom in order that justice will reign." We can say that this is Cobb's conviction as much as it is probably the perception of Jesus himself.[136] We may add, however, that this mode of ethical analysis and reflection is also closer to the perceptions of early Buddhism, and probably of the Buddha, than many may be aware.[137]

Cobb's Christology

It will be helpful at this point to bring into greater sharpness of focus Cobb's use of basic Christological terms and their interrelation. He uses the word "Logos" to denote "the cosmic principle of order, the ground of meaning, and the source of purpose." Cobb acknowledges his indebtedness to Whitehead in perceiving the nature of "this source of the aim at the new." "Logos" seems thus to be equated to the mind of God and is causally efficacious reality both transcendent and immanent (with potentiality for higher degrees of the immanence of the Logos in the created order as the basis of human hope). Christ is the Logos as incarnate.[138] Jesus is Christ or the full incarnation of the Logos. The Logos was distinctively embodied in Jesus. Cobb, however, speaks also of "a concrete particularity of the divine presence and action in him [Jesus] as there is in each of us." The "distinctive" element in Jesus, then, would appear to be a difference of degree of fullness or quality of embodiment rather than of ontology. Cobb takes the language of Ernst Fuchs describing Jesus' uniqueness as that of a man who dares to act in God's stead to support his own (Cobb's) contention that "in some special way the divine Logos was present with and in him."[139] Cobb would have us know that in his own account "the incarnation of the Logos in Jesus is affirmed literally and seriously, as by traditional authority." At the same time he rejects "the supernaturalist and exclusivistic implications that the tradition drew from its correct starting point." Cobb prefers to see Jesus' uniqueness in his overcoming the tension that ordinarily exists between the "I" and "the ever new form that the Logos takes in each moment." "He existed in full unity with God's present purposes for him." Cobb goes on to say that God was therefore "immediately active in the action" but that this is not to be understood in substantialist terms or displacement of the "I."[140]

Cobb insists that Christ as the power of creative transformation (= the Logos incarnate) is "bound up with Jesus" but is not bound to any particular system of religious belief and practice. "The power of transformation, redemption, unification and order," which may be named Christ, "has been apprehended through Jesus and his historical effects," but Cobb will not allow us to absolutize in any way these historical effects. He sees, however, an "increasing efficacy of the story of Jesus" as human beings, who may be agents of the transformation of the world, experience in themselves the supremely important power of Christ "in an increasingly incarnate form." This is to posit the incarnation of the Logos as distinctive in Jesus but potentially a possibility for all other human beings in ever higher degree. Thus whereas the term "Christ," writes Cobb, "has been the symbol of Christian exclusive superiority," Cobb wishes to use it as "identifying the principle of critical overcoming of any such exclusiveness."[141]

Cobb sees the discipline of history of religions as relativizing every sacred form, in contrast to traditional Christian theology, which tended to correlate the theologians' faith with their sacred object. He boldly proposes to name as

Christ precisely that "imminent process" that relativizes "every given object or claim." This is both possible and proper because it is process of which he speaks and, to use Robert Browning's words, "the best is yet to be." At the same time the term "Christ" would be used by Cobb "to name the divine reality as that reality is held to have been present and manifest in Jesus." This means that Jesus also may be called Christ, and Cobb, following Jaroslav Pelikan, holds that our understanding of the nature of the ultimate divine reality is to be regulated by the nature of the personhood of Jesus rather than by assumed axioms of the divine nature such as "absolute," "immutable," "impassible," and so forth. This approach enables Cobb to understand "Christ" as process with potentiality for the new and yet as having rootage in the distinctive qualities of Jesus that, however developed, will not be essentially altered.[142]

CHOAN-SENG SONG

Choan-Seng Song (b. 1929) is one of the most incisive and forthright of contemporary Christian theologians from the so-called Third World. In fact, because of the almost terrible clarity with which he is able and willing to draw out conclusions that others may prefer only to intimate, he could be called an *enfant terrible* of Asian theology. But, as we shall see, he is by no means a naïve or uncritical liberation theologian, and his academic credentials give him as much right to contribute to emerging global Christian theology as do his Asian background and personal spirituality.

Song is Taiwanese in birth and training. As a professor at Tainan Theological College, he first taught Old Testament and then systematic theology, a combination of specialties that has served him well. In 1965 he became the successor of Shoki Coe as principal at Tainan, and later became associate director of the commission on Faith and Order of the World Council of Churches, serving primarily in Geneva. It is significant, however, that for nearly three years (1971–73) he served as secretary for Asian ministries in the General Program Council of the Reformed Church in America.

A major, if not *the* major, existential fact of contemporary history for those of Chinese ethnic and cultural background has been the Communist revolution and political control of mainland China since 1949. For almost all Chinese Christians outside the mainland, the formal rejection of Christianity and—until recent experience has shown otherwise—its apparently complete extermination in China by the Communist government led to profound personal soul-searching and theological questioning. In the case of Song this process-event led him away from an easy or uncritical approval of traditional Chinese culture even as he developed in his theological understanding in the direction of seeing the strongest need to expand the ranges of Western theological thought on the themes of salvation history. He came sharply to question whether there is much profit in finding "points of contact" between Christian faith and "the religious beliefs supposed to be contained in ancient

Chinese writings." His concern is not to deny the fact of such points of contact but to warn against "the adoption of outdated thoughts into Christianity." This latter could mean concretely that "the church comes to associate itself with the conservative forces at work in Taiwan society that resist progress and modernization."[143]

Song believes that the ultimate goal of Christian theology is not just to concern itself with "what is specifically designated as religion" but—while always operating in a particular cultural context in the case of individual theologians—to bring into light "how the creative power of God's saving love is at work in the darkest corner of the world." That is, in every corner no matter how "dark" or remote from previously acknowledged "areas" of salvation history. "The incarnation in Jesus Christ pertains to the whole cosmos as well as to each individual person." Song recognizes both distinction and analogy "between truths scattered in God's creation and the Truth revealed in Jesus Christ." The interaction between the two he describes as "conversation between the deep and the Deep." This means that while the Christ-event in Jesus of Nazareth has normative meaning for Song, he wishes to understand the incarnation also and perhaps primarily as eternally present, "as the powerful creative force" by which "the past is translated to the future, darkness yields to glory, despair gives way to hope, and death is conquered." This is the understanding of the Christian gospel that Song would share with all Asia—and the world—for he believes that "it is the supreme task of the church at this critical juncture to be the apostle of hope" in the particular situations of contemporary human experience.[144]

Song has written elsewhere how he understands what we have just referred to as the normative meaning of Jesus Christ. Rather than to use terms such as "absoluteness" or "uniqueness" or "finality of Christ," he prefers the word "decisiveness." "The decisiveness of Christ" he accepts as integral to the givenness of Christian faith. This reality of the decisiveness of Christ at work in human beings whose minds and lives have been opened by faith puts "under the judgment of God the distortions and corruptions of the gift of the divine creation and salvation by man and his culture." At the same time all persons in whom the decisiveness of Christ is at work will "recognize the love of God and his judgment working dialectically in the life of man and his culture from the beginning of the creation." And, Song contends, "When the decisiveness of Christ is brought to bear on Asian cultures these latter cannot be the same again."[145]

From these perspectives Song has some specific contributions to make to the theme of the present study. He takes history with the utmost seriousness but wants to qualify the usual understanding of history as constituting continuity in an inherently connected story. The task of the historian in this view would be in a special way to discern continuity in the apparent discontinuity of events. Song's view, however, is that the dynamics of history consists more in interruptions than in continuity. Thus he believes that history as represented by the biblical accounts derives its meaning from God's redemptive acts. These acts, however, which are human events and experiences "taken into the orbit of redemption," interrupt more than sustain the normal course of history. This understanding gives Song the basis for his high regard for "revolution," which he speaks of as assuming "the role of introducing new meaning into the life of the people, and of creating a new beginning for the nation. It interrupts history, sometimes peacefully but more often violently." Song sees the death of Jesus Christ on the cross as indeed "the most drastic revolutionary act of God's redemption."[146]

Of course Song has more to say on the meaning of God's redemptive acts in the history of Israel and especially on the meaning of the crucifixion and resurrection of Jesus Christ, but for our present purposes let us note how he sees the history of Israel in connection with the larger history of humankind. As an Old Testament scholar, Song contends that it is actually the great merit of the Hebraic prophetic tradition to refuse to see "the history of Israel as identifiable with the totality of God's acts in the redemption of his creation." The religious seers and prophets of Israel perceived God as working within their own history; they experienced God redemptively in both personal and national crises. But the prophets especially "began to see the hand of God working also outside their limited historical and geographical domains."

Song then comes to the central element of his understanding of the history of Israel as the story of God's redemptive work with a people that is at once redemptive for Israel and also symbolic of wider ranges of divine redemption:

> The people of Israel were singled out, under a divine providence inexplicable to us and even to them, not to present themselves to the rest of the world as the nation through which God's redeeming love would be mediated, *but* to be a symbol of how God would also deal redemptively with other nations. In the light of the experience unique to Israel, other nations should learn how their histories can be interpreted redemptively. An Asian nation would have its own experience of exodus, captivity, rebellion against Heaven, the golden calf. It would have its own long trek in the desert of poverty or dehumanization. . . . An Asian nation will thus be enabled to find its place side by side with Israel in God's salvation.

We have here a manifesto of Asian Christian freedom. This is a call for "Asian Christians to engage in theological reflection on the direct relationship of Asia to God's redemption" in their own historical experience. If the Old Testament is an account written in part to show how the historical experience of any nation can be interpreted as an arena of divine presence and redemptive action, then "the theology which regards Israel and the Christian church as the only bearers and dispensers of God's saving love must be called into question." Song concludes that a "very big theological blunder" was committed by those Western theologians who in the past tried to confine the redemptive work of God within the history of one nation and then the Christian church. This was in effect to try to institutionalize, to confine within the structure of a single human institution and a single stream of human history, the messianic hope of the kingdom of God and God's liberating, saving activity itself. It was an ideologization as well as institutionalization of faith.

This understanding means for Song that we now may, like Second Isaiah (Isa. 44:28; 45:1-4), like the writer of the Melchizedek story (Gen. 14:17-20), or like Ezekiel (29:19-20), "begin to see those alien to our faith as making a contribution to the development of human community, as agents of God." This means that "any Christian understanding of revelation and salvation which fails to give adequate account of the ways in which God has worked positively through the indigenous faiths and ideologies in Asia is woefully inadequate." Song pleads for an ecumenical theological community to be built across the world on the basis of what he calls situational authenticity. This principle gives every people the right to ascribe authentic theological meaning to their own past and present and to look to the future in hope as much as any other people or stream of history. He would replace the characteristically Western theology of essence with a theology of existence, which focuses on what God does in the events and realities in which persons are existentially involved. This perception means that as Christians we shall be concerned to discuss not only what God is doing through the church, but "what he is doing in the world where the church as we normally understand it is non-existent or too weak to have a significant impact."

Song does not deny a unique dimension of meaning and function to the history of Israel and the Christian church. He sees "the Word becomes flesh, the Johannine formulation of God's redeeming love in history" as an "interruption of a radical kind," as constituting a singular divine intervention in history. But this is the very event that "enables us to look at events and happenings within history from a perspective other than that of the historical continuity represented by the Christian church." He would add that "Christian interpretation of history is not complete unless it is tested and corrected by non-Christian, or even anti-Christian, interpretations of history."[147]

A brief final word indicative of Song's understanding may be drawn from his book *Third-Eye Theology*. In a chapter both perceptive and beautiful, entitled "The Cross and the Lotus," he expresses with sensitive specificity his thought regarding Buddhism and Christianity in their historical developments. He reminds his readers who may have been conditioned negatively to the fact and symbols of other religious traditions that a tendency toward demonization of the holy exists within the Christian church as well as without it.[148] And yet the church continues to exist and persons continue to rally to its Christ in spite of its divisions and pettiness. This is all demonstrative to Song that the power of God is stronger than human sin, indeed that "God's love and power have been at work in the world since the beginning of creation." And if "the truth of God has never abandoned the church in spite of the church's failure to measure up to the glory of God," this "must also be true with reference to the whole of creation."

Song fully recognizes "the idolatry and impiety we see in cultures and histories outside Christianity" and acknowledges that "they really do help conceal God's truth. But there are moments and events that still disclose God's continuing presence in a society that has not been shaped by Christianity. These are what we may call redemptive moments and redemptive events. While fragmentary and imperfect, they are nonetheless genuine. They reflect in some way God's redeeming love and power that have become incarnate in Jesus Christ."

Song regards this understanding as the proper and natural consequence of what Paul writes in the first chapters of Romans concerning God's self-disclosure in creation since the world began. Song believes that Gautama the Buddha and the historical movement called Buddhism can be properly understood as functioning within this mode of religious categorization. Such categorization is part of the methodology of Christian theology, and it would not be precisely the way Buddhists would identify themselves. But use of the method intends no disrespect, for it is equally applicable to understanding the Judeo-Christian tradition. Song recognizes, for instance, that the lifelong unselfish toil of the Buddha—from the age of thirty-five to his death at eighty—for the liberation of others from self-centered and ignorant suffering is not without redemptive significance as Christians understand the term (cf. Col. 1:24). He perceives that the teaching of the Buddha on the self points to a transpersonal transformation of self that is actually "a fulfillment of personhood detached from historical bondage and freed from the restrictions of the present life." Therefore Song asks:

Can we not say that Buddha's way is also a part of the drama of salvation which God has acted out fully in the person and work of Jesus Christ? The histories of nations and peoples that are not under the direct impact of Christianity are not just "natural" histories running their course in complete separation from God's redemptive love and power. In this sense, there is no "natural" history. The history of a nation and the dynamics of its rise and fall cannot be explained entirely by natural forces or sociopolitical factors. There are redemptive elements in all nations that condemn human corruption and encourage what is noble and holy. Our evaluation of the history of a nation is not complete until such redemptive elements are properly recognized.

With this bold and "terrible" clarity, which is in turn based on fully open-eyed recourse to what Gayraud S. Wilmore has called "the guts of biblical religion," Song calls the entire Christian church to a truly biblical and Christian view of human history, a view that the narrowed cultural experiences and reductionist theologies of long centuries have obscured. "Viewed in this perspective, religions and cultures outside Christianity cease to be merely objects of Christian condemnation; they begin to acquire an internal relationship with what Christians believe and do."

Song would not have us try to "appreciate the global dimension of redemptive interactions between faith in Jesus Christ and other faiths" merely on the theoretical or doctrinal level. He believes that if with compassionate sensitivity "we realize how ordinary men and women must struggle to cope with the stresses and pressures of life and to find an ultimate meaning in our finite existence, we can begin to discern redemptive events and moments in their lives and to relate them to what God has done in Jesus Christ." In the context of a discussion of the parable of the last judgment in Mt. 25:14–46, Song draws the conclusion that "throughout human history there are men and women who have gone about doing the king's business without being aware that they are in the king's service."

Song therefore sees the mission of the church not as a triumphalist conquest of other faiths but as a "growing with them in the knowledge and experience of God's saving work in the world." At the same time, however, that he asks the whole church to recognize the full theological authenticity of Asian spirituality, which has been shaped by Asian religions and cultures, Song also calls the church to work at informing this spirituality "with the love and compassion of God in Jesus Christ." This means, for Song, among other things, a summons to Christians, specifically Asian Christians, to work together with people of other faiths and ideologies in order "to transform Asian society on the basis of freedom, justice, and equality."[149]

SEIICHI YAGI

We noted in a previous chapter how the early leaders of Protestantism in Japan were vitally concerned to relate their newfound Christian faith to the cultural past and present of their people. They were also concerned to understand that past and present as having Christian theological significance, specifically as playing an authentic role in the larger patterns of divine providence and salvation history that properly belong to faith in "God the Father Almighty, Maker of heaven and earth." As the years passed, however, these perspectives seemed to pass from the forefront of concern in Japanese Protestant theology, perhaps in part because the new generation of leaders had participated less intensively than their predecessors in the traditional modes of education of the land. The influence of Barthian theology in the 1930s and the shock of the World War II years also contributed to a certain narrowing of the range of theological thought.

In order to understand Seiichi Yagi (b. 1932), we should look briefly at the background out of which his work developed. One person from the early postwar years who in a quiet but persistent way carried on the older concerns—and that in keeping with developments in studies in the discipline of history of religions across the world—is Masatoshi Doi (b. 1907). Doi belongs to the Congregational tradition within the United Church of Christ in Japan (*Kyōdan*) and is a theological heir of Hiromichi Kozaki. He was for several decades a professor in the School of Theology of Doshisha University

in Kyoto and has also long been director of the National Council of Churches
Center for the Study of Japanese Religions and editor of its journal, which
appears in English as *Japanese Religions*. Doi is, incidentally, said to have
been the first person to introduce the thought of Paul Tillich to postwar
Japan.

Doi studied deeply the religious traditions of Japan—Shinto, Buddhism,
the older Confucianism, and Neo-Confucianism—and read much in Western
theology and in the wider ranges of the history of religions. His writing is
characterized in a noteworthy way by deep sympathy for other religious traditions. He is able to appreciate in Japanese Buddhism—above all in
Shinran, the great thirteenth-century reformer and pioneer of Japanese Pure
Land Buddhism (*Jōdo Shinshū*)—"a deep insight into the reality of human
existence." Doi sees search for the true meaning of human existence as the
common and proper basis for interfaith dialogue.[150]

After careful study of the relationship between religion and nature as traditionally perceived in East and West, Doi concluded that there is a need to
combine certain aspects of both traditions. On the basis of the Judeo-
Christian doctrine of creation, he feels that the task of Christian theology
must, on the one hand, work to emancipate the mass of the people in Japan
and elsewhere from "the spell of the magical power of nature" by which they
tend yet to be somewhat held in their otherwise commendable feel for solidarity with nature. On the other hand, Japanese Christians, Doi avers, "must,
by emphasizing the solidarity between man and nature, correct the mate-
rialistic view of nature [by which much of the West has been captivated]
which reduces nature into mere 'things' which can be manipulated and exploited ruthlessly for human purposes." For Doi this means that his ancestors in Japan from ancient times were essentially correct in their intuitive
"friendliness and respect for nature and things" even though they may have
expressed this insight in ways that appear naïve to modern persons.[151]

The influence of Doi, however, on the mainstream of Japanese Protestantism has been slight. Both his Congregational origins and heavy commitment
to Tillichian theology have no doubt been factors in limiting his influence.
But also for the reasons briefly indicated at the beginning of this section, the
times were not propitious for wide appreciation of his understanding in the
Japanese Protestant community. A significant example of the long dominant
mentality is the article that Kazō Kitamori wrote in 1960.[152] Kitamori, one of
the most intellectually sophisticated, culturally broad, and spiritually creative of contemporary Japanese theologians, a man who, without being specifically a theological follower of Paul Tillich, has been called the Paul Tillich
of Japan for the breadth and depth of his knowledge of the cultural traditions
of Japan, seemed quite unable at the time to manifest the kind of religious
sympathies that Doi was able to evince.[153]

In depicting the background of Seiichi Yagi, it would be well also to note
his association with John B. Cobb, Jr. Cobb spent most of the spring and
summer of 1978 in Japan, where he taught at the Divinity School of the

Anglican-related Rikkyō University in Tokyo and lectured widely elsewhere. One of the significant products of that activity was a dialogue between Cobb and Yagi on the theme of "Buddhism and Christianity," which was moderated by Professor Yoshinobu Kumazawa of Tokyo Union Theological Seminary and later published in the *Northeast Asia Journal of Theology*. We shall use this as well as other materials in both English and Japanese to introduce Yagi as one of the most seminal theological figures in contemporary Japan.

Seiichi Yagi was born in Yokohama of a distinguished Christian family. His father was a long-time professor in Kantō Gakuin University, a school traditionally associated with the American Baptist Convention. Yagi himself received his doctorate in (Western) Classics from Tokyo University and in the course of his studies spent a period of time at the University of Göttingen in West Germany. Although a long-time professor of German at Tokyo University of Engineering, Yagi has written largely in the area of New Testament studies and in the relationship of Buddhism and Christianity. Yagi's early works—*Shinyaku Shisō no Seiritsu* (The development of New Testament thought), *Seisho no Kirisuto to Jitsuzon* (The Christ of the Bible and existence), *Shinyaku Shisō no Tankyū* (Investigations in the thought of the New Testament), *Iesu* (Jesus), *Kirisuto to Iesu* (Christ and Jesus), and so forth—clearly show the influence of Rudolf Bultmann and his school as well as Yagi's own penchant for a philosophical approach to religious studies. It should be noted that his massive work *Bukkyō to Kirisutokyō no Setten* (Contact points between Buddhism and Christianity) was published by a major Japanese Buddhist publishing house, Hōzōkan.

A key term in Yagi's thought is the Japanese word *tōgō*, which may be translated as "integration," but which has a rich range and depth of meaning in his usage.[154] It has been especially through exploration of the applicability of this term that Yagi has been enabled to come to his conclusion that "primitive Christianity and Buddhism are very close." Actually, Yagi although raised in a Christian family, came to Christian faith "in a very self-conscious way" as a university student in Japan and found his Christian faith significantly deepened by his initial in-depth studies of Buddhism in Germany. Because he was asked many questions in Germany about Buddhism and was at first unable to answer them, he began an intensive course of reading in Zen texts. As a result of struggling with the Zen emphasis upon transcending the human discriminating intellect at the cognitive level in order to reach a more authentic mode of personal awareness and cosmic relationship, he found that he "began to realize the truth of Jesus' word *immediately*." Even though he had previously thought that Buddhism and Christianity were "completely heterogeneous," he began to perceive that they are not so different in their "understanding of authentic human existence." He found that he could interpret both by means of his understanding of the term "integration." This result was made all the more possible by his own growing understanding that the essence of Christian faith lies in the Pauline perception of "Christ who lives in me" (Gal. 2:20) and the concept-practice of "interdependent love."[155]

For Yagi the essence of the human dilemma is the self-centered, alienated self characterized by what he calls egoism.[156] At the cognitive level this condition may be expressed by the discriminating intellect, at a more existential level by lack of love. But for Yagi authentic human existence is manifested in love, which is a term fundamentally relational in its meaning; indeed, it is in its essence other-oriented. This fact leads Yagi to say that the true nature of the human self is polar, to be a pole in fundamental relationship with another pole or poles. This is to be an individual in integration.

In Yagi's faith-understanding there is, to be sure, a transcendent dimension. He believes that "love is given to humanity from the transcendent," that "the work of God is the ground of love" and that the formation of "the community of love" is the will of God. "The act of love thus becomes an event by the work of the transcendent and the free decision of the man who participates in it." This participation is also a process in which individuals experience its realization increasingly as they participate. Like John Cobb, Yagi finds it convenient to use the analogy, from physics, of a "field" to denote the power that makes otherwise separate individuals into poles and thus integrates them in interrelationship. This resultant integration Yagi further denotes by the Hebrew term *emeth*, which is generally translated as "truth" and "faithfulness" but also denotes that which is "whole," that which is in entire accord with its own being.[157]

Yagi believes that "both Christianity and Buddhism understand reality in the frame of integration." This is also to say that the concept of integration as goal is fundamental to both traditions. The Christian experiences this fact insofar as he or she participates in love, and the Buddhist does the same by perceiving the I and Non-I relationship as neither one nor two. This latter is not primarily a matter of objective observation but an intuitive experience, which is to grasp "the immediacy of life." In this knowledge-relationship "beings" are no longer separate entities but "poles," which are characterized by "mutual dependence, mutual implication and mutual reflection."

Primitive Buddhism, according to Yagi, denied the substantiality of human selfhood in order to see the self as the subject of ethical action in a relationship of mutual dependence. That is, "beings" truly exist only in relationship with other beings and to perceive intuitively, to experience, this fact is a central element of the reality of religious salvation. This is to see salvation or liberation not in a theoretical cognition of reality but in the actual "grasp of the immediacy of life." This, we may note, is a legitimate statement of the position of later Tendai or Zen Buddhism, and the fact that Yagi is drawing upon a primarily Mahayana understanding becomes all the clearer through his use of the Sanskrit term *pratītyasamutpāda* (*engi* in Japanese) to denote the linkage of all reality in the cosmos. This Sanskrit term, which may be rendered in English as "dependent origination" or "dependent co-arising," was used frequently in the early Buddhist Scriptures to denote the causal interrelationship of all phenomena in the cosmos. Perception of this principle, especially as descriptive of the process by which human beings come to experience suffering, was an important part of the Buddha's experience called the Enlightenment. But for the Buddha, we must note, the key element in liberation from the "downward" aspect of the process, the dynamic that makes possible the turning, was more narrowly focused than upon "immediate" perception of participation in the whole of things. The focus of the Buddha was upon friendship or intimacy with Dharma, as the "lovely." This relationship was properly prior to and creative of all other authentic relationships, including "immediate" awareness of participation in a linkage with the All.[158]

Yagi, however, is correct in seeing the anthropological goal, or salvation, in both Buddhism and Christianity as fundamentally relational, the "loss" of self at the level of separateness (self-centered, selfish isolation or alienation) and the "finding" of self at the level of other-concerned interrelatedness (cf. Mt. 10:39; 16:25; Rev. 3:20). And, most significantly, he holds that the Buddhist perception of this "new" relationship as *engi* is in fact an envisaging of "personal relations." Yagi recognizes that in much of historic Buddhism, particularly in the Kegon, Tendai, and Zen traditions of the Mahayana, emphasis has generally been given to the more existential aspect of this change, that is, from one level of the self to another, and "authentic communal thinking or interpersonal thinking is comparatively rare." Yagi in particular would contrast this tendency with the biblical *Sitz*, which he sees as fundamentally communal and interpersonal as well as existential in both the Old Testament and the New.[159]

It is necessary to note that both in the early records of the teaching of the Buddha and in other streams of the Mahayana tradition, particularly in the Pure Land schools and in the concept-practice of Bodhisattvas, a strong practical emphasis upon compassionate concern for, and service of, others is to be found. This was an other-oriented perception of authentic "personal relationships" however the world-view or anthropological analysis of the writer or speaker may have been expressed.[160]

Yagi sees "immediacy," in the sense of living in unhindered or immediated relationship both to self and to others, as the essence of Buddhism. He notes that while historically Buddhist perception of the nature and role of the transcendent element in the enabling of this immediacy has varied, there has been consistently an awareness that somehow "the transcendent" has acted to make the change cosmically and humanly possible.

With reference to the life of Christian faith, Yagi sees Christian existence as necessarily including the social dimension and faith as "believing participation in the work of God." He reveals more specifically his sense of the role of the transcendent element in saying that "this participation becomes possible on the ground of the work of God which finds expression in the historical reality through the free decision of the believing man." This statement, however, then becomes for Yagi a way to point Christians toward better modes of understanding and practice of "the immediacy of the work of love." In this process he believes that the historic Buddhist emphasis upon immediacy in the religious life can become for Christians a clue to an enrichment of the quality and a strengthening of the force of their own love for others. The work of life is, for Yagi, of the essence of Christian faith, for it includes both the work of the transcendent and the necessary integration thereof by Christians in life, "the life in which love becomes the event of our historical reality."[161]

Yagi is clearly a probing, seminal theological thinker. He would have Christians move beyond the stark otherness frequently presupposed in concepts of an I-Thou relationship into new modes of understanding and practice of human interrelationship. In his use of the term "immediacy," the issue is not primarily one of ontological perception but of quality of relationship. He uses Jesus' parable of the Good Samaritan as an example of his meaning. The Samaritan in the story did not help the needy person primarily because such was commanded by the law. Rather, the text reads, "when he saw him, he had compassion" (Lk. 10:33). Yagi states that the Samaritan's "having compassion shows an immediacy." This compassion is in keeping with the commandments of God as perceived in the tradition, but it did not really originate with them. It originated in the self of the Samaritan, who was in this instance "immediately" one with God and also with the life situation.[162]

Yagi aims at a transformed Christianity even as he hopes for a self-transformation of Buddhism. His potential for leadership among Japanese Christians is somewhat hindered by his inability in later years to believe in the specifically redemptive aspects of Jesus' life, death, and resurrection. He has continued to believe, as we have seen, in "the work of Christ in me," a phenomenon that he evidently perceives more as an "internal," or existential, reality.[163] His is, however, an outstanding example in Japan of a profound, biblically and theologically informed Christian attempt appreciatively to understand and constructively to relate to the great historical phenomenon of Buddhism.

MIKIZŌ MATSUO

To turn to Mikizō Matsuo is for this writer quite another order of activity. To speak personally, I first met this Japanese Christian gentleman in the early spring of 1946 when I was serving in the American Army of Occupation in Japan. He was the person who asked me to consider returning to Japan as a Christian missionary, and this I later did, believing him to be the Lord's instrument in making such a request. I returned to Japan with my family in 1949 and served there for nearly sixteen years. Throughout this time and also during subsequent years of service in my homeland, Mikizō Matsuo has been my spiritual mentor and practical guide more than any other single Christian leader of his generation.

Mikizō Matsuo was born in a family of Zen Buddhist heritage in Shimabara City on the southwestern island of Kyūshū on March 1, 1890. This means that as of this writing he is ninety-four years of age, but to talk with him is like talking with a person having both the intellectual vigor of younger years and the wisdom of a sage. He is still physically vigorous, with excellent sight and hearing and with a mind as sharp as ever.

Matsuo went to Tokyo for his high school education (under the pre-World War II system wherein "high school" included what is now the first two years of college). The school that he and his parents selected was Meiji Gakuin (now a large university), the old Presbyterian-Reformed church-related school whose origins go back to the beginnings of Protestant educational work in 1865. In Tokyo under the special influence of the pioneer leader among Japanese Presbyterian-Reformed pastors, Masahisa Uemura, he was led to make the commitment of Christian faith and receive baptism. After graduation from Meiji Gakuin, he went on to take the full seminary course at Tokyo Shingakusha, of which Uemura was then president. Uemura was also serving concurrently as pastor of the large Fujimichō Church in Tokyo.

After graduation from the Shingakusha in 1914, Matsuo served for several years in pioneer evangelism in the Tōhoku area (north of Tokyo) in association with a missionary of the Reformed Church in America, Luman Shafer. Shafer later became well known for his service of many years as the Japan secretary of the Board of World Mission of his church. Matsuo then obtained a scholarship to attend Auburn Theological Seminary in Auburn, New York (now a part of Union Theological Seminary in New York City), from which he received the B.D. degree in 1919 and an advanced diploma in 1920 for further work. He next went to the University of Edinburgh in Scotland, where he received a diploma from the Faculty of Divinity in 1921. Later in the same year he returned to Japan to become pastor of the Yukinoshita Church in Kamakura, one of the congregations of the Nippon Kirisuto Kyōkai (of the Presbyterian-Reformed tradition).

Matsuo continued as pastor of this church in Kamakura, which is located about forty miles south of Tokyo and is one of the major cultural centers in Japan, until his retirement shortly after celebration of the fiftieth anniversary of his pastorate. During this period the church became one of the strongest in the denomination (later a part of the United Church of Christ in Japan). This congregation was responsible for sending a considerable number of persons, both men and women, into the professional Christian ministry during those years. Matsuo also served concurrently until the end of World War II as a member of the faculty of a seminary in Yokohama that specialized in the training of women church workers. His was a heroic role during the war. He once told me quietly that he had an item to be added to the list of missionary hardships which the apostle Paul cites in 2 Cor. 11:23–29, namely: "How many times was I taken to the police station for questioning during the war years?" He was one of those Japanese Christian friends who dared to visit John Coventry Smith in his wartime internment in Japan before his repatriation to the United States. Smith later became one of the presidents of the World Council of Churches.

During the period from 1951 to 1962 I myself worked, as a junior partner, in a very close collaboration with Mikizō Matsuo. Together we were key factors in the establishment of about fifteen new Christian churches in the prefecture of Kanagawa, of which Yokohama is the largest city. We worked together to help establish a new Christian Home for the Elderly in Kamakura. We also worked together toward the further development of a variety of Christian institutions in whose founding Matsuo had been a major figure. These included Yokosuka Gakuin (a Christian Junior and Senior High School), Kinugasa Christian Hospital, and the Taura Christian Social Service Center. All these institutions are still thriving, indeed with far better facilities than they had in earlier days. Matsuo continues to serve on the boards of directors of all these institutions, but for many years his personal contributions in leadership went far beyond what is usually considered normal for such a relationship.

Matsuo served as chairman of the board of Yokosuka Gakuin for many years, but after his retirement from the pastorate in 1971, he was asked to become acting president because of a critical personnel situation in the school at that time. Subsequently he was asked to become the president in full status and was so installed. He still serves in this capacity and spends more than half of each day on the job.

I cite these details concerning Mikizō Matsuo partly, of course, for personal reasons. In the preface to an earlier book of mine, *A History of Christianity in Japan*, I wrote of him in the brief preface as "long-time pastor of Yukinoshita Church in Kamakura, perceptive preacher and dedicated pastor, scholar, teacher, author of distinction, valiant and creative laborer in manifold works of the kingdom."[164] But as is clear from the preceding, Mikizō Matsuo is not merely a figure of high distinction in his own right. More than any of the other contemporary Japanese Protestant leaders heretofore cited, he is representative of the mainstream of his church, biblically, theologically, devotionally. His views on the theme of study in this book therefore carry all the more historical significance.

Matsuo is the author of three books, all written within a dozen years. His first was *Epeso Kyōkai ni Manabu* (Learning from the church of Ephesus) (1969), a book wherein he gave expression to his increasingly strong conviction that the best Christian models for the church in a country like Japan lie in the early centuries of the church, in its most culturally cosmopolitan period and situation. His next work was *Kyōiku wo Kangaeru* (Reflections on education) (1978), with the subtitle "Rethinking the Meiji Restoration from a Christian Perspective." The third book, and the one of particular moment for our present concerns, is *Kyōiku wo Kangaeru, Zoku* (Reflections on education 2) (1980), with the subtitle "Evaluating State Shintō from a Christian Perspective."[165]

This last book is difficult for a foreigner to read—difficult, probably, for younger Japanese who have not received Matsuo's extensive education in the older Japanese and Chinese classics as well as continued exposure to the wider ranges of Western culture. The number of Chinese characters (ideograms) in the citations from ancient Shinto texts that are no longer current in contemporary Japanese discourse—or literature—is somewhat daunting. A large lexicon is one's only recourse! But the book is important because it represents a fresh and bold attempt from the mainstream of Japanese Protestant Christianity to work toward a theological understanding and practical modus vivendi with Shinto, which in its relations with the state has been the politico-religious form of the traditional religious faith of the Japanese people. In some ways this kind of rapprochement is in Japan, even now, considerably more delicate, emotionally as well as politically, than attempts to effect relations with Buddhism.

Matsuo first clarifies the fact that in one or more of its forms Shinto has constituted the deepest stream, the very backbone, of Japan's historical life. He defines religion as necessarily involving transcendent elements and thereby some measure of faith in and experience of exalted beings—beings who may be called God or gods (*kami* in Japanese, which is normally used without designation of number for singular or plural). As a Christian he recognizes the morphological and experiential kinships between Shinto and his own faith, in spite of many and important differences. The historical reality of Shinto necessarily becomes "reference material" (*sankō*) for Christian faith.[166]

Matsuo believes that the God of Christian faith, God who is creator of heaven and earth, is the primal origin and initiator of all human religion, however aberrant its forms. He sees progress, an increasing sophistication, in human perception of divine revelation in the total course of human history. Not only historians of religions but also ordinary Christians need to develop, he avers, an imaginative sympathy for this process and recognize that in many cases we confront authentic encounters with God, however varied the levels of human perception and modes of expression. He points out how it is possible to look beyond the often primitive forms of early Shinto polytheism to perceive an underlying reality of profound religious sincerity and even to find models for intimate relationships with God (as perceived by Christians) in the ordinary experiences of life. At the same time he also recognizes in the early Shinto texts attempts to give moral and religious justification to violent battles of aggression, as in the case of the creation of the Yamato state under the emperor Jimmu—a veritable holy war.[167] And in the sharpest language Matsuo notes how the evil of that understanding and spirit has remained with fateful consequences as a part of the nation's corporate history until the present.[168] He acknowledges the lack of an adequate morality of personal conscience in historic Shinto and its tendency to confine its ethical teaching to the duty of subjects to protect the land in support of the imperial family. Yet, he adds, we must not fail to give adequate attention to the historic influence of the harmonious, peace-loving, magnanimous, and patient character, as depicted in the ancient texts, of the chief goddess of the Shinto pantheon, Amaterasu-ō-mi Kami, who is also described in these myths as severely critical of wrongdoing.[169]

We do not have space to consider Matsuo's lengthy treatment of the long course of Shinto development in the history of Japan, its encounters and experiences of mutual influence with Confucianism and Buddhism as they came from the Asian continent. Let us concentrate on his concluding theological and practical observations regarding Shinto with particular reference to the future of the Christian church in Japan.

Matsuo bases his observations upon the conviction of faith that the Japanese people came to settle on the islands of the archipelago by divine providence and destiny. This is to say that they are not there by chance, nor is their subsequent history a reality apart from this divinely structured context. Furthermore, this is the context within which both the future of the nation and the future of Shinto must be viewed. It is particularly interesting and significant to learn how Matsuo as a Japanese Christian sees the future of Shinto. He feels that as a result of the formal disestablishment of Shinto in the early period of the Allied Occupation following the end of World War II, all state Shinto shrine properties should have reverted to the state. This did not happen in fact, but he feels that such would still be the wiser policy.[170] His conviction, strongly and repeatedly stated, is that Shinto must view itself solely in religious terms. But then Matsuo concludes that Shinto as a religious reality, not only in Japan's historic past but in its future, forms the base side of an equilateral triangle, of which the land and the people, respectively, form the other two sides.

Matsuo would have us understand this figure as no other than imagery and as necessarily involving historical dynamism. Within the meaning of the term "historical dynamism" he would also include the "historical influence and contributions of Buddhism and Confucianism to Shinto, and in more recent centuries those of Christianity.[171] The inner body of the figure would be the character and lifestyle of the Japanese people themselves with all the dynamism of their historical changes and developments. Matsuo seems to understand Shinto as properly continuing to form the base side of this triangle in the future, with the emperor at the apex and constituting a primary linkage factor. But this role of Shinto in the future he seems to see not only as a historical probability that Christianity has to accept simply because it cannot be avoided. He also appears to link Shinto with the future meaning, role, and mission of the nation under God, viewed in terms of Christian faith. Therefore, it would seem proper for all Japanese, including Christians, to support and even promote Shinto in some significant sense.

Matsuo, as a sensitive and intelligent modern Japanese, believes that it is only common sense for persons to respect each other's religious faith. At the same time, knowing that Christianity has received more than its share of criticism, not to speak of persecution, in Japanese history, he has some sharp criticisms to offer with regard to the religious record of Shinto. He identifies three areas in which Shinto has significantly yielded to "temptation"—these are inevitably temptations that assail every historic human religion, he adds—indeed, has become a veritable prisoner of such. These are, first, its inability or unwillingness to retain its own character for long periods vis-à-vis Confucianism; second, its long dependence upon political power rather than upon the power of its own religious faith (at this point Matsuo observes that there is nothing more dangerous either for politics or for religion than what is known in the West as the union of church and state, *saisei itchi*); third, its neglect of concern for the religious salvation of individual persons—it has not adequately responded to the quest of individuals for personal faith nor to their need for guidance in daily living.

The significant corollary of these strictures, however, is that Matsuo makes them in the context of his perception, as a Christian, that Shinto—evidently both historically and in the future—is the special religion of the Japanese people. He wants a revival of Shinto as a purer religious activity and grieves over its decline. He looks for its transformation in the direction of coming to possess transnational and transethnic qualities.

Matsuo then begins a most moving paean of praise—extending to several pages in length—for the moral nobility and exalted truth of Christian faith and for its extraordinary contributions to the Japanese nation, not only to Japanese Christians but to all Japan. He writes warmly of the redemptive love of God revealed in the cross of Jesus Christ and the promise of full salvation to human beings who may otherwise be destroyed by the corrupting power of sin. He writes of the simplicity of Christian faith and at the same time of its astonishing depths and heights, its mystical spirituality and its inexhaustible power ever to renew itself and others. But all this in Japan is in the context of interrelationship with the other historic faiths, especially of Christianity with Shinto and Buddhism. He notes, as others have also observed, that there is an emerging monotheistic faith among Japanese of every religious orientation, which without doubt is primarily owing to the influence of Christian faith. But Christianity in Japan has in significant ways also been influenced by both Shinto and Buddhism. Matsuo's theological and practical conclusion is that all three religious traditions have an ongoing role, under God, in the lives and history of the Japanese people. If each were to develop its own special characteristics, they would serve as challenging, stimulating influences upon each other. Matsuo looks for a "conversion" of the Japanese nation to which all traditions would contribute their respective excellences.

Matsuo, in this writer's opinion, is not hereby merely giving theological justification to a massive fait accompli, which, humanly speaking, neither he nor any combination of persons is likely in the near future to be able to change. In support of this view are some of Matsuo's own concluding statements. He concludes his argument with an extensive use of the metaphor of engrafting, which the apostle Paul uses as a means of understanding the respective roles of the Jews and the Gentiles in God's providential order for the salvation of all humankind (Rom. 11:13–36). Matsuo sees Japan as a people to be equivalent not to the wild-olive branch that is engrafted into the original olive tree as in Paul's metaphor, but to a wild-tree trunk that is not to be distinguished from historic Shinto. Into this wild-tree trunk, by divine providence, was first engrafted Buddhism from Asia, then Confucianism. As time passed the effect of the engrafting became weak, and there came to be need for a new engrafting into the ancient trunk. Now, Matsuo avers, is the very best time for the engrafting of Christianity as the true olive *branch* into the old wild trunk of Shinto Japan. Christianity in itself is not a product of the West but the true olive *branch* from heaven above.

But in this hoped-for event-process Matsuo does not anticipate the elimination or disappearance of Shinto. This is not a Kraemerian missiological doctrine of total displacement. Quite the contrary, Matsuo's very last words in this his concluding chapter are that the ongoing interrelationship of Shinto and Christianity will be an eternal problem-challenge for the Japanese people. Here we have a most significant theological as well as missiologically practical contribution from a Japanese Christian to the entire Christian church as to how the church may relate wisely and well to contemporary religious pluralism.[172]

In a letter (1981) to this writer from Matsuo Sensei, he expressed his appreciation for this largely correct understanding of his thought. He feels, however, that unless the Japanese people in some sense turn from historic Shinto to authentic Christian faith, they will continue to experience frustration as a nation. It is still, he wrote, of the core of Shinto to "revere the Emperor and expel foreigners" (*Sonnō-jōi*), in accord with the war cry of the imperial restorationists of the 1860s.[173]

AFRICAN THEOLOGIANS*

African Christianity is increasingly making its influence felt across the world, and, as is well known, it may emerge as the numerically largest continental expression of this faith in the world by the end of the twentieth century. Indeed, it is astonishing to Westerners, especially to Europeans, that "the churches numerically are impressively strong. In a big town church the size of a cathedral, congregation after congregation will assemble on a Sunday for the different services of the day."[174]

Perhaps it would be best to establish continuity with what has preceded in this chapter by brief reference again to John V. Taylor and the Anglican tradition of Christian Presence. Taylor is of course not an African theologian himself, but he has clearly been a significant factor, not only in the contem-

---

*I write last about this increasingly important body of Christian peoples because of my own diffidence. My personal or existential experience here has been the least; my visits to Africa have been limited to two brief sojourns in East Africa. But I have found my readings in this field to be particularly rewarding, and my experiences with African seminary students especially in Dubuque have greatly enriched my life as well as broadened my understanding. R.H.D.

porary development of larger and more sympathetic theological perspectives but also in the larger work of the articulation of current African Christian thinking and feeling. Perhaps we can say that he, as well as Max Warren and others, have helped to give, by both example and sympathy, encouragement to African Christians to be bold in the statement of their case to the larger world of Christian thought.

For one thing, Taylor in the 1960s pointed out what was happening in Africa as is also happening in other parts of the so-called third world, namely, that "Africa's century of acquiescence is coming to an end and the old views and values are reasserting themselves."[175] This reassertion, moreover, is a very widespread reality, as much among African Christians as among those still, in a formal sense, within the traditional faiths. One aspect which has been noted even with anxiety is, among many Africans, "an embarassment, a mistrust, unconscious or overt, towards Christianity. The period of delirious enthusiasm which welcomed the first preachers of the Gospel is over. Now, in proportion as faith grows in depth and breadth, a corrosive discontent ventures to call everything in question." Taylor believes that the bulk of African Christians are remaining faithful, but he goes on to ask, "will they always resist the climate of uneasiness which is being created and maintained by the exciting new awareness, both individual and collective, of the African personality?"[176]

Among the intelligentsia of Africa there is a conscious recovery and reaffirmation of a neo-African culture, which in many cases carries with it a "considered rejection of Western systems of thought and valuation." Also very seriously to be taken into account is the fact that basic elements of the traditional African world-view are still an integral part of the faith-understanding of perhaps the majority of faithful Christians. In this situation, however, a major contribution of Taylor and others of the Christian Presence persuasion has been to show how much of the same situation can be rightly, even warmly, appreciated by Christians everywhere. For one thing, it is now possible for Western Christians to realize that the ancient—shall we say authentic—Christian understanding of being human has far more in common with African perceptions of solidarity with others and the natural world than modern Western notions of individualism. And when African Christian leaders are asking for the right to have spiritually meaningful relationships with their ancestors, it is now possible to find biblical and historico-theological grounds for such, and through this process we of the West gain liberation from the reductive limitations of post-Reformational, post-Enlightenment European and North American rationalism. The time has surely come to appreciate in depth the desire of every body of Christian people to find, with full biblical and theological integrity, the meaning under God—and the Logos of God—of the past of their people and of their culture. This faith-understanding must mean somehow to pull "all the old ones from long ago" into the realm of biblically understood salvation history and even to rethink ancient Christian concepts of the harrowing of hell.[177]

Taylor and his friends have responded to this situation by suggesting and practicing an approach to persons of another faith and culture which is "reverent and attentive, and which consists essentially not of assertion, nor even of action, but of presence." Actually, a great deal of hard theological work is being done in this spirit, as well as no little life-practice. But let us see how African Christians themselves are handling the themes that we are considering in this book.

John S. Mbiti

Probably the first African Christian theologian whom we should consider in this context of thought is John S. Mbiti (b. 1931). Mbiti was born in Kenya and is an outstanding example of those African Christians who have been educated in the "best" of contemporary world cultures, their own and others. Mbiti was educated at Makerere University in Uganda and studied later in the United States and England, receiving a doctorate in theology from Cambridge University. In addition to serving in an English parish, he was also for a time visiting lecturer at the University of Birmingham and later at the University of Hamburg in Germany. In 1968 he became professor of religious studies at Makerere University College; he is now a pastor in the Reformed Church of Switzerland.

Mbiti is a highly sophisticated and learned Christian theologian who is working at the "interface" of theology and history of religions clearly out of profound religious and even missionary concerns as much or even more than academic. He is obviously concerned at the deepest level of his being with the existential situation and need of not only African Christians but also of all Africans. His most important book *African Religions and Philosophy* (1969) was probably written primarily to widen the sympathies as well as deepen the knowledge of Christians everywhere. But this was clearly also with the underlying purpose that the current rapid growth of Christianity in Africa be truly to the best interests of those who are not yet Christian. Those best interests, Mbiti believes, will be served only as Christians of every level of sophistication and professional status, both African and non-African, are enabled to relate to traditional African religions and culture—that is, to Africans as they are, both Christian and traditional—with new modes of understanding and appreciation. The result will probably be transformations of Christian faith and practice, which are, more often than not, moves in the direction of the more authentic Christianity of the early church.

Like most other Africans of the present generation, Mbiti works out of a background of reaction, at times revulsion, to the varying experiences of European colonial rule. Apart from the obvious political and economic aspects of colonialism, Mbiti has seen, as have many others, that the cultural aspects have been as significant, at times far more significant than the other. As he writes:

. . . whether consciously or unconsciously, Europe began to transform Africa and if possible to make it resemble itself in many respects. . . .

In some parts Africans tried to resist but they were overcome by Europeans who slaughtered them like beasts, who burnt down their villages,
who put men and women into prisons, who forced them to quit their
lands and become labourers in European farms or 'house-boys' for
European masters and mistresses. The new change started and continued in blood and tears, in suppression and humiliation, through honest
and dishonest means, by consent and by force, by choice and by subjection. . . . So the revolution came by both peace and force, by choice
and by subjection. . . . So the revolution came by both peace and force,
and Africa could not remain the same any more.[178]

As the latter part of this quotation indicates, Mbiti also knows and acknowledges the positive aspects of Western colonialism. He notes that "some of the
colonial powers developed their African countries educationally, medically
and economically, but others simply coerced Africans to serve them, dug out
African gold, diamonds and copper while doing virtually nothing for the
human welfare of the people." When looked at from a perspective outside, it
is a marvel that Africans began and have continued to become Christian in
such large numbers with this wide spectrum of life-practice by colonizing
European nations, all of whom professed to be Christian. Mbiti himself,
however, would probably be among those Africans, usually with experience
of British or French colonialism, who, somewhat wryly, to be sure, may
make regretful comments about certain African countries because they did
not have "the cultural opportunities" of colonial occupation.[179]

This is not the place to discuss in detail the highly emotion-charged issues
implied in the paragraphs above, but it is vitally important to realize that the
whole range of issues involved in current attempts of Africans of every religious position to relate positively to their traditional religious and cultural
background is at the center of a desperate battle to retain their African identity in the midst of widespread change.

Africans everywhere are almost overwhelmed, albeit with differences in
degree, by the changes that have been coming upon them over the past century. In increasing measure they have been experiencing the life-dislocation
that has been called detribalization and involves on the surface the phenomena of detachment from the land, urbanization, the break-up of tribal and
clan structures, and, perhaps the most deleterious of all, the separation of
men from their families for long periods of time. At deeper levels of the mind
and subconscious, there are changes of anthropological perspective, as from
seeing human beings as primarily tribal to perceiving them as belonging to a
universal family. Above all, there are changes in process, adequately fulfilled
in all too few persons, whereby Africans uprooted from their former participation in tribal, natural, and cosmic solidarities may eventually come to find
their places in a Christianly oriented—for some it will be Islamic—social,
natural, and cosmic solidarity.

Mbiti himself wishes to come to these problems from a distinctly Christian posture of faith and life. He sees the reality and goal of Christian faith to be profound spiritual unity with the Christ of God. Here, he believes, every African and every other human being may find the authentic human identity "which makes nonsense of all other identities in that it claims the whole person and the whole cosmos as the property of Christ. Then deriving from this Christocentric identity, the person is free to become whatever else he wishes, to be identified as an African, nationalist, neutralist, trade unionist or even beggar. That is the height to which Christianity in Africa must soar." Only Jesus Christ, as the Man for others, "deserves to be the goal and standard for individuals and mankind." But this commitment and aspiration do not mean for Mbiti by any means a posture of radical discontinuity with or total rejection of the African past, religiously or culturally. He considers "traditional religions, Islam and the other religious systems to be preparatory and even essential ground in the [African] search for the Ultimate."[180]

There is a dialectical tension here in these words, which in part form the conclusion to Mbiti's book. On the one hand, in the course of his work he does not hesitate to indicate in various ways the flaws, at times grave, of empirical Christianity in Africa over the past century and more. A criticism that he repeats perhaps more than any other is that "mission Christianity" has not penetrated deeply enough into African religiosity. This is at least one of the reasons why he insists that there must be open-ended and respectful theological encounter between Christian faith and the traditional religions and philosophy of Africa. Mbiti, of course, realizes that openness to modes of traditional African religiosity is also openness to anciently traditional Christian religiosity. To ask missionaries and other Christians in the West and elsewhere to be open to the African concern to incorporate within their Christian faith-practice the use of dreams and visions, the guidance and revelation of the Spirit of God, exorcism and healing, deep levels of prayer and meditation, traditional modes of song and dance, even reverence for ancestors with awareness of solidarities beyond mere memory is hardly to move into a world alien to the early church.[181]

On the other hand, Mbiti insists that, more than any other religious activity in contemporary Africa, what he calls "mission Christianity"—as distinguished from the so-called Independent Churches of indigenous provenance and leadership, and also from the traditional religions—has deliberately and steadily attempted to relate Christianity to modern problems in Africa. He sees mission Christianity as "officially and consciously attempting to respond and contribute in form of service to human needs in the slums and refugee camps, schools and hospitals, areas of racial, political and religious tensions, family disintegration and urban loneliness, as far as communities are concerned." Mbiti sums up the larger Christian situation in Africa in the following words:

> The independent Church movements seem to get closer to African traditional aspirations and religiosity than does mission Christianity. But

the latter seems better equipped and concerned to move with the changing times, despite signs of lagging and conservatism. In any case, the
two forms of Christianity need each other, are perhaps necessary for
the moment, and a humble cooperation between them would obviously
enhance the impact of Christianity in Africa. The ancient Church in
Egypt and Ethiopia has its strengths and weaknesses, and both can
contribute to and learn from the two newer forms of Christianity.[182]

Mbiti would also emphasize the distinct theological contributions, expan-
sions of world-view, which Christian faith is making to all Africans. He notes
particularly the Christian introduction of a future dimension of time in the
context of traditional focus upon past and immediate present with the destiny
of human beings seen as merging into the past with perhaps an ultimate loss
of personal identity or individuality. Mbiti sees this introduction, with its
ability to "create new myths of the future," to work for progress, to wait for
realization of hopes, as "perhaps the most dynamic and dangerous discovery
of African peoples in the twentieth century." And in this context Mbiti's
appeal to all Christians, inside and outside of Africa, is that in adding this
third dimension of time—utterly necessary for Africa to cope with contemporary needs—they do so not in the spirit of conquering or coercing traditional religions and philosophy but in the spirit of complementarity, which is
the spirit of Jesus Christ.[183]

African Traditional Religions and Culture

From this point on we shall confine ourselves to brief quotations from and
discussion of a number of African theologians who almost without exception
take a stance similar to that of Mbiti with reference to African traditional
religions and culture. *E. W. Fashole-Luke* (b. 1934) professor at the University of Sierre Leone, for example, states that the widely expressed need to
create indigenous African theologies, "which will satisfy the deepest emotional and spiritual needs of Africans," comes out of a specific background
experience. Western missionaries over most of the past century came from
backgrounds of theological training where "aspects of discontinuity between
Christianity and every culture were stressed to the exclusion of the aspects of
continuity with local cultures. Conversion to Christianity was thus interpreted in terms of a radical breaking away from the past and being set in a
new pattern of life, even if one still continued to live close to one's cultural
and social situation."

Fashole-Luke cites a number of African Christian theologians, such as
Christian Baeta, Harry Sawyerr, and S. G. Williamson, who are in similar
quest for theological understanding that is faithful to the essence of the
Christian past but also applicable to Africa's needs and therefore in a true
sense faithful to Africa's past. As a particularly apt expression of this aspiration he quotes from the Consultation of African Theologians held at Ibadan,
Nigeria, in 1965, which stated:

We believe that the God and Father of our Lord Jesus Christ, Creator of heaven and earth, Lord of history, has been dealing with mankind at all times and in all parts of the world. It is with this conviction that we study the rich heritage of our African peoples, and we have evidence that they know of him and worship him. We recognize the radical quality of God's revelation in Jesus Christ; and yet it is because of this revelation we can discern what is truly of God in our pre-Christian heritage: this knowledge of God is not totally discontinuous with our peoples' previous traditional knowledge of him.[184]

Fashole-Luke, like the others, is not unaware of the fact of elements of discontinuity as well as of continuity. But in accepting the revelation of God in Jesus Christ as unique and constitutive of the criterion by which the nature and quality of all else, religious or cultural, are to be evaluated, he emphasizes that the role of the Christ as criterion works properly only as persons are "in a living relationship with the risen Christ." This primacy of personal relationship gives persons a wholesome flexibility with reference not only to their own and other cultures but also to the Bible and the traditions of specific churches. In this way none of these elements need become instruments of wooden literalism or shackling legalism. Just as there is theological pluralism among the Western churches, the same can be proper for Africa. In this context Fashole-Luke suggests that the previously largely neglected—by most African Christians—theological heritage of the Eastern Orthodox churches should be explored. And what better place to begin than with a study of the ancient Coptic Church of Egypt and the ancient Ethiopian church?

In the July 1975 *Ecumenical Review*, which was published just prior to the World Council of Churches Assembly at Nairobi, Fashole-Luke sums up his thought in the following way. First, "conversion to Christianity must be coupled with cultural continuity." That is, the faith "must become incarnate in the life and thought of Africa and its theologies must bear the distinctive stamp of mature African thinking and reflection." This will mean openness both to traditional African religions and to the Independent Churches. "The quest must therefore be ecumenical and all inclusive" if it is to touch the heart of Africa. For "good theology, like good poetry, is the recollection of powerful emotion in tranquillity."[185]

In the same issue of the *Ecumenical Review* is found a significant article by *Kofi Appiah-Kubi*, executive secretary of the Department of Theology of the All Africa Conference of Churches, on "The Church's Healing Ministry in Africa." It applies in specific ways to some of the principles that we have been discussing. Like almost all Africans, Appiah-Kubi is grateful for the notable work done over the years by the various mission hospitals in Africa in alleviating the physical sickness of Africans. But he feels that this work has been largely done in the context of "total or near total exclusion or rejection of spiritual healing." The consequence has been treatment not only without serious consideration for the world-views of persons but treatment that has left untouched and therefore unhealed many elements of the whole human being. He emphasizes that "in the mind of the African, there is a more unitary concept of psychosomatic interrelationship, that is, an apparent reciprocity between mind and matter."

Appiah-Kubi therefore concludes that a serious study of traditional African beliefs and practices with regard to both health and disease could be of extreme importance to the churches and the communities that they serve. He believes that "the holistic approach to health and disease observed by the priest- and faith-healers of the indigenous African churches can help to renew the whole approach of the Church's healing ministry to the problem of health and disease, at both practical and theoretical levels." He notes that converts to missionary-founded churches have been "effectively conditioned" to consider all traditional medicines and practices of faith-healing as "reprehensible paganism and quackery" but doubts that this is so. Incidentally, Mbiti and almost all other African theologians are currently thinking along these same lines. Appiah-Kubi therefore boldly suggests that the churches make good use of, "integrate into the service," "traditional priest-healers, faith-healers and other local medical experts." The indigenous or Independent Churches, for instance, insist that "our churches are not only churches, they are hospitals."[186]

Another way to perceive what is happening among thoughtful Christians in Africa today is to note the words of *Burgess Carr* (b. 1935), an Anglican from Liberia and secretary of the All Africa Council of Churches. He believes that the task of contemporary African theology is to liberate the Christian gospel from its "Western wrappings in order that the truths which Jesus of Nazareth reveals about God may encounter the spiritual, cultural and intellectual worlds of the African personality: the contours and contents of his mind, his cosmology and eschatology, his institutions and values, his history, politics, philosophy and ideology." But this is not to create another narrowness, a Christianity with "African wrappings." Carr insists that in spite of the tribalism of historic African life, there is a long tradition of the sharing of religious beliefs and practices. Thus he writes: "Universality is at the very heart of traditional African culture. It expresses itself religiously in the corporateness through which men and women relate to the cosmos, and socially in the communality with which they relate to one another in time and eternity." For this reason, as well as from the imperative of the gospel, he sees African Christians as part of the world community in which they "must also share in the redeeming work of Christ" (Col. 1:24; 1 Pet. 4:13).[187]

The last sentence of the previous paragraph must not be understood as a mere theological statement. It is, rather, to be perceived as expressive of the profundity as well as the practicality of contemporary African spirituality. Even the theme of liberation tends to be understood as leading to service of others and to sharing in the sufferings of Christ. Thus *Kenneth D. Kaunda* (b. 1924), the president of Zambia and the son of African missionaries who left their native Nyasaland (now Malawi) and went to serve among the Bemba people to the north, sees the message of the Christ as universal and all-embracing, his work as unifying as well as liberating. By word and deed the Christ imparted also the values of modesty and self-sacrifice. Even as his life of work and suffering for all was according to the principle of "living no longer for ourselves," so we, too, Kaunda tells his fellow Africans, must not only strive to imitate the Christ, "we should genuinely lead his life." As a Christian politician, Kaunda is particularly sensitive to the issues of economic and social justice; he would aim at conditions of equality, at what he calls a humanist society. He sees the honor and dignity of Africans as human beings to belong, like the Christ, to all and urges them to put their work to the service of all.[188]

Roman Catholics are making notable contributions to this context of need and opportunity out of their special breadth and depth of tradition. *Christopher Mwoleka* (b. 1927), bishop of Rulenge, Tanzania, has committed himself, along with perhaps most of his diocese, to the Tanzanian *Ujamaa*, or East African style of political and economic socialism. He sees this commitment as a "down to earth practical" way of imitating the life of the Holy Trinity, which is a life of sharing. He sees the Christ as offering us life, this very life of sharing, of living as he does. The mystery of the Trinity is therefore not to be solved as an intellectual problem but resolved by living it out in practice. Mwoleka sees it a particular responsibility of church members to "supply the interior dispositions needed for this kind of life." This means, as Vatican II exhorted, "to give internal strength to human associations which are just," to commit the mighty weight of Christian dedication to the welfare of the entire community, of the whole world.[189]

Let us conclude this section with a discussion of *Patrick Kalilombe* (b. 1933), Roman Catholic bishop, theologian, and biblical scholar from Malawi.* Kalilombe wrote an article on the theme of our present concerns, which first appeared in the June 1979 issue of *African Ecclesial Review* and which, brief as it is, is as carefully reasoned and as solidly based, biblically and theologically, as any that one might read.

Kalilombe begins by taking note of the tendency in the Christian church over long centuries to take a negative view of the possibility of human salvation outside the bounds of the institutional church. He observes that, in the large, it was not possible to take Cyprian's phrase *Extra ecclesiam nulla salus* with absolute literalness, but the tendency remained and with it a generally negative view of cultures and religions outside historic Christendom. And, as

---

*I had the privilege in 1982 of spending several days in comradely relationship with Kalilombe and found him to be one of the most intellectually brilliant and personally charming persons I have ever met. Indeed, a number of us at the small conference we were attending, both Catholics and Protestants, felt that if ever in the near future there were to be an African pope, Patrick Kalilombe should be the one! R.H.D.

he says, to judge from the normal practice of Christian missionary activity, it was long customary to regard "pagan practices" and systems as essentially aberrations. Little effort was therefore made "to explore the possibility of their providential role in the history of the peoples concerned." In other words, it was rarely asked where God was, God the creator of all as well as redeemer, in all the vast ranges of these histories. The Bible itself was read as supporting these negative evaluations.

Kalilombe takes "reading of the Bible" as one of the themes about which he arranges his thought and asks whether all the relevant elements of the evidence were carefully taken into account: "or was there a tendency to high-light only certain trends of thought appearing in the Scriptures while pushing into the background other important trends which might have modified the nature of the investigation? Were there certain prior working assumptions and attitudes that commanded the selection of the evidence and determined the relative weight given to apparently conflicting lines?" Kalilombe then observes that persons come to the reading of the Bible with all sorts of conditions, including, besides their personal and social histories, the imprint of their own epoch in time. Hitherto most evaluations of African traditional religions, he notes, have been made by non-Africans and, frankly, in the context of a missionary movement that not infrequently bore the ethos of a military expedition.

In this crusading spirit of struggle and conquest, the enemy was seen as primarily Satan. "But Satan was disguised and active through his network of false religions. He and his associates had to be encountered, unmasked in their perfidy, and then engaged in mortal battle." Missionaries may have often had genuine sympathy and love for individuals among the indigenous peoples. "But towards their religious systems and practices, and towards those who were guardians and promoters of these practices, there could be no compromise." In this context of thought and feeling, the most natural selection of biblical passages was of those expressing hostility toward the "pagans." Especially chosen were the diatribes against the idols of the nations, "those in the ridicule style in which Deutero-Isaiah excels."

Kalilombe, however, notes that this tendency, which is only one among several in the Bible, can well be understood as expressive of a defensive spirit prompted by the experiences of captivity and oppression suffered by exilic and postexilic Judaism.[190] Differently from other parts of the tradition, this tendency represented a distortion of the concept of election and a holy people in the direction of an "exclusivist ghetto mentality" prompted by "the need of a socially and politically disadvantaged group to protect itself from corrosive outside forces and to compensate psychologically for its inferiority by exalting whatever redeeming aspects it believes it possesses."

Kalilombe then goes on to show that in both the Old Testament and the New there are other and different trends of thought. "Both the Baptist (cf. Mt. 3:9–10; Lk. 3:8) and Christ went out of their way to stigmatize the misplaced confidence in mere belonging to an ethnic group, albeit a divinely chosen one (cf. Mt. 3:11-12; Jn. 8:37-41)." Kalilombe proceeds, very much in the manner of the early chapters of this book, to demonstrate that the main thrust of the teaching of the Bible is not exclusive but inclusive, that the beginning of all is the "cosmic Covenant of love between God and mankind by the very fact of creation."[191] The special choices of God are "a hopeful sign or proof of what in less evident ways he is doing all along with the whole of mankind, and they are meant to serve this wider Covenant." It is under this rubric and on the basis of the consistent biblical affirmation of "humanity's basic equality before God" that consideration of the "salvific nature of non-Christian religions should start."

On these foundations of biblical understanding Kalilombe develops his thesis that Israel is a "sort of prototype, a light to enlighten the nations and make them realize their God-given destiny." Just as this calling does not necessarily mean that the nations must become a part of the structure of Israel, so Kalilombe questions whether it is "God's intention to introduce every human being into [the] historical Church under pain of not being saved." Following the New Testament witness and the pronouncements of Vatican II, he sees the church as light, salt, leaven, a "City on the mountain whose presence assures the world that God is in the midst of his people (Mt. 5:13-16; Phil. 2:14-16). . . . The Church's destiny is to be inserted into the heart of the world as a sacrament, i.e. visible and effective sign, of the coming Kingdom of God, pointing towards this Kingdom, and proving its efficacious working by acting as a privileged champion of the tenets of the Kingdom." The church's primary concern, therefore, should be, not with mere recruitment of numbers, but with the "authenticity and efficacy of its witness in the world."

Kalilombe would see the situation of African Christians vis-à-vis their traditional religions much as that of the apostle Paul toward that of his fellow kinsmen of Israel who had not yet accepted Jesus of Nazareth as the Messiah of God, similar in both theological structure and intensity of emotion. In both cases the past of the peoples must be sincerely respected. The presence and the work of God therein must be recognized and acknowledged. Every African Christian "would start from the conviction that God has been ever present among his own people, just as he has been in all peoples, cultures, and religious tendencies of the world, not just as a condescension, but because this benevolent presence is in the logic of the cosmic Covenant of creation and re-creation."

Kalilombe insists that this kind of recognition and appreciation does not mean that everything in these religions is good or to be retained. Human nature and all its strivings, as the Bible "strongly" teaches, are under the shadow of sin, and appropriate discrimination is called for in every human setting. But Kalilombe would have us also remember that because God's Spirit is actively present, "it will be necessary to assume that there are also a lot of good and valid elements in this 'grouping'; and these positive elements must be worthy of respect and survival since they are the results of God's activity which is never ultimately defeated by sin and death."[192]

Consultation on Global Solidarity in Theological Education

At this point a final word, drawn from the World Council of Churches-sponsored U.S./Canadian Consultation on Global Solidarity in Theological Education held at the University of Toronto, July 12–15, 1981, is in order. Representative African speakers expressed themselves very much along the lines of what has been cited above, and most significantly, so did the two American black Christians, Samuel Proctor and Deotis Roberts, who were among the main speakers at the conference.

Isaya Guy Otemba, principal of Kima Theological College in Kenya, emphasized that Christian theology has global dimensions and global concerns, that Christian theology speaks of Christ as Lord of the universe as well as Lord of the universal church. "Let us, therefore, seek to maintain those elements of Christian theology which are universal, even as we seek to keep our theological meanings and our methodologies relevant to our particular local situation."

One of the ablest, as well as most clearly articulate, of the African representatives was John S. Pobee, then head of the Department for the Study of Religions and dean of the Faculty of Arts, University of Ghana. Pobee took up the fact that the early emphasis of the entire ecumenical movement was upon the need for cooperation and mutuality among the Christian churches, for mutually respectful and healing attitudes toward Christian denominations hitherto divided. He then stated very strongly that these mutually respectful and healing attitudes must now be directed toward "faiths and whole religious traditions hitherto divided. We now see freshly that we live together in a pluralistic world which was yet created by the one and same God of us all."

Like many other theologians from every major Christian tradition, Pobee insisted that "we need an adequate theology of creation as well as an adequate theology of redemption, in keeping with the fathers of the early church. The post-Reformation over-emphasis upon the individual aspects of salvation has had tragic results." Jean Samuel Zoe-Obeanga, formerly dean of the Protestant Theological Faculty of Yaounde, Cameroun, carried on the same theme with reiteration of the widely shared African perceptions of human solidarity and complementarity. He, like the others, contended that the great need of the day is for these profoundly biblical perceptions to be implemented in the life-practice, even in the sharing, of risks and sacrifices.[193]

8

Theological Epilogue

A NEW AGE IN CHRISTIAN THEOLOGY

Throughout this book, in the process of identification and description of the nature and background of developments leading to the new age into which Christian theology is now moving, we have seen an emerging consensus (and a growing momentum in that emergence) among an increasing number of theologians within every major branch of the Christian church.

Some readers may object that I have included here only those theologians who share the emerging consensus. In fact, many others not mentioned share in the consensus; and among those discussed here are also to be found considerable differences in their larger theological formulations. Their participation in this consensus has more to do with their perception of the nature of the changes taking place and with a general resolve to move away from theological exclusivism to an inclusivism that is in keeping with the best thought of the Judeo-Christian Scriptures and of the church of the first four or five centuries.

Yet it must also be acknowledged that in every major tradition of the Christian church there are those who are resisting mightily the strong contemporary pull in the direction of older theological inclusivism. As Lawrence Nemer has pointed out, we have a comparable case in the "revolutionary" Council of Jerusalem (A.D. 49), when the leaders of the mother church in Jerusalem decided to allow Gentiles to enter the Christian church with less stringent cultic requirements than had previously been considered appropriate for Jews. As then, so now, "not everyone has embraced the new vision of the Church. Some are being dragged into it screaming 'unfaithful to the tradition.' "[1]

In this study, however, in collaboration with many others, we have been able to build a strong case—with massive biblical and theological supportive material—for a theological stance that is distinctly Christian and yet also inclusive. What emerges is a Christian anthropology or doctrine of humanity, a doctrine of God, a doctrine of Jesus Christ as of the Holy Spirit that, taken together, is both true to the best of the Christian past and appropriate to the new age that we are now entering. Let us try to identify for purposes of summation the outlines of these developments.

In keeping with the results of the best biblical scholarship, there has been in Christian theology in the twentieth century a renewed emphasis upon the Old Testament teaching of the fact of the creation of human beings in the image and likeness of God (Gen. 1:26–27; 5:1). In the Gospel of John in the New Testament, along with a "high" Christology, it is increasingly seen that we also have the highest of anthropologies (Jn. 1:1–18; 10:31–39). These are but two elements in a transition in Christian perception, over the past century or more, of the nature of what it means to be human that we can only call radical.

We may note with appreciation the contributions in this area of the movement in Protestant theology from Karl Barth, Emil Brunner, and others that is best known as Neo-orthodoxy. In the United States we may cite in particular the influence of Reinhold Niebuhr (1892–1971), who expressed an anthropological position at points notably different from that of most post-Reformation forms of Calvinism or Puritanism. These latter had long tended to stress the utter unworthiness of sinful human beings before the majesty and holiness of Almighty God. We may recall the common language of confessions of sin, as "and there is no health in us," or the widely influential perception of the Puritan hymnwriter Isaac Watts (1674–1748) of himself as a "worm." These views were in some ways a natural development of the medieval and earlier ascetic tendency to focus on the unworthiness of the creature rather than on the love and glory of God. In part it was influenced by long-traditional Christian ascetic tendencies to focus on sin in physical expression, especially the sexual.

Reinhold Niebuhr and others, without altering significantly the older Protestant perception of the depth and power of sin and evil in human life and in the cosmos, nevertheless came to stress with new force the biblical affirmation that human beings are made in the image of God. This fact meant, for Niebuhr, a new-old reperception of human freedom, to be sure within limits, and of the greatness of human dignity, especially *in potentia*. Niebuhr wrote that "the essence of man is his freedom. . . . His essence is free self-determination." He also affirmed that "the human spirit has the special capacity of standing continually outside itself in terms of indefinite regression. Consciousness is a capacity for surveying the world and determining action from a governing centre. Self-consciousness represents a further degree of transcendence in which the self makes itself its own object in such a way that the ego is finally always subject and not object."[2]

This almost Renaissance-like perception of the nature of human consciousness and freedom was not intended by Niebuhr or any others in the Neo-orthodox tradition to be understood as *properly* leading to a Promethean independence of the human spirit. Quite to the contrary, Niebuhr insisted that in spite of the grandeur and the power of human self-transcendence, human beings are not self-sufficient. The nature of humanity is such that they may find "a harmonious relation of life to life" only in obedient relationship to the divine Source and Center of that life. Thus for Niebuhr the essence of sin is rebelliousness against God, a refusal to seek "harmonious relation of life to life" under the prior aegis of relationship with the Source of all. This is also a refusal to admit one's "creatureliness," that one has been *created* in the image of God, and therefore however exalted the potential inherent in the fact of the creation one must not fail "to acknowledge himself as merely a member of a total unity of life."

This writer would warmly espouse this understanding and emphasis of Reinhold Niebuhr, but would also stress that a somewhat different nuance has emerged within the past generation and more since Niebuhr wrote his great classic. The difference in nuance appears more in a reperception of the larger historical and geographical contexts of "human nature." The strong Neo-orthodox emphasis on the fact of human sin, which members of that movement saw as a necessary counterbalance to their perception of the inadequacies of the older Protestant liberalism in that area, had little to say to the long-dominant Western perceptions of the actual "distribution" of human sin across the world. That is, the Christian world, or Christendom, which in one sense was seen as very sinful indeed, was actually painted in far brighter colors than the "heathen" world.

The older missionary hymns give us a clear picture of the contrast generally held. We note, for example, in Bishop Reginald Heber's famous hymn, "From Greenland's Icy Mountains," written in 1819, how the other lands are bound in "error's chain." Theirs are "men benighted," while we— presumably Western Christians or perhaps all Westerners—are those "whose souls are lighted with wisdom from on high," who dare not deny "the lamp of life" to those benighted. Laura S. Copenhaver (1868–1940) in "Heralds of Christ" comparably wrote of "where once the crooked trail in darkness wound" as characteristic of those other lands.

Another revealing example is seen in the *Minutes of the General Assembly of the Presbyterian Church in the United States of America (1869)*. We find here sharp criticism of the promiscuous sexual practices of Japan of that day, which the missionary writer found "shockingly open" in comparison with Western mores. It was admitted that "Christian countries are not quite free from similar immoralities, but it is in darkness, a work of darkness and shame. Here vice stalks about at noonday."[3] The hypocrisy of this mode of comparison, particularly in light of New Testament teaching about interiority, was evidently apparent to few in Western lands at the time. As late as 1895 the well-known pioneer Protestant missionary-physician in Japan, James C. Hepburn, wrote of the Japanese in general that in morals, "they are like all pagan peoples, untruthful, licentious and unreliable."[4]

The Christian missionaries of the period, representing the prevailing mentality both of their sending churches and of the great bulk of their compatriots, tended—with the sole exception, in Japan, of the Unitarians and perhaps the Germans of liberal theological persuasion—to regard all non-Christians as in spiritual darkness. References were frequently made to "the darkness, the uncleanness and the delusion of heathenism." A church report made in the United States in the 1880s referred to the religion of the Japanese as "worthless and injurious." The victory of Christian faith, whose cultural expression in Japan or any other land both missionaries and their supporters at home expected to be little different from that in the West, was predicated upon the "downfall of idolatry, Buddhism and all false religions and philosophies."[5]

Qualifications to these harsh and unfair views were occasionally (and perhaps increasingly) made, even by their authors, as ongoing experience of living overseas compelled their modification. Given the long course of Western experience since the mid-nineteenth century, however, it is in some ways astonishing that Karl Barth was still able, writing in the early 1930s, to affirm, with many, yet inadequate, qualifications, that "the Christian religion is the true religion," "the right and true religion," over against "the false religions of the Jews and the heathen."[6] Perhaps we can say that the extreme position of Karl Barth and much of Neo-orthodoxy in this respect serves well to cast in sharper focus the nature of the changes that have taken place in the years since then.

A particularly good statement of the changes—we are especially thinking of perceptions of the nature and condition of "non-Christians" in the context of attempts to reformulate an authentic Christian anthropology—made in the twentieth century in Roman Catholic views is that offered by Pietro Rossano. What we have in the words of this director of the Vatican Secretariat for Non-Christians is a new-old "theological vision of humankind" which lays down a basis for dialogue and for a more pastoral approach to Christian evangelization. Rossano writes with special focus on Roman Catholic developments:

> Since the second quarter of the 20th Century, the course of theological reflection has progressively focused on the non-Christian and inculcated respect for him, not only as to his physical identity (which was always there in the Church), not only as to his cultural identity (which has not always been forthcoming, in spite of the clear directives of the ecclesiastical magisterium), but in his own religious identity. This is something which is in fact quite new in the Christian practice of the last centuries. Likewise, Catholic theology progressed from considering the non-Christian as a "being of pure nature," without faith and without divine grace and therefore a question mark as to the very possibility of being associated—*modo Deo cognito*—to the Paschal Mystery (*Gaudium et Spes* 22). There has been, in a word, a theological upgrading of the non-Christian, even in his quality as a religious man: he has been raised to a level of brotherhood and acceptance in the sight of God. It is in this that the theological reason for dialogue is found.[7]

This statement is a brilliant brief summation of what has happened from the 1920s on in Roman Catholic theological thought about the nature of the "non-Christian" and therefore says much about contemporary Catholic thought on the whole anthropological question. Rossano goes on to affirm the theological basis of these new-old convictions to lie in Christian awareness that "God also manifests Himself to those who do not bear the Christian name. The Bible leaves no doubt about this. . . . It is a matter of a multiform revelation which goes beyond the simple 'natural possibility of knowing God.' " Rossano, to be sure, holds that this revelation is "not yet" of the order of the historical revelation that is found in the Old and New Testaments, but he goes on to quote with approval (indeed, as "perfect") the definition given in *Guidelines for Inter-Religious Dialogue* published at Varanasi in 1977 by the Indian Episcopal [Roman Catholic] Commission for Dialogue. "Dialogue is the response of Christian faith in God's saving presence in other religious traditions and the expression of firm hope of their fulfilment in Christ."[8]

The theological position expressed here by Rossano is in fact what has been called the concept of fulfillment and was given one of its best modern expressions by the early twentieth-century Protestant missionary to India J. N. Farquhar.[9] It was conceived, however, and espoused by a number of Christian converts in Asia in the nineteenth century. In Japan, as we have previously seen, the early leaders of Japanese Protestantism of every major tradition— Hiromichi Kozaki, Danjō Ebina, Masahisa Uemura, among others—felt themselves compelled both by their new faith and by their existential knowledge of the religious and cultural heritage of their people to find theological meaning in the past of this people, precisely from the standpoint of the history of salvation.[10]

The concept of fulfillment is not as widely held in the late twentieth century, especially among Protestant theologians, as it was earlier in the century, partly because it seems to have meaning primarily only for Christians. For those who are not Christian it often communicates notions of superiority and religious imperialism. Another reason for the dissatisfaction with the concept, even among Christians, is that persons in espousing it often do not take adequate account of possible divine meaning and value in other religious traditions as continuing realities in contemporary history. Furthermore, the concept, when properly understood, means that Jesus Christ, not the Christian church or Christianity as an empirical movement in history, is the fulfillment of the religions. This is the conclusion, incidentally, to which Karl Barth's theological thought properly leads and which should have prevented him from trying to affirm that "Christianity" is the one true religion.

The fulfillment, moreover, is to be perfectly and visibly realized only as an eschatological reality, at the edge or end of history. At that time, according to Christian faith, Jesus Christ as the Lord of life will fulfill Christianity as well as other religions. He will then deliver the kingdom to God, "that God may be everything to everyone" (1 Cor. 15:24–28). In the meantime both Christianity and the church share in the imperfections and inadequacies of all human experience, as do the other religious traditions of humankind.

At the same time, however, there is an abiding value in the fulfillment theory. It has certainly helped to open the eyes of Western Christians to perceive the reality of the presence and saving work of God in the whole world and among all humankind. It has served as a key to reperceive what the Judeo-Christian Scriptures actually teach about these wider ranges of God's presence and work. It has helped many to find both truth and goodness in other religious traditions to which their previous ideological faith-commitments had blinded them. In a sense, the concept of fulfillment may be seen as one theological expression of the emergence of Western Christians from religious and cultural tribalism. Its abiding value primarily lies in its eschatological aspect, by which the tentative nature of all religious forms and institutions, including the Christian, may be stressed and a due religio-cultural as well as personal modesty retained. This aspect should also keep before all Christians the hope of their glory in Jesus Christ, who is, however, the hope not only of their own fulfillment but also of the fulfillment of many others who "will come from east and west and sit at table with Abraham, Isaac and Jacob in the kingdom of heaven" (Mt. 8:11; cf. Lk. 13:29; Isa. 49:12; Mal. 1:11; Ps. 107:3).[11]

A final word in this section is in order to make clear that the newly positive view of "non-Christian" persons of which Rossano speaks is not to be understood in any easygoing, sentimental way. That is, the affirmation is not of a Jean-Jacques Rousseau-like perception of a kind of universal moral goodness in "natural man." There is no thought here of an all-prevailing moral goodness in the life of human beings. Our twentieth-century experiences of genocide, as well as what seems to be an extremely wide range of testimonies from every culture and every age, rigorously forbid any light view of the reality of evil and human wrongdoing, of what the Judeo-Christian tradition denotes as sin. This is not the place to cite extended support for this thesis, but it is not without significance that Gautama the Buddha used language as strong as the apostle Paul or any Old Testament prophet to describe the empirical self of human beings. He saw the self at this level as characterized by evil desires, as, indeed, in their "thrall." This self is given to self-exaltation, wrath, fault-finding, temper, ill-will, sulkiness. This is the self dominated by self-will, self-centeredness. It is the self-in-isolation, the opposite of the self in relationship with what is Ultimate and therefore oriented toward ethical living.[12]

Yet this language and this understanding are still not to be understood in any totalistic sense, as in the Reformation or post-Reformation concept of the total depravity of human beings, as with the notion that the whole of human life is one totally unrelieved mass of wrongdoing or misery. There is actually a great deal of quiet goodness among persons in this world, in every society, in every age, and it behooves us all to perceive it gladly and to acknowledge it with gratitude. All over the world, even with significant differences in understanding as well as in terminology, most persons perceive and affirm that this goodness can only be wrought in some form of dependent relationship with what they consider Ultimate Reality. The Judeo-Christian Scriptures, like the Buddhist, are far more balanced in their entirety than to give warrant to totalistic views of human evil. It is ironical, however, that these extreme views have served in the past to support the quite unrealistic notion that the "heathen" are somehow worse in their moral life, as in their religious beliefs, than those in traditionally Christian lands. The Bible—for example, in the Psalms—is far more concerned to deal with the actual particularities of life and sees that the issues of faith and unbelief, of moral obedience and disobedience are within Israel as well as without (e.g., Pss. 1, 6, 7, 10, 14–19, 22).

This is therefore the more realistic posture that Christians are now being called to take with reference to the whole world of humankind. We are being asked, for one thing, to remember that the sole criterion that, as recorded in the Gospels of the New Testament, Jesus gives as the test by which to evaluate the religious authenticity of persons is the ethical one. "You will know them by their fruits" (Mt. 7:16).[13] Elsewhere in the New Testament, indeed throughout the Pauline letters and the other literature of the apostolic period, theological as well as ethical criteria are presented. It is significant, however, that nowhere are theological criteria divorced from ethical; a significant example of the correlation of the two is the first letter of John. Therefore, we can well agree with Paul when he wrote, "all who are led by the Spirit of God are sons of God" (Rom. 8:14). So also we may say that all who manifest the Christ-Life, the Spirit of Christ, have received from him and belong to him (cf. Rom. 8:9). This is one aspect of the "new, unheard-of and frightening human unity" that Malachi Martin has seen emerging in our day, a unity that is also presenting Christian theology and the Christian church with almost unprecedented opportunities for new qualities of life, as for new kinds of witness and service.

THE CHRISTIAN DOCTRINE OF GOD

One of the most widely accepted concepts of contemporary theological thinking is that God is present and at work in the secular life of human beings as well as in their traditionally sacred, or religious, spheres of activity. Following Dietrich Bonhoeffer perhaps no single idea has so captured the imagination of, especially, younger Christian theologians in both East and West. Increasingly over the years since the end of World War II, the wider implications of this understanding have come to be seen. That is, if God the Father of Jesus Christ is seen as "free" to act independently of the ecclesial structures and ecclesiastically related personages of the Judeo-Christian tradition, God is free to work and to have worked in widely disparate areas, geographical, cultural, religious. What has happened is a renewed understanding of the universality of God's work, a perception that we have seen, for example, in various expressions of the fulfillment theory, and in the rediscovery of the universal covenants of the Bible, of relationships presumed to exist from the beginning between God and the whole of humanity, indeed with all living things.

This understanding that God is and has been present and at work in the whole world, in every race of humankind and in every culture, has in its background a great amount of solid theological work. It has been made possible by the discovery and reformulation of ancient perspectives of Christian faith. A fresh recognition of the importance to Christian faith of the doctrine of creation, so as to be quite comparable in significance and weight to the doctrine of redemption, as in the more balanced views of early Christian theologians, has contributed to the understanding.[14] It is seen that there is a necessary connection between the orders of creation and of redemption. In this context of thought, creation is also seen to be ongoing. The physical universe appears to be continually expanding. It seems to require the continuous exercise of energy and unceasing renewal by the creative forces of God. This fact has led to a new respect in recent Christian theology for the entire natural order, certainly for all human beings, but also for all living beings, for all that is. No longer is it biblically or theologically permissible to interpret the word to Adam and Eve "fill the earth and subdue it" (Gen. 1:28) as warrant for a ruthless, savage, or domineering approach to the natural order, whether human or other.

Part of this awareness is to sense not only that all human beings live in one world, the creation of one God, but also that in some measure all draw from the same spiritual and moral Source. However broken and imperfect, even distorted, may be the particular manifestations in human life of these manifold drawings from the one Source, loving eyes can usually discern something of their Source in every person, as in every flower. The same eyes can also perceive widespread aspiration to a common fulfillment in the midst of varied "names and forms." On the basis of this understanding, it has become theologically meaningful and, *in potentia*, religiously and ethically helpful to explore more widely and deeply into previously divergent traditions of faith-understanding of the Ultimate Mystery that, we believe, surrounds, permeates, and yet transcends our mortal lot. This is the Mystery that we believe demands love and right living between and among all human persons, and love for all that is.

THE CHRISTIAN DOCTRINE OF JESUS CHRIST

We come now to what is perhaps the most difficult of all Christian doctrines, the doctrine of Jesus Christ. This is also the issue of the significance of particularity within universality. Given the reasons we have noted for recognition of the universality of the presence and work of the God of Christian faith in the whole of his creation, we may ask: Wherein lies theological significance, moral authority, normative quality in the particular? Our answer is that there is much significance in the particular, as has been suggested in earlier chapters, even in the particularity of the election of Israel. Let us then consider, in a recapitulative way, the significance of the particular in Jesus of Nazareth, the Christ.

John Hick has spoken of the "basic awareness of our time that in all the great [religious] traditions at their best the transformation of human existence from self-centeredness to Reality-centeredness is taking place."[15] This statement, which the present writer warmly affirms, is properly understood only in the further awareness that such process of transformation takes place in the context of traditions that have their own modes of affirming particularity. Such particularity, furthermore, almost always includes some concept and practice in the use of criteria, of standards of value and meaning. Even if we may assume an essential similarity of event-meaning in the process of worship and other forms of participation in the various human communities of faith across the world, there are, as we have seen, important differences in the way persons conceive of the Ultimate or express their responses thereto. These conceptions and responses also emerge from within the life of a concrete cumulative tradition, in some cases involving thousands of years of process of cumulation. For the great majority of persons this concrete tradition is a kind of spiritual home in which hallowed persons, objects, and practices are enshrined. Here are family and friends, revered spiritual leaders, sacred Scriptures, familiar phrases and acts of liturgy, music and chantings, creeds and symbols, beloved stories of ancient worthies of the faith. Out of this kaleidoscopically colorful mixture emerges for most persons in communities of faith a single criterion, or focus of criteria, that enables groups and individuals to find order in their lives and to make intelligent ethical choices.

The one single criterion by which persons of Christian faith have historically believed they must order their lives, both individually and collectively, is the person of Jesus Christ. Jesus Christ as criterion has often, and for long centuries, been significantly mediated through both church and Scripture, and we shall consider this aspect of the problem below. We shall also leave out of consideration any question as to the enormous variations in degrees of faithfulness by which either individuals or communities have followed this criterion of Jesus Christ in their life practices. The statement in itself, however, while simple in mode of expression, is by no means simple in application. For one thing, persons never perceive the Christ without mediation or follow him in a social or cultural vacuum.

The very first disciples of Jesus of Nazareth followed him in the context of the religious tradition of Israel, specifically in the multiform variety of religious parties and interpretations of the day. Certainly they perceived his person and interpreted his words and deeds through the filter of their own individual foci of consciousness. The New Testament accounts, however, record a certain general development in the disciples' understanding of Jesus from wandering teacher or rabbi to prophet, from prophet to Messiah and then to transcendent Lord, mysteriously one with and representative of Ultimate Reality as perceived in the historic faith of Israel. Parallel to this development of understanding of the person and role of Jesus seems to have been a development of the disciples' acceptance of him as criterion under God, who is the Source of all divine truth and goodness. In principle, Jesus of Nazareth, once resurrected from the dead, became the disciples' criterion in an absolute sense.

But wise persons then and now know that all truth and goodness received from others are received through the mediation of one's own and others' fallible minds and in the context of one's own and others' tainted as well as limited experiences both past and present. Therefore even in those wondrous forty days of the appearances of Jesus to his disciples, from his resurrection to his ascension, those of the disciples who were wise would not have precisely identified their understanding of Jesus' words with the absoluteness of their criterion. Even more so has been the case in all times and places subsequent to the ascension when Jesus is no longer present quite in the sense of the Palestinian days, however we may interpret experiences such as that of the apostle Paul on the road to Damascus or of Sadhu Sundar Singh on the early morning of December 18, 1904.

Perceptive readers will recognize that the author is engaging in the process of religious dialogue with what may be termed a high Christology of his own. Permit me to speak briefly in the first person singular. I forthrightly accept the resurrection of Jesus of Nazareth as a historical-transhistorical event, as also an event with literally cosmic consequences. I furthermore accept the death of Jesus on the cross, followed by his resurrection, as an event that specifically unleashed divine powers of veritably cosmic consequence unto the forgiveness and liberation of others, of "many" (Mk. 10:45). I can agree with John Hick's demurral that traditional concepts of the Christ-event as divine incarnation, particularly when interpreted as meaning that the Christian religion has been confined "to the single thread of human history documented in the Bible," require some qualification. But I do not feel that it is necessary to follow Hick in his conclusion that "the notion of a special human being as a 'son of God' is a metaphorical idea which belongs to the imaginative language of a number of ancient cultures,"[16] and is therefore not to be taken seriously as having contemporary meaning. I would of course agree with Hick—as with Muhammad—that the notion cannot properly mean that Jesus was begotten by God in the sense of pagan deities who mate. I believe, further, that the main thrust of New Testament teaching with regard to the divine sonship of Jesus Christ is affirmed in the context of further affirmation of a potential continuum, both ontological and functional, between Jesus the elder brother and the rest of humanity. That is the subject for another book, however.

Suffice it to say here that, together with this continuum, there is weighty evidence from the apostolic period and from later centuries to conclude that in Jesus of Nazareth we have to do with a truly exalted being of notably cosmic dimensions both in his origins and his subsequent activities. We have seen in earlier chapters how certain early Jewish Christian groups tried to express faith-perceptions of this kind in keeping with their own background of understanding. The unvaried witness, however varied in mode of expression, of specifically New Testament faith is that in some distinctly experienceable way the risen Jesus continues, as living Lord and ongoing representative of the Most High, to be present and to work, *in potentia*, with all persons in all places and times. Historically this affirmation of faith has been often understood by Christians as a presence limited to those who name the name of Jesus explicitly in conscious and "knowing" continuity with the historic Jesus of Nazareth. We are now able to say that Jesus, as the Christ, "stands at the door of every consciousness of man that seeks to know and will enter if man will but open" (cf. Rev. 3:20). This is the light that "shineth in the hearts and lives of men *everywhere*, in all periods of experience" (cf. Jn. 1:9; italics added). And yet this universally available presence, we would affirm, is in actual continuity in spiritual as well as in ethical quality of life with Jesus of Nazareth, even if not always and everywhere consciously perceived as such.

THE ROLE OF THE HOLY SPIRIT

It is surely an advantage to "know" the living God through this Jesus Christ whom God has sent (cf. Jn. 17:3). As Christians, however, one of our most serious flaws historically is that often we have not adequately perceived or honestly acknowledged the provisional, inadequate nature of our "knowing." We have an absolute criterion whom we know only in part (cf. 1 Cor. 13:12). We Christians who live in the times since the ascension share with one another the varying ambiguities of tradition, much of which in its early forms became canonized in the New Testament. We share the ambiguities of the inspiration-guidance of the Holy Spirit. We share the ambiguities of the fellowship of the church, including its ongoing Tradition or traditions.

Much of the history of the Christian church has been given over to attempts to elevate one or another of these three factors—Bible, guidance of the Holy Spirit, church as institution—into an absolute. We need not pause to consider the sorry details of attempts to regard the Bible as inerrant, the church or bishop as infallible, or the guidance of the Holy Spirit (in human experience) as utterly dependable. In fact, we can consider such attempts as in any case unhappy failures. Only when the three factors are used as what Robert C. Johnson has called reciprocal coefficients, in a reciprocal interworking, can they function in a wholesome, constructive way.[17] The teaching of Jesus as recorded in the New Testament Gospels seems to suggest that a fundamental characteristic of his followers is not only to be teachable, but also to be open to correction from both their Maker and their fellow creatures on the basis of ongoing awareness of personal as well as corporate imperfection in faith-understanding and inadequacy of practice. This posture seems particularly in keeping with our long-experienced need to acknowledge that as Christians our relationship with our Lord is but imperfect, our knowledge but in part, our praxis but faulty. Such awareness is certainly inimical to any kind of triumphalism that puts Christian qua Christian or church qua church in a superior position vis-à-vis others in the world. We have seen also that the main thrust of the teaching of both the Old Testament and the New is to the effect that those who have been given the more will, to that extent, be called to account the more.

Awareness of the inadequacy of human perception, understanding, and practice is equally appropriate, and perhaps as difficult to achieve, among those in other religious traditions. They, too, have varied criteria, although generally with some kind of focus. This is not the place for an extended discussion of this complex theme, but we may note certain instances. As is well known, in both Hindu and Buddhist traditions from very ancient times personal religious experience is often accorded a supremely normative role, although almost never in a total sense. Scriptures also play a role: the Pali canon in Theravada Buddhism, the Pure Land or the Lotus Scriptures in the Mahayana. In historic Hinduism the Vedas are generally normative in a formal sense, while the Upanishads, the Bhagavad Gita, and later writings may constitute more existential criteria. The role of the caste systems in Hinduism, society in particularized form, often constitutes the supreme criterion with regard to external conduct of every kind. Religious teachers, a guru in Hindu context, a Zen master in that tradition, a Sufi master in Islam, may play highly significant normative roles as specific foci of criteria of the particular communities of faith.

In the complex admixture, in varying proportions of all these influences, that constitutes the actual situation in the concrete for each person, family, or community, both individuals and groups struggle to achieve clarity of understanding, order, and consistency in their lives. As Christians we must affirm that the universal Logos of God, whom we confess as one with Jesus of Nazareth, works to protect, guide, correct, and sustain the sincere in any historical context. As we noted in the perceptions of the Spanish cardinal Juan de Lugo already in the seventeenth century, "the soul that in good faith seeks God, His truth and love [whatever be the terminology that individuals use with regard to these Realities], concentrates its attention, under the influence of grace, upon those elements of truth, be they many or few, which are offered to it in the sacred books and religious schools and assemblies of the Church, Sect, or Philosophy in which it has been brought up. It feeds upon these elements, the others are simply passed by; and divine grace, under cover of these elements, feeds and saves the soul."[18] This process of discrimination under God, we may note, given the many and great variations in content of both faith and practice over long centuries of church history, is also applicable to Christian experience.

Affirmation of the resurrection of Jesus of Nazareth, as of his ascension and the coming of the Spirit, perhaps inevitably leads to some form of trinitarian theology. Jesus himself stressed the unity of God (Mk. 12:28–34), and probably this aspect of the Most High is the final word (cf. 1 Cor 3:23; 15:24–28). But under this aegis there seems to be room for distinctions of function and even person that we may call trinitarian. Within this framework of thought, it was of the genius of the fathers of the early church to affirm the identity of Jesus of Nazareth and the universal Logos of God. As we have seen, this understanding enabled Clement of Alexandria to assert a multitude of covenants that God had made with the nations of the world. Rediscovery of this ancient perspective of faith has enabled modern Christians to realize that others than Christians may be in authentic relationship with the Maker of all and receive grace and truth from the Creator in ways uncharted by Christian theology in more recent centuries.

This openness to surprise, surprise that the finest qualities of Christic (Christlike) faith and obedience can be found in what some might call unexpected persons and places, has characterized the most sensitive Christian missionaries of every age, from Gregory Thaumaturgus to Matteo Ricci, from Francis Xavier to Christian Friedrich Schwartz, from Nikolaus von Zinzendorf to Guido Verbeck. We should note, however, that in more recent years many among those not commonly called Christian have had access to and have made use of perhaps all three of the reciprocal coefficients (cited above) by which Christians have traditionally known their Lord. We have referred already to the universal availability of the Logos of God. But in the twentieth century not a few in many lands who do not call themselves Christian have participated in various forms of assembly in Christian worship. Even more—indeed, in numerous cases, far more—have read the Bible. The extraordinary increase in the sale of the Bible and portions of the Bible in Japan since the end of World War II, reaching well beyond eight million a year, according to the statistics of the Japan Bible Society, is a concrete example. This number, given the combined membership of all the Christian churches in the land at roughly one million, means that very large numbers of "non-Christians" are reading the Bible at least to a measure comparable with Bible reading among church members in Western lands.

This is not meant to downgrade the significance of the church of Jesus Christ or membership therein in the institutional sense. Every specific organization of that church is a confessing community of worship and service, often an expression of human life at its highest levels. But we should pull away from any kind of absolutization of the meaning and value of the church as institution. The evidence of the New Testament seems to point to Jesus' having had an instrumental perception of the role and status of his followers, as the tradition of Israel at its best had of its own role and status. Their election was for service, not for privilege. The church of Jesus Christ can thus be viewed metaphorically as the "picked troops" of the Lord, picked for special functions and training, possibly even for special modes of relationship. In this context of understanding, the church has every right to establish specific qualifications for membership and to discipline as well as to instruct its members, even though we must say that the church does not have the right to absolutize its procedures of discipline. The office of the keys (Mt. 16:19; 18:18; Jn. 20:23) has often been interpreted as conveying ultimate authority to the church or to its leaders—with immensely corrupting effect on its holders—but already in the New Testament period such interpretation was implicitly rejected (Rev. 1:18).

The present members of the church are therefore not all of the body to be, nor are they all of the troops presently under command and in the service of the universal Logos. This fact means also that the composition of the followers of Jesus of Nazareth, neither in the days of his flesh nor now, was fixed in any final sense, regardless of the variety of ways the historic church has handled this issue.

From the standpoint of Christian faith, then, the God and Father of our Lord Jesus Christ is sovereignly free within the whole of creation. Not only is God free, however; God has in fact manifested the divine self, will, and saving grace outside as well as within the historic bounds and instrumentation of Israel and the Christian church. As Irenaeus put it, "Where the Spirit of God is, there is the church and all grace." This grand affirmation of faith was turned backwards by the church in the Middle Ages as it presumed to claim control of the Spirit of God. Hence we have come back full swing to affirm with the contemporary Greek Orthodox theologian Georges Khodr that "All who are visited by the Spirit are the people of God."

The foregoing also means that the great religions of human history are, at least potentially, what have been called "training schools of the divine mercy." It means therefore that Christian theologians, and indeed all Christians, are under theological as well as moral obligation to seek to identify all Christic values across the world, in all human history, and specifically in other religious traditions. We are reminded of Karl Rahner's words that heretofore we have looked too ineptly and with too little love at other religious traditions to perceive the traces (*Spuren*) of the divine presence and work outside our medieval-modern theological "confinements" of God and Christ. We are now called to acknowledge and use these findings as potentially authentic source materials for Christian theology, along with the Bible and Christian tradition, even if we do not put them in the category of criteria. The point is that possession of specific criteria (Jesus the Christ, Bible, Guidance of the Holy Spirit, Fellowship of the People of God) should not mean that all else apart from the criteria is of negligible value or meaning.

Raymond Panikkar has written in this context of thought that we have to do with a "universal economy of salvation and a certain mysterious presence of the Lord in a multitude of epiphanies." We have seen in previous chapters that this "wider work of God in the world" is aimed, as the Scriptures proclaim, at all human beings and the restoration of the entire cosmos. We dare not, therefore, limit the ranges of God's work by outmoded theologies of medieval or early modern provenance merely because they have the momentum of some centuries of acceptance behind them.

This line of thought, however, does not mean a universally guaranteed salvation. Like Paul and Origen, we may hope for the ultimate salvation of all, but that does not mean that it is guaranteed. Guaranteed salvation may not be properly proclaimed in advance any more than its reverse, negative pronouncement of details of the Last Judgment, may be given in advance. Human life in all times and places continues to be presented with the challenge given by the Deuteronomist in the words of Moses, "I have set before you life and death, blessing and curse; therefore choose life, that you and your descendants may live, loving the Lord your God, obeying his voice and cleaving to him; for that means life to you and length of days" (Deut. 30:19-20).

I would advocate therefore an Alexandrian theology with "teeth in it," perception of the universal divine love and providence as wise and good and loving but not soft. The merciful, universal Lord continues to stand at the door of every human heart and knock; new every day are God's mercies and opportunities. Those who will not accept them, however, continue to receive the recompense of their choices and of their being-action ("Those whom I love, I reprove and chasten," Rev. 3:19).

The church of Jesus Christ is also still under divine commission to proclaim the gospel as well as to serve all nations to the ends of the earth (Mt. 28:16-20). It is good for all to hear and to heed the gospel, especially when it is taught in an inclusive rather than exclusive way. The best theological thought of our day, in every major Christian tradition, has come to affirm the church, not as the sole ark of salvation, but as a sign, as the eschatological community that points to the consummation of history, the convergence of all truth and goodness, in the Lord Christ. The essence of the meaning of the great commission, as of the gospel, is the offering of intimate relationship with the Lord of life and of participation in the process of discipleship. In fresh ways it is now seen how wide and how deep are the ranges of that process, and members of the church participate in the process with perhaps as many variations in degree as do those who are not of the institutional church. Those who hear and heed the gospel for the first time, say as adults, may do so with a remarkably rich background of sensitive obedience to the previous workings of the universal Logos and may make remarkably rapid progress along the Christian way (cf. Acts 9:2; 19:9). Some who have long been members of the church may not be so far along the same way. How else can we understand "phenomena" like Sundar Singh, Toyohiko Kagawa, and James Aggrey?

Our problem as contemporary Christians is not unlike that of the apostle Paul. In facing the fact that the coming of the Christ had broken down "the dividing wall of hostility" between massively large historic human divisions—between Jew and Gentile (religio-ethnic), between slave and free (socioeconomic), between male and female (physical gender), between Greek and barbarian (cultural-educational)—Paul continued to feel a powerful need to affirm both the historic and the ongoing significance of Israel under God. He forthrightly states, on the one hand, that "he is not a real Jew who is one outwardly, nor is true circumcision something external and physical. He is a Jew who is one inwardly, and real circumcision is a matter of the heart, spiritual and not literal. His praise is not from men but from God" (Rom. 2:28-29). But then he goes on to say that "much in every way" is the "advantage" that the Jew of the historic tradition has (Rom. 3:1-2). The difference is now that this "advantage" is, in Paul's thought, no longer religiously ultimate in any sense of the word. It is no more than instrumental and provisional; in fact, in eschatological perspective it has no final meaning at all (cf. Eph. 2:11-22; Gal. 3:23-29; Rom. 2:28-3:2; 1 Cor. 15:24-28).

The church of Jesus Christ participates in the same advantage and provisionality as historic Israel. When the inner dimensions of life are considered, as Paul wished his fellow Israelites to do, the church may also be led to a sobering and penitent humility. As Christians come to know the rest of the world and its history better, they may very possibly come to the conclusion that in certain places, among some of its "faithful," they have by no means manifested the purest or highest form of divine presence and activity of their age. They may see themselves as but one of several foci or streams of divine revelatory and saving activity in human history. Christians know the "name" of the Lord and Savior of all and, when true to their calling, recognize and heed his voice. The church of Jesus Christ is called to proclaim, in word and life, the name and person of its Lord even though it finds no eschatological ultimacy in its own institutional forms and sees both the structures and the activity of its life to be but one of several "converging" foci of divine presence and activity in human history. This "convergence" is assuredly an eschatological promise to the eyes of faith. To the eyes of love it may be a reality in process.[19]

The way of the Christian church in inner life and outer mission will therefore not be triumphal but modest and, as needful, penitent. This Christian way may be a veritable *via crucis* in unassuming witness and service because the church will look not to its own temporal aggrandizement but to the glorification of the name of the one, true God and the Christ whom God sent. Through the mystery of divine promise the church looks forward to the convergence and manifestation in transformed glory of all strands of divine activity, of which it is one. The Lord who will effect this transformation—which may take much "time"—is the Lord whose name it knows. The church finds its own self, its life purposes and lifestyle in service of the purposes of this Lord but not, for now, its glory. The glory will be known only at the time of consummation, which will also be the time of full convergence. The glory will be shared with others who "will come from east and west, and from north and south, and sit at table in the kingdom of God."

THE CHRISTIAN WORLD MISSION

One final word remains to be said in this context. What of the Christian world mission in its religious specifics, both at home and abroad? Is there no place or need for evangelism, for the proclamation as well as the practice of the Christian gospel, for the good news that "God was in Christ reconciling the world to himself" (2 Cor. 5:19)? There is much need, very much indeed.

The Christian world mission is the singly identifiable most influential activity in all human history, an affirmation that this writer makes even in the face of full recognition of the high moral and spiritual worth of other massive religious movements in the course of human history, such as the slow but widely civilizing as well as spiritually enlightening permeation of Vedic-Brahmanic Hinduism in Asia and other parts of the world; the high religious significance and culturally transforming influence of Buddhism as it moved outward in Asia, to the west and north, to the south and east; the vast impact over long centuries of the expansion of Islam, impelled as it was by a heady mixture of religious zeal, military prowess, and thirst for empire and its appurtenances. Of course, all religious movements work with a mixture of motives and various levels of practice. Yet honesty compels us to acknowledge that the expansion activities of both Islam and Christianity, with their acquisitions of empire and colonies en route, appear in motive and practice to be perhaps the most mixed of all with less than noble qualities in their processes.

But what we are about in these days and in this book is the purification of both motive and practice of the Christian world mission, not its abolition. The affirmation in the previous paragraph of its superlatively massive influence still stands. The Great Commission (Mt. 28:16–20) still operates as a compelling command and privilege for all Christians. What we now see, however, is that no human being is spiritually a blank sheet of paper or morally to be considered totally depraved. Each person has a past and a present worthy of respect, a story worth telling and hearing.

Yet the honesty that compels us to see and acknowledge our own flaws in both past and present compels us also to see the vast ranges of contemporary human need in the world: spiritual, mental, and physical. Even at best persons in every religious tradition know more than they practice, and we all need further instruction. The actual religious and moral condition of every nation or people is fraught with failure and despair. All religious traditions tend to run down, and every generation needs reform and renewal. Modern secularism and naturalistic thought, while by no means as total in their effects as is sometimes claimed, have nonetheless seriously eroded the spiritually enlightening and morally transforming power of religious faith in the lives of vast numbers of persons. In Japan, for instance, while a sense of the unseen world is by no means absent, decisive power in religious faith for the larger ranges of human activity—political, economic, cultural, personal—seems rare. Perhaps the same could be said for every country. The participation of persons in traditional religious activities has become in many cases unnervingly halting.

The role of the Christian world mission is therefore not merely to gain converts to specifically Christian faith, although that remains a legitimate goal in this religiously pluralistic world. The number of persons in almost every country with seriously eroded religious faith—whatever its tradition—

is such as to keep an appeal to specifically Christian faith with organizational commitments a fully legitimate human courtesy. Yet the role of the Christian world mission is also to inspire, to stimulate, perhaps even to shame persons to reform and renew not only their own lives but also their own religious traditions. It is a well-known fact that not a little of the so-called resurgence of ancient religions within the nineteenth and twentieth centuries, as well as the emergence of new ones, has been owed to the challenge of the Christian mission, from the Brāhmo Samāj of India to Sōka Gakkai of Japan and the Independent Churches of Africa.

The primary motivation of the Christian world mission emerges from both the command and the nature of the God whom we see revealed in Jesus Christ. Certainly a primary reason for believing Christians is that they have been commanded to "go" (Mt. 28:16–20; Mk. 13:10; 16:15; Lk. 24:47; Jn. 17:18; 20–21; Acts 1:8).[20] The biblical doctrine of God, God's nature as active, revealing, sending, seeking love impels us.[21] There are those who have found their motivation as deriving, at least in part, from seeing mission as a necessary means to prepare for and hasten the return of Jesus Christ. Others have developed sophisticated concepts of Christian mission as an eschatological work and the church as an eschatological sign of the salvation of the nations. The nature, however, of human need is also a valid and impelling reason.

In the history of the Christian mission, compassion for what we may call the plight of "non-Christians" has generally not been separable from concern for their eternal salvation. We now see that the plight of Christians is comparably ambiguous ("Let any one who thinks that he stands take heed lest he fall," 1 Cor. 10:12) and that the New Testament teaching on salvation is considerably more complex than early modern Western European Pietists or evangelicals thought. Yet this compassion was in actual fact by no means confined to concern for the spiritual state and ultimate destiny of persons. From the very earliest period a spirit-and-practice of wider concerns has characterized the Christian mission at its best and has led to a vast range of life and culture-transforming activities in the areas of personal welfare, education, and health services for persons within and without the church (Gal. 2:10).[22] We have seen that these activities have also not infrequently been mixed with un-Christlike concepts of Western cultural superiority. But the examples of both Jesus and the church over the centuries at its best make it clear that concern for the present physical as well as spiritual condition of persons is an integral part of Christian faith-practice. This is what we may call a pragmatic, or temporal, motivation to mission, in the teaching of Jesus a motive as powerful as any other (Mk. 12:28–34; Mt. 25:40).

It does make a difference, often a quite discernible difference, among individuals and groups in any society if the Christian gospel be faithfully proclaimed and lived in that society. Perhaps a single, simple illustration will give focus to this point. Some years ago this writer—the only foreigner present— had the opportunity to hear the then general secretary of the national YMCA of Japan, Sōichi Saitō, address a gathering largely consisting of Japanese students in the city of Kamakura. In this talk Saitō endeavored to list the contributions of the Christian gospel to Japan, not only to Japanese Christians but in some measure to the whole nation, especially as these had become discernible in the more than one hundred years since the reopening of Japan to foreign intercourse in the 1850s.

The first item that Saitō cited was elevation of the social as well as personal status of women. In spite of the great contributions over long centuries to Japanese life and culture of Buddhism, Confucianism, and native Shinto, here was a vastly significant area of human life that most later observers would agree distinctly needed much improvement. We may add, too, that wherever the Christian gospel has gone, it has consistently brought with it, even if not perfectly or even adequately, the sweet savor of respect for the person as well as concern for the status of both women and children.[23]

Saitō went on to cite Christian contributions with reference to the concept of monotheism, ideals of social and political justice, the concept of personality, the ideal of a single standard of sexual morality, of the transformation of the inner person, one's motives and attitudes. He spoke as a man who had seen most of these contributions—distinctly as concepts and ideals, partly in practice—discernibly in process in his own lifetime. This kind of eyewitness report can be duplicated from almost every part of Asia, Africa, the islands of the seas—and also from almost all parts of the Western world—with the teaching and practice of Jesus always playing a significant role. The accumulation of these reports constitutes for thoughtful persons a weighty testimony to the significance and power of the Christian gospel in human life.

Yet we should be careful not to overstate our case. We have learned from this study, as from others', not to try to correlate the work or the judgments of God with our human institutional or cultural alignments, as not to prejudge the final destinies of persons by our own perceptions of their commitments and performances. John C. Bennett's succinct expression of this understanding can be expressive of our own:

> We must not surround evangelism with the assumption that Christians have a monopoly on the saving grace of God. We may believe that the revelation of God in Christ is normative, not only for us but for all men, but this is quite different from suggesting that God cannot save those who are outside the Christian circle. Belief in the sure mediation of God's grace through Christ is motive enough to seek a Christian witness and a Christian presence in every community, but to stress the importance of this need [does] not mean to deny that non-Christians are in relation to God and receive grace and truth from him in ways uncharted by Christian theology.[24]

This present book represents an attempt to create one kind of Christian chart for exploration of these wider and deeper waters of divine grace.

Perhaps a paradoxical reminder is in order that we should not presume on the gracious mercy of God. There is a lesson to be learned from the experience of the two thieves who were crucified together with Jesus. One was promised paradise, at that last hour of his earthly life, in order that we may not despair. The other was not—for that time—in order that we may not presume (Lk. 23:39–43). The gospel of Jesus Christ also proclaims the grace of God that we may enter the *kingdom* of God—in this earthly life as well as in the next world—so as to live by and under God's authority. But through all Christian witness and service there properly ever moves the spirit expressed in the words of Frederick W. Faber,

> There's a wideness in God's mercy,
> Like the wideness of the sea;
> There's a kindness in His justice,
> Which is more than liberty.
> For the love of God is broader
> Than the measure of man's mind;
> And the heart of the Eternal
> Is most wonderfully kind.

Notes

PREFACE

1. International Congress on Mission I, II, III, *Toward a New Age in Mission: The Good News of God's Kingdom to the Peoples of Asia* (Manila: Theological Conference Office, 1981), I, p. 76; II, pp. 26, 45, 111; III, pp. 90–91, 115–17, 159, 190–92, 197, 217–20, 241–43, 256–66, 273, 344–47, 359.

2. Ibid., I, p. 76.

3. Malachi Martin, *The Final Conclave* (New York: Stein and Day, 1978), p. 19. Roman Catholic theologian and editor Leonard Swidler has expressed the same change as follows: "Like everyone else in the world, Catholics had—until a few short years ago—a static, one-dimensional understanding of reality, of human history, of truth, of the Christian Church, of authority. But modern discoveries of the mind have relativized all aspects of reality, religion, and authority. As a result, the gulf which separates the pre-critical and the critical mentalities is *almost* unbridgeable." He does, however, affirm the existence of a bridge, which persons, having once crossed, "will never be able to cross back again—at least not in good faith." ("Preface: The Critical Divide," *Journal of Ecumenical Studies* 19, no. 2 [Spring 1982]: 1). We may properly recall also that John XXIII, in his proclamation of Vatican Council II on December 25, 1961, wrote that "humanity is on the edge of a new era" *(Humanae salutis).* And in his opening speech to the council he affirmed that "Divine Providence is leading us to a new order of human relations."

4. Martin, *The Final Conclave*, p. 19.

5. Cf. Huston Smith, *Forgotten Truth: The Primordial Tradition* (New York: Harper & Row, 1978); *Beyond the Modern Mind* (New York: Crossroad Publishing Co., 1982); Arthur Koestler, *The Roots of Coincidence* (New York: Random House, 1972).

6. Aleksandr I. Solzhenitsyn, *A World Split Apart* (New York: Harper & Row, 1978), pp. 5–7. Cf. Langdon Gilkey, *Society and the Sacred* (New York: Crossroad Publishing Co., 1981), pp. 3–14.

7. Solzhenitsyn, *A World*, pp. 47–49.

8. Marcello Zago, "Dialogue in a Buddhist Context," in International Congress, *Toward a New Age in Mission*, III, p. 92.

9. Harvey Cox, "The Battle of the Gods? A Concluding Unsystematic Postscript," in Peter L. Berger, ed., *The Other Side of God* (Garden City, N.Y.: Doubleday, 1981), p. 293.

10. Patrick D'Souza, "Church and Mission in Relation to the Kingdom of God Especially in a Third World Context," in International Congress, *Toward a New Age in Mission*, II, pp. 45–46.

1   WHAT IS HAPPENING IN CHRISTIAN THEOLOGY?

1. W. A. Visser 't Hooft, *No Other Name* (Philadelphia: Westminster Press, 1963), p. 114. Cf. *The Finality of Jesus Christ in the Age of Universal History*, World Council of Churches Bulletin, Division of Studies, 8, no. 2 (Autumn 1962): 4–5; Wilfred Cantwell Smith, "An Historian of Faith Reflects on What We Are Doing Here," in Donald G. Dawe and John B. Carman, eds., *Christian Faith in a Religiously Plural World* (Maryknoll, N.Y.: Orbis Books, 1978), p. 145.

2. S. J. Samartha, "More Than an Encounter of Commitments," *International Review of Mission* 59, no. 236 (October 1970): 394, 401–2.

3. Ewert Cousins, "The Trinity and World Religions," *Journal of Ecumenical Studies* 7, no. 3 (Summer 1970): 497.

4. Claude Geffré and Mariasusai Dhavamony, in *Concilium,* vol. 116 (New York: Seabury Press, 1979), p. vii. With reference to the religious dimensions of these developments, Peter Berger has the following to say: "The old agenda of [Christian] liberal theology was the contestation with modernity. That agenda has exhausted itself. The much more pressing agenda today is the contestation with the fulness of human religious possibilities" (Berger, *The Heretical Imperative* [Garden City, N.Y.: Anchor Press/Doubleday, 1979], p. 183). Berger of course uses the term "contestation" here in a nonpolemical sense.

5. Cf. Richard H. Drummond, "Christian Theology and the History of Religions," *Journal of Ecumenical Studies* 12, no. 3 (Summer 1975): 396–97; "Authority in the Church: An Ecumenical Inquiry," *Journal of Bible and Religion* 34, no. 4 (October 1966): 329–45.

6. George E. Mendenhall, "Law and Covenant in Israel and the Ancient Near East" (Pittsburgh: The Biblical Colloquium, 1955), pp. 3–50. Walter Eichrodt, *Theology of the Old Testament*, 6th ed. (Philadelphia: Westminster Press, 1961), passim. There are those, such as D. J. McCarthy and Georg Fohrer, who reject analogies with suzerainty treaties and affirm the covenantal relationship of Yahweh with Israel to rest, rather, on kinship, on Israel as God's family; see Francisco O. Garcia-Treto, "Covenant in Recent Old Testament Studies," *Austin Seminary Bulletin* 96 (March 1981): 10–19.

7. Donald G. Dawe, "Christian Faith in a Religiously Plural World," in Dawe and Carman, eds., *Christian Faith in a Religiously Plural World*, p. 18. See also Dawe, "Religious Pluralism and the Church," *Journal of Ecumenical Studies* 18, no. 4 (Fall 1981): 604–15.

8. Dawe, "Christian Faith," p. 19. Cf. Samuel Amirtham, "The Challenge of New Religions to Christian Theological Thought," *International Review of Mission* 67, no. 268 (October 1978): 401–2.

9. See A. P. Shepherd, *A Scientist of the Invisible* (London: Hodder and Stoughton, 1975), p. 157.

10. Raymond Panikkar, *The Unknown Christ of Hinduism* (London: Darton, Longman and Todd, 1964), pp. 58–59. Cf. Heinz Robert Schlette, *Towards a Theology of Religions* (New York: Herder and Herder, 1966), pp. 71–76.

11. Dawe, "Christian Faith," p. 24. Cf. W. Eugene March, "Because the *Lord* Is Lord: Old Testament Covenant Imagery and Ecumenical Commitment," *Austin Seminary Bulletin* 96 (March 1981): 20–26.

12. Millard C. Lind, "Refocusing Theological Education to Mission: The Old Tes-

tament and Contextualization," *Missiology* 10, no. 2 (April 1982): 141-48.

13. Jeremiah's perception of a "new covenant" is that of a new and different inner relationship between God and his people. It was particularly necessitated because they had broken the old covenant, and the emphasis of the prophet is upon the interiority of the new. Nowhere, however, does he speak of the abrogation of the old in any structured sense, even though he affirms the need for correction of particular popular misunderstandings of God's ways (Jer. 31: 26-34; 32:36-41; cf. Ezek. 36:26-28).

14. Paul Tillich, *The Future of Religions* (New York: Harper & Row, 1966), p. 81. Paul Knitter published in 1975 a study of the views of contemporary continental European Protestant theologians on this theme. He finds that most German-speaking Protestant theologians are now willing to acknowledge the possibility of God's revelatory work outside the "places" and context of explicit Christian faith. He also shows, however, their hesitancy, in contrast with most contemporary Roman Catholic theologians of note, to admit a salvific dimension in this divine work ("European Protestant and Catholic Approaches to the World Religions: Complements and Contrasts," *Journal of Ecumenical Studies* 12, no. 1 [Winter 1975]: 13-28).

15. The English writers Roger T. Forster and V. Paul Marston have shown conclusively by a careful culling of numerous quotations from the early church fathers that the theology of Augustine, particularly with reference to exclusivist understandings of election and predestination (e.g., "double predestination"), was indeed a new theology and not representative of the mainstream of theological understanding of the early church (*God's Strategy in Human History* [Wheaton, Ill.: Tyndale House, 1974], pp. 257-95).

16. Cf. H. H. Rowley, *The Biblical Doctrine of Election* (London: Lutterworth, 1950), p. 52.

17. Statements like Isa. 60:2 are more descriptive of Israel's commission than of judgment of the nations, as the context clearly shows. The foreigners (*ben-hannēkhār*) of Isa. 56:3,6 are presumed to be those who do not reside in Palestine, as distinguished from the *gēr*, or resident aliens, and may refer to others than circumcised proselytes.

2   BIBLICAL BASES FOR THE HAPPENING

1. George E. Mendenhall has shown that the concept of the Israelitic covenant was probably patterned after those widely in use between rulers and their subjects in the Middle East of the second millennium B.C. ("Law and Covenant in Israel and the Ancient Near East" [Pittsburgh: The Biblical Colloquium, 1955], pp. 3-50).

2. Cf. G. E. Wright, *The Old Testament against Its Environment* (Chicago: Henry Regnery, 1950), p. 50.

3. Cf. John Bright, *A History of Israel* (Philadelphia: Westminster Press, 1959), pp. 132-37.

4. Cf. M. M. Thomas, *The Christian Response to the Asian Revolution* (London: SCM Press, 1968), p. 72. Thomas faults A. T. van Leeuwen in his *Christianity in World History* (London: Edinburgh House Press, 1964) for not sufficiently taking account of exceptions of this kind.

5. Johannes Blauw points out that in the historical books of the Old Testament there is a tendency to see the nations as a threat to Israel with regard to its political or national existence as much as a temptation in religion (*The Missionary Nature of the Church* [New York: McGraw-Hill, 1962], p. 23).

6. Cf. Hans Walter Wolff, *Joel and Amos* (Philadelphia: Fortress Press, 1977), pp. 347–48.

7. Cf. also Jer. 25:9; Ezek. 5:6–8; Isa. 41:25; 28:11; Hab. 1:5–6,12; Dan. 9:26. We read in 2 Kings 5:1 that Yahweh is the one who gave military victory to Syria through the valorous Syrian general Naaman. This is the man cited by Jesus, in Luke's account, whose healing by the Hebrew prophet Elisha was a specific example of God's care for persons among the nations as well as within Israel (Lk. 4:25–30).

8. Pietro Rossano concludes that even in passages where the Israelites are warned against turning to the objects of worship of the nations, "a certain validity and legitimacy in the religions of peoples is recognized on principle," as in Deut. 4:19; 29:25 ("The Bible and the Non-Christian Religions," *Bulletin-Secretarius pro non-Christianis* 2, no. 1 [Rome, 1967]: 20.

9. See C. T. Fritsch, "Proverbs," in vol. 4 of Buttrick, ed., *The Interpreter's Bible* (Nashville: Abingdon, 1955), pp. 767, 947; cf. Jer. 49:7; Obad. 8; 1 Kings 5:1–7.

10. G. Ernest Wright, "The Nations in Hebrew Prophecy," *Encounter* 26, no. 2 (Spring 1965): 231–57.

11. Cf. W. F. Albright, *From the Stone Age to Christianity* (Baltimore: Johns Hopkins Press, 1940), pp. 278–80; R. C. Dentan, "Malachi," in vol. 6 of Butterick, ed., *The Interpreter's Bible* (Nashville: Abingdon, 1956), pp. 1120, 1129; John Bright, *History of Israel*, p. 433; Erich Zenger, "Jahwe und die Götter," *Theologie und Philosophie* 43 (1968): 338–59.

12. In the Bhagavad Gita (ca. second century B.C.) we find a similar perception. In this great classic of devotional Hinduism the author affirms that Krishna, as the Lord supreme, accepts every sacrifice of sincere religious devotion. He strengthens the faith of those who worship other gods. In such worship they also worship Krishna, even if not rightly. The paths of human beings are many, but every path is his (Bhagavad Gita 4:11, 32; 7:20–23; 9:22–27).

13. Note must be taken, however, of the existence even in the literary prophets of passages that seem to reflect narrower attitudes. Thus in Ezek. 28:10; 31:18; 32:32 the death of the uncircumcised is seen as a particularly loathesome kind of death, like that of those slain by the sword.

14. Th. C. Vriezen, *Die Erwählung Israels nach dem alten Testament*, p. 32; quoted in Johannes Blauw, *The Missionary Nature of the Church* (New York: McGraw-Hill, 1962), pp. 22–23.

15. Donald G. Dawe and John B. Carman, eds., *Christian Faith in a Religiously Plural World* (Maryknoll, N.Y.: Orbis Books, 1978), p. 22, cf. Isa. 44:5; 45:6,14ff.

16. The Authorized (King James) translation of *ta idia* in Jn. 1:11 as "his own," and therefore to be naturally understood by readers as identical in meaning with "his own" (*hoi idioi*, "his own people") in the second part of the verse, was unfortunate. The RSV's "his own home" is little better. The Jerusalem Bible's "his own domain" gives better the sense of the original Greek, which by the use of the neuter plural was evidently intended to denote the whole of creation; cf. Jn. 4:21–24. Jn. 19:27 uses the expression in a more restricted sense.

17. This statement is also found in Lk. 9:50. The thought negatively phrased occurs in Lk. 11:23; Mt. 12:30; cf. Num. 11:27–29.

18. H. J. Cadbury, *Jesus: What Manner of Man?* (New York: Macmillan, 1947), p. 23; cf. *1 Clement* 41:4; Justin Martyr, *First Apology* 17, 43.

19. Ibid., p. 25.

20. Ibid., pp. 26–30.

21. We may say of Jesus' use of Scripture in the Gospel of Matthew that it is both selective and corrective; cf. Mt. 5:17–48.

22. Cf. Alan Richardson, ed., *A Theological Word Book of the Bible* (New York: Macmillan, 1960), p. 220; G. Friedrich, *Theologisches Wörterbuch zum Neuen Testament* (Stuttgart: W. Kohlhammer, 1964), VII, 15–16, pp. 989ff.; John A. T. Robinson, *Truth Is Two-Eyed* (Philadelphia: Westminster Press, 1979), pp. 105–6. Krister Stendahl, "Notes for Three Bible Studies," in Gerald H. Anderson and Thomas F. Stransky, eds., *Christ's Lordship and Religious Pluralism* (Maryknoll, N.Y.: Orbis Books, 1981), pp. 11–15.

23. Cf. C. J. Bleeker, *Christ in Modern Athens* (Leiden: E. J. Brill, 1965), pp. 1–25, 54.

24. Jean Héring understands Paul's use of lords (*kurioi*) to refer to the angels of the nations concealed behind political powers (*The First Epistle of Paul to the Corinthians* [London: Epworth Press, 1962], p. 69). Paul gives us insight into his views on this theme, even if not systematically, in his letter to the Colossians, written in a detention situation near the end of his life. In all his letters Paul reveals a consistently high view of the role of angels in the divine order in the cosmos, but in this letter, quite in accord with his faith-understanding of the sole lordship of God and his Christ (cf. Col. 2:1—3:3), he disallows the worship of angels as inappropriate to Christian faith (Col. 2:18). Paul also assumes that the utter committal of Christian faith, which he describes with the imagery of dying with Christ, means to die to, to withdraw from the power of, what he calls *ta stoicheia*, "the elemental spirits of the universe." This term literally means "elements," and one aspect of its meaning may be what Helena Petrovna Blavatsky and other Theosophists call "elementals." The word was also used in Hellenistic culture to denote the twelve signs of the Zodiac as well as the personal beings to whom were assigned, it was believed, by the God who is over all, the control of the movements of the heavenly bodies (Col. 2:8,20).

Paul's language clearly indicates that by Christian faith-committal persons no longer live, in the essence of their lives, in this world (*en kosmo*). This understanding is expressed also in the phrase, "your life is hid with Christ in God," and Christ is above, "seated at the right hand of God" (Col. 3:1–3). In language that is paradoxical more in word than in fact, Paul speaks also of "Christ in you" (Col. 1:27). His larger purpose, however, is to affirm that those "in Christ" accept worshipfully the ultimate control of naught in this entire universe except the one God and his Christ. Paul is not, however, as we have already seen, totally negative about "this world," which is of course a state of mind or spiritual-condition realm rather than a "place." In the letters that are generally recognized as authentically of Paul, he does not speak of this world as totally under satanic control. His culminating affirmation is, rather, that God in Christ "disarmed the principalities and powers and made a public example of them, triumphing over them in him" (Col. 2:15). This is the victory that is available to all who will accept it in faith and obedience (cf. Rom. 1:5) even while they live—externally—in this world (1 Cor. 5:9–11).

If Romans 13 can be considered authentically Pauline, we have a positive affirmation on Paul's part that the governing authorities of the Roman empire are rulers in a structure instituted by God and as such deserve the obedience of Christians, even though Paul nowhere says this obedience should be absolute or unqualified (Rom. 13:1–7). And if he disallowed the worship of angels, he was certainly not of a mind to encourage worship of the Roman emperor.

Paul does share with other New Testament writers a view of the cosmos which sees "this world" as significantly under the domination of subordinate powers that are disobedient to the Most High. In 2 Cor. 4:4 he refers to such a "blinding" power as the god of this world (Gr. *aion,* "of this age," which in Gal. 1:4 Paul calls "the present evil age"). In Ephesians, which probably does not consist totally of Pauline material, we find a somewhat more negative nuance. The continuing "wrestling" of Christians is said to be "against the principalities, against the powers, against the world rulers (*kosmokratores*) of this present darkness, against the spiritual hosts of wickedness in the heavenly places" (Eph. 6:12; cf. 1 Pet. 5:8–9). The author of the Gospel of John, who sharply differentiates between "this world"—although God loves it (Jn. 3:16)—and the realm of light and life, nevertheless uses language similar in intent to Paul's about the victory wrought by Christ Jesus. The ruler of "this world" is about to be cast out, he has no power over Jesus, he is already judged (Jn. 12:31; 14:30; 16:11). Indeed, Jesus has overcome the world and has been given power of the Father "over all flesh." Therefore the disciples are not to be taken out of the world but sent into the world. The concern of Jesus is primarily that they be protected from the evil one's influence in the world. Therefore they no longer belong to the world even though they are in it (Jn. 16:33; 17:2,14–18). The perception is of a world ultimately under God's control and of an effective victory won over all subordinate powers by his Christ. But because these subordinate powers are still relatively effective in their influence in this world, the disciples of Jesus are said to be "not of the world." Their allegiance is higher (cf. Col. 3:1–4) (cf. Eduard Lohse, *Colossians and Philemon* [Philadelphia: Fortress Press, 1971], pp. 92–131).

25. The letter to the Ephesians in its present form is probably not an authentic letter of Paul. While containing much Pauline material, it ascribes to the nations a total alienation from God, which is not characteristic of the mainstream of thought in either the Old Testament or the New (cf. Eph. 2:12; 4:17ff.). The New English Bible translation of Rom. 11:36 is helpful as to Paul's mind: "Source, Guide, and Goal of all that is—to him be glory for ever! Amen." (I should add that my friend Benedict Ashley prefers to interpret these passages in Ephesians less literally as referring to "the generally pessimistic and agnostic condition of much Hellenistic religion." The author would then be contrasting a kind of "vague religiosity" with "the vibrant faith of the early Church.")

26. Jn. 14:17 should properly be understood as indicative of moral-spiritual refusal to accept the Spirit of truth, not as total lack of light (cf. Raymond E. Brown, *The Gospel according to John,* The Anchor Bible [Garden City, N.Y.: Doubleday, 1970], vol. 2, p. 639; cf. Jn. 3:19; 7:7). John 10:8 is also not to be interpreted in an exclusivist sense. Quite apart from the textual ambiguity of the words "before me," in this Gospel the precursors of Jesus (Abraham, Moses, and the prophets, specifically Isaiah), are cited as authentic witnesses to Jesus (Jn. 1:45; 5:46; 8:56; 12:41). Similarly, Jn. 14:6, "I am the way and the truth and the life; no one comes to the Father, but by me," is properly understood in the context of Jn. 1:9, "The true light that enlightens every man was coming into the world."

3 HISTORICO-THEOLOGICAL BASES FOR THE HAPPENING

1. The question of Peter as recorded in Acts 15:10 ("Now therefore why do you make trial of God by putting a yoke upon the neck of the disciples which neither our fathers nor we have been able to bear?") reveals another side, a self-questioning,

querulous sense of inadequacy and failure in contemporary popular Judaism; cf. Acts 15:19; Mt. 23:4; Gal. 5:1; 6:13; 1 Pet. 1:18.

2. Cf. T. R. Glover, *The Jesus of History* (New York: Association Press, 1922), pp. 192–94.

3. Cf. Samuel Angus, *The Religious Quests of the Graeco-Roman World* (New York: Charles Scribner's Sons, 1929), pp. 54, 98. The vision of Second Isaiah looks toward the preserved of Israel as a light to the nations that the salvation of the Lord may "reach to the end of the earth" (Isa. 49:6; 45:22), whereas in Deuteronomy the prophecy for Joseph is that "he shall push the peoples, all of them, to the ends of the earth" (Deut. 33:17; cf. the function of the Gentiles as agents of curse: Deut. 28:49, 64–68). The Septuagint adds to the Hebrew of Deut. 33:19 the promise that Zebulun and Issachar will utterly destroy the nations. The Book of Jubilees (late second century B.C.) refers in a total way to the uncleanness and the shame of the Gentiles, who will be to Israel "an offence and a tribulation and a snare" (I, 9, 21–25); cf. John Bright, *The Kingdom of God* (Nashville: Abingdon, 1953), pp. 160–62.

4. H. G. May, "Synagogues in Palestine," *Biblical Archaeologist* 7 (February 1944): 6–7.

5. *"Ton hierotaton Platona,"* Philo, *Every Good Man Is Free* 13.

6. Tertullian, *De prescriptione haereticorum* 7, 9. Tertullian, of course, like all other early Christian writers, affirmed the universal presence and rule of God in the world (*Ad nationes* 2, 8). Another aspect of this complex figure is revealed in his work *On Prayer*, in which he acknowledges the effectiveness of prayer in ancient times apart from the "form" of Christ and affirms that all creation, even cattle and wild beasts, pray authentically, each in its own way. The birds soar up to the sky in the morning and in place of hands spread their wings in the shape of a cross and cry out something that seems like prayer (*De oratione* 29). He also used the pregnant phrase "testimonium animae naturaliter Christianae," *Apologeticum* 17, 5–6.

7. The issue as stated here should be distinguished from that of relations with the Roman state and, in particular, the issue of worship of the emperor. See Charles N. Cochrane, *Christianity and Classical Culture* (New York: Oxford University Press, 1944), passim.

8. Cf. John Foster, *After the Apostles* (London: SCM Press, 1951), p. 100; 1 Clement 7, 5–7; 20, 11.

9. As we have noted above, pagan practices in the area of personal and family morality, particularly sexual practices, came under strong Christian criticism. Adolf von Harnack, after stressing the "inextricable medley of conservatism and radicalism characteristic of the earliest expressions of Christianity," goes on to state that "in one point, undoubtedly, all Christians worthy of the name were radical, namely, in their opposition to the world of idolatry, of impurity, of sensuality, of debasing pleasures, of cruelty and hardheartedness, by which they were surrounded" (*Essays on the Social Gospel* [London: Williams & Norgate, 1907], pp. 22–25).

10. Origen, *Contra Celsum* 3:15.

11. Lactantius, *De ira dei* 2.

12. A. C. Bouquet, *The Christian Faith and Non-Christian Religions* (New York: Harper, 1958), p. 138; cf. also Bouquet's "Revelation and the Divine Logos," in Gerald H. Anderson, ed., *The Theology of the Christian Mission* (New York: McGraw-Hill, 1961), pp. 183–98. See also Étienne Cornelis, *Valeurs Chrétiennes des Religions Non Chrétiennes* (Paris: Les Editions du Cerf, 1965), pp. 67–74.

13. Justin Martyr, *The First Apology* 46. Cf. Basil of Caesarea, *Homily XXII (Ad*

adolescentes), who cites certain examples of pagan conduct as on a par with Christian conduct and worthy of emulation. Basil's exhortation to a discriminating study of classical literature, as Johannes Quasten has put it, shows "extraordinary feeling for the leading values of Hellenistic learning, and its broadmindedness has had a strong influence on the attitude of the Church toward the classical tradition" (*Patrology* [Utrecht: Spectrum Publishers, 1966], pp. 214–15).

14. Justin Martyr, *The Second Apology* 13; cf. Seneca, *Ad Lucilium epistulae morales* I, 106.

15. Justin Martyr, *The First Apology* 10; cf. Peter Gerlitz, "Der *Logos Spermatikos* als Voraussetzung für eine ökumenische Theologie," *Zeitschrift für Religions und Geistesgeschichte* 22 (1970): 1–18.

16. Irenaeus, *Contra haereses* III, 24; III, 12–13; III, 18, 1; IV, 6–7; IV, 20, 6 (Deus . . . incognitus autem nequaquam). Irenaeus taught also that God had made a number of covenants with humankind (ibid., I, 10, 3).

17. Clement, *Stromateis* VI, 7, VII, 2.

18. Theophilus Antiochenus, *Ad Autolycum* II, 32, 36–38; II, 22.

19. Minucius Felix, *Octavius* 19.

20. *Recognitions* (Pseudo-Clementine) IV, 20.

21. Ibid., I, 52.

22. Origen, *Commentarius in Ioannem* I, 39; *Commentarius in Canticum Canticorum* II, 62; cf. Gregory Thaumaturgus, *In Origenem oratio panegyrica* XIII; cf. 1 Clement 32:4. The view long current in the Middle Ages and into modern times that Origen was condemned by the Sixth Ecumenical Council held in Constantinople in 553 has been shown to be erroneous; see F. Prat, "Origen and Origenism," in *The Catholic Encyclopedia*, vol. 11 (New York: The Gilmary Society, 1939), pp. 306–12.

23. Post-Reformation Protestant theological polemics against "synergism," indeed, the whole contestation as to how faith may be distinguished, even separated, from works (practical morality) would have seemed absurd to the bulk of Christians of the first three centuries. This is one reason why the trend denoted by German scholars as early Catholicism has been extended to earlier and earlier periods in the history of the church, indeed quite into the period when the New Testament was written.

24. Already in First Isaiah this perception of the religious life as one of long-range growth is expressed in the striking words: "For it is precept upon precept, precept upon precept, line upon line, line upon line, here a little, there a little" that the Lord of hosts would teach his people, even "by men of strange lips and with an alien tongue" (Isa. 28:9–13).

25. Clement, *Stromateis* VII, 82. The translation is from John E. L. Oulton and Henry Chadwick, eds., *Alexandrian Christianity* (Philadelphia: Westminster Press, 1954), pp. 38–39.

26. Cf. Jean Daniélou, *Origéne* (Paris: La Table Ronde, 1948), pp. 203–5, 208.

27. Henry Chadwick, *Early Christian Thought and the Classical Tradition* (London: Oxford University Press, 1966), pp. 88–89, 114–16. With regard to the problem of interpretation of the extant materials of Origen, part of which has come down to us only in Latin translation, Chadwick warns against the admitted editorializing of Rufinus, Origen's Latin translator, to make the content palatable to the Latin orthodoxy of his own time. Some key passages in Origen are *Contra Celsum* VII, 50; *De principiis* I, 7, 4; I, 8, 1; I, 8, 4; III, 3, 5; III, 5, 5; *Commentarius in Ioannem* II, 24–25.

28. Origen, *De principiis*, II, 9, 7; *Commentarius in Ioannem* II, 25; Clement, *Stromateis* VI, 6; VII, 6.

29. Donald G. Bloesch, *Essentials of Evangelical Theology*; vol. 1: *God, Authority, Salvation* (New York: Harper & Row, 1978), p. 246. Various forms of this concept were widely held in the early church. Cf. J. A. MacCulloch, *The Harrowing of Hell* (Edinburgh: T. & T. Clark, 1930), pp. 253-87.

30. Joseph Head and S. L. Cranston, eds., *Reincarnation: The Phoenix Fire Mystery* (New York: Warner Books, 1978), pp. 198-201, passim.

31. Examples are Geddes MacGregor, *Reincarnation in Christianity* (Wheaton, Ill.: Theosophical Publishing House, 1978); Quincy Howe, Jr., *Reincarnation for the Christian* (Philadelphia: Westminster Press, 1974); Nels F. S. Ferré, *The Universal Word* (Philadelphia: Westminster Press, 1969), pp. 246-71. Karl Rahner entertains the concept of reincarnation as a live possibility for Christian faith and theology in correlation with the ancient Catholic notion of an "interval" after death and a more sophisticated understanding of purgatory (*Foundations of Christian Faith* [New York: Seabury Press, 1978], pp. 441-42).

32. Flavius Josephus, *Jewish War* III, 374; *Against Apion* II, 218; *Jewish Antiquities* XVIII, 15(3). The editor of the last volume in the Loeb series (*Jewish Antiquities*), L. H. Feldman, says in a note that the citation does not refer to "metempsychosis which was not a tenet of the Pharisees." The scholar, however, who edited more of the volumes in the Loeb series on Josephus than any other, H. St. J. Thackeray, forthrightly affirms that the passages do mean metempsychosis (reincarnation), severally and even more when collated.

33. F. L. Cross, *The Early Christian Fathers* (London: Gerald Duckworth, 1960), pp. 98-99. Cyril Richardson, however, believes that the Pseudo-Clementine materials are not of Syrian Jewish Christian provenance, but are more likely Alexandrian.

34. *Homilies* (Pseudo-Clementine) III, 20; cf. *Recognitions* V, 10, where we may have a significant example of the self-admitted editorializing of Rufinus.

35. *Newsweek*, May 26, 1980, p. 94; cf. Adin Steinsaltz, *The Thirteen Petalled Rose* (New York: Basic Books, 1980), pp. 53-65.

36. Herbert Weiner, "Report from Israel," *Parapsychology Review* (March–April, 1973), pp. 13-16; cf. Jean Daniélou, *The Theology of Jewish Christianity* (Chicago: Henry Regnery, 1964), p. 85; Henri-Charles Puech, "Gnosis and Time," in Joseph Campbell, ed., *Man and Time*, Bollingen Series XXX, Papers from the Eranos Yearbooks, vol. 3 (New York: Pantheon Books, 1957), p. 65; Samuel J. Fox, *Hell in Jewish Literature* (Northbrook, Ill.: Whitehall, 1972), pp. 129-46. Mention should also be made that reincarnation was a belief widely held in Christian Gnostic circles. Clement and Origen, who as we have seen apparently also shared this belief, felt impelled, however, to write critically of some of the Christian positions called Gnostic; cf. Richard H. Drummond, "Studies in Christian Gnosticism," *Religion in Life* (Spring 1976), pp. 16-19.

37. Jerome, *Letters* CXXX (*Epistula ad Demetriadem*), 16. The context of this statement of Jerome is that at this time of his life he no longer believed in reincarnation himself. The crotchety old man had given up his youthful enthusiasm for Origen! Incidentally, one more clarification may be in order with reference to Origen. As Ernst Benz has shown, a number of passages from Origen, both in the original Greek and in Latin translation, indicate Origen's opposition to the notion of transmigration, which apparently quite a number of Christians of the time believed, namely, that human souls may be reborn in animal bodies (cf., however, G. W. Butterworth, ed., *Origen on First Principles* [Gloucester, Mass., Peter Smith, 1973], pp. 70-75; *De principiis* I, 8, 4). Benz, however, confines himself to these passages and concludes therefrom that Origen did not believe in reincarnation, the essence of his argument

being that at this time in Western civilization it is not possible to believe in such a concept (Ernst Benz, *Indische Einflüsse auf die frühchristliche Theologie* [Wiesbaden: Verlag der Akademie der Wissenschaften und der Literatur in Mainz, 1951], pp. 185–90; cf. Origen, *Commentarius in Ioannem* II, 24–25; *Contra celsum* I, 32).

4 SOME SUGGESTED "WHYS" FOR REDUCTIONISM IN THE HISTORICAL PROCESS

1. Cf. John R. Hale, *Age of Exploration* (New York: Time-Life Books, 1970), p. 17.

2. Cf. Sarvapalli Radhakrishnan, *Eastern Religions and Western Thought* (New York: Oxford University Press, 1960), pp. 372–75.

3. Arnold Toynbee, *The World and the West* (New York: Meridian Books, 1960), pp. 262–63.

4. Thomas Babington Macaulay, "Lord Clive," in *Critical, Historical, and Miscellaneous Essays and Poems* (New York: John B. Alden, n.d.), vol. 2, p. 391.

5. G. B. Sansom, *The Western World and Japan* (New York: Alfred A. Knopf, 1962), pp. 54–86.

6. The statement of the British field marshal who became famous in the Boer War, Frederick, Lord Roberts, is quite clear as to the role of attitudes of superiority in the process of colonial expansion: "It is this consciousness of the inherent superiority of the European which has won us India" (Louis Fischer, *Gandhi, His Life and Message for the World* [New York: New American Library, 1954], p. 62).

7. The apostle Paul also expected obedience to himself and his co-workers (2 Cor. 7:13–15; 1 Thess. 5:12; Philem. 21); cf. the thesis of Elaine Pagels, *The Gnostic Gospels* (New York: Random House, 1979), pp. 28–47, 102–18.

8. Cyril C. Richardson, *Early Church Fathers* (Philadelphia: Westminster Press, 1953), p. 76.

9. Ignatius, *Ephesians* 4–6.

10. Augustine, *Contra Faustum* 19, 2 ("Dubitandum non est, et Gentes suos habere prophetas. Necnon et veritatem habere prophetas suos, tam idem Paulus significat, quam etiam Iesus").

11. Augustine, *Retractiones* I, 12, 3; *De civitate dei* V, 21; XII, 28; X, 32. Augustine expresses the more humane view in *Epistulae CII*, 12–15; *De doctrina christiana* II, 18.

12. Fulgentius, *De fide* I, 27, 38; cf. Philip Schaff, *History of the Christian Church* (Grand Rapids, Mich.: Wm. B. Eerdmans, 1957), vol. 3, p. 866.

13. Augustine, *Enchiridion* 107.

14. T. Paul Verghese, *The Freedom of Man* (Philadelphia: Westminster Press, 1972), pp. 51–52.

15. The kingdom of Armenia, while a vassal state under the Roman empire during the first four centuries of the latter's history, maintained its own sovereigns as well as its language and culture. This state was historically the first to have a Christian ruler. King Tiridates (ca. 238–314) was baptized evidently some years before the end of the third century and thus well before the Christian profession of Constantine.

16. Prosperus Aquitanus, *De vocatione omnium gentium* II, 4–5, 29, 31.

17. Cf. Hendrik Kraemer, *World Cultures and World Religions: The Coming Dialogue* (London: Lutterworth, 1960), pp. 29–55.

18. Henri Pirenne, *Mohammed and Charlemagne* (New York: Meridian Books, 1958), pp. 147–85.

19. Johannes Damascenus, in J. P. Migne, ed., *Patrologia Graeca*, XCIV, 761–80; 1585–97; cf. Richard H. Drummond, "Toward Theological Understanding of Islam," *Journal of Ecumenical Studies* 9, no. 4 (Fall 1972): 777–99.

20. Cyprian, *De catholicae ecclesiae unitate* 6. In this passage Cyprian rigorously develops the theme: "Habere non potest Deum patrem, qui ecclesiam non habet matrem." The actual phrase "salus extra ecclesiam non est" occurs in *Epistulae* LXXIII, 21.

21. Henry Bettenson, *Documents of the Christian Church* (New York: Oxford University Press, 1947), pp. 161–63.

22. Cf. Karl Adam, *The Spirit of Catholicism* (Garden City, N.Y.: Doubleday, 1962), pp. 172–75; quotation from Henry Denzinger, *The Sources of Catholic Dogma* (Enchiridion Symbolorum) (St. Louis: B. Herder, 1957), p. 230.

5 THE LONG WAY OUT AND UP

1. George J. Dyer, *Limbo: Unsettled Question* (New York: Sheed and Ward, 1964), pp. 39–60.

2. St. Thomas Aquinas, *Summa theologica*, pt. III, q. 61, art. 1; pt. II, q. 2, art. 7. Cf. *Quaestiones disputatae, de veritate*, q. 14, art. 11. Cf. Yves Congar, *The Wide World My Parish* (Baltimore: Helicon Press, 1961), pp. 93–154.

3. Cf. Ewert Cousins, "The Trinity and World Religions," *Journal of Ecumenical Studies* 7, no. 3 (Summer 1970): 490.

4. Cf. Philippe Maury, ed., *History's Lessons for Tomorrow's Mission* (Geneva: World Student Christian Federation, 1960), pp. 76–77; Ramon Lull, *Obres essencials,* 2 vols. (Barcelona, 1957, 1960), p. 1138; quoted in R. Panikkar, *The Intrareligious Dialogue* (New York: Paulist Press, 1978), pp. xi–xiii.

5. Cf. Benedict M. Ashley, O.P., "Three Strands in the Thought of Eckhart, the Scholastic Theologian," *The Thomist* 42, no. 2 (April 1978): 236; Edmund Colledge, O.S.A., "Meister Eckhart: His Times and His Writings," ibid., pp. 247–48; John D. Caputo, "Fundamental Themes in Meister Eckhart's Mysticism," ibid., pp. 207–8. The same openendedness can be affirmed of Johannes Tauler, who in his Sermon XIX quoted both Augustine and Thomas Aquinas in support of this thesis.

6. Joseph Head and S. L. Cranston, *Reincarnation: The Phoenix Fire Mystery* (New York: Warner Books, 1977), pp. 242–56. There is at least one affirmation of the concept in Dante, *Paradiso* XX; cf. Head and Cranston, pp. 240–41.

7. Cf. Christopher Dawson, *The Dynamics of World History* (New York: New American Library, 1962), pp. 241–42.

8. Great care is needed in the interpretation of traditional materials regarding these groups, inasmuch as the bulk of the materials available is usually that of the prosecuting agencies; cf. Arthur Guirdham, *The Cathars and Reincarnation* (London: Neville Spearman, 1970), pp. 131–33, 145–58.

9. Cf. John D. Caputo, "Meister Eckhart's Mysticism," p. 212.

10. Cf. Marie-Louise von Franz, *C. G. Jung, His Myth in Our Time* (New York: G. P. Putnam's Sons, 1975), pp. 31–32.

11. Cf. H. Richard Niebuhr, *Christ and Culture* (New York: Harper & Brothers, 1956), p. 135.

12. John Calvin, *Institutes of the Christian Religion*, I, 3, 1.

13. Cf. Reinhold Niebuhr, *The Nature and Destiny of Man* (New York: Charles Scribner's Sons, 1949), vol. 1, p. 284.

14. G. H. Williams, *Spiritual and Anabaptist Writers* (Philadelphia: Westminster Press, 1957), pp. 129, 150.

15. H. E. Jacobs, ed., *Large Catechism, The Book of Concord* (Philadelphia: General Council Publication Board, 1911), p. 186. Luther wrote in his *Large Catechism* that the true honor and service of God, which he sharply distinguished from the false worship and idolatry of the heathen, is commanded under penalty of eternal wrath (ibid., pp. 392-93, 395). Calvin, on the basis that the name of the one God was everywhere known, concluded that "the heathen, to a man, by their own vanity either were dragged or slipped back into false inventions" and were therefore without excuse (John Calvin, *Institutes of the Christian Religion* I, 10, 3).

16. Cf. Hans Küng, *Freedom Today* (New York: Sheed and Ward, 1966), p. 119.

17. Georg Schurhammer, S.J., and Joseph Wicki, S.J., eds., *Epistolae S. Francisci Xavierii* (Rome: Monumenta Historica Societatis Iesu, 1945), vol. 1, pp. 164-65, 274.

18. Ibid., pp. 123, 148.

19. Ibid., pp. 382, 466; cf. James Broderick, S.J., *St. Francis Xavier* (London: Burns and Oates, 1958), pp. 437, 357.

20. Schurhammer and Wicki, eds., *Epistolae*, vol. 2, pp. 262-67; 187-88, 201; cf. Richard H. Drummond, *A History of Christianity in Japan* (Grand Rapids, Mich.: Wm. B. Eerdmans, 1971), pp. 31-35.

21. Nicholas of Cusa, *De pace fidei*, 10-12, 16-18, 68.

22. Emanuel Kellerhals, *Der Islam* (Basel: Basler Missionsbuchhandlung, 1945), p. 316.

23. Alfred North Whitehead, *Science and the Modern World* (New York: New American Library, 1958), p. 6.

24. This quotation constitutes the summary of de Lugo's views given by Friedrich von Hügel, *Essays and Addresses on the Philosophy of Religion* (London: Dent, 1921), p. 252. This understanding and spirit were expressed in comparable language by Pope Pius IX in an encyclical of 1863, *Quanto conficiamur moerore*. Cf. Jean L. Jadot, "The Growth in Roman Catholic Commitment to Interreligious Dialogue since Vatican II," *Journal of Ecumenical Studies* 20, no. 3 (Summer 1983): 369.

25. Louis Gardet, *Experiences Mystiques en Terres Non-Chretiénnes* (Paris: Alsatia, 1953), pp. 174-75; J.A. Cuttat, *The Encounter of Religions* (Tournai, Belgium: Desclée, 1960), pp. 41-42; cf. Heinrich Dumoulin, S.J., *A History of Zen Buddhism* (New York: Random House, 1963), pp. 198-224, 269-90; published in German in 1959.

26. Walter M. Abbott, ed., *The Documents of Vatican II* (New York: Guild Press, 1966), pp. 656-71.

27. Adrianus de Groot, "The Mission after Vatican II," *Concilium* 36 (1968): 174; cf. Peter Schreiner, "Roman Catholic Theology and Non-Christian Religion," *Journal of Ecumenical Studies* 6 (Summer 1969): 376-99.

28. Gregory Baum, "The Jews, Faith and Ideology," *The Ecumenist* 10 (July-August 1972): 74-75.

29. Raymond Panikkar, "Toward an Ecumenical Theandric Spirituality," *Journal of Ecumenical Studies* 5, no. 3 (Summer 1968): 527-528; cf. Panikkar, "Faith and Belief: On the Multireligious Experience (An Objectified Autobiographical Fragment)," *Anglican Theological Review* 53, no. 4 (October 1971): 219-37; J.A. Cuttat, "Experience Chrétienne et Spiritualité Orientale," *La Mystique et Les Mystiques* (Paris: Desclée de Brouwer, 1965), pp. 825-27.

30. Abbott, ed., *The Documents of Vatican II*, pp. 661-63. In note 11 on page 662

is found the observation that a basis for this appreciative thinking is found both in the New Testament and in the theologians of the early church. Indeed, it is "an understanding that is traditional in the Catholic Church." The editor then proceeds to say: "Through the centuries, however, missionaries often adopted the attitude that non-Christian religions were simply the work of Satan and the missionaries' task was to convert from error to knowledge of truth. This Declaration marks an authoritative change in approach. Now, for the first time, there is recognition of other religions as entities with which the Church can and should enter into dialogue."

31. Pope John Paul II, *First Encyclical Letter, Redemptor Hominis* (March 4, 1979) (Washington, D.C.: United States Catholic Conference, 1979), pp. 18, 24–25, 30–31, 34, 39–40.

32. Cf. Hans Joachim Margull, "The Awakening of Protestant Missions," in Maury, ed., *History's Lessons for Tomorrow's Missions*, pp. 142–46. We should note, however, that once missionaries of Pietist background came to have actual experience of other cultures, they sometimes also developed more sensitive appreciation of the wider work of God in the world in particulars. Thus Bartholomäus Ziegenbalg, who was one of the first of the German University of Halle pioneer Pietist missionaries in India, wrote in 1710 that he did not reject everything taught by the Hindus but, rather, rejoiced that for them "long ago a small light of the Gospel began to shine" and that "One will find here and there such teachings and passages in their writings, which are not only according to human reason but also according to God's Word" (W. Richey Hogg, "Edinburgh 1910—Perspective 1980," *Occasional Bulletin of Missionary Research* 4, no. 4 (October 1980): 149.

33. Rufus M. Jones, *The Journal of George Fox* (New York: Capricorn, 1963), pp. 100–101; Rosalie L. Colie, *Light and Enlightenment, A Study of the Cambridge Platonists and the Dutch Arminians* (Cambridge, England: Cambridge University Press, 1956), pp. ix–xii, 1–21. John Donne's famous words, "No man is an island," are also indicative of this humane spirit.

34. Akio Dohi, "Nihon ni okeru Fukuin no Dochaku," *Fukuin to Sekai* 21, no. 10 (October 1966): 10–13. A concept of vicarious suffering is an old and persistent feature of folk religion in Japan. Cf. Joseph M. Kitagawa, *Religion in Japanese History* (New York: Columbia University Press, 1966), pp. 319–21.

35. Inazō Nitobe, *Bushido, the Soul of Japan* (Los Angeles: Ohara Publications, 1969), p. 128.

36. Louis J. Gallagher, S.J., *China in the Sixteenth Century: The Journals of Matthew Ricci: 1583–1610* (New York: Random House, 1953), p. 93.

37. There is reason to believe that the problem here outlined existed from the early Reformation period. Luther himself, for all his stress on faith alone as the means of salvation (from the human side), had expected that the pure preaching of justification by faith alone would lead to a moral reformation and the transformation of the total social and political life of the Protestant lands. His own understanding of "faith" was so rich, varied, and lively in content that the ethical dimension was indeed largely contained therein. The fact, however, that, as is well known, he was greatly saddened in his last years by his failure to see any notable change in the public life of Protestants can be attributed in part to inadequate communication of his understanding of the gospel, as well as to ordinary human lethargy and perversity (cf. Paul Althaus, *The Theology of Martin Luther*, trans. Robert C. Schultz [Philadelphia: Fortress Press, 1966], pp. 245–50).

38. Cf. Williston Walker, *A History of the Christian Church*, 3rd ed., rev. Robert

T. Handy (New York: Charles Scribner's Sons, 1970), pp. 428–30, 479–83.

39. Mircea Eliade, "Review of 'La Franc-Maçonnerie Templiere et Occultiste aux XVIIIᵉ et XIXᵉ siècle,' by René Le Forestier," *History of Religions* 13, no. 1 (August 1973): 89–91.

40. Friedrich Schleiermacher, *The Christian Faith*, ed. H. R. Mackintosh and J. S. Stewart (Edinburgh: T. and T. Clark, 1948), pp. 31–34.

41. Cf. Jacques Waardenburg, *Classical Approaches to the Study of Religion* (The Hague: Mouton, 1973), pp. 7–78.

42. For a discussion of the meaning of the term "history of religions," see Joseph M. Kitagawa, "The History of Religions in America," in Mircea Eliade and Joseph M. Kitagawa, eds., *The History of Religions, Essays in Methodology* (Chicago: University of Chicago Press, 1959), p. 15.

43. Mircea Eliade, "Methodological Remarks on the Study of Religious Symbolism," in Eliade and Kitagawa, eds., *The History of Religions, Essays in Methodology*, p. 91.

44. Quotation from IMC official statement from "The Christian Life and Message in Relation to Non-Christian Systems of Thought and Life," *The Jerusalem Meeting of the International Missionary Council*, 8 vols., March 24–April 8, 1928 (New York: IMC, 1928), vol. 1, pp. 410–11 (cf. pp. 126–29, 210–11, 273). Cf. also E. C. Dewick, *The Christian Attitude to Other Religions* (Cambridge, England: Cambridge University Press, 1953), pp. 52–53, 105–6. It has been pointed out that the World Missionary Conference at Edinburgh in 1910 was much more in accord with the tradition of the Logos theology of the early church than has been generally known (cf. W. Richey Hogg, "Edinburgh 1910—Perspective 1980," *Occasional Bulletin of Missionary Research* 4, no. 4 [October 1980]: 149).

45. William E. Hocking, ed., *Re-Thinking Missions* (New York: Harper & Brothers, 1932), pp. 31, 37, 40, 327. Hocking himself later wrote that the Christian mission, as indeed every religious tradition, needs institutionalized modes of what he called "reconception." This is participation in a process of learning as well as teaching, contemplation as well as study, in short to receive as well as to give, from both the Most High God and fellow human beings of whatever background (*Living Religions and a World Faith* [New York: Macmillan, 1940], pp. 198–208).

46. Kraemer's views were expressed in detail in his book written for the Tambaram meeting, *The Christian Message in a Non-Christian World*. There were only nonsubstantive changes in his later books, *Religion and the Christian Faith*, *World Cultures and World Religions*, and *Why Christianity of All Religions?* Ernst Benz subsequently wrote of the "frightening isolation" into which much Christian thought fell as a result of the "unfounded claims of dialectical theology" ("Ideas for a Theology of the History of Religion," in Gerald H. Anderson, ed., *The Theology of the Christian Mission* [New York: McGraw-Hill, 1961], pp. 135–47; Benz, *Ideen zu einer Theologie der Religionsgeschichte* [Mainz: Verlag der Akademie der Wissenschaften und der Literatur, 1961], p. 36). A key reference for the thought of Karl Barth on this theme is *Die Kirchliche Dogmatik* (Zollikon-Zurich: Evangelischer Verlag, 1945), vol. 1, 2, pp. 356–97. Eng. ed., *Church Dogmatics* (Edinburgh: T. and T. Clark, 1956), vol. 1, 2, pp. 325–61. A number of scholars (e.g., Choan-Sen Song) have pointed out more recently, however, that in the later writings of Barth on anthropology he seems to affirm much in other religions as both true and edifying and to imply that even the term "divine revelation" may be appropriate in some cases.

47. Cf. S. J. Samartha, "Christian Study Centres and Asian Churches," *International Review of Mission* 59, no. 234 (April 1970): 173–79.

48. Cf. Rodger C. Bassham, "Mission Theology: 1948-1975," *Occasional Bulletin of Missionary Research* 2, no. 4 (April 1980): 52.

49. Ronald K. Orchard, ed., *Witness in Six Continents* (London: Edinburgh House Press, 1964), p. 174.

50. W. A. Visser 't Hooft, ed., *New Delhi Speaks about Christian Witness, Service, Unity* (New York: Association Press, 1962), pp. 27-30, 34, 32.

51. "Christian Encounter with Men of Other Beliefs," *The Ecumenical Review* 16, no. 4 (July 1964): 451-55.

52. "Christians in Dialogue with Men of Other Faiths," *International Review of Missions* 56, no. 223 (July 1967): 338-43.

53. *The Constitution of the United Presbyterian Church, U.S.A., Part I, Book of Confessions,* 2nd ed. (Philadelphia: Office of the General Assembly, U.P.C.U.S.A., 1970), sec. 3 (9.42).

54. "Statement from the East Asia Christian Conference of July 1970," *International Review of Mission* 59, no. 236 (October 1970): 428.

55. Norman Goodall, ed., *The Uppsala Report 1968* (Geneva: World Council of Churches, 1968), p. 29. There is a misprint in the text of the last sentence quoted, which I have altered, from "connecting" to "correcting." Carl F. Hallencreutz has also made this correction.

56. S. J. Samartha, "The World Council of Churches and Men of Other Faiths and Ideologies," in Samartha, ed., *Living Faiths and the Ecumenical Movement* (Geneva: World Council of Churches, 1971), p. 78.

57. S. J. Samartha, "More Than an Encounter of Commitments," *International Review of Mission* 59, no. 236 (October 1970): 392-403; cf. David Jenkins, "Commitment and Openness, A Theological Reflection," ibid., pp. 404-13.

58. "Christians in Dialogue with Men of Other Faiths," *International Review of Mission* 59, no. 236 (October 1970): 382-91; cf. M. M. Thomas, "Report of the Executive Committee by the Chairman," *The Ecumenical Review* 23, no. 2 (April 1971): 89-104.

59. S. J. Samartha and J. B. Taylor, eds., *Christian-Muslim Dialogue* (Geneva: World Council of Churches, 1973), pp. 145-63. All references to the Broumana Consultation and the memorandum, including Cragg's statement, are taken from these pages.

60. "A Letter to the Churches," from the CWME Assembly, Bangkok 1973, *International Review of Mission* 62, no. 246 (April 1973): pp. 180-82; cf. "An Affirmation on Salvation Today," ibid., pp. 183-84; *Bangkok Assembly 1973* (WCC Commission on World Mission and Evangelism) (Geneva: World Council of Churches, 1973), pp. 70-80.

61. "Towards World Community," *Study Encounter* 10, no. 3 (1974): 1-14; cf. S. J. Samartha, "Reflections on a Multilateral Dialogue," *The Ecumenical Review* 26, no. 4 (October 1974): 637-46. All references to the Colombo Dialogue are taken from these pages.

62. David M. Paton, ed., *Breaking Barriers, Nairobi 1975* (London: SPCK, 1976), pp. 70-85. All references to the Nairobi Report are taken from these pages.

63. David Allan Hubbard, *What We Evangelicals Believe* (Pasadena, Calif.: Fuller Theological Seminary, 1979), pp. 7-16.

64. Stransky used this figure during a lecture at a U.S. section meeting of the WCC at Madison, Wisconsin, in 1981.

65. Cf. Rodger C. Bassham, "Mission Theology: 1948-1975," *Occasional Bulletin of Missionary Research* 2, no. 4 (April 1980): 53-55. The Lausanne Congress

Covenant, section 5, affirms that "Evangelism and socio-political involvement are both part of our Christian duty," and that "we should share God's concern for justice and reconciliation throughout human society and for the liberation of men from every kind of oppression." It should be added that a "Statement of Concerns" was unofficially issued at the Consultation on World Evangelism held at Pattaya, Thailand, in June 1980 under the auspices of the continuing Lausanne Committee for World Evangelization. The Lausanne Committee was rather sharply criticized in this statement for lack of serious concern in implementing the affirmations of the Lausanne Covenant.

66. Donald G. Bloesch, *Essentials of Evangelical Theology*, 2 vols. (San Francisco: Harper & Row, 1978), vol. 1, pp. 245–46. Hendrikus Berkhof concludes that "a concentration on an eternal punishment in hell does not belong to the core of the [apostolic] kerygma" and that the intent of Paul was to communicate that "salvation in Christ extends as far as the lostness in Adam." His own personal position is succinctly expressed as a mode of hope: "For God's sake we hope that hell will be a form of purification" (*Christian Faith* [Grand Rapids, Mich.: Wm. B. Eerdmans, 1979], pp. 532–33). The mysterious verse Mk. 9:49, when viewed in its immediate context, seems helpful in this regard.

67. Quoted by Paul S. Rees, "Evangelicals/Resurgent," *World Vision* 21, no. 10 (October 1977): p. 23. The full text is found in *The Nottingham Statement* (Over Wallop, Hampshire, England: BAS Printers, 1977), p. 15.

68. Leon Howell has written in his report on Melbourne: "What seems likely is that this will be the last international conference of the WCC where only one imperialism will be attacked" ("Melbourne on Mission: Joining with the Poor," *Christianity and Crisis* 40, no. 13 [August 18, 1980]: 231).

69. "Melbourne Conference Section Reports," *International Review of Mission* 69, nos. 276–77 (October 1980–January 1981): 388–436; all references to the Melbourne Conference are taken from these pages. Simon Barrington-Ward has contrasted Melbourne with the consultation on World Evangelization (under Protestant evangelical auspices) held at Pattaya, Thailand, a month later as follows: "At Melbourne we had focussed on the world's pain, though in places we had touched on the healing. At Pattaya, for some at least, the healing of Christ became apparent in its fulness. An integral Gospel emerged, with healing for individuals and society" (*CMS News-Letter*, no. 436, October 1980, p. 7). Cf. Stanley J. Samartha, "Guidelines on Dialogue," *The Ecumenical Review* 31, no. 2 (April 1979): 155–62.

70. "Christians in Dialogue with Men of Other Faiths," *International Review of Mission* 59, no. 236 (October 1970), pp. 383–85, 391. Cf. David Jenkins, "Commitment and Openness," ibid., p. 411; Troy Organ, "A Cosmological Christology," *Christian Century* 88, no. 44 (November 3, 1971): 1293–95.

71. Karl Rahner, "Das Christentum und die nichtchristlichen Religionen," *Schriften zur Theologie*, 12 vols. (Einsiedeln: Benziger Verlag, 1964), vol. 5, p. 153. Eng. ed., *Theological Investigations* (Baltimore: Helicon Press, 1966), vol. 5, p. 130.

72. One is reminded of an early cosmopolitanism in the Roman playwright Terence (ca. 195?–159 B.C.): "Homo sum: humani nil a me alienum puto."

73. Cf. Vladimir Lossky, *The Mystical Theology of the Eastern Church* (London: James Clarke, 1957), pp. 135–73; John Meyendorff, *Christ in Eastern Christian Thought* (Washington, D.C.: Corpus Books, 1969), pp. 85–115, 149–61; Jaroslav Pelikan, *The Spirit of Eastern Christendom (600–1700)* (Chicago: University of Chicago Press, 1974), pp. 252–98; Timothy Ware, *The Orthodox Church* (Baltimore: Penguin Books, 1964), pp. 216–80.

74. Georges Khodr, "Christianity in a Pluralistic World—The Economy of the Holy Spirit," *The Ecumenical Review* 23 (April 1971): 118–19.

75. Khodr does not develop this point, but he is probably referring to the thesis held by a number of scholars that the presence and activity of the Nestorian church in central Asia was a significant causal factor in the development of the Pure Land School of Mahayana Buddhism in the direction of a trinitarian theism. With Shan-tao (d. 681) the concept of eternal life and of a vicarious, victorious savior was clarified as an integral part of Amitabha (Japan. Amida) Buddhist faith, and the holy Trinity of the Western Paradise (the *locus* of the goal in the tradition) appeared in distinctive form. Shan-tao lived near the Nestorian sphere of activity at the very time the Persian church was proclaiming the message with pristine power. Kwan-yin, one member of the Trinity, was depicted as sending down the white dove symbolic of pure Spirit, imagery characteristic of Nestorianism, as of the early church (cf. Karl Ludwig Reichelt, *Truth and Tradition in Chinese Buddhism* [Shanghai: Commercial Press, 1927], pp. 131–32, 179).

76. Georges Khodr, "Christianity in a Pluralistic World—The Economy of the Holy Spirit," pp. 118–28; cf. Paul Verghese, "Christ and All Men," in S. J. Samartha, ed., *Living Faiths and the Ecumenical Movement* (Geneva: World Council of Churches, 1971), pp. 159–64.

6 VIEWS OF CONTEMPORARY THEOLOGIANS: ROMAN CATHOLIC

1. Raymond Panikkar, *The Unknown Christ of Hinduism* (London: Darton, Longman and Todd, 1968), pp. vii–ix.

2. Ibid., pp. x, 4.

3. Ibid., p. 51.

4. Ibid., pp. 16–17.

5. Ibid., pp. 17–19, 41.

6. Ibid., pp. 25–28.

7. Ibid., pp. 29, 32–34, 49, 51.

8. Ibid., pp. 49, 54.

9. Ibid., pp. 58–59, 38–39. In this context Panikkar notes that Christianity itself does not appear without a "long 'economical' and 'pedagogical' education." He affirms that two key patristic theological concepts were to "explain divine providence from the beginning of mankind and the coming of the Christian message at the 'end of time.' "

10. Ibid., pp. 50–51, 59.

11. Raymond Panikkar, *The Trinity and World Religions* (Madras, India: Christian Literature Society, 1970), pp. 1–3. The content of this booklet of eighty pages is given in shortened form in "Toward an Ecumenical Theandric Spirituality," *Journal of Ecumenical Studies* 5, no. 3 (Summer 1968): 507–34.

12. Ibid., pp. 54–55, 4–6.

13. Panikkar, "Toward an Ecumenical Theandric Spirituality," p. 534.

14. Panikkar, "Faith and Belief: A Multireligious Experience," *Anglican Theological Review* 53, no. 4 (October 1971): 223, 230, 236–37.

15. Panikkar, "The Hindu Ecclesial Consciousness—Some Ecclesiological Reflections," *Jeevadhara, Journal of Christian Interpretation* 4, no. 21 (May–June 1974): 203–5 (published in Alleppey, Kerala, India).

16. Panikkar, *The Intrareligious Dialogue* (New York: Paulist Press, 1978), pp.

xviii-xx, xxii, 54-61; cf. Nalini Devdas, "The Theandrism of Raimundo Panikkar and Trinitarian Parallels in Modern Hindu Thought," *Journal of Ecumenical Studies* 17, no. 4 (Fall 1980): pp. 606-20. Panikkar has developed his thought somewhat further in the introduction to the revised and enlarged edition of his *The Unknown Christ of Hinduism* (Maryknoll, N.Y.: Orbis Books, 1981), pp. 1-30. Cf. also his "A Preface to a Hindu-Christian Theology," *Jeevadhara* 9, no. 49 (January-February 1979): 6-63.

17. J.G. Weber, ed., *In Quest of the Absolute: The Life and Work of Jules Monchanin* (Kalamazoo, Mich.: Cistercian Publications, 1977), pp. 1-2.

18. Cf. Henri Le Saux, *Hindu-Christian Meeting Point* (Bangalore-Bombay, 1969); *Prayer* (Philadelphia: Westminister Press, 1972).

19. Cf. Bede Griffiths, *Christ in India, Essays toward a Hindu-Christian Dialogue* (New York: Charles Scribner's Sons, 1966); *Return to the Center* (Springfield, Ill.: Templegate, 1976).

20. Cf. Klaus Klostermaier, *In the Paradise of Krishna* (Philadelphia: Westminster Press, 1971); *Kristvidya, a Sketch of an Indian Christology* (Bangalore, India, 1967); "Hṛdayavidyā: A Sketch of a Hindu-Christian Theology of Love," *Journal of Ecumenical Studies* 9, no. 4 (Fall 1972): 750-76.

21. Edward Schillebeeckx had written earlier that all religion presupposes "an at least anonymous supernatural revelation and faith" and that pagan religious rites can be the manifestation of "an anonymous but nonetheless effective operation of grace." He called the concept of a purely "natural religion" a fiction *(Christ the Sacrament of the Encounter with God* [New York: Sheed and Ward, 1963], pp. 8-9, fn. 2). The book was originally published in Dutch in 1960.

22. Karl Rahner, "Das Christentum und die nichtchristlichen Religionen," *Schriften zur Theologie,* 15 vols. (Einsiedeln: Benziger Verlag, 1964), vol. 5, pp. 136-39.

23. Ibid., p. 140.

24. Cf. Hendrik Kraemer, *Why Christianity of All Religions?* (Philadelphia: Westminster Press, 1962), pp. 114-19.

25. Rahner, "Das Christentum," pp. 147, 154.

26. Ibid., pp. 145-46, 151.

27. Ibid., p. 143. Jean Daniélou, however, is able to affirm only, for example, that the highest in Hinduism is the highest in the human order, infinitely below the revelation of the trinitarian God of Christian faith, who is love *(The Salvation of the Nations* [Notre Dame, Ind.: University of Notre Dame Press, 1962], p. 40; first published in 1949).

28. Ibid., pp. 150, 155.

29. Ibid., pp. 141-42, 148.

30. Ibid., p. 153.

31. Ibid., pp. 146, 155.

32. Ibid., p. 153.

33. Ibid., p. 152.

34. Ibid., pp. 144, 142.

35. Ibid., p. 157.

36. Ibid., pp. 154-55. Rahner acknowledges that the term "anonymous Christian" is subject to interpretation by non-Christians as presumptuous. Hans Küng prefers not to use the term at all *(Freedom Today* [New York: Sheed and Ward, 1966], p. 144). Cf., however, Edward Schillebeeckx, *The Church and Mankind,* Concilium, Dogma, vol. 1 (Glen Rock, N.J.: Paulist Press, 1965), pp. 88-89; Maurice Boutin,

"Anonymous Christianity: A Paradigm for Interreligious Encounter?" *Journal of Ecumenical Studies* 20, no. 4 (Fall 1983): 602–29.

37. Heinz Robert Schlette, whose thought we shall subsequently consider, specifically rejects the notion of a "more advantageous chance of salvation" *(Towards a Theology of Religions* [New York: Herder and Herder, 1966], p. 93). I once had the opportunity to discuss this point with Fr. Rahner personally (Oct. 27, 1967). He assured me that he agrees with Schlette and apparently wishes to qualify the language of this passage of his essay.

38. Rahner, "Das Christentum," pp. 156–58.

39. Other Catholic theologians of somewhat lesser note, however, such as Paul de Surgy and Joseph Masson, acknowledge the possibility of salvation outside the institutional church but consider the situation of non-Christians as "precarious and obviously less favorable to salvation." The means of salvation available to the Christian makes the person's task "infinitely easier, his path infinitely more secure, his future infinitely more favorable" (quoted in Eugene Hillman, "The Wider Ecumenism," unpublished manuscript, 1967, p. 5). H. van Straelen represents an older position strongly critical of Rahner et al. (*The Catholic Encounter with World Religions* [Westminster, Md.: Newman Press, 1966], pp. 95–132).

40. Karl Rahner, *Foundations of Christian Faith* (New York: Seabury Press, 1978), pp. 142–61, 311–21; cf. Jerome P. Theisen, *The Ultimate Church and the Promise of Salvation* (Collegeville, Minn.: St. John's University Press, 1976), pp. 65–121.

41. Schlette, *Towards a Theology of Religions,* pp. 32, 70.

42. Ibid., p. 64.

43. Ibid., pp. 35, 70, 73, 36, 71–75.

44. Ibid., pp. 80–81, 94. Schlette defines salvation as "the whole life and existence of mankind as ordered according to God's intention"; it is not merely the salvation of the soul after death (ibid., pp. 75–76, 85, 37).

45. Ibid., p. 37.

46. Ibid., pp. 93–94, 96, 114, 116, 85–86, 82. Schlette acknowledges in another passage, however, that the empirical catholicity of the church is never absolute and perfect (ibid., p. 101).

47. Ibid., pp. 106, 112–13.

48. Hans Küng, *Freedom Today* (New York: Sheed and Ward, 1966), pp. 121–24. The essay appeared in German under the title *Christenheit als Minderheit* (Einsiedeln: Benziger Verlag, 1965), and represents the revision of an address given at the World Eucharistic Congress in Bombay in November 1964.

49. Walter M. Abbott and Joseph Gallagher, eds., *The Documents of Vatican II* (New York: America Press, 1966), p. 35 (Dogmatic Constitution on the Church, no. 2.16).

50. Küng, *Freedom Today,* pp. 139–41, 144. Cf. Hans Küng, "The World's Religions in God's Plan of Salvation," in Joseph Neuner, ed., *Christian Revelation and World Religions* (London: Burns and Oates, 1967), pp. 25–66.

51. Ibid., pp. 152–55, 158–61.

52. Hans Küng, *On Being a Christian,* trans. Edward Quinn (Garden City, N.Y.: Doubleday, 1976), p. 91.

53. Ibid., pp. 92–93, 99–100.

54. Ibid., pp. 101–7. Küng also is mistaken in saying that the Qur'ān "contains a great deal of later, adventitious material," even though it certainly "includes a very

human history" (p. 107). At several points from pages 101 to 110 Küng has committed himself to generalization that cannot be substantiated. Other examples are under his understanding of *māyā* in the Hindu tradition, statements of the "far-reaching cosmic *pessimism* of Buddhism and its "supreme *indifference toward the social needs of men,"* etc.

55. Kenneth Scott Latourette, *A History of the Expansion of Christianity,* 7 vols. (New York: Harper, 1937-45).

56. Cf. Richard H. Drummond, *A History of Christianity in Japan* (Grand Rapids, Mich.: Wm. B. Eerdmans, 1971), pp. 117-25, 184-93.

57. Küng, *On Being a Christian,* pp. 106, 111-12.

58. Ibid., pp. 112-15. A more recent work by a German Catholic missiological theologian is Walbert Bühlmann, *The Search for God, An Encounter with the Peoples and Religions of Asia* (Maryknoll, N.Y.: Orbis Books, 1980).

59. Paul F. Knitter, *Towards a Protestant Theology of Religions* (Marburg, 1974), in H. Grass and W.G. Kümmel, eds., Marburger Theologische Studien.

60. Paul F. Knitter, "World Religions and the Finality of Christ: A Critique of Hans Küng's *On Being a Christian,"* *Horizons,* 5, no. 2 (Fall 1978): 151-64.

61. Cf. Paul F. Knitter, "Jesus—Buddha—Krishna: Still Present?" *Journal of Ecumenical Studies* 16, no. 4 (Fall 1979): 669.

62. Paul F. Knitter, "Jesus and Buddha: A New Conversation," unpublished paper given at the annual convention of the College Theology Society, May 1980. Knitter develops this theme with further precision in his article, "Christianity as Religion: True and Absolute? A Roman Catholic Perspective," in *Concilium,* vol. 136 (New York: Seabury Press, 1980); cf. his "Roman Catholic Approaches to Other Religions: Developments and Tensions," *International Bulletin of Missionary Research* 8, no. 2 (April 1984): 50-54; *No Other Name* (Maryknoll, N.Y.: Orbis Books, 1985), pp. 169-231.

63. Cf. Edward Conze, *Buddhist Thought in India* (Ann Arbor: University of Michigan Press, 1967), pp. 21-25.

64. Heinrich Dumoulin, "Buddhism—A Religion of Liberation," in *Concilium,* vol. 116 (New York: Seabury Press, 1979), pp. 22-30.

65. Heinrich Dumoulin, *Christianity Meets Buddhism* (La Salle, Ill.: Open Court Publishing Co., 1974), pp. 3, 11, 112, 198.

66. Ibid., pp. 19, 22-26, 34-37, 127-29.

67. This last phrase is cited as a quotation from Thomas Aquinas, *Summa theologica* IIa-IIae, q. 138, a. 2, ad 1. The citation seems to be in error. The thought, however, is certainly Thomistic. Cf. "et communicatio bonorum operum quae est per caritatem, ut bonum unius alteri prosit" (In III *sententiarum* 25, 1, 2.co/42); "caritas, id est communicabilis bonitas" *(Liber de fide trinitatis* 1.12/65). Joseph J. Spae, *East Challenges West: Towards a Convergence of Spiritualities* (Chicago: Chicago Institute of Theology and Culture, 1979), p. 11.

68. Again, there is a problem with the citation. In Augustine, *In Psalm.* CXXII, 2, there is a phrase similar to this but apparently used in a different way. In any case, the quotation as it stands in the text is expressive of the thought of Spae, and that is what we are considering.

69. Actually, even though Thomas Aquinas *(De potentia* quest. 1, art. 3, obj. 6) cites this sentence as from Ambrose, it is from the so-called Ambrosiaster, an otherwise unknown but able Christian in Rome who wrote a commentary in Latin in the last quarter of the fourth century on the letters of Paul. In Ambrosiaster the Latin original is: "quicquid enim verum a quocumque dicitur, a sancto dicitur spiritu" *(In*

epistulas ad Corinthios 12, 3, in Heinrich J. Vogels, ed., *Corpus Scriptorum Ecclesiasticorum Latinorum* [Vienna: Hoelder-Pichler-Tempsky, 1968], vol. 81, p. 132).

70. Spae, *East Challenges West,* pp. 11–12.

71. Ibid., pp. 15–29, 33. According to Spae "Emptiness" is called "Wondrous Being" by Nāgārjuna, the great Indian early Mahayana Buddhist philosopher and mystic (ca. A.D. 150–250), and as such is "the basis for human freedom, creative activity, and the ethical life" (ibid., p. 40).

72. Ibid., pp. 37–39.

73. Ibid., pp. 43, 49.

74. Ibid., pp. 43, 49, 53, 61.

75. Ibid., pp. 63–65, 78–81.

76. Joseph J. Spae, *Buddhist-Christian Empathy* (Chicago: Chicago Institute of Theology and Culture, 1980), pp. 206, 227, 233, 239–41; cf. Joseph J. Spae, "Eastern Cults in Western Culture," *International Review of Mission* 67, no. 268 (October 1978): 227–35.

77. Cf. Thomas Merton, *Mystics and Zen Masters* (New York: Farrar, Straus and Giroux, 1967), passim, but especially pp. 3–44, 281–88.

78. H.M. Enomiya-Lassalle, *Zen—Way to Enlightenment* (London: Burns and Oates, 1967), pp. 125–26; cf. his *Zen Meditation for Christians* (La Salle, Ill.: Open Court Publishing Co., 1974), pp. 23–38, 149–67. In this later book Lassalle confesses that he hopes to "discover a synthesis" of the way of Zen meditation and the way of Christian meditation.

79. William Johnston, *The Still Point* (New York: Fordham University Press, 1970), pp. xi–xii.

80. Ibid., pp. 15–16, 171–74.

81. Ibid., pp. 175–82.

82. William Johnston, *The Inner Eye of Love* (New York: Harper & Row, 1978), pp. 73–78, 105, 141; cf. his *Christian Zen* (New York: Harper & Row, 1974), pp. 30–56; *The Mirror Mind* (New York: Harper & Row, 1981), pp. 33–41, 97–102, 126–27, 132–76. It is well to note how these perceptions of William Johnston, and indeed of the other Roman Catholic theologians described in this chapter, are closely in accord with a consensus already emergent within the leadership of the Roman Catholic Church throughout the whole of Asia. Cf. the Report of the International Congress on Mission, 2–7 December, 1979, *Toward a New Age in Mission* (Manila: Theological Conference Office, 1981), vol. 1, pp. 32–45; vol. 2, pp. 45–48, 59–67, III–14; vol. 3, pp. 46–100, 119–23, 208–16.

7 VIEWS OF CONTEMPORARY THEOLOGIANS: PROTESTANT

1. Julius Richter, "Missionary Apologetic," *International Review of Missions* 2, no. 7 (July 1913): 522–23.

2. Cf. Ludwig Wiedenmann, *Mission und Eschatologie* (Paderborn, Germany: Verlag Bonifacius-Druckerei, 1965), p. 11.

3. Cf. Martin Schlunk "Theology and Missions in Germany in Recent Years," *International Review of Missions* 27, no. 59 (July 1938): 465, 470–71; *Die Weltreligionen und das Christentum* (Frankfurt am Main: Anker-Verlag, 1953), pp. 170–78; and Georg Vicedom, *The Challenge of the World Religions* (Philadelphia: Fortress Press, 1963), pp. 120–53, especially p. 125. Vicedom's criticisms of the religions are frequently inept as well as unfair. One should add, however, that much of the missionary work of

German Protestants has been among peoples of preliterate cultures, and a number of mass movements have occurred whereby large sociological units were converted to Christian faith, e.g., in Sumatra. The issue of religious displacement alters considerably in this context, since the cultural momentum of the past is carried on, as formerly in the case of central and northern Europe, to an appreciable extent regardless of the intent of missionaries.

4. Wolfhart Pannenberg, *Basic Questions in Theology*, trans. George H. Kehm (Philadelphia: Fortress Press, 1971), pp. 65–118 (note especially p. 70). Cf. Ernst Benz, *Ideen zu einer Theologie der Religionsgeschichte* (Wiesbaden: Akademie der Wissenschaften und der Literatur in Mainz, 1961), p. 36.

5. Paul F. Knitter, "European Protestant and Catholic Approaches to the World Religions: Complements and Contrasts," *Journal of Ecumenical Studies* 12, no. 1 (Winter 1975): 13–28.

6. Cf. E.C. Dewick, *The Christian Attitude to Other Religions* (Cambridge, England: Cambridge University Press, 1953), pp. 41–43.

7. Hendrik Kraemer, *The Christian Message in a Non-Christian World* (Grand Rapids, Mich.: Kregel Publications, 1963), p. 104.

8. Ibid., p. 109.

9. Cf. ibid., p. 300.

10. Ibid., p. 113; quotation from p. 101.

11. Ibid., pp. 113, 125.

12. Ibid., p. 126.

13. Ibid., p. 136 (Kraemer's italics).

14. Ibid., pp. 111, 132.

15. Ibid., pp. 124, 130–37.

16. Hendrik Kraemer, *Religion and the Christian Faith* (London: Lutterworth Press, 1956), pp. 339, 340–41, 350, 352, 358–59.

17. Hendrik Kraemer, *Why Christianity of All Religions?* trans. Hubert Hoskins (Philadelphia: Westminster Press, 1962), pp. 15, 72, 77.

18. Ibid., p. 79.

19. Ibid., pp. 115–16.

20. Ibid., pp. 90, 93.

21. Ibid., pp. 93–95. Cf. Antonio R. Gualtieri, "The Failure of Dialectic in Hendrik Kraemer's Evaluation of Non-Christian Faith," *Journal of Ecumenical Studies* 15, no. 2 (Spring 1978): 274–90.

22. Ibid., p. 96.

23. Ibid., pp. 103, 97–99. The italicized *openly* is Kraemer's.

24. Ibid., pp. 122–24. Kenneth Cragg writes regarding Kraemer's book *World Cultures and World Religions* that in the conclusion Kraemer "seemed to move away from the issue of truth in theology towards the obligation of truth in community." But the evidence that Cragg adduces from the book does not appear to substantiate his view (Kenneth Cragg, *The Christian and Other Religion* [London: Mowbrays, 1977], p. 72).

25. Paul Tillich, *Biblical Religion and the Search for Ultimate Reality* (Chicago: University of Chicago Press, 1964), pp. 45–46.

26. Paul Tillich, *Christianity and the Encounter of the World Religions* (New York: Columbia University Press, 1963), pp. 2, 32–33, 63–64.

27. Ibid., pp. 53–54, 79–80.

28. Ibid., p. 37.

29. Tillich does not use the term "universalism" in the sense of a guaranteed universal salvation but of universal divine activity.

30. Tillich, *Christianity and the Encounter of the World Religions*, pp. 77–78.

31. Ibid., pp. 81–82, 97.

32. Ibid., pp. 31–32. At one point Tillich speaks of the universal principle of justice as producing in Israel the exclusive monotheism of the God of justice.

33. Ibid., pp. 94, 83.

34. Ibid., pp. 85–89, 22.

35. Ibid., pp. 23–24.

36. Ibid., pp. 68–70.

37. Tillich is also mistaken in his affirmation that Buddhist compassion lacks the will to transform (ibid., p. 71).

38. Ibid., pp. 63–66, 70–73.

39. Ibid., pp. 66–67.

40. Ibid., p. 95. Tillich elsewhere strongly emphasizes the need of conversion as a necessity of ontology. This he understands as an "opening of the eyes, a revelatory experience." This, however, does not mean for Tillich conversion from one religious affiliation to another (*Biblical Religion and the Search for Ultimate Reality*, p. 65).

41. Paul Tillich, *Systematic Theology*, 3 vols. (Chicago: University of Chicago Press, 1971), vol. 3, pp. 224–28.

42. Paul Tillich, *The Future of Religions* (New York: Harper & Row, 1966), p. 91.

43. Ibid., p. 81.

44. Ibid., p. 85.

45. Ibid., pp. 86–88.

46. Ibid., pp. 88–89.

47. Ibid., p. 90.

48. W.A. Visser 't Hooft, ed., *New Delhi Speaks about Christian Witness, Service, Unity* (New York: Association Press, 1962), p. 18.

49. Ibid., pp. 27–33.

50. David Gnanaprakasam Moses, *Religious Truth and the Relation between Religions* (Madras: Christian Literature Society for India, 1950), pp. 122, 142, 159. It is very likely that twentieth-century Indian Christian thought on these themes has been significantly influenced by the nineteenth-century Hindu of the Brahmo Samaj, Keshub Chunder Sen, who in his lectures and writings developed seminal thoughts of extraordinary perception and potency on the significance of Jesus Christ. (Cf. Clifford G. Hospital, "The Contribution of Keshub Chunder Sen toward a Global and Inductive Christology," *Journal of Ecumenical Studies* 19, no. 1 [Winter 1982]: 1–17.)

51. *A Christian Theological Approach to Hinduism* (Madras: Christian Literature Society, 1956), pp. 21, 11, 8, 21–28. Appasamy earlier wrote *Christianity as Bhakti Marga* (1926), *What is Moksha* (1931), and *The Gospel and India's Heritage* (1942). Cf. his "Warum indische Theologie?" in *Neue Zeitschrift für systematische Theologie and Religionsphilosophie* 6 (1964): 343–59.

52. Ibid., pp. 29–30.

53. Ibid., pp. 32–33.

54. Ibid., pp. 36–38, 45, 34.

55. Ibid., pp. 50–54.

56. Ibid., pp. 55–58, 60–61.

57. Ibid., pp. 70, 72–73.

58. Ibid., pp. 66-67; cf. Rajah B. Manikam, ed., *Christianity and the Asian Revolution* (New York: Friendship Press, 1955), pp. 207-9.

59. Paul David Devanandan, *The Gospel and Renascent Hinduism* (London: SCM Press, 1959), pp. 54-55, 57-62.

60. Quoted in Carl F. Hallencreutz, "A Long-Standing Concern: Dialogue in Ecumenical History 1910-1971," in S.J. Samartha, ed., *Living Faiths and the Ecumenical Movement* (Geneva: World Council of Churches, 1971), pp. 62-63.

61. Quoted in M.M. Thomas, *Man and the Universe of Faiths* (Madras, India: Christian Literature Society, 1975), pp. 149-50.

62. Vinjamuri E. Devadutt, *The Bible and the Faiths of Men* (New York: Friendship Press, 1967), pp. 42-47, 52.

63. M.M. Thomas, *The Christian Response to the Asian Revolution* (London: SCM Press, 1966), pp. 93-95.

64. M.M. Thomas, *The Acknowledged Christ of the Indian Renaissance* (London, SCM Press, 1969), pp. 239-53.

65. Ibid., pp. 283-87. Reference has already been made to Paul Tillich's hope, expressed only a few days before his death, for the future of theology to move beyond the compass of his *Systematic Theology* into a long and intensive "interpenetration of systematic theological study and religious historical studies." A similar aspiration is reported to have been expressed by D.T. Niles shortly before his death in 1970.

66. Ibid., p. 305; cf. Burnett Hillman Streeter, *The Buddha and the Christ* (London: Macmillan, 1932), p. 71.

67. Ibid., pp. 298-301; cf. M.M. Thomas, *Towards a Theology of Contemporary Ecumenism* (Madras, India: Christian Literature Society, 1978), pp. 188-89, 235-37, 303-7.

68. M.M. Thomas, *Man and the Universe of Faiths* (Madras, India: Christian Literature Society, 1975), pp. vi, 148-57. In an earlier work Thomas had written that, following Keshub Chunder Sen and Manilal Parekh, he wished to state that "the Church can take form as a Christ-centered fellowship of faith and ethics in the Hindu religious community." He felt that this meant the presence of Christ within this Hindu community and included "in the long run" authentic "unity and historical continuity with the whole Church." The effect would be to allow Jesus Christ to function within the community so as "to judge and fulfill not merely the cultural and social but also the religious life of the Hindu" (*Salvation and Humanisation* [Madras: Christian Literature Society, 1971], pp. 40, 18).

69. S.J. Samartha, ed., *Living Faiths and the Ecumenical Movement* (Geneva: World Council of Churches, 1971); *Dialogue between Men of Living Faiths* (Geneva: World Council of Churches, 1971); *Christian-Muslim Dialogue* (Geneva: World Council of Churches, 1973); *Living Faiths and Ultimate Goals* (Maryknoll, N.Y.: Orbis Books, 1974); *Faith in the Midst of Faiths* (Geneva: World Council of Churches, 1977).

70. S.J. Samartha, *"More* than an Encounter of Commitments," *International Review of Mission* 59, no. 236 (October 1970): 402.

71. S.J. Samartha, "Dialogue as a Continuing Christian Concern," *The Ecumenical Review* 23, no. 2 (April 1971): 138-42.

72. S.J. Samartha, "Living Faiths and Ultimate Goals: Introducing a Discussion," in *Living Faiths and Ultimate Goals,* pp. vii, xvii; cf. *The Ecumenical Review* 25, no. 2 (April 1973): 137-47.

73. S.J. Samartha, "A Pause for Reflection," in *Faith in the Midst of Faiths*

(Geneva: World Council of Churches, 1977), pp. 8–15. Cf. S.J. Samartha, "Mission and Movements of Innovation," in Gerald H. Anderson and Thomas F. Stransky, eds., *Mission Trends, No. 3* (New York: Paulist Press, 1976), pp. 233–44; "Partners in Community: Some Reflections on Hindu-Christian Relations Today," *Occasional Bulletin of Missionary Research* 4, no. 2 (April 1980): 78–82.

74. The statement adopted at Chiang Mai is entitled "Dialogue in Community" and is found in *Faith in the Midst of Faiths*, pp. 134–49 and in *The Ecumenical Review* 29, no. 3 (July 1977): 254–64.

75. S.J. Samartha, "Dialogue in Community: A Step Forward," *Faith in the Midst of Faiths*, pp. 183–90. For another, similar Indian Christian discussion of our theme, see Samuel Amirtham, "The Challenge of New Religions to Christian Theological Thought," *International Review of Mission* 67, no. 268 (October 1978): 399–406.

76. Cf. Owen C. Thomas, ed., *Attitudes toward Other Religions* (New York: Harper & Row, 1969), pp. 26, 219–21.

77. John V. Taylor, *CMS News-Letter*, no. 303 (April 1967), p. 2. Taylor identifies Ralph Harper as a person who has expressed with singular beauty "the world of presence"; cf. Ralph Harper, *The Sleeping Beauty* (London: Harvill, 1955), especially pp. 111, 122.

78. John V. Taylor, *CMS News-Letter*, no. 330 (September 1969), pp. 1–4.

79. Ibid., no. 382 (June 1974), pp. 5–6; cf. W.F. Albright, *From the Stone Age to Christianity* (Baltimore: Johns Hopkins Press, 1940), pp. 232–40.

80. John V. Taylor, *The Primal Vision: Christian Presence amid African Religion* (Philadelphia: Fortress Press, 1963), pp. 196–205.

81. George Appleton, *On the Eightfold Path*, Christian Presence amid Buddhism (London: SCM Press, 1961); Kenneth Cragg, *Sandals at the Mosque*, Christian Presence amid Islam (London: SCM Press, 1959). The periodical *Ends and Odds*, published under the auspices of the Anglican Archbishopric of Jerusalem as a newsletter of theology and dialogue in the Middle East, is clearly expressive of the same concern for a "quickened intercession and a larger, more alert compassion." The massive work of A.C. Bouquet, *The Christian Faith and Non-Christian Religions* (New York: Harper & Brothers, 1958), rightly belongs in this category of contemporary Anglican thought. Bouquet was for many years lecturer in history and history of religions at Cambridge University.

82. M.A.C. Warren, in John V. Taylor's *The Primal Vision*, pp. 10–11. Warren's views are given in more extended form in *I Believe in the Great Commission* (Grand Rapids, Mich.: Wm. B. Eerdmans, 1976), pp. 153–70. Here near the end of his life he affirmed his conviction that what "we are, indeed, seeing is a convergence of religious men. And they are converging on the Man, Jesus." He held, with the Greek church fathers, that the risen Christ "is the heart of all [authentic human] spirituality" and that one significant element of Christian mission is the humble role of unveiling "the unknown Christ," for it is "response to him which saves, even when, as may often be the case, he is unrecognized as the Saviour." "The more I claim for Jesus Christ and the inspiring activity of his Holy Spirit in creating and redeeming and sanctifying human life, the more profound is my reverence and regard for what I see him doing in history *and* in the lives of those who do not know him."

83. Schubert Ogden, *Christ without Myth* (New York: Harper & Brothers, 1961), p. 154.

84. Ibid., p. 153.

85. Ibid.

86. Ibid., pp. 156–57, 160–61.

87. Schubert Ogden, *The Reality of God* (New York: Harper·& Row, 1966), pp. 192–203.

88. Ibid., p. 173.

89. Ibid., p. 181.

90. Ibid., pp. 202–3.

91. Schubert Ogden, "The Point of Christology," *Journal of Religion* 55, no. 4 (October 1975): pp. 378–79, 387, 391.

92. Ogden, *The Reality of God*, pp. 197–98. Ogden has written negatively of traditional concepts of "subjective immortality" in favor of hope in the "ultimate reality of God's love, which alone . . . embraces our future" ("The Meaning of Christian Hope," in Harry James Cargas and Bernard Lee, eds., *Religious Experience and Process Theology* [New York: Paulist Press, 1976], pp. 195–212).

93. John Hick, *God and the Universe of Faiths* (London: Macmillan, 1973), p. 131. Hick has written briefly of his personal pilgrimage of faith in *God Has Many Names* (London: Macmillan, 1980), pp. 1–9.

94. Ibid., pp. 174–75, 191, 197, 118.

95. Ibid., pp. 101–2. We shall meet with the term "field of force" again in John B. Cobb, Jr., as in Wolfgang Pannenberg. It is significant, however, that Hick uses the term in the plural number.

96. Ibid., pp. 135–36; cf. Bouquet, *The Christian Faith*, pp. 56–100.

97. Ibid., pp. 103, 106–7.

98. John Hick, "Jesus and the World Religions," in John Hick, ed., *The Myth of God Incarnate* (Philadelphia: Westminster Press, 1977), p. 181.

99. Hick, *God and the Universe of Faiths*, p. 141.

100. Hick, *The Myth of God Incarnate*, p. 180.

101. Hick, *God and the Universe of Faiths,* pp. 112–13; cf. John Hick, *Death and Eternal Life* (London: Collins, 1976), pp. 171–77.

102. Ibid., p. 152.

103. Ibid., pp. 172–74, 176–78. A recent summation of Hick's thought on this theme is found in his "Whatever Path Men Choose Is Mine," in John Hick and Brian Hebblethwaite, eds., *Christianity and Other Religions* (Philadelphia: Fortress Press, 1980), pp. 171–90. Wilfred Cantwell Smith has similarities with Hick's theocentrism but perhaps more concern for continuity with the Christian past; cf. *Towards a World Theology* (Philadelphia: Westminster Press, 1981), pp. 152–79.

104. Don Cupitt, "The Finality of Christ," *Theology* 78, no. 666 (December 1975): 626–27.

105. Ibid., p. 627.

106. Ibid., p. 625; cf. Cupitt, "The Christ of Christendom," in John Hick, ed., *The Myth of God Incarnate*, p. 140.

107. Don Cupitt, "One Jesus, Many Christs," in S.W. Sykes and J.P. Clayton, eds., *Christ, Faith and History* (Cambridge, England: Cambridge University Press, 1972), pp. 131–44.

108. Cupitt, "The Finality of Christ," p. 627.

109. Ibid., pp. 627–28.

110. "The criterion of religious adequacy, rightly understood, itself demands that christology be not any kind of man-cult: it must be theocentric, not christocentric" (Cupitt, "The Christ of Christendom," p. 146).

111. John A.T. Robinson, *The Human Face of God* (Philadelphia: Westminster Press, 1973), p. 213.

112. Ibid., pp. 215–18.

113. Ibid., pp. 221–22.

114. Ibid., pp. 223, 225, 227, 229, 231–32, 234.

115. Ibid., pp. 237–40. The last phrase "all begin to make . . ." of Robinson's sentence is from Harvey Cox, *Feast of Fools* (Cambridge, Mass.: Harvard University Press, 1969), p. 141.

116. John A.T. Robinson, *Can We Trust the New Testament?* (Grand Rapids, Mich.: Wm. B. Eerdmans, 1977), pp. 120–29.

117. John A.T. Robinson, *Truth Is Two-Eyed* (Philadelphia: Westminster Press, 1978), pp. 22–25, 35–37.

118. Ibid., pp. 42, 64–65.

119. Ibid., pp. 71, 98–99.

120. Ibid., pp. 99–129.

121. John B. Cobb, Jr., *Christ in a Pluralistic Age* (Philadelphia: Westminster Press, 1975), pp. 18–19.

122. Ibid., p. 19.

123. Ibid., p. 21.

124. Cf. David L. Miller, *The New Polytheism: Rebirth of the Gods and Goddesses* (New York: Harper & Row, 1974), pp. 64–83.

125. Cobb, *Christ in a Pluralistic Age*, pp. 21–22.

126. Ibid., pp. 204–5, 54.

127. Ibid., p. 264.

128. Ibid., p. 220. Cobb seems to qualify this understanding in a later article, where he notes that there is "a strong connectedness among successive experiences of a single person," and also states that in the Buddhist concept of *karma* "the factuality of a personal self" is really affirmed but that in Buddhism no formal metaphysical basis or "common subject" is presumed in the connection of experience ("Buddhism and Christianity as Complementary," *Northeast Asia Journal of Theology* [March/September 1978]: 24–25).

129. Cf. Richard H. Drummond, *Gautama the Buddha* (Grand Rapids, Mich.: Wm. B. Eerdmans, 1974), pp. 138–52.

130. Cobb, *Christ in a Pluralistic Age*, p. 220.

131. Ibid., p. 242, 245–46, 258.

132. Ibid., p. 24.

133. Ibid., pp. 212–13, 140.

134. Cf. the review by Wolfhart Pannenberg of Cobb's book, in which he gives particular attention to Christological issues and to the degree of Cobb's variations from the philosophy of Whitehead (Wolfhart Pannenberg, "A Liberal Logos Christology: The Christology of John Cobb," in David Ray Griffin and Thomas J.J. Altizer, eds., *John Cobb's Theology in Process* [Philadelphia: Westminster Press, 1977], pp. 133–49).

135. Cobb, *Christ in a Pluralistic Age*, pp. 212, 220.

136. Ibid., p. 228.

137. Cf. Drummond, *Gautama the Buddha*, pp. 86–88.

138. Cobb, *Christ in a Pluralistic Age*, pp. 71–72.

139. Ibid., pp. 24, 130–31, 134–35.

140. Ibid., pp. 27, 139–41.

141. Ibid., pp. 33, 43, 28, 54. Cobb develops this theme further in a brilliant article, which also constitutes an appeal to Buddhists to take with fresh seriousness for the development of their own tradition of faith-practice the historical data focused on Jesus of Nazareth ("Can a Buddhist Be a Christian, Too?" *Japanese Religions* 11, nos. 2-3 [September 1980]: 35-55; cf. "Can a Christian Be a Buddhist, Too?" *Japanese Religions* 10, no. 3 [December 1978]: 1-20). Only after writing this section was I able to read Cobb's full book on this theme, *Beyond Dialogue: Toward Mutual Transformation of Christianity and Buddhism* (Philadelphia: Fortress Press, 1982), especially pp. 75-143.

142. Ibid., pp. 54-55, cf. Jaroslav Pelikan, *The Christian Tradition: A History of the Development of Doctrine*; vol. 1, *The Emergence of the Catholic Tradition (100-600)* (Chicago: University of Chicago Press, 1971), p. 229.

143. Choan-Seng Song, "Theology of the Incarnation," in Gerald H. Anderson, ed., *Asian Voices in Christian Theology* (Maryknoll, N.Y.: Orbis Books, 1976), pp. 147-53.

144. Ibid., pp. 149, 154-59.

145. Choan-Seng Song, "The Decisiveness of Christ," in Douglas J. Elwood, ed., *What Asian Christians Are Thinking* (Quezon City, Philippines: New Day Publishers, 1976), pp. 240-64.

146. Choan-Seng Song, "From Israel to Asia: A Theological Leap," in Gerald H. Anderson and Thomas F. Stransky, eds., *Mission Trends No. 3* (New York: Paulist Press, 1976), pp. 212-14.

147. Ibid., pp. 214-22. Song develops these views more fully in his *Christian Mission in Reconstruction* (Maryknoll, N.Y.: Orbis Books, 1977), pp. 174-276.

148. Cf. Gregory Baum, "The Jews, Faith and Ideology," *The Ecumenist* 10, no. 5 (July-August 1972): 74-76.

149. Choan-Seng Song, *Third-Eye Theology* (Maryknoll, N.Y.: Orbis Books, 1979), pp. 48-54, 101-23; cf. C.S. Song, *The Compassionate God* (Maryknoll, N.Y.: Orbis Books, 1982), pp. 21-141.

150. Masatoshi Doi, "Christianity and Buddhism in Encounter," *Studies in the Christian Religion* (Kirisuto-kyo Kenkyu) 35, no. 4 (November 1968): 10-22.

151. Masatoshi Doi, "Religion and Nature," in Elwood, ed., *What Asian Christians Are Thinking*, pp. 119-30; cf. "Dynamics of Faith," *Japanese Religions* 9, no. 243 (September 1980): 56-73.

152. Kazō Kitamori, "Christianity and Other Religions," *Japan Christian Quarterly* 26, no. 4 (October 1960): 230-38.

153. Kitamori is best known in the West for his significantly original work entitled *Theology of the Pain of God* (Richmond, Va.: John Knox Press, 1965); in Japanese, *Kami no Itami no Shingaku*. His early volume of essays, *Kami to Ningen* (Tokyo: Gendai Bungeisha, 1956), is an excellent example of the wide range of his cultural interests; he writes on Socrates, Marx, and the Japanese novelist Sōseki Natsume, on the problem of God in contemporary literature, on Luther and Calvin, etc. Kitamori in later work has written somewhat more sympathetically of Buddhism. He sees the Zen experience of "Emptiness" *(Kū)* as having significant correlation with Christian experience of reconciliation with God, which latter is the overcoming—by divine grace—of the human sin of alienation from God ("Kū to Jūjika, Zen Bukkyō to Kirisuto Kyō," *Shinto no Tomo*, no. 386 (March 1979): 16-19.

154. Yagi's work *Bukkyō to Kirisutokyō no Setten* (Kyoto: Hōzōkan, 1976) largely revolves around the use of this term *tōgō* (see especially pp. 26-62, 122-67, 275-363).

Yagi has said that "the highest realization of integration is the community of saints as the Body of Christ" (cf. 1 Corinthians 12). The latter is from a paper entitled "East and West in Encounter" and delivered by Yagi at the University of Hawaii in July 1980.

155. Seiichi Yagi, "Buddhism and Christianity" (a dialogue with John B. Cobb, Jr.), *Northeast Asia Journal of Theology* 20-21 (March/September 1978): 34-37.

156. Yagi has given considerable attention to the theme of egoism. See his *Ai to Egoisumu* (Love and Egoism) (Tokyo: Tōkai Daigaku Shuppankai, 1979), pp. 115-40.

157. Cf. Johannes Pedersen, *Israel, Its Life and Culture* (London: Oxford University Press, 1954), vol. 2, p. 338.

158. Seiichi Yagi, "Buddhism and Christianity," pp. 7-13.

159. Ibid., pp. 34-41.

160. Cf. Beatrice Lane Suzuki, *Mahayana Buddhism* (London: Allen and Unwin, 1959), p. 12; Karl Ludwig Reichelt, *Truth and Tradition in Chinese Buddhism* (Shanghai: Commercial Press, 1927), pp. 38-39. A moving account of Buddhist compassionate social action in Japan is given by Shōkō Watanabe, *Nippon no Bukkyō* (Tokyo: Iwanami Shoten, 1958), pp. 31-54.

161. Yagi, "Buddhism and Christianity," pp. 10-18.

162. Ibid., pp. 41-42.

163. Ibid., pp. 34-37.

164. Richard H. Drummond, *A History of Christianity in Japan* (Grand Rapids, Mich.: Wm. B. Eerdmans, 1971), p. 12.

165. Mikizō Matsuo, *Epeso Kyōkai ni Manabu* (Tokyo: Kirisuto Shimbunsha, 1969); *Kyōiku wo Kangaeru*, "Kirisutokyō kara Meiji Ishin wo Minaosu" (Yokosuka: Yokosuka Gakuin, 1978); *Kyōiku wo Kangaeru, Zoku*, "Kirisutokyō kara Kokka Shintō wo Kōsatsu Suru" (Yokosuka: Yokosuka Gakuin, 1980).

166. Matsuo, *Kyōiku wo Kangaeru, Zoku*, pp. 13-25.

167. Jimmu is the emperor traditionally identified as the founder of the present imperial line with a time focus in the year 660 B.C. Modern historians, however, prefer to set the date of Jimmu's activity in the fourth century A.D. (cf. Joseph M. Kitagawa, *Religion in Japanese History* [New York: Columbia University Press, 1966], pp. 7-8).

168. One must regrettably also note similar incitements to "holy war" in the Old Testament (e.g., Josh. 11:6-23).

169. Matsuo, *Kyōiku wo Kangaeru, Zoku*, pp. 25-38. He notes elsewhere the character of certain Buddhist priests as true glories of Japanese history (ibid., pp. 46-47).

170. Such a policy would, of course, not mean confiscation but the enabling of the priests and supporters of former state Shinto shrines to buy the properties on a long-term basis. For a succinct account of the constitutional changes effected in the early period of the Allied Occupation, see Edwin O. Reischauer, *Japan, Past and Present* (Tokyo: Charles E. Tuttle, 1962), pp. 229-35.

171. For possible early Christian influences upon Shinto, especially upon sectarian Shinto but also upon state Shinto, see Drummond, *A History of Christianity in Japan*, pp. 120-23.

172. Matsuo, *Kyōiku wo Kangaeru, Zoku*, pp. 121-36; cf. Sokyo Ono, *The Kami Way* (Tokyo: International Institute for the Study of Religions, 1959); H. Byron Earhart, *Japanese Religion: Unity and Diversity* (Belmont, Calif.: Dickenson, 1969).

173. Matsuo, personal letter, Sept. 29, 1981; cf. the editorial review, "Kyūjū Issai

Ō Kempitsu wo Furuu," *Kirisuto Shimbum* (The Christ Weekly), Jan. 31, 1981.

174. Simon Barrington-Ward, "Soyinka's Dream," *CMS News-Letter*, no. 453 (March 1983), p. 3.

175. John V. Taylor, *The Primal Vision*, p. 90.

176. Ibid., pp. 22–23, 29.

177. Ibid., pp. 93, 117, 154–71; cf. John V. Taylor, *The Go-Between God* (Philadelphia: Fortress Press, 1973), pp. 179–97.

178. John S. Mbiti, *African Religions and Philosophy* (Garden City, N.Y.: Doubleday, 1970), pp. 284–85; *New Testament Eschatology in an African Background* (London: Oxford University Press, 1971), pp. 1–23, 182–91.

179. With regard to the vexing problem of long-range evaluation of the pros and cons of Western colonialism, see Stephen Charles Neill, *Colonialism and Christian Missions* (New York: McGraw-Hill, 1966), passim.

180. Mbiti, *African Religions and Philosophy*, pp. 349, 362–63; "On the Article of John W. Kinney: A Comment," *Occasional Bulletin of Missionary Research* 3, no. 2 (April 1979): 68; cf. John W. Kinney, "The Theology of John Mbiti: His Sources, Norms, and Methods," ibid., pp. 65–67.

181. Mbiti, *African Religions,* pp. 305–11; cf. Vincent Donavan, "The Naked Gospel: Stamping Out Ready-to-Wear Christianity," *U.S. Catholic* 46, no. 6 (June 1981): 24–31; John S. Mbiti, *The Prayers of African Religion* (Maryknoll, N.Y.: Orbis Books, 1976), pp. 1–26; *Love and Marriage in Africa* (London: Longman, 1973), passim.

182. Mbiti, *African Religions,* pp. 309, 315, 358; cf. John V. Taylor and Dorothea Lehmann, *Christians of the Copperbelt* (London: SCM Press, 1961), pp. 94–118, 216–68, 271–91; Bengt Sundkler, *The Christian Ministry in Africa* (London: SCM Press, 1962), pp. 50–98.

183. Mbiti, *African Religions,* pp. 128, 289, 357; cf. John S. Mbiti, "Theological Impotence and the Universality of the Church," in Gerald H. Anderson and Thomas F. Stransky, eds., *Mission Trends No. 3* (New York: Paulist Press, 1976), pp. 6–18; "The Biblical Basis for Present Trends in African Theology," *Occasional Bulletin of Missionary Research* 4, no. 3 (July 1980): 119–24.

184. E. W. Fashole-Luke, "The Quest for an African Christian Theology," *The Ecumenical Review* 27, no. 3 (July 1975): 260–63; cf. Gabriel M. Setiloane, "I Am an African," in *Mission Trends No. 3*, pp. 128–31, where Setiloane in poetic form sings: "Our fathers and theirs, many generations before, knew Him. / They bowed the knee to Him, / By many names they knew Him, / And yet 'tis He the One and only God." With reference to Jesus of Nazareth, "that *Lamb*, His blood cleanses," Setiloane proclaims that the Lamb is also the ancient sacrifice "making peace between us and our fathers long passed away."

185. Fashole-Luke, "The Quest," pp. 263–69. With reference to the potential role of Eastern Orthodoxy in Africa, see Anastasios Yannoulatos, "Christian Awareness of Primal World-Views," in Gerald H. Anderson and Thomas F. Stransky, eds., *Mission Trends No. 5* (New York: Paulist Press, 1981), pp. 249–57.

186. Kofi Appiah-Kubi, "The Church's Healing Ministry in Africa," *The Ecumenical Review* 27, no. 3 (July 1975): 230–39; cf. Jacques Ngally, "Jesus Christ and Liberation in Africa," ibid., pp. 215–16.

187. Burgess Carr, "The Relation of Union to Mission," in *Mission Trends No. 3*, pp. 158–68. This theme of human suffering after the model of Christ's suffering is developed in a significant way by Manas Buthelezi, general secretary of the Evangeli-

cal Lutheran Church in South Africa. Buthelezi sees this suffering as becoming truly redemptive as black Africans transmute their present suffering into the medium of liberation of both self and others through authentic self-esteem ("Daring to Live for Christ," ibid., pp. 176–80). He would also emphasize that the God of Christian faith has always been in Africa, "already there protecting and sustaining life as Creator," and black and white are one before God ("Change in the Church," in Gerald H. Anderson and Thomas F. Stransky, eds., *Mission Trends No. 1* (New York: Paulist Press, 1974), pp. 195–204.

188. Kenneth D. Kaunda, "The Challenge of Our Stewardship in Africa," in *Mission Trends No. 3*, pp. 169–75. Julius Nyerere, Roman Catholic president of Tanzania, makes a similar appeal for Christian commitment to the welfare of all ("The Development of Peoples and the Meaning of Service," in *Mission Trends No. 1*, pp. 143–53.

189. Christopher Mwoleka, "Trinity and Community," in *Mission Trends No. 3*, pp. 151–55.

190. Gregory Baum has in several writings explored this thesis of the role of defensiveness in the development of theological postures; cf. "The Jews, Faith and Ideology," *The Ecumenist* 10, no. 5 (July–August 1972): 71–76.

191. It is worthy of note that Kalilombe uses the term "Cosmic Covenant" for the covenant established by creation, while Jean Daniélou and Raymond Panikkar use the term as descriptive of the universal scope of the Noachian covenant.

192. Patrick Kalilombe, "The Salvific Value of African Religions," in *Mission Trends No. 5*, pp. 50–68; cf. Harry Sawyerr, *Creative Evangelism: Towards a New Christian Encounter with Africa* (London: Lutterworth Press, 1968), pp. 33–158.

193. Cf. F. Ross Kinsler, "U.S./Canadian Consultation on Global Solidarity in Theological Education: An Introduction," and Robert W. Martin and Fredrica Harris Thompsett, "A Report of the U.S./Canadian Consultation," *Ministerial Formation* 16 (October 1981): 3–11; cf. also *Global Solidarity in Theological Education Report*, Programme on Theological Education (Geneva: World Council of Churches 1981); and John S. Pobee, *Toward an African Theology* (Nashville: Abingdon, 1979), pp. 24–119.

8 THEOLOGICAL EPILOGUE

1. Lawrence Nemer, Commencement Address given at Divine Word College, Epworth, Iowa, on May 15, 1982, pp. 1–3.

2. Reinhold Niebuhr, *The Nature and Destiny of Man*, 2 vols. (New York: Charles Scribner's Sons, 1949), vol. 1, pp. 12–18.

3. *Minutes of the General Assembly of the Presbyterian Church in the United States of America* (1869), 18:41.

4. William Elliot Griffis, *Hepburn of Japan* (Philadelphia: Westminster Press, 1913), p. 97. The sentiments expressed by Alfred Tennyson in his poem *Locksley Hall* may fairly be considered as representative of many sensitive and humane Westerners of his day:

> But I count the gray barbarian lower than the Christian child.
> . . . with narrow foreheads, vacant of our glorious gains,
> like a beast with lower pleasures, like a beast with lower pains.
> Thro' the shadow of the globe we sweep into the younger day:
> Better fifty years of Europe than a cycle of Cathay.

5. Cf. Richard H. Drummond, *A History of Christianity in Japan* (Grand Rapids, Mich.: Wm. B. Eerdmans, 1971), pp. 156–59.

6. Karl Barth, *Church Dogmatics*, ed. G. W. Bromiley and T. F. Torrance (Edinburgh: T. and T. Clark, 1963), I, 2, pp. 326, 330, 339, 356–57. In this context of thought Barth also affirmed that Christianity "alone has the commission and the authority to be a missionary religion, i.e. to confront the world of religions as the one true religion, with absolute self-confidence to invite and challenge it to abandon its ways and to start on the Christian way" (p. 357).

7. Pietro Rossano, "Probleme théologique du dialogue entre le christianisme et les religions non chrétiennes," *Bulletin* (Secretariatus pro non-Christianis) 13, no. 2 (1978): 88; the English translation is by Marcello Zago. Rossano later wrote that the attitude of every Christian to the religions of the world ought to be "one of humility and respect," that of a person *"paratus semper nuntiare, paratus semper doceri,* always ready to announce, always ready to be taught" ("Christ's Lordship and Religious Pluralism in Roman Catholic Perspective," in *Christ's Lordship and Religious Pluralism*, Gerald H. Anderson and Thomas F. Stransky, eds. [Maryknoll, NY: Orbis Books, 1981], p. 109).

8. Rossano, "Probleme théologique," pp. 89–90. Another pertinent Roman Catholic statement is that of Joseph A. DiNoia, a Dominican from the United States, who writes of the "determination [among Christians in the United States and in the West generally] to be respectful of the values enshrined in other traditions and of the upright lives of their adherents." He sees it as a major task of Catholic theologians "to articulate a more generally sympathetic and just account of other religions and a more confident view of the state of their adherents than have prevailed in Christian communities in the past" (in Mary Motte and Joseph R. Lang, eds., *Mission in Dialogue* [Maryknoll, N.Y.: Orbis Books, 1982], pp. 377–78).

9. J. N. Farquhar, *The Crown of Hinduism* (London: Oxford University Press, 1915).

10. Cf. Drummond, *A History of Christianity in Japan*, pp. 200–205.

11. The biblical parable of the pearl of great price can be understood as pointing to a concept of fulfillment. The merchant in the parable was a professional, seeking pearls, and he presumably already had pearls, perhaps very good ones. But for "the one pearl of great value" he was willing to sell all that he had (Mt. 13: 45–46).

12. *Majjhima-Nikāya* I, 97–100; *Sutta-Nipāta* 272, 592, 436–39, 585, 659; cf. Rom. 1: 18–32; Isa. 64: 6; Pss. 10: 2–11; 12: 1–2; 14: 2–4.

13. Cf. Mt. 7: 15–23; 11: 9; 12: 33–35; 25: 31–46; Lk. 6: 43–45; Jn. 14: 11; Didache 11, 8–12. This criterion was also the one that Jeremiah used as primary in his evaluation of contemporary "false prophets" in Judah (Jer. 23: 14–22).

14. Cf. Col. 1: 16–17; Isa. 46: 4. It was a central element of the Greek-speaking theological tradition to see "creation as a Trinitarian act: from the Father, through the Son and in the Spirit." For this reason the major Greek theologians had the theological tools by which they could perceive and freely acknowledge the action of the Trinity in the whole universe and in all human history. Cf. Ewert Cousins, "The Trinity and World Religions," *Journal of Ecumenical Studies* 7, no. 3 (Summer 1970): pp. 488–89; Hans Urs von Balthasar, *A Theology of History* (New York: Sheed and Ward, 1963), pp. 49–75.

15. John Hick, *God Has Many Names* (Philadelphia: Westminster Press, 1982), p. 9. This quotation is from the preface to the American edition of this work.

16. Ibid., pp. 8, 19.

17. Robert C. Johnson, *Authority in Protestant Theology* (Philadelphia: Westminster Press, 1959), p. 193 and passim; cf. Richard H. Drummond, "Authority in the Church: An Ecumenical Inquiry," *Journal of Bible and Religion* 34, no. 4 (October 1966): 329–45.

18. See Friedrich von Hügel, *Essays and Addresses on the Philosophy of Religion* (London: Dent, 1921), p. 252.

19. The concept of eschatological convergence seems to be an appropriate application of the thought of P. Teilhard de Chardin. See his *The Phenomenon of Man* (New York: Harper, 1959), pp. 262–63; *The Future of Man* (New York: Harper, 1964), pp. 89–96, 120–23. Cf. Wolfhart Pannenberg, *Basic Questions in Theology*, trans. George H. Kehm (Philadelphia, Fortress Press, 1971), vol. 2, pp. 92–96; Nels F. S. Ferré, *The Universal Word* (Philadelphia: Westminster Press, 1969), pp. 170–71, and passim; Paul S. Minear, *Images of the Church in the New Testament* (Philadelphia: Westminster Press, 1975), pp. 221–67.

20. The reflections of Karl Barth on the Matthean passage are well worthy of study; cf. "An Exegetical Study of Matthew 28: 16–20," in Gerald H. Anderson, ed., *The Theology of the Christian Mission* (New York: McGraw-Hill, 1961), pp. 55–71.

21. Cf. Johannes Blauw, *The Missionary Nature of the Church* (New York: McGraw-Hill, 1962), p. 30.

22. Cf. Kenneth Scott Latourette, *The First Five Centuries* (New York: Harper, 1937), pp. 239–97; Gerhard Uhlhorn, *Die christliche Liebestätigkeit in der alten Kirche* (Stuttgart: n.p., 1882), passim.

23. The role of missionaries in the abolition of slavery is a notable one, as it has been in the emancipation of women and children in various countries. Cf. V. A. Smith, *The Oxford History of India* (London: Oxford University Press, 1958), p. 725.

24. John C. Bennett, "The Future of Evangelism," *Christianity Today* 10, no. 7 (Jan. 7, 1966) : 45.

Bibliography

Abbott, Walter M., ed. *The Documents of Vatican II*. New York: America Press, 1966. *See also* Flannery, Austin.

Adam, Karl. *The Spirit of Catholicism*. New York: Doubleday, 1962.

"An Affirmation on Salvation Today," Commission on World Mission and Evangelism Assembly, Bangkok, 1973. *International Review of Mission*, 62, no. 246 (April 1973).

Albright, W.F. *From the Stone Age to Christianity*. Baltimore: Johns Hopkins Press, 1940.

Althaus, Paul. *The Theology of Martin Luther*, trans. Robert C. Schultz. Philadelphia: Fortress Press, 1966.

Ambrosiaster. *In Epistulas ad Corinthios 12, 3. Corpus Scriptorum Ecclesiasticorum Latinorum*, 81, ed. Heinrich J. Vogels. Vienna: Hoelder-Pichler-Tempsky, 1968.

Amirtham, Samuel. "The Challenge of New Religions to Christian Theological Thought." *International Review of Mission*, 67, no. 268 (October 1978).

Anderson, Gerald H. *Christ's Lordship and Religious Pluralism*. Maryknoll, N.Y.: Orbis Books, 1981.

———— and Thomas F. Stransky, eds. *Mission Trends, No. 1* (1974); *No. 2* (1975); *No. 3* (1976); *No. 4* (1979); *No. 5* (1981). New York: Paulist Press.

Angus, Samuel. *The Religious Quests of the Graeco-Roman World*. New York: Charles Scribner's Sons, 1929.

Appasamy, A.J. *Christianity as Bhakti Marga*. London: Macmillan & Co., 1927.

————. *The Gospel and India's Heritage*. New York: Macmillan, 1942.

————. "Warum indische Theologie?" *Neue Zeitschrift für systematische Theologie und Religionsphilosophie* 6 (1964).

Appiah-Kubi, Kofi. "The Church's Healing Ministry in Africa." *The Ecumenical Review* 27, no. 3 (July 1975).

Appleton, George. *On the Eightfold Path*, Christian Presence amid Buddhism. London: SCM Press, 1961.

Aquinas, Thomas. *De potentia*.

————. *In III sententiarum*.

————. *Liber de fide trinitatis*.

————. *Quaestiones disputatae, de veritate*.

————. *Summa theologica*.

Ashley, Benedict M., O.P. "Three Strands in the Thought of Eckhart the Scholastic Theologian." *The Thomist* 42 (April 1978).

Augustine. *Contra Faustum*.

————. *De civitate dei*.

————. *De doctrina christiana*.

————. *Enchiridion*.

————. *Epistulae*.

————. *Retractiones.*

Balthasar, Hans Urs von. *A Theology of History.* New York: Sheed and Ward, 1963.

Bangkok Assembly 1973 (World Council of Churches, Commission on World Mission and Evangelism). Geneva: World Council of Churches, 1973.

Bareau, André. *Die Religionen Indiens*, ed. C. M. Schroeder. Stuttgart: Kohlhammer Verlag, 1964.

Barrington-Ward, Simon. "In Search of a Whole Gospel." *CMS News-Letter* 436 (October 1980).

————. "Soyinka's Dream." *CMS News-Letter* 453 (March 1983).

Barth, Karl. "An Exegetical Study of Matthew 28: 16–20." Gerald H. Anderson, ed., *The Theology of the Christian Mission.* New York: McGraw-Hill, 1961.

————. *Church Dogmatics*, ed. G.W. Bromiley and T.F. Torrance. Edinburgh: T. and T. Clark, 1963. Originally published as *Die Kirchliche Dogmatik.* Zollikon-Zürich: Evangelischer Verlag, 1945.

Basil of Caesarea. *Homilies.*

Bassham, Rodger C. "Mission Theology: 1948–1975." *Occasional Bulletin of Missionary Research* 2, no. 4 (April 1980).

Baum, Gregory. "The Jews, Faith and Ideology." *The Ecumenist* 10, no. 5 (July–August 1972).

Bennett, John C. "The Future of Evangelism." *Christianity Today* 10, no. 7 (Jan. 7, 1966).

Benz, Ernst. "Ideas for a Theology of the History of Religion." Gerald H. Anderson, ed., *The Theology of the Christian Mission.* New York: McGraw-Hill, 1961. Originally published as *Ideen zu einer Theologie der Religionsgeschichte.* Mainz: Verlag der Akademie der Wissenschaften und der Literatur, 1961.

————. *Indische Einflüsse auf die frühchristliche Theologie.* Wiesbaden: Verlag der Akademie der Wissenschaften und der Literatur in Mainz, 1951.

Berger, Peter L. *The Heretical Imperative.* Garden City, N.Y.: Doubleday/Anchor Press, 1979.

Berkhof, Hendrikus. *Christian Faith.* Grand Rapids, Mich.: Wm. B. Eerdmans, 1979.

Bettenson, Henry. *Documents of the Christian Church.* New York: Oxford University Press, 1947.

Bhagavad-Gītā, trans. Juan Mascaro. Baltimore: Penguin Books, 1962.

Blauw, Johannes. *The Missionary Nature of the Church.* New York: McGraw-Hill, 1962.

Bleeker, C.J. *Christ in Modern Athens.* Leiden: E. J. Brill, 1965.

Bloesch, Donald G. *Essentials of Evangelical Theology.* 2 vols. New York: Harper & Row, 1978.

Bouquet, A.C. "Revelation and the Divine Logos." Gerald H. Anderson, ed., *The Theology of the Christian Mission.* New York: McGraw-Hill, 1961.

————. *The Christian Faith and Non-Christian Religions.* New York: Harper, 1958.

Boutin, Maurice. "Anonymous Christianity: A Paradigm for Interreligious Encounter?" *Journal of Ecumenical Studies* 20, no. 4 (Fall 1984).

Bright, John. *A History of Israel.* Philadelphia: Westminster Press, 1959.

————. *The Kingdom of God.* New York: Abingdon, 1953.

Broderick, James, S.J. *St. Francis Xavier.* London: Burns and Oates, 1958.

Brown, Raymond E. *The Gospel according to John*, the Anchor Bible. 2 vols. Garden City, N.Y.: Doubleday, 1970.

Bühlmann, Walbert. *The Search for God: An Encounter with the Peoples and Religions of Asia.* Maryknoll, N.Y.: Orbis Books, 1980.

Butterworth, G.W., ed. *Origen on First Principles.* Gloucester, Mass.: Peter Smith, 1973.

Cadbury, H.J. *Jesus: What Manner of Man?* New York: Macmillan, 1947.

Calvin, John. *Institutes of the Christian Religion,* ed. John T. McNeill; trans. Ford Lewis Battles. 2 vols. Philadelphia: Westminster Press, 1960.

Camps, Arnulf. *Partners in Dialogue: Christianity and Other Religions,* trans. John Drury. Maryknoll, N.Y.: Orbis Books, 1983.

Caputo, John D. "Fundamental Themes in Meister Eckhart's Mysticism." *The Thomist* 2 (April 1978).

Cargas, Harry James and Barnard Lee. *Religious Experience and Process Theology.* New York: Paulist Press, 1976.

Carr, Burgess. "The Relation of Union to Mission." Gerald H. Anderson and Thomas F. Stransky, eds., *Mission Trends, No. 3.* New York: Paulist Press, 1976.

Chadwick, Henry. *Early Christian Thought and the Classical Tradition.* London: Oxford University Press, 1966.

"Christians in Dialogue with Men of Other Faiths." *International Review of Missions* 56, no. 223 (July 1967).

Christian Theological Approach to Hinduism. Madras: Christian Literature Society, 1956.

Clement of Alexandria. *Stromateis.*

Clement of Rome. 1 Clement.

Cobb, John B., Jr. *Beyond Dialogue.* Philadelphia: Fortress Press, 1982.

———. "Buddhism and Christianity as Complementary." *Northeast Asia Journal of Theology* (March/September 1978).

———. "Can a Buddhist Be a Christian, Too?" *Japanese Religions* 11, nos. 2 and 3 (September 1980).

———. "Can a Christian Be a Buddhist, Too?" *Japanese Religions* 10, no. 3 (December 1978).

———. *Christ in a Pluralistic Age.* Philadelphia: Westminster Press, 1975.

Cochrane, Charles N. *Christianity and Classical Culture.* New York: Oxford University Press, 1944.

Colie, Rosalie L. *Light and Enlightenment, a Study of the Cambridge Platonists and the Dutch Arminians.* Cambridge, England: Cambridge University Press, 1956.

Colledge, Edmund, O.S.A. "Meister Eckhart: His Time and His Writings." *The Thomist* 42, no. 2 (April 1978).

Congar, Yves. *The Wide World My Parish.* Baltimore: Helicon Press, 1961.

The Constitution of the United Presbyterian Church, U.S.A. Part 1: Book of Confessions. 2nd ed. Philadelphia: Office of the General Assembly, U.P.C.U.S.A., 1970.

Conze, Edward. *Buddhist Thought in India.* Ann Arbor: University of Michigan Press, 1967.

Cousins, Ewert. trans. *Bonaventure.* New York: Paulist Press, 1978.

———. "The Trinity and World Religions." *Journal of Ecumenical Studies* 7, no. 3 (Summer 1970).

Coward, Harold. *Pluralism: Challenge to World Religions.* Maryknoll, N.Y.: Orbis Books, 1984.

Cox, Harvey. "The Battle of the Gods? A Concluding Unsystematic Postscript."

Peter L. Berger, ed., *The Other Side of God*. Garden City, N.Y.: Doubleday, 1981.

Cragg, Kenneth. *The Christian and Other Religion*. London: Mowbrays, 1977.

———. *Sandals at the Mosque*, Christian Presence amid Islam. London: SCM Press, 1959.

Cross, F.L. *The Early Christian Fathers*. London: Gerald Duckworth, 1960.

Cupitt, Don. "The Christ of Christendom." John Hick, ed., *The Myth of God Incarnate*. Philadelphia: Westminster Press, 1977.

———. "The Finality of Christ." *Theology* 78, no. 666 (December 1975).

———. "One Jesus, Many Christs." S.W. Sykes and J.P. Clayton, eds., *Christ, Faith and History*. Cambridge, England: Cambridge University Press, 1972.

Cuttat, Jacques-Albert. *The Encounter of Religions*. Tournai, Belgium: Desclée, 1960.

———. "Experience Chrétienne et Spiritualité Orientale." *La Mystique et Les Mystiques*. Paris: Desclée de Brouwer, 1965.

Cyprian. *De catholicae ecclesiae unitate*.

———. *Epistulae*.

Daniélou, Jean. *Origéne*. Paris: La Table Ronde, 1948.

———. *The Salvation of the Nations*. Notre Dame, Ind.: University of Notre Dame Press, 1962.

———. *The Theology of Jewish Christianity*. Chicago: Henry Regnery, 1964.

Dante. *Paradiso*.

Dawe, Donald G. "Christian Faith in a Religiously Plural World." Donald G. Dawe and John B. Carman, eds., *Christian Faith in a Religiously Plural World*. Maryknoll, N.Y.: Orbis Books, 1978.

———. "Religious Pluralism and the Church," *Journal of Ecumenical Studies* 18, no. 4 (Fall 1981).

Dawson, Christopher. *The Dynamics of World History*. New York: New American Library, 1962.

Dentan, R.C. "Malachi." Vol. 6 of George A. Buttrick, ed., *The Interpreter's Bible*. 12 vols. Nashville: Abingdon, 1956.

Denzinger, Henry. *The Sources of Catholic Dogma* (Enchiridion Symbolorum). St. Louis: B. Herder, 1957.

Devadutt, Vinjamuri E. *The Bible and the Faiths of Men*. New York: Friendship Press, 1967.

Devanandan, Paul David. *The Gospel and Renascent Hinduism*. London: SCM Press, 1959.

Devdas, Nalini. "The Theandrism of Raimundo Panikkar and Trinitarian Parallels in Modern Hindu Thought." *Journal of Ecumenical Studies* 17, no. 4 (Fall 1980).

Dewick, E.C. *The Christian Attitude to Other Religions*. Cambridge, England: Cambridge University Press, 1953.

Dohi, Akio. "Nihon ni okeru Fukuin no Dochaku." *Fukuin to Sekai* 21, no. 10 (October 1966).

DiNoia, Joseph A. "The Universality of Salvation and the Diversity of Religious Aims." *Mission in Dialogue*. Mary Motte and Joseph R. Lang, eds. Maryknoll, N.Y.: Orbis Books, 1982.

Doi, Masatoshi. "Christianity and Buddhism in Encounter." *Studies in the Christian Religion* (*Kirisuto-kyō Kenkyū*), 35, no. 4 (November 1968).

———. "Dynamics of Faith." *Japanese Religions* 11, nos. 2 and 3 (September 1980).

———. "Religion and Nature." Douglas J. Elwood, ed., *What Asian Christians Are Thinking*. Quezon City, Philippines: New Day Publishers, 1976.

Donavan, Vincent. "The Naked Gospel: Stamping Out Ready-to-Wear Christianity." *U.S. Catholic* 46, no. 6 (June 1981).

Drummond, Richard H. "Authority in the Church: An Ecumenical Inquiry." *Journal of Bible and Religion* 34, no. 4 (October 1966).

———. "Christian Theology and the History of Religions." *Journal of Ecumenical Studies* 12, no. 3 (Summer 1975).

———. *Gautama the Buddha*. Grand Rapids, Mich.: Wm. B. Eerdmans, 1974.

———. *A History of Christianity in Japan*. Grand Rapids, Mich.: Wm. B. Eerdmans, 1971.

———. "Studies in Christian Gnosticism." *Religion in Life*. Spring 1976.

———. "Toward Theological Understanding of Islam." *Journal of Ecumenical Studies* 9, no. 4 (Fall 1972).

Dumoulin, Heinrich, S.J. "Buddhism—A Religion of Liberation." *Concilium,* vol. 116. New York: Seabury Press, 1979.

———. *Christianity Meets Buddhism*. La Salle, Ill.: Open Court Publishing Co., 1974.

———. *A History of Zen Buddhism*. New York: Random House, 1963.

Dyer, George J. *Limbo: Unsettled Question*. New York: Sheed and Ward, 1964.

Earhart, Byron H. *Japanese Religion: Unity and Diversity*. Belmont, Calif.: Dickenson, 1969.

Eichrodt, Walter. *Theology of the Old Testament*. 6th ed. Philadelphia: Westminster Press, 1961.

Eliade, Mircea. Review of "La Franc-Maçonnerie Templiere et Occultiste aux XVIIIe et XIXe siècle," by René Le Forestier. *History of Religions* 13, no. 1 (August 1973).

———. "Methodological Remarks on the Study of Religious Symbolism." Mircea Eliade and Joseph M. Kitagawa, eds., *The History of Religions, Essays in Methodology*. Chicago: University of Chicago Press, 1959.

Enomiya-Lassalle, H.M. *Zen Meditation for Christians*. La Salle, Ill.: Open Court Publishing Co., 1974.

———. *Zen—Way to Enlightenment*. London: Burns and Oates, 1967.

Farquhar, J.N. *The Crown of Hinduism*. London: Oxford University Press, 1915.

Fashole-Luke, E.W. "The Quest for an African Christian Theology." *The Ecumenical Review* 27, no. 3 (July 1975).

Ferré, Nels F.S. *The Universal Word*. Philadelphia: Westminster Press, 1969.

Fischer, Louis. *Gandhi, His Life and Message for the World*. New York: New American Library, 1954.

Flannery, Austin, O.P., ed. *Vatican Council II: The Conciliar and Post-Conciliar Documents*. Boston, Mass.: St. Paul Editions, 1975. *See also* Abbott, Walter M.

Forster, Roger T. and Paul V. Marston. *God's Strategy in Human History*. Wheaton, Ill.: Tyndale House, 1974.

Foster, John. *After the Apostles*. London: SCM Press, 1951.

Fox, Samuel J. *Hell in Jewish Literature*. Northbrook, Ill.: Whitehall, 1972.

Franz, Marie-Louise von. *C.G. Jung, His Myth in Our Time*. New York: G.P. Putnam's Sons, 1975.

Friedrich, Gerhard, ed. *Theologisches Wörterbuch zum Neuen Testament,* vol. 7, Stuttgart: W. Kohlhammer, 1957.

Fritsch, C.H. "Psalms and Proverbs." George A. Butterick, ed., vol. 4 of *The Interpreter's Bible*. 12 vols. New York: Abingdon, 1955.

Fulgentius. *De fide.*

Gallagher, Louis J., S.J. *China in the Sixteénth Century: The Journals of Matthew Ricci: 1583-1610.* New York: Random House, 1953.

Garcia-Treto, Francisco O. "Covenant in Recent Old Testament Studies." *Austin Seminary Bulletin* 96 (March 1981).

Gardet, Louis. *Experiences Mystiques en Terres Non-Chretiénnes.* Paris: Alsatia, 1953.

Geffré, Claude and Mariasusai Dhavamony, eds. *Buddhism and Christianity. Concilium* 116. New York: Seabury, 1979.

Gerlitz, Peter. "Der *Logos Spermatikos* als Voraussetzung für eine ökumenische Theologie." *Zeitschrift für Religions und Geistesgeschichte* 22 (1970).

Gilkey, Langdon. *Society and the Sacred.* New York: Crossroad Publishing Co., 1981.

Glover, T.R. *The Jesus of History.* New York: Association Press, 1922.

Goodall, Norman, ed. *The Uppsala Report 1968.* Geneva: World Council of Churches, 1968.

Gregory Thaumaturgus. *In Origenem oratio panegyrica.*

Griffis, William Elliot. *Hepburn of Japan.* Philadelphia: Westminster Press, 1913.

Griffiths, Bede. *Christ in India, Essays toward a Hindu-Christian Dialogue.* New York: Charles Scribner's Sons, 1966.

———. *Return to the Center.* Springfield, Ill.: Templegate, 1976.

de Groot, Adrianus. "The Mission after Vatican II." *Concilium,* vol. 36 (1968).

Gualtiere, Antonio R. "The Failure of Dialectic in Hendrik Kraemer's Evaluation of Non-Christian Faith." *Journal of Ecumenical Studies* 15, no. 2 (Spring 1978).

Guirdham, Arthur. *The Cathars and Reincarnation.* London: Neville Spearman, 1970.

Hale, John R. *Age of Exploration.* New York: Time-Life Books, 1970.

Hallencreutz, Carl F. "A Long Standing Concern: Dialogue in Ecumenical History 1910-1971." S.J. Samartha, ed., *Living Faiths and the Ecumenical Movement.* Geneva: World Council of Churches, 1971.

Harper, Ralph. *The Sleeping Beauty.* London: Harvill, 1955.

Head, Joseph and S.L. Cranston, eds. *Reincarnation: The Phoenix Fire Mystery.* New York: Warner Books, 1977.

Héring, Jean. *The Epistle of Paul to the Corinthians.* London: Epworth Press, 1962.

Hick, John. *Death and Eternal Life.* London: Collins, 1976.

———. *God and the Universe of Faiths.* London: Macmillan, 1973.

———. *God Has Many Names.* London: Macmillan, 1980; Philadelphia: Westminster Press, 1982.

———. "Jesus and the World Religions." John Hick, ed., *The Myth of God Incarnate.* Philadelphia: Westminster Press, 1977.

———. "Whatever Path Men Choose Is Mine." John Hick and Brian Hebblethwaite, eds., *Christianity and Other Religions.* Philadelphia: Fortress Press, 1980.

Hocking, William Ernest. *Living Religions and a World Faith.* New York: Macmillan, 1940.

———. *Re-Thinking Missions.* New York: Harper, 1932.

Hogg, Richey W. "Edinburgh 1910—Perspective 1980." *Occasional Bulletin of Missionary Research* 4, no. 4 (October 1980).

Homilies (Pseudo-Clementine).

Hospital, Clifford G. "The Contribution of Keshub Chudar Sen toward a Global and Inductive Christology." *Journal of Ecumenical Studies* 19, no. 1 (Winter 1982).

————. *Breakthrough: Insights of the Great Religious Discoverers*. Maryknoll, N.Y.: Orbis Books, 1985.

Howe, Quincy, Jr. *Reincarnation for the Christian*. Philadelphia: Westminster Press, 1974.

Howell, Leon. "Melbourne on Mission: Joining with the Poor." *Christianity and Crisis* 40, no. 13 (Aug. 18, 1980).

Hubbard, David Allan. *What We Evangelicals Believe*. Pasadena, Calif.: Fuller Theological Seminary, 1979.

Hügel, Friedrich von. *Essays and Addresses on the Philosophy of Religion*. London: Dent, 1921.

Ignatius. *Ephesians*.

International Congress on Mission, I, II, III. *Toward a New Age in Mission: The Good News of God's Kingdom to the Peoples of Asia*. Manila: Theological Conference Office, 1981.

Irenaeus. *Contra haereses*.

Jacobs, H.E., ed. *Large Catechism, The Book of Concord*. Philadelphia: General Council Publication Board, 1911.

Jadot, Jean L. "The Growth in Roman Catholic Commitment to Interreligious Dialogue since Vatican II." *Journal of Ecumenical Studies* 20, no. 3 (Summer 1983).

Jenkins, David. "Commitment and Openness, A Theological Reflection." *International Review of Mission* 59, no. 236 (October 1970).

Jerome. *Epistula ad Demetriadem*.

The Jerusalem Meeting of the International Missionary Council (March 24–April 8, 1928). New York: IMC, 1928.

Johannes Damascenus. J.P. Migne, ed., *Patrologia Graeca*, vol. 94.

John Paul II. *First Encyclical Letter, Redemptor Hominis* (March 4, 1979). Washington, D.C., United States Catholic Conference, 1979.

Johnson, Robert C. *Authority in Protestant Theology*. Philadelphia: Westminster Press, 1959.

Johnston, William. *Christian Zen*. New York: Harper & Row, 1974.

————. *The Inner Eye of Love*. New York: Harper & Row, 1978.

————. *The Mirror Mind*. New York: Harper & Row, 1981.

————. *The Still Point*. New York: Fordham University Press, 1970.

Jones, Rufus M. *The Journal of George Fox*. New York: Capricorn, 1963.

Josephus, Flavius, *Against Apion*.

————. *Jewish Antiquities*.

————. *Jewish War*.

Justin Martyr. *The First Apology*.

————. *The Second Apology*.

Kalilombe, Patrick. "The Salvific Value of African Religions." Gerald H. Anderson and Thomas F. Stransky, eds. *Mission Trends, No. 5*. New York: Paulist Press, 1981.

Kaunda, Kenneth D. "The Challenge of Our Stewardship in Africa." Gerald H. Anderson and Thomas F. Stransky, eds., *Mission Trends, No. 3*. New York: Paulist Press, 1976.

Kellerhals, Emanuel. *Der Islam*. Basel: Basler Missionsbuchhandlung, 1945.

Khodr, Georges. "Christianity in a Pluralistic World—The Economy of the Holy Spirit." *The Ecumenical Review* 23 (April 1971).

Kinney, John W. "The Theology of John Mbiti: His Sources, Norms, and Method." *Occasional Bulletin of Missionary Research* 3, no. 2 (April 1979).

Kinsler, F. Ross. "U.S./Canadian Consultation on Global Solidarity in Theological Education: An Introduction." *Ministerial Formation* 16 (October 1981).

Kirisuto Shimbun, "Kyūjū Issai Ō Kempitsu wo Furuu" (editorial review of Mikizō Matsuo's *Kyōiku wo Kangaeru, Zoku*), Jan. 31, 1981.

Kitagawa, Joseph M. "The History of Religions in America." Mircea Eliade and Joseph M. Kitagawa, eds., *The History of Religions, Essays in Methodology*. Chicago: University of Chicago Press, 1959.

———. *Religion in Japanese History*. New York: Columbia University Press, 1966.

Kitamori, Kazō, "Christianity and Other Religions." *Japan Christian Quarterly* 26 (Oct. 4, 1960).

———. *Kami to Ningen*. Tokyo: Gendai Bungeisha, 1956.

———. *Theology of the Pain of God*. Richmond, Va.: John Knox Press, 1965.

———. "Kū to Jūjika, Zen Bukkyō to Kiritsuo Kyō." *Shinto no Tomo* 386 (March 1979).

Klostermaier, Klaus. "Hṛdayavidyā: A Sketch of a Hindu-Christian Theology of Love." *Journal of Ecumenical Studies* 9, no. 4 (Fall 1972).

———. *In the Paradise of Krishna*. Philadelphia: Westminster Press, 1971.

———. *Kristvidya: A Sketch of an Indian Christology*. Bangalore, India: n.p., 1967.

Knitter, Paul F. "Christianity as Religion: True and Absolute? A Roman Catholic Perspective." *Concilium*, vol. 136. New York: Seabury Press, 1980.

———. "Christianity's New Dialogue with Buddhism." *Horizons* 8, no. 1 (Winter 1981).

———. "European Protestant and Catholic Approaches to the World Religions: Complements and Contrasts." *Journal of Ecumenical Studies* 12, no. 1 (Winter 1975).

———. "Jesus—Buddha—Krishna: Still Present?" *Journal of Ecumenical Studies* 16, no. 4 (Fall 1979).

———. *No Other Name? A Critical Survey of Christian Attitudes Toward the World Religions*. American Society of Missiology Series, no. 7. Maryknoll, N.Y.: Orbis Books, 1985.

———. *Towards a Protestant Theology of Religions*. Marburger Theologische Studien, ed. H. Grass and W.G. Kümmel. Marburg: n.p., 1974.

———. "World Religions and the Finality of Christ: A Critique of Hans Küng's *On Being a Christian*." *Horizons* 16, no. 4 (Fall 1979).

———. "Roman Catholic Approaches to Other Religions: Developments and Tensions." *International Bulletin of Missionary Research* 8, no. 2 (April 1984).

Koestler, Arthur. *The Roots of Coincidence*. New York: Random House, 1972.

Kraemer, Hendrick. *The Christian Message in a Non-Christian World*. New York: International Missionary Council, 1947.

———. *Religion and the Christian Faith*. Philadelphia: Westminster Press, 1957.

———. *Why Christianity of All Religions?* trans. Hubert Hoskins. Philadelphia: Westminster Press, 1962.

———. *World Cultures and World Religions: The Coming Dialogue*. London: Lutterworth, 1960.

Küng, Hans. *Christenheit als Minderheit*. Einsiedeln: Benziger Verlag, 1965.

———. *Freedom Today*, New York: Sheed and Ward, 1966.

———. *On Being a Christian*, trans. Edward Quinn. Garden City, N.Y.: Doubleday, 1976.

———. "The World's Religions in God's Plan of Salvation." Joseph Neuner, ed., *Christian Revelation and the World Religions*. London: Burns and Oates, 1967.

Lactantius. *De ira dei.*

Latourette, Kenneth Scott. *The First Five Centuries.* New York: Harper, 1937.

———. *A History of the Expansion of Christianity.* 7 vols. New York: Harper, 1937–45.

Leeuwen, A.T. van. *Christianity in World History.* London: Edinburgh House Press, 1964.

Le Saux, Henri. *Hindu-Christian Meeting Point.* Bangalore-Bombay: n.p., 1969.

———. *Prayer.* Philadelphia: Westminster Press, 1972.

"A Letter to the Churches," from the CWME Assembly, Bangkok, 1973. *International Review of Missions* 62, no. 246 (April 1973).

Lull, Ramon. *Obres essencials.* Barcelona: n.p., 1957.

Lohse, Eduard. *Colossians and Philemon.* Philadelphia: Fortress Press, 1971.

Lossky, V. *The Mystical Theology of the Eastern Church.* London: James Clarke, 1957.

Luther, Martin. *Large Catechism, The Book of Concord,* Henry E. Jacobs, ed., Philadelphia: General Council Publication Board, 1911.

Macaulay, Thomas Babington. "Lord Clive." *Critical, Historical, and Miscellaneous Essays and Poems.* 2 vols. New York: John B. Alden, n.d.

MacColluch, J.A. *The Harrowing of Hell.* Edinburgh: T. & T. Clark, 1930.

MacGregor, Geddes. *Reincarnation in Christianity.* Wheaton, Ill.: Theosophical Publishing House, 1978.

Majjhima-Nikāya 1; *The Middle Length Sayings* I, trans. I.B. Horner. London: Luzac, 1967.

Manikam, Rajah B., ed. *Christianity and the Asian Revolution.* New York: Friendship Press, 1955.

March, W. Eugene. "Because the *Lord* is Lord: Old Testment Covenant Imagery and Ecumenical Commitment." *Austin Seminary Bulletin* 96 (March 1981).

Margull, Hans Joachim. "The Awakening of Protestant Missions." Philippe Maury, ed., *History's Lessons for Tomorrow's Missions.* Geneva: World Student Christian Federation, 1960.

Martin, Malachi. *The Final Conclave.* New York: Stein and Day, 1978.

Martin, Robert W. and Fredrica Harris Thompsett. "A Report of the U.S./Canadian Consultation." *Ministerial Formation* 16 (October 1981).

Mascaró, Juan. *The Upanishads.* Harmondsworth, England: Penguin Books, 1971.

Matsuo, Mikizō. *Epeso Kyōkai ni Manabu.* Tokyo: Kirisuto Shimbunsha, 1969.

———. *Kyōiku wo Kangaeru,* Kirisutokyō kara Meiji Ishin wo Minaosu. Yokosuka: Yokosuka Gakuin, 1978.

———. *Kyōiku wo Kangaeru, Zoku,* Kirisutokyō kara Kokka Shintō wo Kōsatsu Suru. Yokosuka: Yokosuka Gakuin, 1980.

Maury, Philippe, ed. *History's Lessons for Tomorrow's Missions,* Geneva: World Student Christian Federation, 1960.

May, H.G. "Synagogues in Palestine." *The Biblical Archaeologist* 7 (February 1944).

Mbiti, John S. *African Religions and Philosophy.* Garden City, N.Y.: Doubleday, 1970.

———. "The Biblical Basis for Present Trends in African Theology." *Occasional Bulletin for Missionary Research* 4, no. 3 (July 1980).

———. *Love and Marriage in Africa.* London: Longman, 1973.

———. *New Testament Eschatology in an African Background.* London: Oxford University Press, 1971.

———. "On the Article of John W. Kinney: A Comment." *Occasional Bulletin of Missionary Research* 3, no. 2 (April 1979).

———. *The Prayers of African Religion*. Maryknoll, N.Y.: Orbis Books, 1976.

"Melbourne Conference Section Reports," *International Review of Mission* 69, nos. 276–77 (October 1980–January 1981).

Mendenhall, George E. "Law and Covenant in Israel and the Ancient Near East." Pittsburgh: The Biblical Colloquium, 1955.

Merton, Thomas. *Mystics and Zen Masters*. New York: Farrar, Straus and Giroux, 1967.

Meyendorff, John. *Christ in Eastern Christian Thought*. Washington, D.C.: Corpus Books, 1969.

Miller, David L. *The New Polytheism: Rebirth of the Gods and Goddesses*. New York: Harper & Row, 1974.

Minear, Paul S. *Images of the Church in the New Testament*. Philadelphia: Westminster Press, 1975.

Minucius Felix. *Octavius*.

Minutes of the General Assembly of the Presbyterian Church in the United States of America, vol. 18 (1869).

Moses, David Gnanaprakasam. *Religious Truth and the Relation between Religions*. Madras: Christian Literature Society for India, 1950.

Mwoleka, Christopher. "Trinity and Community." Gerald H. Anderson and Thomas F. Stransky, eds., *Mission Trends, No. 3*. New York: Paulist Press, 1976.

Neill, Stephen C. *Colonialism and Christian Missions*. New York: McGraw-Hill, 1966.

Nemer, Lawrence. Commencement address, given at Divine Word College, Epworth, Iowa, May 15, 1982.

Ngally, Jacques. "Jesus Christ and Liberation in Africa." *The Ecumenical Review* 27, no. 3 (July 1975).

Nicholas of Cusa. *De pace fidei*.

Niebuhr, H. Richard. *Christ and Culture*. New York: Harper, 1956.

Niebuhr, Reinhold. *The Nature and Destiny of Man*. 2 vols. New York: Charles Scribner's Sons, 1949.

Nikhilananda, Swami. *The Upanishads*. New York: Harper & Row, 1963.

Nitobe, Inazō. *Bushido: The Soul of Japan*. Los Angeles: Ohara Publications, 1969.

The Nottingham Statement. Over Wallop, Hampshire, England: BAS Printers, 1977.

Nyerere, Julius. "The Development of Peoples and the Meaning of Service." Gerald H. Anderson and Thomas F. Stransky, eds. *Mission Trends, No. 1*. New York: Paulist Press, 1974.

Ogden, Schubert. *Christ without Myth*. New York: Harper & Brothers, 1961.

———. "The Meaning of Christian Hope." Harry James Cargas and Bernard Lee, eds., *Religious Experience and Process Theology*. New York: Paulist Press, 1976.

———. "The Point of Christology." *Journal of Religion* 55, no. 4 (October 1975).

———. *The Reality of God*. New York: Harper & Row, 1966.

Ono, Sokyo. *The Kami Way*. Tokyo: International Institute for the Study of Religions, 1959.

Orchard, Ronald K., ed. *Witness in Six Continents*. London: Edinburgh House Press, 1964.

Organ, Troy. "A Cosmological Christology." *Christian Century* 88 no. 44 (Nov. 3, 1971).

Origen. *Commentarius in Canticum Canticorum*.

——. *Commentarius in Ioannem.*

——. *Contra Celsum.*

——. *De principiis.*

Oulton, John E.L. and Henry Chadwick, eds. *Alexandrian Christianity.* Philadelphia: Westminster Press, 1954.

Pagels, Elaine. *The Gnostic Gospels.* New York: Random House, 1979.

Panikkar, Raymond. "Faith and Belief: On the Multi-Religious Experience (an Objectified Autobiographical Fragment)." *Anglican Theological Review* 53, no. 4 (October 1971).

——. "The Hindu Ecclesial Consciousness—Some Ecclesiological Reflections." *Jeevadhara*, a Journal of Christian Interpretation (Alleppey, Kerala, India), vol. 4, no. 21 (May–June 1974).

——. *The Intrareligious Dialogue.* New York: Paulist Press, 1978.

——. "A Preface to a Hindu-Christian Theology." *Jeevadhara* 9, no. 49 (January–February 1979).

——. "Toward an Ecumenical Theandric Spirituality." *Journal of Ecumenical Studies* 5, no. 3 (Summer 1968).

——. *The Trinity and World Religions.* Madras, India: Christian Literature Society, 1970.

——. *The Unknown Christ of Hinduism.* London: Darton, Longman and Todd, 1964. Revised and enlarged edition. Maryknoll, N.Y.: Orbis Books, 1981.

Pannenberg, Wolfhart. *Basic Questions in Theology,* trans. George H. Kehm. Philadelphia: Fortress Press, 1971.

——. "A Liberal Logos Christology: The Christology of John Cobb." David Ray Griffin and Thomas J.J. Altizer, eds., *John Cobb's Theology in Process.* Philadelphia: Westminster Press, 1977.

——. *Theology and the Philosophy of Science.* Philadelphia: Westminster Press, 1976.

Paton, David M., ed., *Breaking Barriers,* Nairobi 1975 Assembly. London: SPCK, 1976.

Pedersen, Johannes. *Israel, Its Life and Culture.* 2 vols. London: Oxford University Press, 1954.

Pelikan, Jaroslav. *The Christian Tradition: A History of the Development of Doctrine.* Vol. 1, *The Emergence of the Catholic Tradition (100–600).* Chicago: University of Chicago Press, 1971.

——. *The Christian Tradition: A History of the Development of Doctrine.* Vol. 2, *The Spirit of Eastern Christendom (600–1700).* Chicago: University of Chicago Press, 1974.

Philo Judaeus, *Every Good Man Is Free.*

Pirenne, Henri. *Mohammed and Charlemagne.* New York: Meridian Books, 1958.

Pobee, John S. *Toward an African Theology.* Nashville: Abingdon, 1979.

Prat, F. "Origen and Origenism." Vol. 11 of *The Catholic Encyclopedia.* New York: The Gilmary Society, 1939.

Prosperus Aquitanus, *De vocatione omnium gentium.*

Puech, Henri-Charles. "Gnosis and Time." Joseph Campbell, ed., *Man and Time,* Bollingen Series XXX, Papers from the Eranos Yearbooks, vol. 3. New York: Pantheon Books, 1957.

Quasten, Johannes. *Patrology.* 3 vols. Utrecht: Spectrum Publishers, 1966.

Race, Alan. *Christians and Religious Pluralism: Patterns in the Christian Theology of Religions.* Maryknoll, N.Y.: Orbis Books, 1983.

Radhakrishnan, Sarvapalli. *Eastern Religions and Western Thought.* New York: Oxford University Press, 1960.

Rahner, Karl. "Das Christentum und die nichtchristlichen Religionen." *Schriften zur Theologie.* Einsiedeln: Benziger Verlag, 1964. Vol. 5.

————. *Theological Investigations.* Trans. Karl H. Kruger. 15 vols. Baltimore: Helicon Press, 1966.

————. *Foundations of Christian Faith.* New York: Seabury Press, 1978.

Rees, Paul S. "Evangelicals Resurgent." *World Vision* 21, no. 10 (October 1977).

Reichelt, Karl Ludwig. *Truth and Tradition in Chinese Buddhism.* Shanghai: The Commercial Press, 1927.

Reischauer, Edwin O. *Japan, Past and Present.* Tokyo: Charles E. Tuttle, 1962.

Richardson, Alan, ed. *A Theological Word Book of the Bible.* New York: Macmillan, 1960.

Richardson, Cyril C. *Early Church Fathers.* Philadelphia: Westminster Press, 1953.

Richter, Julius. "Missionary Apologetic." *International Review of Missions* 2, no. 7 (July 1913).

Robinson, John A.T. *Can We Trust the New Testament?* Grand Rapids, Mich.: Wm. B. Eerdmans, 1977.

————. *Truth Is Two-Eyed.* Philadelphia: Westminster Press, 1979.

Rossano, Pietro. "The Bible and the Non-Christian Religions." *Bulletin,* Secretariat for Non-Christians, vol. 2, no. 1 (1967).

————. "Probleme theólogique du dialogue entre le christianisme et les religions non chrétiennes," *Bulletin,* Secretariat for Non-Christians, vol. 13, no. 2 (1978).

Rowley, H.H. *The Biblical Doctrine of Election.* London: Lutterworth, 1950.

Samartha, Stanley J. "Christian Study Centres and Asian Churches." *International Review of Mission* 59, no. 234 (April 1970).

————. "Dialogue as a Continuing Christian Concern." *The Ecumenical Review* 25, no. 2 (April 1973).

————. *Dialogue between Men of Living Faiths.* Geneva: World Council of Churches, 1971.

————. "Dialogue in Community: A Step Forward." Samartha, ed., *Faith in the Midst of Faiths.* Geneva: World Council of Churches, 1977.

————. "Guidelines on Dialogue." *Ecumenical Review* 21, no. 2 (April 1979).

————. *Living Faiths and Ultimate Goals.* Maryknoll, N.Y.: Orbis Books, 1974.

————. "Mission and Movements of Innovation." Gerald H. Anderson and Thomas F. Stransky, eds., *Mission Trends, No. 3.* New York: Paulist Press, 1976.

————. "*More* than an Encounter of Commitments." *International Review of Mission* 59, no. 236 (October 1970).

————. "Partners in Community: Some Reflections on Hindu-Christian Relations Today." *Occasional Bulletin of Missionary Research* 4, no. 2 (April 1980).

————. "A Pause for Reflection." Samartha, ed., *Faith in the Midst of Faiths.* Geneva: World Council of Churches, 1977.

————. "Reflections on a Multilateral Dialogue." *The Ecumenical Review* 26, no. 4 (October 1974).

————. "The World Council of Churches and Men of Other Faiths and Ideologies." Samartha, ed., *Living Faiths and the Ecumenical Movement.* Geneva: World Council of Churches, 1971.

Samartha, Stanley J., and John V. Taylor. *Christian-Muslim Dialogue.* Geneva: World Council of Churches, 1973.

Sansom, G.B. *The Western World and Japan.* New York: Alfred A. Knopf, 1962.

Sawyerr, Harry. *Creative Evangelism: Towards a New Christian Encounter with Africa.* London: Lutterworth Press, 1968.

Schaff, Philip. *History of the Christian Church.* 8 vols. Grand Rapids, Mich.: Wm. B. Eerdmans, 1957.

Schillebeeckx, Edward. *Christ, the Sacrament of the Encounter with God.* New York: Sheed and Ward, 1963.

———. *The Church and Mankind*, Concilium, Dogma I. Glen Rock, N.J.: Paulist Press, 1965.

Schleiermacher, Friedrich. *The Christian Faith*, ed. H.R. Mackintosh and J.S. Stewart. Edinburgh: T. and T. Clark, 1948.

Schlette, Heinz Robert. *Towards a Theology of Religions.* New York: Herder and Herder, 1966.

Schlunk, Martin. "Theology and Missions in Germany in Recent Years," *International Review of Missions* 27, no. 59 (July 1938).

———. *Die Weltreligionen und das Christentum.* Frankfurt am Main: Anker-Verlag, 1953.

Schneider, Peter, ed. *Ends and Odds.* Arundel, England: Burpham Vicarage, n.d.

Schurhammer, Georg, S.J. and Joseph Wicki, S.J., eds. *Epistolae S. Francisci Xavierii.* 8 vols. Rome: Monumenta Historica Societatis Iesu, 1945.

Seneca. *Ad Lucilium epistulae morales.*

Setiloane, Gabriel M. "I Am an African." Gerald H. Anderson and Thomas F. Stransky, eds., *Mission Trends, No. 2.* New York: Paulist Press, 1975.

Shepherd, A.P. *A Scientist of the Invisible.* London: Hodder and Stoughton, 1975.

Smith, Huston. *Beyond the Modern Mind.* New York: Crossroad Publishing Co., 1982.

———. *Forgotten Truth, the Primordial Tradition.* New York: Harper & Row, 1977.

Smith, V.A. *The Oxford History of India.* London: Oxford University Press, 1958.

Smith, Wilfred Cantwell. "An Historian of Faith Reflects on What We Are Doing Here." Donald G. Dawe and John B. Carman, eds., *Christian Faith in a Religiously Plural World.* Maryknoll, N.Y.: Orbis Books, 1978.

———. *Towards a World Theology.* Philadelphia: Westminster Press, 1981.

Solzhenitsyn, Aleksandr I. *A World Split Apart.* New York: Harper & Row, 1978.

Song, Choan-Seng. *Christian Mission in Reconstruction.* Maryknoll, N.Y.: Orbis Books, 1977.

———. *The Compassionate God.* Maryknoll, N.Y.: Orbis Books, 1982.

———. "The Decisiveness of Christ." Douglas J. Elwood, ed., *What Asian Christians Are Thinking.* Quezon City, Philippines: New Day Publishers, 1976.

———. "From Israel to Asia: A Theological Leap." Gerald H. Anderson and Thomas F. Stransky, eds., *Mission Trends, No. 3.* New York: Paulist Press, 1976.

———. "Theology of the Incarnation." Gerald H. Anderson, ed., *Asian Voices in Christian Theology.* Maryknoll, N.Y.: Orbis Books, 1976.

———. *Third-Eye Theology.* Maryknoll, N.Y.: Orbis Books, 1979.

Spae, Joseph J. *Buddhist-Christian Empathy.* Chicago: Chicago Institute of Theology and Culture, 1980.

———. *East Challenges West: Towards a Convergence of Spiritualities.* Chicago: Chicago Institute of Theology and Culture, 1979.

———. "Eastern Cults in Western Culture." *International Review of Mission* 67, no. 268 (October 1978).

Steinsaltz, Adin. *The Thirteen Petalled Rose.* New York: Basic Books, 1980.

Stendahl, Krister. "Notes for Three Bible Studies." Gerald H. Anderson and Thomas

F. Stransky, eds., *Christ's Lordship and Religious Pluralism*, Maryknoll, N.Y.: Orbis Books, 1981.

Streeter, Burnett Hillman. *The Buddha and the Christ*. London: Macmillan, 1932.

Study Encounter 10, no. 3 (1974).

Sundkler, Bengt. *The Christian Ministry in Africa*. London: SCM Press, 1962.

Sutta Nipāta: Woven Cadences of Early Buddhists, trans. E.M. Hare. London: Oxford University Press, 1947.

Suzuki, Beatrice Lane. *Mahayana Buddhism*. London: Allen and Unwin, 1959.

Swidler, Leonard. "Preface: The Critical Divide." *Journal of Ecumenical Studies* 19, no. 2 (Spring 1982).

Taylor, John V. *CMS News-Letter* 303 (April 1967); 330 (September 1969); 382 (June 1974).

———. *The Go-Between God*. Philadelphia: Fortress Press, 1973.

———. *The Primal Vision: Christian Presence amid African Religion*. Philadelphia: Fortress Press, 1963.

Teilhard de Chardin, Pierre. *The Future of Man*. New York: Harper, 1964.

———. *The Phenomenon of Man*. New York: Harper, 1959.

Tertullian. *Ad nationes*.

———. *Apologeticum*.

———. *De oratione*.

———. *De prescriptione haereticorum*.

Theisen, Jerome P. *The Ultimate Church and the Promise of Salvation*. Collegeville, Minn.: St. John's University Press, 1976.

Theophilus, Antiochenus. *Ad Autolycum*.

Thomas, M.M. *The Acknowledged Christ of the Indian Renaissance*. London: SCM Press, 1969.

———. *The Christian Response to the Asian Revolution*. London: SCM Press, 1968.

———. *Man and the Universe of Faiths*. Madras, India: Christian Literature Society, 1975.

———. "Report of the Executive Committee by the Chairman," *The Ecumenical Review* 23, no. 2 (April 1971).

———. *Salvation and Humanisation*. Madras, India: Christian Literature Society, 1971.

———. *Towards a Theology of Contemporary Ecumenism*. Madras, India: Christian Literature Society, 1978.

Thomas, Owen C., ed. *Attitudes toward Other Religions*. New York: Harper & Row, 1969.

Tillich, Paul. *Biblical Religion and the Search for Ultimate Reality*. Chicago: University of Chicago Press, 1964.

———. *Christianity and the Encounter of the World Religions*. New York: Columbia University Press, 1963.

———. *The Future of Religions*, ed. Jerald C. Brauer. New York: Harper & Row, 1966.

———. *Systematic Theology*. 3 vols. Chicago: University of Chicago Press, 1971.

Toynbee, Arnold. *The World and the West*. New York: Meridian Books, 1960.

Uhlhorn, Gerhard. *Die christliche Liebestätigkeit in der alten Kirche*. Stuttgart, 1882.

Verghese, Paul T. "Christ and All Men." S.J. Samartha, ed., *Living Faiths and the Ecumenical Movement*. Geneva: World Council of Churches, 1971.

———. *The Freedom of Man*. Philadelphia: Westminster Press, 1972.

Vicedom, Georg. *The Challenge of the World Religions.* Philadelphia: Fortress Press, 1963.

Visser 't Hooft, W.A., ed. *New Delhi Speaks about Christian Witness, Service, Unity.* New York: Association Press, 1962.

———. *No Other Name.* Philadelphia: Westminster Press, 1963.

Vriezen, Th. C. *Die Erwählung Israels nach dem Alten Testament.* Zurich: Zwingli Verlag, 1953.

Waardenburg, Jacques. *Classical Approaches to the Study of Religion.* The Hague: Mouton, 1973.

Ware, Timothy. *The Orthodox Church.* Baltimore: Penguin Books, 1964.

Warren, M.A.C. *I Believe in the Great Commission.* Grand Rapids, Mich.: Wm. B. Eerdmans, 1976.

Watanabe, Shōkō. *Nippon no Bukkyō.* Tokyo: Iwanami Shoten, 1958.

Weber, J.G., ed. *In Quest of the Absolute: The Life and Work of Jules Menchanin.* Kalamazoo, Mich.: Cistercian Publications, 1977.

Weiner, Herbert. "Report from Israel." *Parapsychology Review.* (March–April 1973).

Whitehead, Alfred North. *Science and the Modern World.* New York: New American Library, 1958.

Wiedenmann, Ludwig. *Mission und Eschatologie.* Paderborn: Verlag Bonifacius-Druckerei, 1965.

Williams, G.H. *Spiritual and Anabaptist Writers.* Philadelphia: Westminster Press, 1957.

Winkworth, Susannah. *The History and Life of the Reverend Doctor John Tauler with Twenty-Five of His Sermons.* London: Allenson, n.d.

Wolf, Hans Walter. *Joel and Amos.* Philadelphia: Fortress Press, 1977.

World Council of Churches. "The Finality of Jesus Christ in the Age of Universal History." *WCC Bulletin* (Division of Studies) 8, no. 2 (Autumn 1962).

Wright, G. Ernest. "The Nations in Hebrew Prophecy." *Encounter* 26, no. 2 (Spring 1965).

———. *The Old Testament against Its Environment.* Chicago: Henry Regnery, 1950.

Yagi, Seiichi. *Ai to Egoisumu.* Tokyo: Tōkai Daigaku Shuppankai, 1979.

———. "Buddhism and Christianity," a dialogue with John Cobb, Jr. *Northeast Asia Journal of Theology* 20–22 (March/September 1978).

———. *Bukkyō to Kirisutokyō no Setten.* Kyoto: Hōzōkan, 1976.

———. "East and West in Encounter" (paper delivered by Yagi at the University of Hawaii in July 1980).

Yannoulatos, Anastasios. "Christian Awareness of Primal World-Views." Gerald H. Anderson and Thomas F. Stransky, eds., *Mission Trends, No. 5.* New York: Paulist Press, 1981.

Zago, Marcello. "Dialogue in a Buddhist Context." International Congress on Mission, III, *Toward a New Age in Mission: The Good News of God's Kingdom to the Peoples of Asia.* Manila: Theological Conference Office, 1981.

Zenger, Erich. "Jahwe und die Götter." *Theologie und Philosophie* 43 (1968).

INDEX

Abel, 11
Abelard, 46, 48
Abraham, 4-6, 18, 84, 188, 208
Abram, 4
Adam, 4-6, 190, 218
  man, 5
Adullam, 11
Agape, Johannine, 85
Aggrey, James, 197
Alaric, Visigoth chieftain, 38
Albertus Magnus, 46, 48
Albigenses (Cathari), 47, 49
Alchemists, 48
Alcott, Bronson, 63
Alexandria, 13, 26, 29, 30, 38
Alexandrian Theology, 197
Ambrose of Milan, 38
Americas, 2
Amitābha (Amida) Buddha, 219
Amos, 10
Anabaptist(s), 49
Anaximenes, 29
Angels, 22, 207
Anquetil-Duperron, A.H., 63
Anthropocentricity, xi
Anthropologies, 184-189
  Calvinist-Puritan, 184
  and concepts of total depravity, 188-189
  highest of, 184
  and new-old theological vision of human-
    kind, 186
anthropos ("man," human being), 5
Appasamy, Aiyadurai Jesudasen, 123
Appiah-Kubi, Kofi, 177-178
Aquinas, Thomas, 46, 48
Arabia, 11
Archimedes, 52
Arianism, 43
Armenia, 43, 212
Arndt, Johann, 55
Aryan invaders, 37
Ashley, Benedict, 208
Asia, mission in, xii
Athenagoras, 28
Augsburg Confession, 49
Augustine, xii, 6, 30, 38, 41-43, 46, 50, 205
  ambivalent aspects of, 41
  as *doctor gratiae*, 41
Avicenna (Ibn Sina), 48
Baal,
  prophets of, 8
  worship of, 9
Baalism, and Ashtarōt, 13
Babylonian, 5, 11

Bacon, Roger, 47
Balaam, 11
Baptism, 42, 45, 50
  unbaptized children, 45, 50
Barth, Karl, 65-66, 186, 187
Basil of Caesarea, 209-210
Baum, Gregory, 54
Beghards, 49
Beguines, 49
Bellarmine, Robert, 50
Bennett, John C., 201
Benz, Ernst, 211-212, 216
Berger, Peter L., 204
Berkhof, Hendrikus, 218
Bhagavad-Gita, 194, 206
Bible, 1, 3-5, 8-24, 35, 73, 75, 77, 193, 195
  biblical covenants, 1-7
  biblical inerrancy, 77
  Latin Vulgate, 135
  New Testament, 16-24, 33, 35
  Old Testament, 8-16
  one of three reciprocal coefficients, 193
  Septuagint, 209
Blauw, Johannes, 205
Blavatsky, Helena Petrovna, 207
Bloesch, Donald G., 32, 79
Blondel, Maurice, 53
Böhme, Jakob, 55
Bonaventura (John Fidanza), 46
  concept of "appropriations," 47
Bonhoeffer, Dietrich, 67, 189
Boniface VIII, Pope, 45
Bouquet, A.C., 28
Brahe, Tycho, 52
Brahmans, 30
Brāhmo Samāj, 200
Brethren of the Common Life, 49
Broad-Church Movement (Church of Eng-
  land), 64
Brunner, Emil, 65
Bruno, Giordano, 47
Buddha, Gautama the, xii, 34, 188
  anthropology of, 188
Buddhism, xii, 33, 54, 65, 84, 170-171, 199, 201
  Mahāyāna, 53, 194, 215
  Pure Land School of, 194, 219
Buddhists, 71, 74, 84, 194, 219
Bushidō (The Way of the Warrior), 57
Byzantine Empire (Greek), 83
Cabala, 34
Cabazilas, Nicholas, 83
Cadbury, H.J., 18
Calvin, John, 6, 48, 214
Campanus, John, 49

Canaanite(s), 9, 11
Caphtor (Crete?), 10
Carey, William, 56
Carmel, Mt., 9
Carr, Burgess, 178
Cartier, Jacques, 37, 49
Caste system (of India), 9
Cathari, *see* Albigenses
Catholic Church, Roman, 49-55, 66, 78, 203, 215
Catholic (Roman) theologians, 86-113, 179-182
Catholicism, early, 210
Celsus (pagan philosopher), 27
Chadwick, Henry, 32, 210
Chakkarai, Vengal, 123-124
Chaldeans, 12
Chandran, Russel, 76
Chantepie de la Saussaye, Pierre D., 63
Chenchiah, Pandipeddi, 124-125
China, 51, 58-59
Chinese, 37
Chinese civilization, 59, 62
Chinese culture, European enthusiasm for, 59
Chinese socialism, 11
Christ, *see* Jesus Christ
Christian(s), ix-x, 3, 6, 16, 29, 34, 37, 41, 43, 74
    Jewish, 11, 33-34
    as pilgrim people, 35
Christian Institute for the Study of Religion and Society, 70
Christian-Muslim Dialogue, 71-73
    interrelationships, 43-44
Christianity, 12, 35, 66, 209
    Arian, *see* Arianism
    as fulfillment, 57
    Jewish, 11, 30, 33-34
    Protestant, 12, 77
Church(es) (Christian), ix, x, 1, 15, 23, 35, 39, 47, 59, 65-83
    from beginning of time, 30
    as body of Christ, 72, 197
    early, 25-35, 38-45, 51, 61, 80, 216
    Eastern Orthodox, 83-85
    as emergency residence (*paroikia*), 81
    as instrument of salvation, 84, 196, 198
    and mission of God, 67, 198-202
    as one reciprocal inefficient, 193
    as "picked troops," 195, 198
    Protestant, *see* Protestantism
    Roman Catholic, *see* Catholic Church, Roman
    as sign, 197
    and Spirit, 85
    visible Catholic, 42
Cicero, 51
Civilization, Western, xi-xii, 25, 36, 38
    and colonialism, xi-xii, 36-38
    exclusivist views of, 25
    sense of superiority of, 36-38, 66, 212
Clavius, Christopher, 52
Clement, First, 11, 40
Clement of Alexandria, 28, 29, 30-32, 211
Cobb, John B., Jr., 149-155
Collegium Romanum (Jesuit), 52
Colonialism, *see* Civilization, Western
Colossians, letter to the, 207-208
Columbus, Christopher, 37, 49
Confucius, 57

Confucianism, 56, 65, 169, 201
Congar, Yves, 53
Conquistadores, 37
Constantine (Roman Emperor), 2, 38, 41, 43
Constantinople, 51
Consultation on World Evangelism, Pattaya (Thailand-1980), 218
Copenhaver, Laura S., 185
Cornelius, 21, 25
Cosmos, x, 9, 14, 16
    hierarchy of values in, 19
    restoration of, 16
Council of Jerusalem, 183
Counter-Reformation, 50
Covenant(s), 1, 2-8, 13-14, 23, 29, 55, 84, 204, 205
    cosmic, 5
    ethical aspects of, 12-13
    Lausanne, *see* International Congress on World Evangelization
    universal, 5, 12, 29, 84
    unto service, 23
Cox, Harvey, xii
Creation, 5, 23, 76, 84, 206, 209
    of human beings in likeness of God, 184
    ongoing, 190
    respect for the natural order of, 190
    spiritual adoption of whole of, 84
Creed(s), Apostles', 40
Crusades, 47, 49
Cudworth, Ralph, 56
Cupitt, Don, 143-145
Cuttat, Albert, 53
Cyprian, 44, 50, 213
    formula of, 44, 50
Cyrus, 12-13
Damascus, 32, 44
Damnation, 56
Daniel, 11
Daniélou, Jean, 5, 31, 53
Dante, 47
Davidic King, 39
Dawe, Donald G., 4, 6, 14
Day of the Lord, *see* Lord, Day of the
Deism, 59
Deutero-Isaiah, 12, 14, 23, 209
Deuteronomy, 8, 12, 209
Devadutt, Vinjamuri E., 126-127
Devanandan, Paul, 125-126
Dewey, John, 63
Dialogue among religions, 67-76
Diaspora (Dispersion), 14, 26, 39
Diogenes of Apollonia, 30
Dispersion, *see* Diaspora
Doi, Masatoshi, 160-161
Donatism, 40
Donne, John, 215
Drake, Francis, 37, 49
D'Souza, Patrick (Bishop of Varanasi, India), XII
Dumoulin, Heinrich, 104-107
Ebina, Danjō, 187
Eckhart, Meister, 47
Economy
    of Christ, 84-85
    of God, 83-85
    of the Spirit, 85
Ecumenical Council, sixth, 210

Edict of Milan, 38
Edom, 11, 13
Edomite sages, three, 11
Edwards, Jonathan, 79
Egypt, 8, 11
Eichrodt, Walther, 3
Êl (Semitic term for deities), 12
Election, 6-7, 13-16, 18, 84, 205
Eliade, Mircea, 61, 63
Elijah, 8-9
Elisha, 206
Emerson, Ralph Waldo, 63
Emperor worship, 207-208
Engstrom, Olle, 75
Enlightenment (Age of), xi, 51, 53, 58-61
    as protest against Protestant orthodoxy,
      60-61
    religious views of, 60-61
Enoch, 11
Enoch, second, 26
Enosh, 5
Epoché, 63
Er, 11
Esau, 32
Esotericism, 26, 61
Ethiopians, 10
Europe, 37, 46
    western, xi, 1-2, 43
    isolation of, 43
Evangelical Foreign Missions Association, *see*
    Evangelicalism
Evangelicalism, 55-57, 76-80
    Evangelical Foreign Missions Association,
      77
    Interdenominational Foreign Mission
      Association of N.A., 77
    International Congress on World Evangeli-
      zation (Lausanne 1974), 78; (Pattaya
      1981), 218
    National Association of Evangelicals, 77
    National Evangelical Anglican Congress,
      Second, 79
Eve, 5-6, 190
Exodus, 6, 8
    liberation experience of, 6
Ezekiel, 10, 11
Ezra, 26
Faber, Frederick W., 202
Faith(s), x, xi, 3, 38, 43, 56, 60, 76, 80, 206,
    208, 211, 215
    biblical, 12
    Christian, x, xi, 3, 20, 29, 30, 31, 39, 43, 46,
      56, 67, 71, 75
    justification by, 60, 189
    leading toward transformation, 31, 60, 215
Farguhar, J.N., 64, 187
Farrar, Frederick William, 64
Fashole-Luke, E.W., 176-177
Feldman, L.H., 211
da Fiore, Gioachino, 61
Ferrara and Florence, Council of, 45, 51
Fohrer, Georg, 204
Forster, Roger T., 205
Forsyth, P.T., 32, 79
Fox, George, 56
Francis of Assisi, 47
Franciscan(s), xiii
Franck, Sebastian, 49, 55

Freud, Sigmund, 48
Friends of God, 49
Fulfillment theory, 57, 187-189
Fuller Theological Seminary, 77
Fulgentius of Ruspe, 42
Fundamentalism, 65, 77
Gairdner, Temple, 64
Galilei, Galileo, 52
da Gama, Vasco, 49
Gardet, Louis, 53
Genocide, 12
Gentile(s), 15, 17, 19, 22, 46, 209
German National Socialism, 36
Gibbon, Edward, 42
Gnosticism, Christian, 40
God, xii, xiii, 4-7, 8-15, 16-24, 25-35, 68, 79-83,
    84, 208, 216
    of all living beings, 5, 19, 22
    as Creator and Controller, 22, 41
    covenanting action of, 5-7
    as Father, 23, 29, 44, 54, 57, 64
    generosity of, 19, 21, 22
    goodness of, 50
    grace of, 29, 31, 84
    impartiality of, 18, 19, 21-23, 49
    knowledge of, 47, 49, 56, 79
    known in creation, 22
    life of, 84
    lordship of, 207-208
    love toward, 26
    loving concern of, 10, 17, 19, 23, 56, 72, 84,
      200, 206
    mercy of, 50, 56, 79, 202
    and *missio Dei*, 67
    as patron deity of Western peoples, 44, 57
    and presence in secular realm, 29, 67-67
    providence of, *see* Providence
    reconciling work of, 68
    relationship with, 75
    revelatory work of, 6, 14-15, 22, 24, 28, 29,
      35, 46, 52, 64, 65, 205
    righteousness of, 29
    saving work of, 6, 14, 15, 32, 35, 44, 46, 52,
      56, 188, 205
    Trinity, *see* Trinity
    unity of, 29, 48, 194
    wider work of, 10, 21-22, 27-35, 43, 49, 65,
      68, 72-85, 188, 189, 215
    will of, 6, 9, 48
    word of, 10
Gods, 19, 23, 27, 207-208
    as demons, 8, 23, 50
Grace, 6-7, 41, 56, 60
    biblical theme of, 6-7
    gratia imputata, 60
    gratia infusa, 60
Gratian, 38
Great Commission (Mt. 28:16-20), 78, 199-200
Greece, 1
Greek, 28, 32, 33
Greeks, 37
Gregory Thaumaturgus, 195
Guillaume de Paris, 48
Habakkuk, 12
Hallencreutz, Carl F., 217
van Harnack, Adolf, 209
Hasidim, 34
Heber, Reginald, 185

Hebrew (Hebraic),
    people, 4
    tradition, 5, 6
Heiler, Friedrich, 64
Hell, 79, 218
Hellenism, 26
Henry the Navigator, 49
Hepburn, James C., 185
Heraclitus of Ephesus, 17, 28
Heraclius (Byzantine emperor), 44
von Herder, Johann Gottfried, 62
Héring, Jean, 207
Hick, John, 140-143, 191, 192
Hijrah, 44
Hinduism, 33, 54, 65
    Vedic-Brahmanic, 199
Hindu religious tradition, 70
Hindu scripture, 194
Hindus, 71, 74, 215
Hippo (North Africa), 38, 42
History, x, 2
    Christian, 38
    of Christian theology, *see* Theology
    of ecumenical movement, 75
    human, 3, 4, 21, 47, 56, 81, 83
    of Israel, *see* Israel
    of religions, xii, 66, 216
    Religionsgeschichtliche Schule religious, 2,
        71
    universal sacred, 53
Hocking, William Ernest, 64, 216
Holy Spirit, 3, 48, 56, 84, 85
Homer, 51
Homilies, see Pseudo-Clementine writings
Howell, Leon, 218
Hubbard, David A., 77
Hubmaier, Balthasar, 49, 55
Humanism, xi, 52, 55, 60-61
    humanist perspectives of other religions,
        51-53
Hume, David, 60
Ignatius, 212
Independent Churches (of Africa), 200
India, 9, 33, 44, 212, 215
    British in, 37
Indians, 30
Interdenominational Foreign Mission Associa-
    tion of North America, *see* Evangelicalism
International Congress on Mission (Manila,
    December 2-7, 1979), 203
    Toward a New Age in Mission, 203
International Congress on World Evangeliza-
    tion, Lausanne, 1974, 78
    Lausanne Covenant, 217
International Missionary Council (IMC), 67
    Jerusalem Meeting, 1928, 64
    Tambaram Meeting, 1938, 66
Intertestamental period, 14
Irenaeus, 28, 28, 42, 85, 196, 210
Isaac, 18, 188
Isaiah, 208
    First, 210
    Second, *see* Deutero-Isaiah
Islam, 55, 58, 61, 64, 71, 74, 199, 213
Israel, 4, 5, 7, 8, 9, 10, 12, 14, 15, 19, 22-23,
    39, 206, 209
    commission of, 205
    covental relationship of, 23

    election of, 7, 84, 190
    history of, 8, 10, 13, 22, 38, 191
    symbolized as prophet, 15
Israel, people of, 4, 5, 8, 9, 11, 13, 14, 15, 19,
    23
    establishment of, 5
    self-understanding of, 4, 23
Israelites, 12
Issachar, 209
Jacob, 11, 18, 32, 188
James, William, 63
Japan, xiii, 50, 57, 187, 195, 200
Japanese, 37, 50
    language, xii
    studies, xii
Jeremiah, 6, 11, 205
Jericho, 11
Jerome, 35
Jerusalem, 18
Jerusalem meeting, *see* International Mission-
    ary Council
Jesus Christ, xii, 4, 17-20, 27, 30, 40, 44, 54,
    55, 66, 68, 69, 76, 79, 80, 86
    anthropology of, 19
    atoning sacrifice of, 60
    as the Christ, xii, 3, 34, 191-193
    and Christ event, 35, 79
    and contemporary Judaism, 17
    as cosmic Christ, xii
    as criterion, 191-192
    cross and resurrection of, 56, 192
    crucified and risen, 82, 192
    crucifixion of, 82
    as elder brother, 192
    ethical concerns of, 17
    and final revelation of God, 81
    and Gentiles, 17
    gospel of, 202
    hope in, 188
    Incarnation of, 55
    incarnations of, 34
    inclusiveness of, 17-20
    as Logos, 17, 28, 31, 194
    as Lord, 23, 27, 39, 65, 76, 79, 191, 197
    and Messiahship and early church, 20, 191
    name of, 20-21, 79
    of Nazareth, 6, 16, 20, 39, 191-194, 196
    new life in, 73
    the power of, 20
    presence and work in the whole world of,
        56, 68, 80, 197
    and prophetic tradition, 17
    redemptive sacrifice of, 60
    resurrection of, and early church, 20
    as Savior, 27, 29, 65, 76
    as Son of God, 29, 55, 81, 83, 192
    as suffering servant, 76
    uniqueness of, 75
    and use of Scripture, 19, 207
    as wisdom, 30
    as Word of God, 83
Jesuits, 50, 51, 58
Lettres curieuses et édifiantes, 58
Jethro, 11
Jews, 15, 17, 22, 26, 33, 34
    Hellenistic, 26
    of Palestine, 25, 33
    Sephardic, 34

Job, 11
Joel, 9
John (apostle), 20
John the Baptist, 33
John of Damascus, 44
John Paul II, Pope, ix, 55, 57
    Redemptor Hominis, 55
John XXIII, Pope, x, 203
John, Gospel of, 16, 19, 24, 208
Johnson, Robert C., 193
Johnston, William, 111-113
Jonah, 15
Jones, Rufus, 65
Joseph, 209
Josephus, Flavius, 33, 211
Judah, son of Jacob, 11
Judaism, 11, 13, 38, 39, 74, 209
    Alexandrian, 26
    and ethical concerns, 26
    Iranian influence upon, 13
    missionary activities of, 26
    as mystery religion, 26
    pre-Christian, 4, 12, 17, 22, 25
Judeo-Christian,
    faith, *see* Faith
tradition, 4, 6, 16, 33, 34
Judgment, 10, 12, 22, 24, 29
    as biblical theme, 6
    and ethical conduct, 14, 18, 19
Justice, economic and social, 2, 9
Justin Martyr, 28-29, 35, 42
Kagawa, Toyohiko, 197
Kalilombe, Patrick, 179-182
Kant, Immanuel, 60
Karaite Movement, Jewish, 34
Kaunda, Kenneth D., 178-179
Kepler, Johann, 52
Khodr, Georges, 83-85, 196, 219
Kingdom, 17
    of God, 18, 20, 31, 57, 80, 81, 202
    of heaven, 6, 18
Kir, 10
Knitter, Paul, 102-104, 205
Kozaki, Hiromichi, 57, 187
Kraemer, Hendrik, 66, 114-118, 216
    The Christian Message in a Non-Christian World, 216
    Why Christianity of All Religions?, 216
    World Cultures and World Religions, 216
Krishna, 206
Küng, Hans, 53, 96-101
Kwan-yin (Kannon), 219
Lactantius, 27
Land, conquest of the, 8
Lateran Council, Fourth, 45
Law,
    Mosaic, 22
    natural, doctrine of, 48, 53, 58, 59
Leibnitz, Gottfried Wilhelm, 59, 60
Leipzig, 45
Lessing, Gotthold Ephraim, 61
    Education of the Human Race, 61
    Nathan the Wise, 61
Lewis, C.S., 80
Licinius, 38
Limbo, 46
Lind, Millard, 6
Llull, Ramon, 47

Locke, John, 59
Logos (word), 17, 24, 35
    doctrine of, 51, 57-58, 189, 195
    Justin Martyr on, 28
    Minucius Felix on, 29
    Nicholas of Cusa on, 51
    Origen on, 31
    as seed (*sperma*), 28
    Theophilus of Antioch on, 29
    as universal, 196
    as universal Reason, 17
Lombard, Peter, 46
Lord, 5, 10, 12, 23, 29, 50, 85, 206
    Day of the, 10, 13
    of hosts, 210
    Jesus Christ as, *see* Jesus Christ
    lords, 207-208
    name of the, 5
    word of the, 10
Lot, 11
Loyola, Ignatius, 50
de Lubac, Henri, 53
de Lugo, Juan Cardinal, 52, 55, 194, 214
Luria, Rabbi Isaac, 34
Luther, Martin, 7, 45, 214, 215
    Large Catechism, 214
Lutheran Church, Missouri Synod, 77
Lystra of Lycaonia, 21
Macauley, Lord, 37
Maccabean rule, 39
Macccabean struggle, 25
Maccabees, Second Book of, 33
Magellan, Ferdinand, 37, 49
Maier, Johann (of Eck), 45
Malachi, 13, 32
Manichaeism, 41, 44
"Manifest destiny," 8
Marston, V. Paul, 205
Martin, Malachi, x, 189, 203
Massignon, Louis, 53
Matsuo, Mikizō, 165, 171
Maxentius, 38
Mazzini, Giovanni Antonio, 52
Mbiti, John S., 173-176
McCarthy, D.J., 204
McCord, James I., ix, x, xiii
Mecca, 44
Medes, 12
Medina, 44
Mediterranean, 38, 49
    as a "Muslim lake," 44
Melchizedek, 11
Mendenhall, George, 4, 205
Messiah, 14
Metaphysical Movement, *see* New Thought Movement
Metempsychosis, *see* Reincarnation
Methodist Church, of Sri Lanka, 76
Mirandola, Pico della, 47
Minicius Felix, xii, 29-30
Missiology, viii, 11, 67, 84
    and Christian world mission, 198-202
    and mission, 67, 81, 216
    new age in, ix
    and pragmatic motivation to mission, 200
Mission, *see* Missiology
Missionaries, 215
    Pietist, 215

Protestant evangelical, 77
Roman Catholic, 77
Mission Covenant Church (Sweden), 75
"Modernism," 53, 65
Monotheism, ethical, 12, 26
Montanism, 40
Moor, see Muslim(s)
Moravians, 56
More, Henry, 56
Moses, 5, 11, 26, 197, 208
Moses, David G., 122-123
Mozart, Wolfgang, 61
    The Magic Flute, 61
Muhammad, 44, 51, 84
Müller, F. Max, 63, 65
Muslim(s), ix, 37, 44, 50, 55, 72
Mwoleka, Christopher, 179
Mystery religions, Greek, 39
Mystical tradition(s), German, 55
Naaman, 206
Napoleonic period, 53
National Association of Evangelicals (U.S.A.),
    see Evangelicalism
National Council of Churches (U.S.A.), 77
National Evangelical Anglican Congress, see
    Evangelicalism
Nazareth, 19
Nebuchadnezzar, 11
Nemer, Laurence, 183
Neo-Confucians, 57
Neo-Orthodoxy, Protestant, 26, 66, 184-186
    and crisis (dialectical) theology, 65, 216
Neo-Platonism, 41
Neqamah, 12
Nestorian Church, 84, 219
Newman, John Henry, 52
New Thought Movement, 63
Nicholas of Cusa, 47, 51, 55
    De Pace Fidei, 51
Niebuhr, Reinhold, 184-185
Nineveh, 15
Nitobe, Inazō, 57
Noah, 4, 5, 6, 11
Obadiah, 11
Octavius, 29
Ogden, Schubert, 138-140
Origen, 29, 30-32, 196, 209, 210, 211
Orthodox Church(es), Eastern, 78, 83
    Greek, 83
    Romanian, 83
    Slavic, 83
Otemba, Isaya Guy, 182
Otto, Rudolph, 64
Paganism,
    Hellenistic, 27
    philosophy of, 30
Paideusis, 31
Palestine, 25, 34, 39, 44
Panikkar, Raimundo (Raymond), 5, 53, 87-93,
    196, 213, 214
Pantheism, 17
Paul (apostle), 6, 15, 21-23, 197, 207, 208, 218
    anthropology of, 188-189
    Athenian address of, 21
    and faith working through love, 60
    and God and the world, 21
    and obedience, 212
    on the road to Damascus, 192

and salvation, 60, 218
    universal perspectives of, 21-23, 196
Pax Romana, 42
Pentateuch, 6
Pentecostal church, of Chile, 77
People of God
    as broader than the church as institution,
        196
    the economy of, 85
    as those visited by the Spirit, 85, 196
Persia, 44
Persian Empire, 13
Persians, 12
Peter, 20-21, 38, 208
Petrarch, 47
Pharisaism, 25
Pharisees, 33, 211
Phenomenology of religions, 67
Philippi, 32
Philippidis, Leonidas J., 83
Philistines, 10
Philo, 26, 35
Photius, patriarch of Constantinople, 32
Physics, new, x
Pietism, 20, 50, 56, 57, 59, 61
Pirenne, Henri, 44
Pius IX, Pope, 214
Plato, 26, 30, 35, 51
Platonists, Cambridge, 56
Pluralism, religious, xii, 54
Plutarch, 51
Pobee, John S., 182
Polytheism, 51
Pragmatism, 63
Predestination, 43, 205
Preparatio evangelica, 80
Presbyterian Church, U.S.A. Minutes of the
    General Assembly (1869), 185
Pronoia, 31
Prophecy, biblical, 12-13, 25
Prophets,
    of the nations, 41
    Hebrew, 9-14, 206
Prosperus of Aquitaine, 43
Philosopher(s), 21, 27, 29
    Epicurean, 21
    Greek, 29, 47
    humanistic, 1, 3
    Muslim, 48
    Platonist, 48
    scholastic, 48
    Stoic, 1
Protestantism, 55-57, 64-83
    German, 59
    Japanese, 57
    and orthodoxy, 60, 65
Providence, xiii, 11, 12, 20, 21, 23, 29, 31, 46,
    68, 79, 81
Psalms, 12
Pseudo-Clementine writings, 33, 211
    Homilies, 30, 211
    Recognitions, 11, 30
Psychology, Jungian, 34
Pure Land School, see Buddhism
Purgatory, 80, 211
Qur'ān, 73, 84
Quasten, Johannes, 210
Rabbi(s), 34

Rabbinical tradition, 34
Rahab, 11
Rahner, Karl, 53, 83, 93-96, 196, 211
Rationalism, 59
Rawlinson, George, 64
Reason (*intellectus, intellegere*), 48, 52
Rebellion, as biblical theme, 6
Reformation, 48, 49, 55-56, 59, 215
Reformers, Protestant, 49
Reichelt, Karl Ludwig, 64
Reincarnation, 31, 33-35, 47, 211
    metempsychosis, 31, 211
    transmigration, 211
Relandus, Hadrianus, 58
    De religione Mohammadanica libri due, 58
Religionsgeschichtliche Schule, see History
Religious texts, Asian, 63
Remonstrants, Dutch Arminian, 56
Renaissance, xi, 47, 50, 51, 53, 56, 58, 59, 61
Resurrection, 20, 56, 79
Revolution, French, 53
Revivalism, *see* Evangelicalism
Rhys Davids, C.A.F., 63
Ricci, Matteo, 58, 195
Richardson, Cyril, 211
Roberts, Frederick Lord, 212
Robinson, John A.T., 145-149
Roman Empire, 26, 30, 38, 40, 43, 44
Romans, 37, 38
Rome, 1, 11, 42, 48
    bishop of, 38
    church of, 12, 40, 45, 50
Rossano, Pietro, 186-188, 206
Rousseau, Jean-Jacques, 188
Rufinus, 30, 210
Ruth, 11
Saitō, Sōichi, 200-201
Salvation, 4, 5, 6, 14, 16, 20, 22, 32, 34, 39, 41,
    50, 60, 69, 72, 78, 79-80, 82, 84, 188, 209
    as biblical theme, 6
    and the Church, 41, 44
    from death and danger,
    final (*salutem beatitudinis*) 41, 43, 200
    found in natural revelation and law, 58
    of Gentiles, 46
    and healings of Jesus, 21, 32
    history of, 53, 66, 84
    Jesus' name and, 79
Samaritan, 19
Samartha, Stanley J., 130-134, 216
Sansom, G.B., 37
Satan, 215
Saunders, Kenneth J., 65
Schleiermacher, Friedrich, 61
Schlette, Heinz Robert, 96-101
Scriptures, 5, 6, 12, 16, 19, 34, 77,
Schwartz, Christian Friedrich, 195
Seneca, 51
Sensus naturae ("unconscious, instinctive, su-
    pernatural knowledge"), 48
Septuagint, *see* Bible
Seth, 5
Shan-tao, 219
Sheba, Queen of, 11
Shedd, William Ambrose, 64
Shintō, 57, 167-171, 201
Shua, 11
Sidon, 19

de Silva, Lynn A., 76
Simon the Pharisee, 18
Sinai, Mt.,
    revelatory events of, 6
    covenant at, 8
Singh, Sundar (Sadhu), 192, 197
Sirach, ben, 5, 6
Socialism, xi
Socrates, 28, 35
Söderblom, Nathan, 64
Sodom, 19
Sōka Gakkai, 200
Solomon, 6, 11
Solzhenitsyn, Aleksandr, xi
Song, Choan-Seng, 155-160
Southern Baptist Convention, 77
Soviet Union, 36
Spae, Joseph J., 107-111
Spener, Philipp Jakob, 55
Spirit, the Holy
    coming of, 194
    doctrine of, 183
    guidance of, 193
    as one of three reciprocal inefficients, 193
    role of, 193, 196
Spirituality, 47, 50, 61, 82
Steiner, Rudolf, 5
Steinsaltz, Rabbi Adin, 34
Stoicism, 48
Stoics, 17
Stott, John R.W., 76, 78
Stransky, Thomas, 77, 80
Suarez, 50
Sullivan, Louis, 63
Swidler, Leonard, 203
Synagogue, 25, 39
Syria, 11, 44, 206
Syrians, 10
Tambaram Meeting, *see* International Mission-
    ary Council
Tamor, 11
Tatian of Syria, 26
Taylor, John V., 134-138, 171-173
Temple, William, 64
Tertullian, xii, 26, 209
    On Prayer, 209
Terence, 218
Thackeray, H. St. J., 211
Thales, 29
Theism, 17
Theocracy, 39
Theodosius, 38
Theology, xii, 15, 38, 63, 204
    American liberal, 63
    Barthian, 65, 70
    Christian, ix, xi, 1, 2, 3, 4, 48, 66
    crisis (dialectical), *see* Neo-orthodoxy, 66
    Eastern Orthodox, x
    historical, x
    history of Christian, 3, 4
    of Israel, 8
    liberal, 65, 204
    new, 38
    new age in, ix
    and non-Christian religions, 46-85
    Protestant, 66
    Roman Catholic, 46, 66
    speculative, 55

Theologian(s), 27, 30, 65-71
    Alexandrian, 42
    early Greek patristic, 83
    Orthodox, 32, 71, 83-85
    Protestant, 32, 55, 79, 83, 114-182
    Roman Catholic, 2, 32, 53-55, 71, 79, 83,
        86-113
Theophilus of Antioch, 28, 29
Thieves, the two (Luke 23:39-43), 202
Thomasius, Christian, 59
Thoreau, Henry David, 63
Tiele, Cornelis P., 63
Thomas, M. (Madathilparampil) M., 66, 70,
    127-130
Tillich, Paul, 6, 118-122
Tiridates, King, 212
Toynbee, Arnold, 37
Transcendentalism, 63
Transcendentalists, 63
Transmigration, see Reincarnation
Trent, Council of, 50
Trigault, Nicola, 59
Trinity, 48, 194
    Buddhist, 219
    Christian Theology of, 194
Troeltsch, Ernst, 62, 64
Tyre, 11, 19
Uemura, Masahisa, 57, 187
Unitarianism, 59
United Presbyterian Church, U.S.A., 69
    "The Confession of 1967," 69
Upanishads, 194
Vandals, 38, 42
Vatican Council, Second (Vatican II), ix, 53-
    55, 69, 78
    "Declaration on the Relationship of the
        Church to Non-Christian Religions," 53
Vedas, 37, 194
Verbeck, Guido, 195
Verghese, T. Paul, 42, 83
Via crucis, 198
Viatte, Auguste, 61
    Les sources occultes du romatisme:
        Illuminisme-Theosophi, 61
Visigoths, 43
Visser't Hooft, W.A., 1
Voltaire, 59
Voyages of discovery (exploration), 37, 49, 52,
    56, 58, 59
Vriezen, Th. C., 14
Wakō, Japanese, 37
Waldenses, 47
Warren, M.A.C., 134-138
Watts, Isaac, 184
"Way, the," 39
Weiner, Rabbi Herbert, 34

Whitehead, Alfred North, 51
William of Conches (Normandy), 48
Wolff, Christian, 59, 60
World Council of Churches (WCC), 67-77, 78,
    79-83, 218
    Addis Abba Meeting (1971), 72
    aide-mémoire, 72
    Ajaltoun Consultation, Beirut (1970), 71,
        74
    Assembly of the East Asia Conference
        (Christian Conference of Asia), Bangkok
        (1964-1970), 68
    Broumana Consultation (1972), 72
    "Christian Encounter with Men of Other
        Beliefs," 68
    "Christians in Dialogue with Men of Other
        Faiths" (Kandy), 69
    Colombo Memorandum, 74
    "Dialogue with Men of Living Faiths," 71
    Division of World Mission and Evangelism,
        67, 70
    Fifth Assembly, Nairobi (1975), 75
    Fourth Assembly, Uppsala (1968), 70, 73,
        76, 78
    Multi-Lateral Dialogue, Colombo, 73
    "Seeking Community: The Common
        Search of People of Various Faiths, Cul-
        tures, and Ideologies," 75
    Third Assembly, New Delhi (1961), 67
    "The Word of God and the Living Faiths of
        Man," 67
    World Mission and Evangelism Confer-
        ence, Bangkok (1973), 73
    World Mission and Evangelism Confer-
        ence, Melbourne (1980), 80
    Zürich Consultation (1970), 71
World Missionary Conference, Edinburgh
    (1910), 216
World War,
    First (I), 65
    Second (II), 66
Wright, Frank Lloyd, 63
Wright, G. Ernest, 12
Wycliffe Bible Translators, 77
Xavier, Francis, 50, 57, 58, 195
Yagi, Seiichi, 160-165
Yahweh, 6, 10, 12-15, 14, 204
Zago, Marcello, xii
Zebulon, 209
Zeno, 17
Ziegenbalg, Bartholomäus, 215
von Zinzendorf, Nikolaus, 195
Zodiac, twelve signs of the, 207
Zoe-Obeanga, Jean Samuel, 183
Zoroastrianism, 12
Zwingli, Huldreich, 49, 55